The Volume and Dynamics of
and Transnational Social Spaces

The Volume and Dynamics of International Migration and Transnational Social Spaces

THOMAS FAIST

CLARENDON PRESS · OXFORD

OXFORD
UNIVERSITY PRESS

Great Clarendon Street, Oxford OX2 6DP

Oxford University Press is a department of the University of Oxford.
It furthers the University's objective of excellence in research, scholarship, and education by publishing worldwide in

Oxford New York

Athens Auckland Bangkok Bogotá Buenos Aires Calcutta
Cape Town Chennai Dar es Salaam Delhi Florence Hong Kong Istanbul
Karachi Kuala Lumpur Madrid Melbourne Mexico City Mumbai
Nairobi Paris São Paulo Singapore Taipei Tokyo Toronto Warsaw

and associated companies in Berlin Ibadan

Oxford is a registered trade mark of Oxford University Press
in the UK and certain other countries

Published in the United States
by Oxford University Press Inc., New York

First published 2000

British Library Cataloguing in Publication Data

Data available

Library of Congress Cataloging in Publication Data

Faist, Thomas, 1959–
The volume and dynamics of international migration and transnational social spaces/Thomas Faist.
Includes bibliographical references and index.
1. Emmigration and immigration. I. Title.
JV6035.F35 2000 304.8′2′01–dc21 99-048709

ISBN 0–19–829391–7
ISBN 0–19–829726–2 (Pbk)

1 3 5 7 9 10 8 6 4 2

Typeset by J&L Composition Ltd, Filey, North Yorkshire
Printed in Great Britain
on acid-free paper by
Biddles Ltd, Guildford and King's Lynn

In Memory of
My Parents, Anton and Gertrud Faist

Acknowledgements

Like all original works, this book owes a great deal of its content to the thoughts and efforts of persons other than the author. I would especially like to mention the participants in the project on theories of international migration and development that was part of a research programme 'Migration, Population and Poverty'. The project was mainly based at the Centre for Research in International Migration and Ethnic Relations (CEIFO), University of Stockholm. We—an interdisciplinary group of economists, anthropologists, sociologists, and political scientists—had a chance to develop our thoughts revolving around the central question: Why do most people stay immobile? Although the question of immobility among potential migrants had been repeatedly posed, it had never received a systematic treatment. While writing a disciplinary chapter and the concluding chapter of our group book, I developed the basis of some of the main thoughts presented here. The results of the group work appeared in *International Migration, Immobility and Development. Multidisciplinary Perspectives* (1997), edited jointly by Tomas Hammar, Grete Brochmann, Kristof Tamas, and myself.

It goes without saying that this experience provided some of the tools used in this book, such as the concept of space. Discussion in the group also gave me the opportunity to finally go one step further, and extend my explorations into a more detailed study of immobility and mobility: Why are there so few migrants out of most places? and: Why are there so many migrants out of a few places? Furthermore, the common work stimulated me to think about the border-crossing expansion of migrants' spaces, so-called transnational social spaces. This concept connects my study to a strand of work I have been engaged for the past years, the analysis of immigrant integration in advanced welfare states.

This volume has benefited from exceptional research assistance by Jürgen Gerdes who also provided valuable suggestions. Ute Bitzer, Judith Quintern, Ilja Mertens, and Lars Heinemann carefully looked through the whole manuscript. Several colleagues read specific chapters. They helped me to correct some mistakes and tighten up the analysis, although I obviously take full responsibility for this final version. My gratitude goes to: Tomas Hammar, Carsten Ullrich, Svenja Falk, Madeleine Tress, Sabine Dreher, Eyüp Özveren, Bernhard Peters,

John Mollenkopf, John Rex, and Aristide Zolberg. My colleagues at the Institute for Intercultural and International Studies (InIIS) at the University of Bremen discussed and criticized the two chapters on transnational social spaces in research seminars. At Oxford University Press I have been very fortunate to receeive the advice of Dominic Byatt and the generous help of Amanda Watkins. Anne-Helene Seedorff provided secretarial assistance. As usual, Rita and Bernhard Stadler afforded me a quiet place to finalize this study. And throughout the writing my wife Süreyya supported me in more ways than one.

Bremen
February 1999 T. F.

Contents

List of Figures

List of Tables

Abbreviations

AMGT	Avrupa Milli Görüş Teşkilatlam
BA	Bundesanstalt für Arbeit
DİB	Diyanet İşleri Başkanlığı
DİTİB	Diyanet İşleri Türk İslam Birlığı
GATT	General Agreement on Trade and Tariffs
GCC	Gulf Cooperation Council
ILO	International Labour Organisation
IMF	International Monetary Fund
INGOs	international non-governmental organizations
INS	Immigration and Naturalization Service
IRCA	Immigration Reform and Control Act (USA)
NAFTA	North American Free Trade Agreement
NATO	North Atlantic Treaty Organization
NGOs	non-governmental organizations
OECD	Organization for Economic Coopertion and Development
PKK	Partiya Karkarên Kurdistan
SAW	Special Agricultural Workers
SSA	Social Security Administration
TES	Turkish Employment Service
UNHCR	United Nations High Commissioner for Refugees
USCR	United States Committee for Refugees
VIKZ	İslam Kültür Merkezleri Birliği

1

Lacunae of Migration and Post-Migration Research

There is a baffling puzzle in international migration: Why are there so few migrants from so many places and so many from only a few places? On the one hand, there is relative immobility—only a very small percentage of potential migrants are moving abroad. Most persons migrate domestically, and an even greater share never move considerable distances for extended periods of time at all. And, on the other hand, we can undeniably speak of international chain migration. Once migration processes have started, more and more people move. A process of chain reaction unfolds which sometimes leads to mass migration, involving a large part of the population in specific regions of an emigration country. The question is: How can these two, at first sight, opposite interpretations of contemporary international migration be reconciled—massive relative immobility and equally widespread mass migration?

This book claims that both relative immobility and mass migration go hand in hand: resources inherent in ties between people—within networks, groups, and communities—are often locally specific. These ties and the corresponding resources are not easily transferred from one place to another, especially across borders of nation-states. Ties carry resources such as obligations, reciprocity, and solidarity and people derive benefits from them—access to resources of significant others, information, and control over other people. The ties people develop with each other, the attachments they have to groups and communities, and the corresponding resources contribute to relative immobility of potential migrants. This applies both to situations such as labour recruitment policies or the hideous persecution of minorities. However, once mechanisms such as migrant networks have evolved which make these resources more easily transferable across nation-state borders, chain migration develops in situations characterized by relatively high degrees of choice among potential migrants.

These processes are not restricted to pioneer and chain migration. We know that international migrants do not travel along one-way streets but on two-lane highways. People staying in the immigration country sometimes not only maintain and build up relations within the new place of settlement but also maintain ties to the country of emigration. In some cases these ties and the unfolding strong and dense circular flows of persons, goods, ideas, and symbols within a migration system—transnational social spaces—even extend beyond the first generation. Phenomena such as diasporas have attested to this for centuries. This leads us to the second puzzle, concomitant transnational ties and adaptation in the countries of destination. Although many situations of international migration in the contemporary world clearly point towards at least partial adaptation of labour migrants and refugees from the South in the immigration countries of the North, transnational ties among many of the migrant groups show no signs of abiding in the first and sometimes not even in the second generation. Unfolding immigrant adaptation and the formation of transnational social spaces proceed simultaneously. The main set of questions derived from the puzzle of concomitant transnationalization of ties and unfolding adaptation is: How do transnational social spaces emerge out of labour migrants' and refugees' ties to their country of origin, and what are the implications of transnational ties for the adaptation of newcomers in the states of destination?

The two puzzles are intimately related. Potential migrants in the original emigration areas usually do not easily transfer resources, especially if they lack financial resources and skills sought after in the destination areas. We cannot study migration and its aftermath without taking into account the ties of migrants in their living contexts. And migrants need ties in the countries of destination to find work, housing, and a congenial cultural environment. Only within functioning migrant and migration networks we do observe international chain and mass migration. Likewise, it would be short-sighted to describe and explain immigrant adaptation without considering the ties migrants maintain to their countries of origin. Networks of migrants, stayers, brokers, and organizations do not simply vanish proportionally to the density and strength of new ties in the country of immigration. They are operative in return migration, in the formation of immigrant communities, and inside established ethnic and religious minority groups.

Even in one of the most cherished laudations on immigration in the Americas around the turn of the nineteenth to the twentieth century, Emma Lazarus's imagery of the 'huddled masses', seeking refuge in the promised land has another side to it. In her words, America not only receives the 'poor and the downtrodden' but also holds open her arms as the 'Mother of Exiles' (see also Daniels 1990: 17). This suggests that many immigrants have left their countries of origin only reluctantly. It does not brush aside the feelings of loss and enduring devotion to the countries of emigration. Migration entails departure as well as arrival—exit from the old and adaptation in the new country. The presence abroad implies a poignant absence from the former home. Packing off to the North means taking up residence in the former periphery of one's world; and yet the former centres do not necessarily lose their centrality.

In sum, there are two puzzles, breaking down into four hard questions for migration research to address when trying to explain relative immobility and mass migration, and its consequences for movers and non-movers—concomitant transnationalization of ties and immigrant adaptation: Why are there so few migrants from most places? And why are there so many from only a few places? How do transnational social spaces emerge out of labour migrants' and refugees' ties to the countries of origin? And what are the implications of transnational ties for the incorporation of newcomers in the immigration states? Up until now theories of international migration and immigrant adaptation have avoided directly addressing the four questions which make up these two puzzles. The facts are known but insufficiently theorized. Written at the turn of the twentieth to the twenty-first century, this study seeks a unified approach that can deal with both migration and post-migration processes through unpacking the two puzzles.

The First Puzzle: Relative Immobility and Mass Migration

We now need to describe the puzzles and questions in more detail. The first two questions relate to the puzzle of relative immobility and mass migration.

Why Are There So Few Migrants Out of Most Places?

In the early to mid-1990s, the number of people on the move looked impressive. According to recent estimates by the United Nations, there were 120 million international migrants in 1990 (United Nations 1993); more than 70 million people worked legally and illegally in other countries (Bilsborrow et al. 1997: p. v). This number has been increasing by about 2 to 4 million a year throughout the remainder of the 1990s. If merged into a single country, this 'nation of migrants' would be the world's tenth largest nation-state. Various approaches have presented an impressive array of plausible arguments in trying to explain why people could be motivated or forced to move from one place to another, especially if it involves crossing the borders of nation-states. Yet the total migrant population in the world is estimated to constitute only about 2% of the world's population—a number that looks much less impressive than the total figure mentioned before.

Most potential migrants in the South either migrate internally, or do not migrate at all. The largest part of migrants, virtually impossible to estimate, are internal migrants. There is a considerable amount of internal migration, especially associated with rural–urban migration. Within this category one needs to differentiate rural–rural and rural–urban migration. 'As a matter of fact in many developing countries rural–rural migration is quantitatively more important than rural–urban migration. But whereas the former is usually seasonal and short term, the latter is generally more permanent and often tends to attract those who are relatively better off in terms of education and income' (Oberai 1981, cited in Bulutay 1995: 130). And international migration is often part of a migration sequence. International migration often has been a second step after a successful internal migration—step migration. But most potential labour migrants and refugees never cross the borders of nation-states to live or work in another country. In essence, a large proportion of potential migrants in the South have never considered moving although they would have gained by doing so (Speare 1974: 174). This is puzzling because about half of the world's population constitute potential international migrants. They are supposed to have the necessary motivation to migrate since they do not belong to the upper income echelons and have the necessary resources to migrate because they are not absolutely poor. None the less, even many of those who are forced to move due to war, political instability, ecological disasters, economic catastrophes, or ethnic, religious, and tribal conflict never leave their country. At best they move to other developing countries—but not to the North. In general, when citizens rebel against the very institutions that contribute or cause their poverty and oppression, some may become international refugees and asylum seekers. Most, however, remain in their nation-states. One recent estimate puts the number of internal refugees or displaced persons in 1993 in excess of 24 million, most of whom are women and children (US Committee for Refugees (USCR) 1993: 52).

At least half of those who migrate move from one developing country to another and not to developed countries. South–South migration flows are numerically more significant than South–North streams. This is even true for refugee flows, albeit for somewhat different reasons. Overall, in 1990, about 55% of the world's estimated 130 million migrants resided in developing countries (UNHCR 1997). Specifically, it is estimated that 97% of the world's refugees remain in developing countries. It is imperative to include refugees in any analysis of migration, since they are the majority of international migrants.

The same picture emerges if we look at migrant stocks. Overall, including labour migrants and refugees, some developing countries hosted the highest percentages of migrants in their populations: Côte d'Ivoire had close to 30% foreign-born persons, while it amounted to 26% in Jordan, and 19% in Costa Rica (Farrag 1997: 317), compared to about 8% in Germany and 9% in the United States (see also Table 1.1). In 1996, over half of the world's refugees and asylum seekers lived in the Middle East and South Asia. Two groups, Palestinians (3.7 million) and Afghanis (2.6 million) constitute over 40% of the world's refugees and asylum seekers, and the top five countries from which refugees and asylum seekers came, Palestine and Afghanistan plus Bosnia-Herzegovina, Liberia, and Iraq accounted for over 60% of the

TABLE 1.1. *World population born abroad, divided by regions*

Region	Million persons 1965	Million persons 1985	Per cent of total population 1965	Per cent of total population 1985
WORLD TOTAL	75.9	105.5	2.3	2.2
Industrialized countries, Eastern Europe and former Soviet Union	31.0	47.4	3.5	4.5
Europe	15.6	23.0	3.5	4.7
Former Soviet Union	0.1	0.2	0.1	0.1
North America	12.7	20.4	6.0	7.8
Oceania	2.6	3.9	14.8	16.0
Low and middle income countries	45.0	58.1	1.9	1.5
Caribbean and Central America	0.5	0.9	2.0	2.7
China	0.3	0.3	0.0	0.0
East and South-East Asia	7.6	7.5	1.9	1.2
North Africa and West Asian States of Gulf Cooperation Council	5.5	13.4	4.0	5.7
South America	5.4	5.6	2.4	1.5
South Asia	18.7	19.2	2.8	1.8
Sub-Saharan Africa	7.1	11.3	3.0	2.7

Source: World Bank 1995.

total. And on the destination side, one unlikely country, Iran, included almost one-fourth of the world's more than 20 million refugees (USCR 1997).

Even increasing chain and mass migration—about 2 to 4 million more each year—are not at an unprecedented high when viewed in comparative historical perspective. There is no conclusive evidence that would support the widespread expectations concerning steadily increasing volumes of international migration during the twentieth century. For example, in the period from 1919 until 1980 the relative volume of international migration in the case of voluntary migration was considerably lower compared to the 'long nineteenth century' from 1814 to 1914 (own calculations, based on Segal 1993: 16–21).

In sum, more than 65 million migrants in the economically developed nation-states are a significant number but very little compared to domestic migration within the South and border-crossing from South to South. But all these figures dwindle when compared to the huge percentage of potential movers who never migrate despite ever more incentives to do so, such as revolutions in transportation and communication that cut travel costs, a heightened perception of economic inequalities, and the ever-present demographic pressures. The developed nation-states in the North-West are not being overrun by a tidal wave of immigrants.

Existing theories have—with few exceptions—not directly addressed the question of why so few people migrate out of most communities, and why there is sometimes a high rate of return migration (Hammar et al. 1997; Uhlenberg 1973). This is a curious shortcoming because the problem of how potentials may be actualized is an old problem in the research on social movements. In most cases, the number of potential movement participants—the latitude of acceptance—is much higher than the number of those actually participating in events (McPhail and Miller 1973). Crucially, the question is how potential participants in social movements and migration networks turn into actual ones. In this way research in international migration shares important characteristics also with the vast majority of studies on status attainment and social class mobility. So far, virtually all analyses have been concerned with change of position. However, in social mobility research, for example, most analysts never took account of the fact that most people are not very mobile or not mobile at all. Thus, one challenging problem is why so many people do not change their position.

Why Are There So Many Migrants Out of a Few Places?

What is noteworthy is that under propitious circumstances international migration surges out of selected places in the South; hence the question: Why so many international migrants out of a few places? It is clear that most South–North labour migration has been from former colonies or dependent territories to the dominant centres of the North (Portes and Walton 1981), or has been instigated through selective recruitment by states in the North short of cheap and docile labour. Not only have most migrants been out of a few places but also to a few places. The direction of contemporary international migration is quite clear: about 65 million international migrants have settled in nation-states with a high degree of industrialization and in oil-rich countries. Six of the world's wealthiest countries—France, Germany, Italy, Japan, the United Kingdom, and the United States—count for about one-third of the world's migrants (Martin and Widgren 1996) and more than two-thirds in the North. And in the Middle East, migrants form the backbone of the labour force.

Some migration theories talk about about macro-structural conditions that explain why we find migration from certain countries of the South to the North, but they do not talk about movements from other developing countries to the economically more developed centres. They do not address the question of vast differences in emigration rates from within developing countries: in one and the same country, we find both villages which have ceased to exist because their inhabitants congregate abroad, and communities from which none or very few members migrated North. Micro-theories, especially extended rational choice theories such as value-expectancy theories, emphasize the values, viz. desires, of people and how such preferences translate into decisions to stay or go. Such individual-level approaches, however, cannot account for why a potential migrant moves from Turkey to Germany whereas individuals in a similar situation in Mali do not take the same route.

Macro-theories concentrate on structural constraints and opportunities, such as income differences between countries of emigration and immigration and the legal-institutional regulation of exit and entry. These latter approaches can explain plausibly, for example, that in the case of countries such as Turkey labour recruitment in a first period and family reunification policies in a second period stimulated international migration to Germany. In contrast, such policies were absent vis-à-vis Mali. Malians were much more likely to move to France if they decided to move at all; presumably because it was easier to gain entry due to legal regulations and established migrant networks linking Mali and

France. However, even these explanations are limited in that they say very little about differential migration rates within the same country or even region. For example, imagine two villages in Central Anatolia with substantial emigration rates over years. From one village more than half the population migrates to Germany whereas very few do from the other. In the latter, for example, it could be that more do migrate domestically, for example, to other cities in Turkey. Then there may be households within communities that do migrate, others do not; some may migrate earlier than others (Engelbrektsson 1978; for other examples, see Farrag 1997: 323).

Even fewer studies deal with the process of migration itself and address the endogenous dynamics of international movement such as the functions of migrant networks. These meso-level studies have unearthed important insights into the dynamics of migration. Yet they have focused exclusively on the second part of our puzzle. They devoted attention to the functions of migrant networks as facilitators of chain migration and, eventually, mass migration across international borders. These theories give us important clues as to some causes that are, in the end, not sufficient: to postulate the existence of migrant networks and to insist on their importance is not the same as showing how they come into being and how they function. It is not persuasive to assume that, all of a sudden, in the process of migration, migrants have resources at their disposal that did not exist before. It is therefore plausible to look at the resources available to potential and actual migrants. Then we can ask: What is the specificity of these resources? How may they encourage or prevent migration? To what extent can migrants transfer them across international borders? How may they be used to build migrant networks? How do they affect the process of adaptation in the immigration country?

The Second Puzzle: Transnational Social Spaces and Immigrant Adaptation

The second puzzle refers to the simultaneous existence of flourishing transnational ties and the adaptation of immigrants in the countries of origin and destination. International migration is not a discrete event constituted by a permanent move from one nation-state to another. Rather, it is a multi-dimensional economic, political, cultural, and demographic process which encapsulates various links between two or more settings in various nation-states and manifold ties of movers and stayers between them. In bi-directional migration systems, stayers, returnees, and those in the immigration countries frequently engage in border-crossing activities. Examples are plentiful: Muslims from Morocco and Algeria who reside in France exchange religious instructors with the countries of emigration (Wihtol de Wenden 1997). These imams contribute to a pluralization of the French religious landscape. Kurdish organizations in Germany, the Netherlands, and Sweden actively intervene in Turkish politics. Many of the participants have grown roots in Germany and have established families (Falk 1998). Politicians from Mexico, the Dominican Republic, and Haiti campaign in Los Angeles and New York City before national elections. Their prospective voters are often permanent residents or even citizens of the USA (Levitt 1996). And quite often, some migrant groups are likely to engage in recurrent international migration, pendulating between locations in two different countries. Nurses from Jamaica work in New York City hospitals while their mothers rear their children in the Caribbean. The children, in turn, spend some of their time in the 'Big Apple' (Pessar 1997). Moreover, the second generation sometimes crosses borders and transfers its syncretist practices. The German-based and now disbanded rap group 'Cartel', made up of children of former Turkish contract workers in Germany, toured Turkey in the summer of 1995 and replaced Michael Jackson as number 1 in the Turkish hit charts. They succeeded in addressing youthful audiences in both Germany and Turkey. All these examples of dense social relations that commonly accompany long-distance migration and subsequent adaptation contradict the standard vision of the immigrant as someone who leaves the old country's security, passes through a period of risk and turmoil, and then establishes a definite equilibrium in the new nation-state.

How Do Lasting Cross-Border Linkages Evolve Out of Migration?

The question therefore is: How do these transnational social migrant spaces emerge, function, and how are they maintained? Not only when international migrants engage in recurrent migration but also when they eventually return to the country of origin or stay in the country of immigration, the connections to both do not automatically vanish. Instead, we observe multi-stranded ties; sometimes labour migration and refugee movements even give rise to a cyclical exchange between the emigration and immigration countries including not only migrants but also material goods, information, symbols and cultural practices. These phenomena challenge the assumptions about clear-cut distinctions between emigrant and immigrant in the case of recurrent migrants. It also raises questions about the formation of these transnational migrant spaces in migration systems.

Simultaneous Transnational Ties and Immigrant Adaptation?

The question reads: What are the implications of transnational social ties upon the incorporation of labour migrants and refugees? It is quite obvious that dominant theories of incorporation of labour migrants such as the canonical and refined theories of assimilation and ethnic pluralism espouse naive conceptions of transnational ties. Most versions of assimilation theory are silent about transnational ties. Implicitly, these ties are deemed to gradually vanish, often proportionally to the intensity of new ties immigrants build in the immigration country. Consequently, emigration country specific norms, values, and practices are thought to slowly evaporate in the process of successful adaptation to the new country. Immigrants and their descendants supposedly maintain remnants of those ties which are compatible with the mainstream culture(s). While criticizing assimilation theories for looking upon immigrant resources as useless baggage weighed down by the exigencies of the new circumstances of life, concepts of ethnic pluralism have fallen into equally problematic assumptions. Insofar as ethnic pluralists maintain that immigrants mainly transplant traits, resources, cultural characteristics from the old country to the new, they are not capable of explaining new and syncretist forms of immigrant life. Ethnic pluralists assert that the ties of immigrants do not melt away but are still vivid among the second and third generations. For example, children of immigrants often speak their mother tongue at home. In a period of increasing demands among immigrants for cultural rights and heightened tolerance of immigration countries towards multiculturalism—expressed in forms such as public recognition of immigrant religious practices and mother tongue instruction of immigrant children at school—this train of thought has experienced a revival.

How can we start to understand the seemingly simultaneous existence of trends towards both adaptation and the maintenance of social, religious, national, and ethnic attachments? Is this a case of yet incomplete melting into the core of society, as the assimilation theorists would like to have it? Or, is it a sure sign of increasingly multicultural polities, as the ethnic pluralists claim? The jury is still out on this question because recent migration flows after World War Two and new immigrant generations are still too fresh to convincingly muster empirical evidence speaking for one or the other interpretation. What is feasible at this point is to ask how migrants' ties across nation-state borders impact upon processes of adaptation or incorporation of immigrants that could eventually lead to assimilation or ethnic pluralism—or to new forms of adaptation characterized by activities in transnational social spaces, the border-crossing expansion of social space. Transnational spaces consist of migrant networks cutting across discrete organizations such as nation-states. They are thus interstitial, even though they may congeal into bounded groups such as transnational communities, as for example, diasporas.

Participation of international migrants in transnational spaces that span two or several nation-states raises serious challenges to the conceptualization of immigrant membership in nationally bounded societies. This could mean that immigrant organizations in cumulatively developing transnational spaces cannot easily be controlled by the nation-states of emigration and immigration. Think of the various projects exiles and transnational communities entertain to form nation-states in or out of their homelands. We need to ask whether the whole of transmigrant associations influences the course of state politics and policies, shapes and modifies them to a significant degree. Taking into account the vastly improved means of transportation and communication during the past decades, the feasibility of such developments is obvious. Consider the activities of the Islamic *umma* in wide parts of the Western world, and the various movements for political independence and reconquest among exiled groups of Kurds, Sikhs, Iranians, and numerous other groups around the globe. Finally, the question arises whether associations populated and run by international migrants form a coherent whole that can structure itself and coordinate itself in transnationalizing civil societies.

Three Generations of Migration Scholarship

Theoretically, migration in transnational social spaces denotes a third generation of conceptualizing international migration. In the first phase, models emphasized the push–pull nature of migration in the context of developments such as demographic transition in the age of industrialization. These and other push factors are analysed together with pull factors emanating from the immigration countries, such as efforts at labour recruitment. Flows were seen as distinct movements from emigration to immigration regions, with counter-streams developing, such as return migration (Figure 1.1).

Those analysts who upgraded this conceptualization in a second

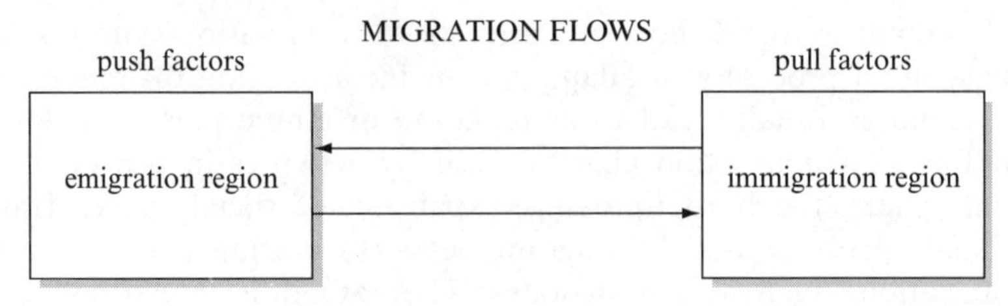

FIG. 1.1. *Stylized push–pull model of migration*

phase argued that labour migration and refugee flows occur in structured relationships between emigration and immigration states; embedded in structural dependence between core and periphery regions of the capitalist world economy. Generally, emigration states are post-colonial regions of the economically less developed and politically penetrated periphery, while the immigration states are thought to occupy the higher echelons in the politico-economic hierarchy of the world economy. Emigration and immigration states form regional migration systems, tied by manifold linkages—of trade, military, and cultural cooperation—which are necessary requirements for international migration to take off at all. Migratory flows are but one form of linkage that connect centres and peripheries (Figure 1.2). While the penetration of the periphery is the ultimate cause of South–North migration, the 'Third World' comes to the North through migration and leads to conflicts when migrants primarily act as and are seen by the natives not only as economic but also as political and cultural agents.

A third generation of scholarship is in the making. Instead of mere linkages that connect emigration and immigration regions, the concept of transnational social space aims towards a recognition of the practices of migrants and stayers connecting both worlds and the activities of institutions such as nation-states that try to control these spaces. This approach complements but does not substitute for the earlier ones. International migrants—transmigrants if recurrent migration is exten-

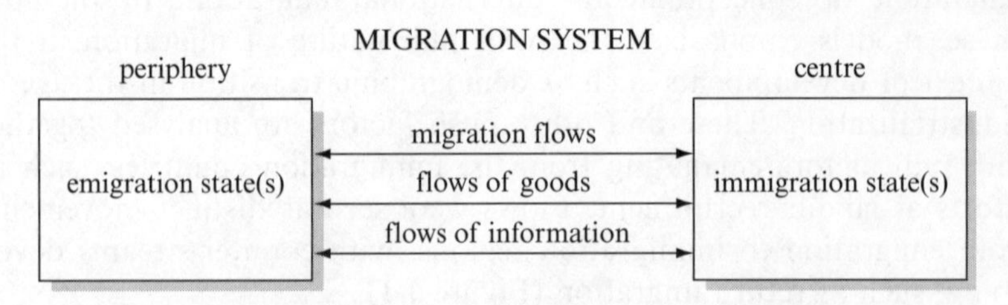

FIG. 1.2. *Stylized centre–periphery model of migration*

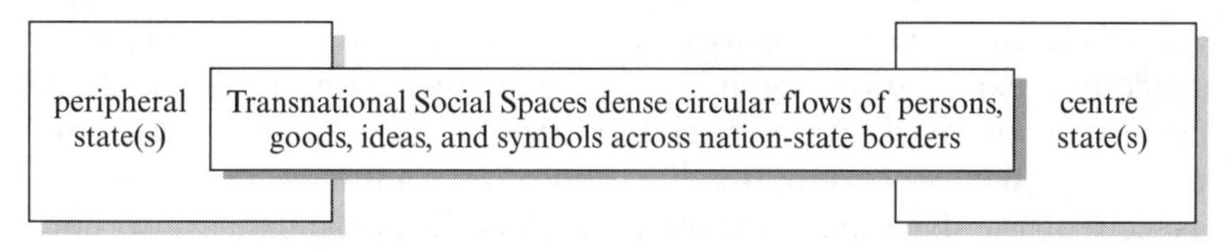

FIG. 1.3. *Stylized model of migration in transnational social spaces*

sive—build ties that cross political borders by maintaining multiple and border-transgressing familial, economic, social, religious, cultural, and political relationships. This also entails the circuitous movement of goods, ideas, information, symbols, and persons—transnational exchanges. Also, migrations are not singular journeys but tend to become an integral part of migrants' lives (Figure 1.3). Moreover, the distinction between countries of origin and destination blurs even further. As the migration process is proceeding, it is becoming increasingly difficult to classify countries as either senders or receivers. At a late stage most are both because of generally high rates of return migration and, sometimes, transmigrants who travel back and forth. The metaphor of transnational social spaces helps to broaden the scope of migration studies to include the circulation of ideas, symbols, and material culture, not only the movement of people (Goldring 1996*b*: 77). In doing so, it reconnects with the second approach that focuses on macro-structural linkages between emigration and immigration countries.

The Approach Taken

The proposition made here to unpack the two puzzles—ranging from relative immobility and mass migration to transnational ties and adaptation—is that the decisions of potential migrants to stay or go have to be considered within the context of their ties. At the forefront of the analysis stand two aspects, social and symbolic ties and social capital. Social resources, viz. capital within ties, are necessary requirements for ties concatenating into networks.

Migration Networks and Social Capital

This study draws on two literatures in migration studies. Both network analysis and the concept of social capital have been applied. Yet they are still somewhat awkward dance partners. The task is to choreograph them in a more systematic way. A rich and impressive literature gives suggestive explanations of migration dynamics with the help of the network concept (Kritz and Zlotnik 1992). These analyses are most plausible when explaining the direction of international migration and aspects of the dynamics of migration flows. In particular, it also considers feedback effects that help to explain why even more migration occurs once it has taken off. From Arensberg and Kimball (1940) to Massey and his collaborators (1987: 170), researchers have admirably accounted for the fact that migrant networks become self-sustaining over time because of the social support that they provide to prospective migrants.

Yet migration network analysis has two major deficiencies. First, it is silent when it comes to explaining relative immobility. Oddly, these researches do not raise the question at all. Second, accounts of how migrant networks come into existence are also absent. Here, another strand helps. Alejandro Portes and his collabourators have begun to connect network analyses with concepts from economic sociology, especially on the economic success of self-employed immigrants in the United States (Portes 1995). The argument goes that the higher the stock of social capital in the form of reciprocity and solidarity, the more successful these self-employed immigrants are in inserting themselves into the American economy. We can use this idea, improve upon the conceptualization of social capital and apply it to the transfer of social capital from emigration to immigration countries. In particular, we need to consider the character of social capital as a local asset that limits mobility in the beginning stages of migration, while it may function as a transmission belt and help accelerate international movement in the later stages.

The two literatures on migrant networks and social capital have made a resourceful and exigent case for dynamic analyses with which this analysis is in keen sympathy and much agreement. This book disputes the encircled qualities of their research programme, taking issue with its neglect of the resources immigrants transfer transnationally. This omission cobbles their persuasiveness in solving the two substantial puzzles of international migration and immigrant adaptation outlined earlier. Instead, this study connects the structure of ties in networks, and the content of ties—social capital. This conceptual sinew helps to delineate the concrete mechanisms of transfer and convertibility of migrants' capital across nation-state borders. It produces a tight and rich coupling between mobility and immobility, between migration and post-migration processes.

Towards an Expanded Relational Approach: Ties and Social Capital

The social and symbolic ties between individual and collective agents influence the decisions made by potential and actual migrants. Moreover, people take certain positions within a web of ties. The analysis of such ties and positions is the hallmark of network analysis. In this view, structure is conceptualized as lasting patterns of relations, viz. ties, among people. Regularities or patterns in interaction give rise to social structures in which positions determine access to resources such as money, authority, and power. Since it is not only face-to-face contacts and friends of friends that are important—especially in large groups or across borders—we also need to consider symbolic ties, embodied in shared or common meanings, memories, future expectations, and symbols.

Network analysis does not consider the content of social and symbolic ties—obligations, reciprocity, and solidarity, and those that can be mobilized through these ties, such as resources of others, information, and social control. Obligations, reciprocity, and solidarity are dimensions of social capital; resources of others, information, and control are benefits derived from social capital (for differing definitions, see Bourdieu 1983; Coleman 1990: ch. 12; and Putnam 1993). These dimensions and benefits of social capital are visible in kinship groups, neighbourhoods, formal organizations, and specific migrant networks.

Social capital is location-specific. Local assets include economic resources, such as money or physical capital, human capital, such as educational credentials, vocational training and professional skills, and social capital, i.e. the content of ties and the resources inherent in social transactions. Local assets in the communities and countries of origin translate into specific advantages of potential migrants. Territorial assets may refer to economic capital such as financial assets, human or educational capital such as degrees, professional skills, and—the focus of this analysis—social capital. The question comes up under which conditions local assets are transferable and under which they are not, and thus contribute to immobility, domestic, or international migration.

Social capital denotes the transactions between individuals and groups that facilitate social action, and the benefits derived from these mechanisms. It is primarily a local asset and can be transferred cross-nationally only under specific conditions. Especially for pioneer migrants the expected costs and risks in international movement are high. They face the task of maintaining social and symbolic ties with those in the country of origin and of building new contacts in the destination country. They often need to come up with at least a modicum of ties in the new country in order to deploy their human and economic capital, for example, finding jobs and housing. Political engagement of migrants abroad needs a basis in ties and social capital, too. Therefore, the hypothesis is that social capital contributes to low relative mobility across borders. However, once official policies and other groups support migration, pioneer migrants and other facilitators take heart. Their actions help to establish migration networks, in themselves crystallized social capital. International migration takes off.

The approach taken here is not simply an application of network analysis. In empirical research it has nearly become routine to include network factors in the analysis of whatever phenomenon as a kind of turbo-chaser. It nicely boosts explained variance in accounting for almost any kind of phenomenon. However, there is a gap. The theoretical underpinning for all these models and analyses is missing (Granovetter 1979: 501). Network theory is more of an empirical methodology than a substantive theory. The theoretical assumptions often come in only implicitly. The most general claim is that a particular network structure has a specific effect on the actions of certain people participating in these webs of ties: individual behaviour is influenced through relationships if the individual interacts with others (Rogers and Kincaid 1981: 83). In other words, the position of a participant in a set of ties determines her behaviour (White, Boorman, and Breiger 1976). This is the same as saying that syntax is the whole of grammar, a truly preposterous statement. What about the meaning of words, semantics? Likewise, a purely structural approach overlooks how potential migrants organize staying and moving within close and remote connectivities in paying attention to the content of ties. Moreover, not only social ties matter but also symbolic ones.

While the relational approach can be applied to all levels of analysis—macro, meso, or micro—this study concentrates on the meso level. On this level, the attempt is to understand the fundamental internal dynamics driving immobility and mobility and at times, subverting structural factors inducing migration, such as economic conditions in the countries of emigration and destination. It truly provides a meso link because the resources inherent in social and symbolic ties tie people to larger collectives, and enable collectives to bond people in groups.

The Goal: A Meso-Link Analysis

The purpose of this book is to design a wider theoretical and analytical template for dynamic migration analysis. The approach presented in the chapters to follow is not a superior alternative to existing micro-, meso-, and macro-levels of analysis and to existing research on migrant networks. Instead, it is an opportunity to sharpen and deepen our research capacities in providing a meso link. It is both more modest and more assertive than existing approaches. It is more modest because each level of analysis has its inherent limitation. No one set of 'nuts and bolts' can claim exclusive purchase on the two substantive puzzles of international migration. This analysis is additive, it seeks to fill substantial gaps, while building on the fundaments of studies on migrant networks and social capital.

Yet it is also more assertive than preceding studies because it claims that an enlarged meso-level analysis with social and symbolic ties leads us to better understand the characteristics of one of the main resources of migrants, social capital. The focus of this analysis is on the structure and the content of the ties between people. This all means that migration can be analysed as a matter of social and symbolic ties. The terrain on which migration processes play out lies beyond the agents themselves. A relational analysis neither denies individual agency nor disregards macro-structures. By contrast, it helps us to appreciate the localized or territorialized, ambiguous, and contradictory character of migrants' lives. Broadly conceived, the relational approach taken here radically differs from social science based on categories and attributes.

An expanded relational approach builds on two more guiding concepts—local assets and transnational social spaces. In a nutshell, the two puzzles of simultaneous relative immobility and mass migration, and concomitant transnational spaces and immigrant adaptation are inextricably related. Migrants usually cannot transfer social capital abroad without pioneer migrants and brokers who help in establishing migrant networks and link up with institutions in migration networks. Chain and mass migration develop when social capital does not function as a local asset but as a transnational transmission belt. Once social capital is internationally transferable, adaptation in the country of destination or readaptation in the emigration country proceeds on a new level—in transnational social spaces. Importantly, there is no linear reciprocal relationship between immigrant adaptation, on the one hand, and ties within transnational spaces developing out of international migration, on the other.

Towards a Working Definition of Migration

In its most general form spatial movement can be understood as a transfer from one place to another, from one social or political unit to another. This concept rests upon the understanding of space as a sort of container to a socially, politically, and economically relevant construct. Migration is a permanent or semi-permanent change of residence, usually across some type of administrative boundary. Unlike the singular demographic events of birth and death, a person can migrate many times, for varied duration, and across numerous territorial divisions. This transfer may strain, rupture, change, or reinforce previous ties. A similar definition states that in 'its most general sense "migration" is ordinarily defined as the relatively permanent movement of persons over a significant distance. But this definition, or any paraphrase of it, merely begins to delimit the subject, for the exact meaning of the most important terms ("permanent", "significant") is still to be specified' (Petersen 1968: 286). Other definitions exclude certain types of movement: 'human migration, the permanent change of residence by an individual or group; it excludes such movements as nomadism, migrant labour, commuting and tourism, all of which are transitory in nature' (*The New Encyclopedia Britannica* 1991: vi. 137).

Who is a Migrant?

Importantly, we find some differentiation between change of residence between nation-states—immigration and emigration—and between subunits of a nation-state—in-migration and out-migration (*The Social Science Encyclopedia* 1985: 524). On the most rudimentary level, one can use administratively defined territorial units to distinguish between internal and international migration. Then movement within the same administrative unit is not regarded as migration anymore, it is relocation. The number of persons who are classified in censuses as migrant are an artefact that is produced by territorial boundaries (Husa 1990/1: 37). Generally, international movement poses higher barriers or intervening obstacles than internal movements in terms of borders. International migration raises pertinent issues regarding claims of people vis-à-vis states, citizenship, integration into labour, educational, and housing markets and cultural adaptation.

In this study the term 'migrant' refers to a person who moves from one country to another with the intention of taking up residence there for a relevant period of time. All those are migrants who reside and stay abroad for more than three months, be they primary migrants—those migrating for the first time—return migrants, or circular and recurrent migrants. A return migrant is a person who moves back to the original country of emigration with the intention of taking up residence again there for a relevant period of time. This could mean that she moves again—back to the immigration country—re-emigration—or yet another third country—second-time emigration. Sometimes returnees do not endure living in the original emigration countries upon return or are forced to leave again. We speak of return migration as repatriation when the initiative to return is not of the migrants themselves but of the political authorities (Bovenkerk 1974: 4–6). Return migration is different from transilient and circular migration: transilient migration or *Weiterwanderung* happens when people move on to a second destination. Recurrent or circular migration is characterized by frequent movement between two or more places, such as in seasonal labour migration. Circular migrants are different from transmigrants: the latter are persons who live in either the country of emigration or destination, and commute back and forth between the two locations. However, this is not seasonal as in the case of circular migrants. Rather, it pertains to life-periods or a whole life among categories such as hypermobile businessmen.

Mobility and Immobility: Anthropological and Social Science Views

To emphasize the high rate of relative immobility is not to make an anthropological statement about the allegedly sedentary nature of human beings as against the notion of women and men as inherently nomadic beings, having an innate *Wanderlust*. It makes sense to focus on the very conditions enabling, prompting, hindering, and continuing geographical mobility and immobility. In most migration theories, however, the assumption is that human beings are inherently sedentary. More specifically, the sedentarist norm is an image prevalent in much of the literature on refugees. For example, there is the assumption that the country of origin is not only the normal but the ideal habitat for any person (Stein 1981). It is considered the place where one fits in, lives in peace, and has an unproblematic culture and individual or collective identity. This assumption can already be discerned in the semantics used. In order to turn into migrants, people need to be 'pushed' by factors in their home regions and 'pulled' away by the lures of the immigration regions. However, these anthropological assumptions can neither be confirmed nor disconfirmed by social science enquiries.

Looking through a historical lense, we forcefully debunk the myth of an allegedly sedentary lifestyle in the pre-industrial period and place the study of migration in the context of history. This means to take the challenge seriously to write the history of mankind as the history of migration (Sombart 1969: i/2, 883). As a historian of migration reminds us:

Our image of a sedentary Europe . . . is seriously flawed. People were on the move; and where and why they traveled tells us a good bit about the past and about the pressures and processes that produced the world with which we are familiar. Human movement is connected to every level of life in western Europe—from the intimacy of family decisions about how cash will be earned to the global scale, where it reflects Europe's place in the world economy. Migration, in short, connects the changes in European history with the lives of men and women in the past.

(Moch 1992: 1)

Moreover, a sophisticated anthropological approach argues that human beings are first of all open towards their social and cultural environment (Gehlen 1957; see Hoffmann-Nowotny 1988: 31–2).

Options for Migrants: Exit, Voice, Loyalty—and Despondence

It is useful to look upon the types of choices available to potential migrants. Moving, exit, and staying are the main options for migrants. The concept of local assets helps us to structure the alternatives. We can distinguish various options of exit, voice, and loyalty. In addition to exit, two responses are common in the case of schools, governments, and other organizations whose performances fluctuate. The relevant public may voice its dissatisfaction, with implicit or explicit threats of exit. Or it may tolerate unsatisfactory performance for awhile because the costs of exit or voice are greater than the loss of quality. Tolerance reflects the subjective returns a person derives from the organization. It is an indicator of loyalty (Hirschman 1970).

Exit can mean a variety of strategies of geographical mobility, ranging from internal migration within a nation-state to international migration. Exit of potential movers is often coupled with members of households or other groups who stay. This indicates that moving and staying always have to be considered jointly and can thus constitute complementary strategies (Goldscheider 1971: 57). Indeed, territorial exit can actually constitute a way to reinforce staying for others within a family or network of significant others in the country of emigration, and economic betterment through the remission of money, goods, and skills from abroad. This strategy is often coupled with family members engaging in short-term cyclical migration, such as seasonal work. In the rural areas of many developing countries seasonal migration supplements subsistence agriculture. In the case of international migration, the exit option allows for the accumulation of additional resources to be used upon return in the country of origin. For example, the returnee may invest money, political know-how and transfer skills acquired abroad. Resources transferred from abroad may also serve to increase insider-specific local assets. Think of small entrepreneurs who use remittances to set up shops in the countries of origin.

Voice means political expression and action in the place of origin or in the immigration country. The options of potential migrants to exercise exit and voice strategies are constrained by nation-state policies and international policies. Importantly, exit and voice are not exclusive alternatives. Instead, they can be used in a sequence, such as migration and political voice upon return, or at the same time, such as political activities in both the immigration state and influence on domestic politics in the emigration country. Also, emigration to a democratic nation-state often enhances political opposition in the state of origin that otherwise might not be possible. It could be argued, for example, that at times exit is not an alternative for voice but even a necessary condition for the use of voice (Hirschman 1993). This certainly applies to exile and diaspora communities that are vividly engaged in the politics of the emigration states. The voice option may be used to exert political pressure in the country of origin to improve living conditions, both by stayers and by movers after their return. In the case of transnational communities the immigration country may even serve as a platform from which to influence politics in the country of origin.

The importance of loyalty is that it can neutralize within certain limits the tendency of the most quality-conscious customers or members to be the first to exit (Hirschman 1970: 79). The concept of loyalty has to be taken two steps further to be fruitful for migration analysis. If local assets are available, then their specificity makes people try to improve life *in situ* or use voice before exiting. If local assets are nonexistent, then people cannot make meaningful choices about exit and voice, and loyalty is an irrelevant category.

First, in our case, we recur to the specificity of local assets. Local assets mediate the probability of exit and voice. Local assets that are hard to transfer geographically attenuate the tendency to exit a country. Local assets may also increase the possibility that potential refugees resort to voice before exiting. Because of the specificity of certain types of assets, people generally try *in situ* adaptation first. They seek to improve their life at home. Among the types of assets, economic capital is the most easy to transfer. To take an extreme example, some immigration countries grant permanent residence and citizenship to immigrants who agree to invest a certain amount of money. Human capital is harder to transfer abroad. For example, educational credentials of professionals may not be recognized or a new language has to be learned in order to deploy human capital. Social capital is hardest to transfer because it depends on fragile systems of social transaction. It is the most locally specific among all sorts of capital. Local assets can also lead potential migrants to remain loyal to their country and exercise voice—trying to change their situation politically. In general, potential movers will not move to the degree that their assets are locally bound or can only be fruitfully applied in the local or regional context where the mover or stayer lives. In the case of potential refugees, such local assets may include symbolic ties such as loyalty to a polity or community in the political realm and resources in social ties that cannot be transferred abroad in the social realm; for example, affective ties to kin and friends.

Second, there are cases in which local assets are destroyed or simply non-existent. Exit and voice occur under varying degrees of freedom or choice; ranging on a continuum from involuntary to voluntary forms of migration. One of the far end points along the continuum is of particular relevance: the majority of people in developing countries have practically no choice because they completely lack resources for exit and voice. They are despondent, in a state of resignation to a hostile environment around them (Ahmed 1997: 176). Often, the degree of autonomy for persons is close to zero because individuals do not have sufficient resources such as money, information, and connections available. They cannot engage in a weighed decision to either move or stay, to choose exit or voice. In these situations people only move because their very physical survival is threatened by violent conflicts, civil war, persecution, economic or ecological disasters. This does not mean that they are not moving at all, as many refugee movements in contemporary Africa attest. Yet we would expect most of these movers to exit to the nearest location possible.

Forced and Voluntary Movements vs. Labour Migrants and Refugees

One of the most widespread typologies of migrants includes permanent settlers, temporary contract workers, temporary professional transients, clandestine or illegal workers, respectively, asylum seekers and refugees (Appleyard 1991: 22–3). The criteria involved to construct such categories encompass: (1) territory: domestic–international, (2) time: temporary–permanent, (3) size of flow: individual, group, mass migration, (4) cause: voluntary labour migration–involuntary or forced refugee flight and (5) legal status: illegal–legal. While the first three categories are undoubtedly easy to establish and necessary to define international movers—if data are collected and made available—legal status is a set of devices established by the state bureaucracies of emigration and immigration countries and hence subject to permanent redefinition. The fourth dimension is the most problematic for our meso-link analysis. Let us focus on the forced and voluntary distinction because nation-states use distinct criteria to separate forced migrants as refugees from voluntary migrants as labour migrants.

Basically, we can use the voluntary–involuntary distinction as a point of departure. But instead of seeing it as a dichotomous category, we will use it to denote a continuum. This continuum should not be confused with another distinction, labour migrants vs. refugees. It would be misleading to equate involuntary migrants with refugees and voluntary migrants with labour migrants. The terms 'refugees' and 'labour migrants', when used exclusively, are best reserved for analyses focusing on the nation-state's vantage point, while the continuum between forced and voluntary migration can be used as an analytical device to determine the degrees of choice or freedom available to potential migrants.

The most basic distinction is between voluntary and forced (Fairchild 1925). The emphasis is on the presence or absence of physical coercion. It is certainly undisputed to characterize phenomena such as deportation, exile, expulsion of groups as well as displacement, and deportment—often associated with slavery and torture—as forced movement. And there is a second category including forms of violence against ethnic, cultural, or religious minorities, allowed or even supported by the nation-state authorities that induce a sort of quasi-'voluntary' departure. While these two categories can be subsumed under forced migration and refugee flows, albeit with an even higher degree of involuntariness when we move from category one to two, other phenomena are much harder to classify. For example, are peasants fleeing droughts in the Sahara voluntary or forced migrants? Are migrants who try to escape the high rate of unemployment in their countries of origin really purely voluntary migrants? It may also be difficult to draw the line between economic migrants and refugees because as the crisis phenomena in developing countries worsens, all sectors of society are hit. Yet it would be all too easy to oversimplify the relationship between poverty and refugee flows. The idea that extreme poverty produces refugees is inconsistent with the fact that situations of extreme economic deprivation usually have not resulted in masses of persons claiming international refugee status (Zolberg, Suhrke, and Aguayo 1989: 260). The forced–voluntary distinction was elabourated and refined by Petersen who identified a middle category. He distinguished between '*impelled* migration when the migrants retain some power to decide whether or not to leave and *forced* migration when they do not have this power' (1958: 261).

We should look upon the forced–voluntary distinction as a graded scale and not as a dichotomy. Therefore, we now move from cardinal distinctions to an ordinal scale. It then makes sense to think of degrees of freedom as ranging from high to low, from involuntary or forced to voluntary. As to the exit option, mobility of persons is best viewed as ranging on a continuum from totally voluntary exit—in which the choice of the migrants within a web of ties is the overwhelmingly decisive element encouraging people to move—to totally forced exit, where the migrants are faced with death if they remain in their present place of residence. The same idea stands behind the distinction between proactive and reactive movement: in the proactive case refugees do indeed have a wider and richer opportunity structure than in the reactive case where they have to respond very quickly in order to save their lives (Richmond 1988 and 1993). Along this voluntary–forced continuum we can place labour migrants and refugees but also movers who are involved in family migration, overstaying tourists or visitors that turn into permanent settlers, and illicit immigrants.

Nation-states accepting refugees do not employ a continuous scale when classifying new entrants. De jure distinctions made by nation-states and international regimes distinguish between labour migrants and refugees. The notion of refugees is therefore restricted to those persons fleeing persecution and massive disasters. The de jure definition of refugee as used by most nation-states is tied to the Geneva Convention (1951). The most commonly cited part of the basic legal definition of refugee status reads:

> [T]he term 'refugee' shall apply to any person who [,] . . . owing to well-founded fear of being persecuted for reasons of race, religion, nationality, membership of a particular social group or political opinion, is outside the country of his nationality and is unable or, owing to such fear, is unwilling to avail himself of the protection of that country; or who, not having a nationality and being outside the country of his former habitual residence as a result of such events, is unable or, owing to such fear, is unwilling to return to it.

The Geneva Convention was more encompassing than the case-by-case treaties of the pre-World War Two period, but it was only intended to address the European refugee situation. The 1967 'Protocol Relating to the Status of Refugees' removed the Eurocentric geographical restriction and the war-linked time restriction. Now the Geneva Convention became the universal instrument of refugee law.

In sum, refugees are not synonymous with involuntary migrants and labour migrants not with voluntary migrants. Refugees and labour migrants are dichotomous distinctions applied by authoritative collective agents to international migrants. What is even more crucial is that the continuum of forced to voluntary can apply to either refugees or labour migrants. To take an extreme example, forced migrants may apply as labour migrants. Therefore, the terms 'labour migrants' and 'refugees' are used when we speak from the point of view of nation-states and other collective actors; the range from involuntary to voluntary applies to the degrees of freedom available to people.

The Three *Longues Durées* of International Migration in Modern Times

The South–North migration streams are currently the most visible international manifestations of one of the three *longues durées* of international migration since the late sixteenth century. The focus is on the South–North and not South–South and North–North or European East–West dimensions. It encompasses all kinds of movements from the so-called developing countries in the South to the economically more developed countries in the North.

A historical perspective helps to identify the relative migration potential and the particular circumstances under which South–North migration has unfolded in the past decades. The scope of theoretical concepts such as local assets and transnational social spaces is meant to apply to a specific historical period. In South–North migration, we talk about migration from economically less developed to more developed countries. Throughout most of modern history, for example, the majority of international migrants moved into the opposite direction, from colonizing countries to subjected areas of the world. This is of importance because the structural conditions and the motivations of the movers were quite different. Migrations from economically more highly developed to less developed countries are attractive to a quite different sort of group than in the opposite direction. For example, it is not really very attractive for a labourer to move to a less developed country because lower costs of production would cause him to migrate in the other direction. However, it may be more attractive for farmers, merchants or academics and has been so throughout most of the nineteenth century. If such individuals and groups with higher amounts of economic, human, and social capital move abroad, the terms of adaptation are also likely to differ from those of manual labour. In contemporary migration, we encounter both manual labour, highly skilled human capital migrants such as professionals and economic capital migrants such as business entrepreneurs; albeit with a clear numerical overrepresentation of the first category.

At least three periods of large-scale migration movements can be distinguished in modern times (K. Davis 1989):

(1) *European Colonization*

During the Age of Discovery, the early stages of European colonization of what was later called the Third World, the use of involuntary labour by European colonizers constituted a mechanism of economic penetration. Colonizers turned to two main forms of forced labour, slavery—Africans in the Americas from the seventeenth to the nineteenth century or in the Middle East—and so-called contract labour, such as Indians in Australia in the nineteenth century.

(2) *Transatlantic Migration to White Settler Colonies*

The second long period covers the main phase of the industrialization of Europe and the attendant settlement of white settlers in the Americas, Australia and South Africa during the second half of the nineteenth and early twentieth century. It was a sort of compass migration in a growing Atlantic world-economy. Craftspersons and artisans from urban areas and at a later stage, peasants from the rural countryside in peripheral regions of Europe, made up the majority of economically motivated migrants (Morawska 1990). Yet there was also a substantial number of minorities discriminated against because of religious belonging who came to the New World, such as the Hutterites in nineteenth-century Russia and political dissidents from Europe, among them activists in the 1848/9 revolutions. The net flows of international migration went from countries in the North, mostly Europe, to the rapidly developing classical immigration countries, the Anglo-Saxon settler colonies and Latin America, and—to a lesser extent—to colonies in Africa and Asia.

(3) *South–North Migration after World War Two*

The contemporary period set in roughly in the early 1960s. Labour migrants and increasingly refugee flows moved from economically less developed to more developed countries. Even more than in the phase of transatlantic migration, these current movements are characterized by grossly different population growth rates between the developed and the developing countries. So far, this spread is noteworthy not so much in the relative magnitude of flows that have increased since the second half of the 1980s. As we have already noted, the relative magnitude of flows has not surpassed the levels of Europe–settler colony movements in the second period; when we measure movers as a percentage of the total population potentially involved. But it is of import above all in its direction. Since the mid-1960s more than two-thirds of all people applying for immigrant visas in the USA come from developing countries of the South, mostly Asia and Latin America. The situation is not much different for many European immigration countries, where Africa, Asia, and Eastern Europe have turned into major suppliers of new migrants. Since the 1970s the Near East has developed into a major centre of attraction for hundreds of thousands of labour migrants. Also, the economic prosperity of Japan and other South-East Asian countries has begun to attract migrants from poorer South Asian countries. The contemporary configuration is without precedent in four respects. All of them suggest that the migration potential is higher now than ever before in modern times—while the actual rates are not.

First, there are huge, and in many cases still growing, international differentials in income per head and quality of life. This difference seems to be wider now than ever in the past. These differentials are widely, almost universally, known. Mass communication, pioneer migrants, and transnational circuits of recurrent migrants create the impression that the relative volume of international migration has achieved an extent not reached before.

Second, rates of population growth in the South are much higher than the potential for labour market absorption in the North (Castles and Miller 1993: ch. 4). In the case of Europe and North America during the second *longue durée*, the migration that made the greatest contribution to dynamic economic transformation occurred at the time when there was a general shortage of population and the industrial process was labour-intensive and expanding rapidly. Since the demand for labour was high in the face of its limited supply, urban migrants could be productively incorporated into the industrial process of the receivers. The dismantling of the feudal remnants and the capitalization of agriculture in the countries of origin drove labour into urban areas and propelled economic growth. Later, when the increasingly capital-intensive industrial process produced a relative population surplus, the European industrial powers had ready access to the colonies of Africa and Asia, where they could profitably employ both excess population and vagabond capital. Growth and full employment in the more industrialized countries depended on the availability of an abundant supply of labour, and the problems of the poorer countries could be more easily overcome if they were able to reduce the pressure of their manpower surpluses on their society and economy (Lewis 1954). Yet, this felicitous coincidence of immigration country demand and emigration country supply was limited to fortuitous and specific historical circumstances in the late nineteenth and early twentieth century that do not seem to have been applicable to the third *longue durée*. For example, in the European–North African scenario, studies project striking discrepancies in labour force growth between neighbouring regions that differ in wealth; the EU labour force is projected to rise by 1% in the 1990s, while the labour force of the Southern and Eastern Mediterranean is likely to increase by 27% (Stalker 1994: 27).

Thus, the very conditions and forces that characterized the European development experience are conspicuously absent in most contemporary nation-states in the South. Developing countries are trapped in a situation of low labour demands and high labour supplies. Despite some outlets for external migrations, migrants in the South are not in a position to enjoy the kind of colonial migration and settlement that European migrants of the nineteenth century did. In essence, contemporary migration in the South is proceeding under the conditions of rapid population growth, agricultural underdevelopment, generally capital-intensive industrialization, and uncongenial socio-economic structures which have their roots both in internal institutions and colonial policies. Irrespective of the rate of population growth, such economies are inherently incapable of gainfully employing their citizenry. As a result, the dynamic economic energy embodied in them remains suppressed, unable to make any tangible contribution to the process of development (Amin 1974).

Outline of the Book

Chapter 2 discusses the most elabourate theoretical approaches, micro- and macro-level theories, especially theories of rational choice and migration systems theories. On the meso level, the analysis traces network theories. These latter theories only conceptualize the dynamics of migration once it has started, they help to answer our question 'why are there so many international migrants out of a few places?'. They have to be extended to account for relative immobility.

The subsequent two chapters set the stage for analysis. Chapter 3 sketches the macro-context of opportunity structures. Structural factors may initiate international migration. These factors provide partial answers to the puzzle of relative immobility and chain migration. Chapter 4 details the conceptual framework for a meso-link analysis, with a particular focus on ties and social capital. It distinguishes two aspects of social capital. The dimensions are obligations as a pattern of exchange, reciprocity as a norm, and solidarity. The benefits of social capital come into focus: information, access to resources of others, and social control. The analysis explains why social capital is mainly a local asset; but it can turn into a transmission belt when it crystallizes in migrant networks. Social capital fulfils certain functions in selecting migrants, contributes to diffusion, bridges contexts of origin and destination, and helps migrants to adapt to their new environments and transnational life.

The two following chapters explore the first puzzle. Chapter 5 discusses the first question of 'why are there so few migrants out of most places?'. It emphasizes that the costs of maintaining ties and building new ones in the immigration countries are very high in the absence of established migrant networks. Chapter 6 then continues to detail the selection and diffusion functions of social capital in addressing the second question of 'why are there so many out of very few places?'. In particular, the adapted critical mass approach emphasizes the pivotal role of pioneer migrants and brokers, the formation of migrant and migration networks, and processes of cumulative mobility that result in S-shaped migration curves.

The next part plunges into the second puzzle. Chapter 7 deals with the bridging functions of social capital in asking the third question of how transnational social spaces emerge out of former homeland ties and processes of adaptation in the country of immigration. This concerns a typology of transnational spaces, factors contributing to their development, stages of their formation, and their expressions in the economic, political, and cultural life of migrants. Turning to the adaptive functions of social capital, Chapter 8 elaborates on the fourth question of how we can explain the concomitant processes of immigrant adaptation and continuing transnationalization in economic, political and cultural realms. An apocryphal gospel, the concept of border-crossing expansion of social space, supplements the canonical concepts of assimilation and ethnic pluralism theories in order to describe the various trajectories of immigrant adaptation following contemporary migration.

Building upon the meso-link analysis of international migration and its consequences, Chapter 9 reassembles the findings of this study. It provides elements for a multi-level theory of migration and post-migration on all three ideal-typical levels of analysis, micro, meso, and macro. Thus, the function of the resources and mechanisms of the meso link become more obvious. In conclusion, the discussion singles out the political dimension of continuing transnationalization through international migration because it is the most problematic in terms of membership.

2

A Review of Dominant Theories of International Migration

The greater part of the research on international migration has dealt with the question of why people migrate and, to a lesser extent, the dynamics of migration, such as chain migration in migrant networks. This chapter appraises both micro- and macro-level theories about the volume of international South–North movement. In addition, it considers network or meso-level theories concerning the dynamics of migration. The goal of this chapter is to disclose the unsatisfactory features of existing migration theories regarding the puzzles of relative immobility and mass migration. The analysis is divided into three parts. It first elaborates a familiar and ideal-typical distinction—micro: the individual decision-making level, meso: people within the web and content of ties on the intermediate level, and macro: the highly aggregated and broader structural level. Second, the literature review moves from micro to macro and macro to micro. Third, this helps to identify the theoretical gap in the meso-analysis, the occlusion of resources inherent in social and symbolic ties. Finally, the discussion turns to the relationship between theory and empirical evidence used in the following chapters.

Three Stylized Levels of Analysis: Micro, Macro, and Meso

Three levels of analysis offer a starting ground (Figure 2.1):

(1) The degree of freedom or autonomy of a potential migrant, the individual or micro-level. This is the degree to which she has the ability to decide on moving or staying.

(2) The political-economic-cultural structures on the level of the nation-states, the country of origin and the country of destination, and the world system constitute the macro-level. On this plane, the analysis turns to the inter- and transnational structures and the relations between nation-states. For example, we can speak of the Atlantic world-system in the nineteenth century which connected North America and Europe.

MICRO values or desires and expectancies	*MESO* collectives and social networks	*MACRO* macro-level opportunity structures
individual values and *expectancies* – improving and securing survival, wealth, status, comfort, stimulation, autonomy, affiliation, and morality	*social ties* – strong ties families and households – weak ties networks of potential movers, brokers, and stayers; *symbolic ties* kin, ethnic, national, political, and religious organizations; symbolic communities *content of ties – transactions* obligations, reciprocity, and solidarity; information, control, and access to resources of others	*economics* – income and unemployment differentials *politics* – regulation of spatial mobility through nation-states and international regimes; – political repression, ethnic, national, and religious conflicts *cultural setting* – dominant norms and discourses *demography and ecology* – population growth; – availability of arable land – level of technology

FIG. 2.1. *The three stylized levels of migration analysis*

(3) The set of social and symbolic ties among movers and groups, and the resources inherent in these relations constitute the meso-level. This refers to the structure, strength, and density of social ties, on the one hand, and their content, on the other. This relational dimension concerns the social and symbolic ties among stayers and migrants with units and networks in the areas of origin and destination, and relations between relevant collective actors; *inter alia*, kin groups, households, religious groups, ethnic communities, and nations. It also contains the resources inherent in these ties that facilitate cooperation, namely social capital.

(1) *The Micro Level*

Whatever is taken into account on this level, the focus solidly rests on the decision-making individual. On the most fine-grained dimension, international movements can be characterized by a continuum along the degrees of freedom or choice for potential migrants. On the one end, in some instances, the essential decision-maker is not the migrant him- or herself; think of slaves, convicts, some refugees, contract workers, sometimes children and spouses. On the other end, there are individuals with a high degree of autonomy, based on resources such as money, information, and connections. The degree of freedom or autonomy is circumscribed in a context in which the main sets of parties involved in migration decision-making and the dynamics of migration are: people themselves, enmeshed in a web of significant others in the places of origin and destination, collectives and social networks of potential and actual movers and stayers such as families, households, friendship and kinship circles, neighbourhoods, ethnic, religious, and professional associations. Furthermore, there are also interested collective actors in the countries of origin and destination, such as non-governmental organizations (NGOs), supra-national organizations such as the United Nations High Commissioner for Refugees (UNHCR), emigration and immigration country governments, political parties, unions and employer organizations.

(2) *The Macro Level*

Political-economic-cultural structures denote an array of factors in the emigration and destination countries and in the international political and economic system of nation-states. Macro-structural analyses of international migration imply a triadic relationship between governments and authorities in the emigration countries, their counterparts in the destination country, and the migrants' associations—and sometimes international organizations. Along all these dimensions we find a considerable degree of variation affecting migration decisions: nation-states differ regarding factors such as external power in the international system, internal administrative capacity, efficiency, and political stability. This has consequences for the emergence of migrant flows. The admission and integration policies of emigration countries vary from open to restrictive. Moreover, nation-states tend to favour the admission of certain immigrant categories and newcomers from certain countries, while making it harder for people from other groups and territorial origins. And, fundamentally, international migration cannot be conceived without nation-states in the South and in the North, potential senders and receivers, who differ along economic characteristics such as living standards, jobs, working conditions, unemployment rates, and wages in the emigration and immigration countries. Such differentials are important prerequisites for migration to occur between nation-states. International norms and organizations also have an impact on the mobility of persons. Consider the international covenants on human and social rights by the International Labour Organisation (ILO) and the Geneva Convention on refugees and asylum seekers. Finally, in the cultural realm, there are differences in normative expectations and collective identity. For example, in some areas of the world, 'cultures of migration' have developed, in which international migration forms an accepted and widely practised form of life.

(3) *The Meso Level*

A relational analysis obviates the rigid micro vs. macro distinction because it focuses more on the form and content of the relationship rather than on the properties or attributes of the actors or positions. On the meso level, the social and symbolic ties of the movers and stayers vary with respect to their structure, such as density and strength and their content. The emphasis clearly is on the ties people entertain with others. The ties may reach to the immigration or the emigration countries or to both at the same time. Among international migrants, the ties can range from a dense network to the emigration country to a total break. This implies no bonds to the origin anymore and a complete reorientation to the immigration country. Yet even in the case of permanent settlement abroad, old ties to the country of origin can be maintained or new ones established—both in the country of origin and in the immigration country. Therefore, permanent settlement in the country of immigration does not necessarily mean fewer ties to the area of origin. If these ties are systematically patterned in networks and collectives, we can link the relational to the macro-structural level. Migrants use resources inherent in these ties, such as various dimensions of social capital—exchange-based obligations, the norm of reciprocity and solidarity, and benefits derived from them, such as access to the resources of others, information, and control.

Among the three levels considered here, the meso level is the most vague. However, for explaining processes of immobility and mobility and the mechanisms involved, it is the most notable. Situated in between micro- and macro-level analysis, meso approaches establish firm links to both—forming a meso link. Addressing the ties of individuals, meso-level analysis focuses on how social action is facilitated and on resources such as social capital that people can muster to achieve goals. At the interstices of individual and collective action, it connects with larger aggregates: groups, formal organizations, social movements, and institutions. It concerns associations (Tocqueville 1988) and 'secondary groups near enough to the individuals to attract them strongly in their sphere of action and drag them . . . into the general torrent of social life' (Durkheim 1964: 28). It refers to what can be labelled as intermediary—community life, voluntary associations, trade unions, and political parties. These collectives form constitutive elements of civic community or civil society, that complex of political groups and institutions mediating between individual citizens and the polity (Putnam 1993).

The three levels of migration analysis discussed—micro, macro, and meso—do not embody necessarily valid distinctions, or reflect some readily identifiable social or political reality. No major migration scholar's oeuvre fits comfortably into the Procrustean bed provided by the oversimplified and heavily stylized categories of analysis—micro, macro, and meso. Instead, reviewing these researches along this triad enables us to define more closely the conceptual elements needed to solve the two puzzles. Thus, distinguishing among these three levels is analytically convenient at best and theoretically misleading at worst. On the convenient side, the distinctions yield a reasonable way of organizing a discussion of the volume and dynamics of international migration. The difficulty is, however, that the problems appear at more than one analytical level. On the misleading side, the threefold distinction lends itself to reification, to the view that the macro, meso, and micro levels are separable and separate kinds of migratory reality. Throughout this analysis, which focuses on the meso level and the meso link, there are many problems that arise from transitions among different levels. In any kind of process and organization do we observe the interpenetration of the three levels.

As we will see in the following review, both micro- and macro-level analyses disregard the relational nature of migration decision-making and dynamics. Existing micro-theoretical approaches view either individuals or households as homogeneous decision-makers. This is true for rational choice approaches and for social psychological stress-awareness concepts. Yet, as abundant empirical research has demonstrated, decision-making involving international migration often occurs within kinship systems such as families and in households that do not necessarily represent homogeneous interests or desires. Such a deficit can be addressed when employing a decidedly relational perspective. At the macro-level, migration systems theories have so far rightly emphasized the linkages between emigration and immigration countries. These theories have come to use network analysis to address the problems of migration dynamics. The configuration of relations at the upper structural levels—international and global—set the limits of the possible and the impossible within which people stay and move, but it is at the level of the more proximate surroundings that people evaluate their situations, define purposes, and undertake actions. But while network elements help to explain the dynamics of migration once it has taken off, they have not been very useful for understanding relative immobility, the formation of migrant networks, and the kind of resources that make up these webs of transactions. In order to overcome this shortcoming, we need to ask about the resources inherent in social and symbolic ties.

The focus then shifts to issues such as exchange of information and goods, obligations, reciprocity, and solidarity among actors.

Both rational choice and social psychological approaches emphasize the motives of individual migrants. They focus upon the capacities people have to make decisions, the preferences or desires that drive potential migrants, the expectations they hold about places abroad, and the importance of these subjective evaluations in their life course.

Micro—The Rational Choice Approach: Moving from Preferences to Opportunities

One of the first such models that shifted the lens from geographical distance to individual decision-making convoked the intervening opportunities: 'the number of persons going a given distance is directly proportional to the number of opportunities at that distance and inversely proportional to the number of intervening opportunities' (Stouffer 1940: 846). This means the following: if opportunities are distributed relatively homogeneously over geographical space, then the number of intervening opportunities—obstacles such as nation-state frontiers—is a simple inverse function of distance. However, empirical studies have repeatedly shown that using intervening opportunities instead of distance adds little to predicting the volume of migration (Speare 1974: 86).

Economistic Cost-Benefit Models

Economistic cost-benefit models were another precursor. In the simplest form of the cost-benefit model, a potential migrant is likely to move if the present value of all future monetary benefits from moving is greater than the monetary costs of moving. It is assumed that the decisive benefits are the differences in income between the origin and the destination and that the only costs are those of transporting the migrant, his family if they also move, and his belongings between the two places. The model thus includes one factor at the emigration country, one factor at the immigration country, and one intervening obstacle. The underlying assumption of the economic cost-benefit model can be expressed by the following equation. A person will move if:

$$\sum_{j=1}^{N} \frac{(Y_{dj} - Y_{0}j)}{(1 + r)^{j}} - T > 0$$

where: Y(dj) = earnings in the *j*th year at the destination
Y(0j) = earnings in the *j*th year at the origin
T = cost of moving
N = total number of years in which future returns are expected
r = rate of interest used to discount future earnings

This logic also underlies more sophisticated cost-benefit models (Sjaastad 1962 and Todaro 1969). But even if wage or income levels between countries of emigration and immigration constitute the most important factor, the reasoning is faulty. For example, in the case of North African/Turkish–West European migration in the 1960s the same factor was there before and after 1973, the year immigration of recruited workers virtually ceased. The effective reason, however, was the demand of West European countries for foreign migrant workers. Also, if what counted were the wage differentials, then the persons most ready to migrate would be the poorest members of the emigrant communities. Evidence from all around the world does not support this conclusion (Albrecht 1972: 74–5).

Another problem with these models is that they are purely economic. Yet, obviously, many other factors go into the decision to move or to stay. There is a large literature on problems with this economic approach because it does not take into account macro-political factors. After all, governments in the immigration states admit certain categories of migrants and exclude others (Zolberg 1987). These rulers also largely determine the size of immigration and the conditions under which newcomers are allowed to stay.

Value-Expectancy Models and Structural Individualism

The basic instrumental statement that extends the economistic reasoning is: in deciding between at least two alternative courses of action, a person is apt to choose the one for which the perceived value of the result is the greater. The actor is able to make rational decisions on the basis of a set of value or preference orderings. In the value-expectancy model, values or preferences are supplemented by the expectancies—the subjective probabilities—a potential mover holds (DeJong and Fawcett 1981). The basic value-expectancy model is straightforward:

$$MM = \Sigma_i P_i E_i$$

where: MM = the strength of the motivation to migrate
P = the preferred outcome
E = the expectancy that migration will lead to the desired outcome
i = the specific values potential movers hold (see Kulu-Glasgow 1992)

The values or desires can be most diverse. We readily see: 'It is close to impossible to think of a cause which influences the behavior of people—without this cause having an impact on the decision of the people to emigrate' (author's translation; Sadler, cited in von Waltershausen 1909: 274). They may be related to improving and securing: wealth (e.g. income), status (e.g. prestigious job), comfort (e.g. better working and living conditions), stimulation (e.g. experience, adventure, and pleasure), autonomy (e.g. high degree of personal freedom), affiliation (e.g. joining friends or family), exit from oppression of all kinds, meaningful life (e.g. improving society), better life for one's children, and morality (e.g. leading a virtuous life for religious reasons). In this view the potential migrant could not only be a worker, a member of a household or a kinship group, but also a voter, a member of ethnic, linguistic, religious, and political groups, a member of a persecuted minority, or a devotee of arts or sports.

However, potential migrants often rationalize their actions *ex post* rather than reason *ex ante* to take them, as the instrumental value-expectancy model suggests. To infer preferences of potential migrants requires the researcher to devise a plausible common metric of utility for actors. Rationality here becomes such a broad covering term that it encompasses virtually every type of motive. But revealed preferences—the basis for inferring trade-offs across goals—exist only *post hoc*. Thus, it is exceedingly difficult to use this kind of approach in order to make specific *ex ante* predictions on migratory movements and to thus empirically verify these motives. Detailed analyses show that often not clearly specified feelings of insecurity and dissatisfaction induce migration. However, when migrants are interviewed after moving, one of the above-named more specific factors is usually used to 'rationalize' the decision (Mälich 1989: 878). This problem is rather serious. In a nutshell, it avers that reason works to rationalize action rather than guide it. The point is that potential migrants sometimes seem to have no reason for acting the way they do. Or, rather, the researcher sees no reason. For instance, potential migrants may recognize one reason for acting in a particular way, but they can equally rationalize acting in a contrary fashion. Alternatively, potential migrants may simply see no reason for acting one way rather than another. In such circumstances, as cognitive dissonance theory would suggest, potential migrants experience psychological distress. It comes from the dissonance between potential migrants' self-image as individuals who are authors of their own scripts and their manifest lack of reason for acting. It is like a crisis of self-respect and the actors seek to remove it by creating reasons (see Festinger 1957 for a general statement).

These micro-level choice theories can be extended. For example, we can use value-expectancy theory and develop such a model for social movement theory (Klandermans 1997). This approach could be translated into migration decision-making in the following way: the individual is a rational, calculating actor weighing costs and benefits of action—staying or moving. The expected costs and benefits are not independent of the individual's evaluation of the likely actions of others. Instead, the perceived efficacy of participation in migration for the individual will depend upon the expectations about one's own contribution to the probability of success. Also, we need to consider the individual's expectations about the probability of success if many persons from the relevant social group such as the family participate. We then expect the person to take a decision when she has high expectations on both of these probabilities. One problem with such a quasi game-theoretic approach is that the act of decision is usually made in well-knit reference groups. Decisions made within such groups depend primarily on trust towards significant others; and cost-benefit calculations enter at a later stage.

More sophisticated renditions of rational choice theory do not only take into account preferences and expectancies—that may, in turn, again shape preferences—but also the opportunity structure, based on the situation encountered by actors. One example is structural individualism. The theoretical premisses, meant to shed light upon the assimilation and acculturation of migrants in the immigration country (Esser 1980: 210–11), can be rephrased for our purposes in the following way: the more intensive the motives of a migrant are regarding a specific goal, the stronger the expectation that she can fulfil her goals by territorial exit, the higher the propensity to attribute a high value to exit; and the fewer the constraints working against exit, the more likely a potential mover will choose the exit option. These constraints and opportunities could include factors such as societal and cultural norms (e.g. gender roles), state exit and admission policies, and economic differentials related to income or employment.

This extension of neo-classical theory takes care of a commonly waged criticism, namely that migration is often determined in great part by external forces—structural opportunities and access to resources—which are not mediated by the crudely modelled social psychological variables in the original rational choice approach (Simmons 1985–6: 133). Viewed from a structural individualist perspective, the question is not so much whether macro- or micro-factors account more or less in general or in specific situations for the decision to migrate. Instead, it matters very much how the two levels of analysis can be bridged by suitable hypotheses and assumptions that specifically consider time, place, and the logic of the situation in which actors are bound to act. Unfortunately, structural individualists have not presented us with a coherent model along these lines. None the less, we can easily establish such a bridging hypothesis: 'The greater differences in unemployment and wages between two countries, the higher opportunities for exit from the emigration and entry in the immigration country—then the more likely it is that potential migrants undertake an international move.' Such a hypothesis takes for granted that macro-level factors such as unemployment and wage differentials are perceived—correctly or incorrectly—by potential migrants, that these persons evaluate this information and form expectancies about the realization based on prior preferences, and that potential migrants eventually decide whether to stay or to go.

Yet, this hypothesis does not explicitly take into account the social and symbolic ties of the potential migrant. In this view her relations to significant others are just one more variable to be considered. Such an approach still divorces the individual actor and the subjective utilities that shape her choices from the network ties and collective settings in which these utilities are derived. In addition, and this is pivotal, the generation of expectancies, on which the stay or go decision depends, is a profoundly transactional process requiring attention not only to information about other relevant actors but also about the kind of relationship between the relevant actors involved in the migration process. Therefore, it is necessary to know more about the contents of the relationships involved, such as trust, authority relations and reciprocity.

Seen in this way, one of the major problems with individual structuralism is that it does not go beyond ad hoc hypotheses about 'micro–macro' linkages. Taking social and symbolic ties as an explicit point of departure, we are better able to link macro and micro aspects. All available empirical evidence in migration research corroborates the primacy of what takes place between agents. For example, studies in Mexican–USA labour migration found that for rural fathers the strongest determinants of migration reflect patterns of socio-economic organization such as the system of land tenure, access to credit, the extent of urban primacy, and the economic organization of agriculture rather than individual characteristics such as age, education, and occupation (Massey et al. 1987: 294). These socio-economic characteristics are reflected in household patterns and thus social relations among its members (Klaver 1997).

Instead of taking ad hoc hypotheses to link micro- and macro-levels, we can start from the insight of rational choice models that information plays an important role for migration decision-making. It is one element to help us pay more attention to the bonds between movers and stayers, pioneer migrants, migration brokers, and followers. Depending on the availability of information on transportation and opportunities for jobs and housing potential, migrants can optimize their benefits. Such information may flow along various communication channels, such as mass media and friends who migrated before, but also pioneer migrants outside the inner circle of relatives and friends. Different channels of information are likely to be used at different stages in the process. Mass media information is relatively more important at the information-gathering stage while interpersonal channels are crucial at the persuasion stage (cf. Rogers and Kincaid 1981).

Social Choice: The New Economics of Migration

Social choice accounts, in this case the so-called new economics of migration, have reacted to findings that migration decisions are taken in social units such as the family, households, or even whole communities. The problem of defining a supra-individual decision-making unit is partly remedied by the new economics of migration, whose theorists do not prejudge the sole social unit of decision-making to be the individual actor but try to aggregate the utilities of the individuals involved, especially in the case of rural economies. Basically, it is a portfolio strategy of potential migrant households who try to diversify their sources of income (Stark 1991). The new economics of migration and approaches that focus on the household view migration as a collective strategy to ensure the economic viability of the domestic unit through the strategic allocation of labour and investments. The household uses available resources in their perceived self-interest (D. Wolf 1992). Often, in patriarchal systems, the male head decides at the expense of females and younger members of the family.

Yet the solution of rational choice theories to extend rationality beyond individual actors to collective units is not sufficient. The main problem with social choice approaches to migration has been that they are only concerned with transactions between the collective units and not with what goes on within them. It does not consider the social embeddedness of potential migrants' behaviour. While it examines situational features such as economic inequalities between emigration and immigration countries—such as perceived unemployment and income differentials—ties, norms embedded gender roles, identity, and past relations of actors do not figure prominently. Since now the household itself is transformed into an actor, we face three difficulties:

(1) The conflicts and negotiations—the contentions within the household—are unexamined as yet. By considering family utility in aggregate terms, social choice theorists have ignored or simplified the relations between family members, the ties that bind or separate family or household members. If basic social relations are disregarded in this way, we do not get a good grasp of power and authority relations, (mis)trust, obligations, reciprocity, and solidarity. For example, who decides which member of a social unit such as a household migrates and what is the legitimation of the decision-maker?
(2) Ethnographic research indicates that household members often exercise rights and are subject to obligations that go beyond the household. Ties of obligations, reciprocity, and solidarity may extend to whole kinship systems (Guyer 1981). Also, ties with extra-household kin are sometimes stronger and more enduring than the marital ties that link wives and husbands in households (Kerns 1983). And, last, we should not forget the evidence indicating that informal networks of social support play an especially critical role among women in developing countries of the contemporary South (Chant 1992).
(3) Rational choice theories are heavily future-oriented. If the shadow of the future is dominant, the past is too unimportant. We may wonder if rational individuals are just interested in future discounts. People are likely to be interested very much in how particular others deal with them honestly—and not just in general reputations (Granovetter 1985: 491). People scheme on the foil of perceived trustworthiness of those they encounter. Trust develops in repeated transactions; it is a product of past relations. Among the institutions, in which these social relationships concerning migration show, are kinship groups, especially extended and smaller families, local and symbolic communities. They constitute the most important realms for non-market transactions and are probably still the least specialized.

Other criticisms waged against individual and social choice approaches cannot be dealt with here extensively. One concerns the reduction of rationality to instrumental rationality. This objection says that instrumental rationality is only one form of rationality. Often, the differentiation of rationality as instrumental or norm-oriented is cited, recurring to Max Weber (Weber 1980). Also, the distinction between strategic and communicative action enters the picture (Habermas 1981). Suffice it to say that the fundamental assumption of utility-maximizing individuals of rational choice approaches can at least be used as one element in more complex approaches; namely where rationality can be relaxed, as in the concept of bounded rationality. Therefore, it is of little explanatory importance when the respective aficionados claim a fundamental inconsistency between rational choice approaches and social structural approaches such as network analysis. In their strong versions both approaches err in ignoring the contents of ties—rational choice in prioritizing individual decisions and network analysis in hypostasizing the structural position of people and collectives.

Insights Derived: Location-Specific Assets

One fruitful addendum of the general cost-benefit approach is to look attentively at the kind of resources available to migrants and whether these resources are spatially transferable, in this case from one country to another. In a micro-perspective an important explanation for immobility, given sufficient information, is asking what goals can be better accomplished in the emigration or the immigration country. If a potential migrant decides to be mobile, the question arises whether the necessary resources can be transferred abroad. The territorial restriction of certain assets has been termed location-specific capital (DaVanzo 1981: 116). It is a widespread phenomenon that highly educated and trained movers, for example among refugees, cannot enter at the same occupational level in the immigration country as they occupied in the emigration country. For example, lawyers, physicians, and engineers may not get accredited to practice law, medicine, and mechanics and have to look for work outside their field. Information about these and other limitations prohibits international movements, while they generally do not discourage the internal movement of migrants—for obvious reasons. In these cases, it is more likely that internal and not international migration occurs.

If we want to know more about relative immobility and the dynamics of migration, we need to move to the analysis of the transferability and convertibility of resources from a purely individual basis to also include those inherent in social relationships. This supplement to the rational choice approach shifts our attention to the transferability and convertibility of human capital, the risks and costs associated with transferring specific individual assets. This makes us aware of difficulties in transferring human capital and local or territorially bounded assets more generally. It is thus a first step towards answering the 'out of many' and 'out of few places' questions.

More Micro-Social Psychological Models: Bounded Rationalities in Social Spaces

Psychologically-oriented models start from potential migrants as being rationally bound. For example, the individual decision-maker is limited in the capacity to formulate and solve problems and to acquire and retain information (Simon 1957). To cope with these problems the individual uses a simplified model of the situation at hand and acts rationally with respect to that personal model. Only a subset of the alternatives are perceived and payoffs are evaluated only as satisfactory or unsatisfactory. No action is taken if the current state is judged to be satisfactory. If it is unsatisfactory, a search is made for outcomes which are satisfactory, and the search is terminated when a satisfactory alternative is found. Viewed from a psychological angle, it is simply a strategy of satisficing.

The Stress-Threshold Model

One could interpret the so-called stress-threshold model to be based on this thought (Wolpert 1975). According to this view, a potential migrant assigns—in a satisficing manner—a place utility to the current place of residence which represents the social, economic, psychological, and other costs and benefits derived from that location. The individual evaluates this place utility relative to a threshold which is a function of his experience or attainments at a particular place and the attainments of his peers (Wolpert 1965: 162).

This idea has been made more explicit by dividing geographical mobility into two stages. First, potential migrants take account of their situation. This does not necessarily commit them to moving. They look for alternatives. Second, they may decide to relocate or to adjust to their current location. These stages are described as being highly dependent on how the potential migrant processes the information available in the local place. The term 'awareness space' refers to those places to which the potential migrant has knowledge about through direct contact, through friends and relatives, the mass media, or links through intermediary agencies such as employment services. In most cases the awareness space includes only a small subset of the sum total of opportunities which are available (Brown and Moore 1971); a clear indication of the boundedness of rationality.

The concepts of stress and awareness seem to be applicable to the continuum from free through impelled to forced migration. Where stress is extreme, little choice is left; where stress is high, most people move and their moves are viewed as impelled migration. And where stress is low, few people will move and their moves can be viewed as free migration—although stress may be important in initiating the mobility decision-making process. Like other theories, stress-awareness models do not take account of alternatives to moving. After all, there are many alternatives to geographical exit besides voice; for example, *in situ* adjustment by searching for alternate economic sources of income at home.

Relative Deprivation and Relative Frustration

Another version of this model—actually developed in social movement studies—emphasizes the role of relative deprivation. The theory of relative deprivation posits that there is an unfavourable gap between: (1) what a person feels he is entitled to and what, in fact, (2) he is receiving that encourages activism. It encourages activism if:

(1) a person is relatively deprived of *x* when he does not have *x*,
(2) he sees some other person(s)—possibly including himself at some previous or future time—as having *x* (whether or not that is or will be in fact the case),
(3) he sees it feasible that he should have *x* (Runciman 1966: 10).

Again, similar to stress-awareness models, this theory leads us to search for an underlying state of individual psychological tension which people relieve by migrating. The problem is that we do not learn why people relieve stress or tension by migrating, as opposed to a variety of other ameliorating mechanisms such as voice or *in situ* adjustment.

We can fuse a rational choice approach with relative deprivation in emphasizing relative frustration. We hypothesize that the example migration sets for others results in a self-reinforcing process in which individual motivations become correspondingly less important than the collective expectation to use exit complementary to voice. The change of migrants' values or desires is central in any such explanation (Mackie 1995): migrants encounter expanding opportunities. As a consequence, migrants' desires expand. Opportunities and desires are connected by the 'Tocqueville effect': as opportunities for migration increase, frustration among the stayers increases even faster. This is a special instance of relative deprivation. Large gains with limited migration opportunities lead to frustration, quarrels, and illicit migration. Eminently, migration as a self-sustaining process depends not only on decreasing information costs inside expanding networks of migration, as conventional rational choice accounts would predict, but also on transformation of preferences of the stayers who feel the feedback effects—such as growing scarcity of land and lower social status associated with not migrating abroad. Of course, the ultimate preference change would be the settlement of migrants abroad. The provocative implication of the relative frustration model is that very restrictive or very open borders do not set in motion ratcheting opportunity-desire cycles—while partial opening and closure actually do: if, say, destination countries hire foreign labour, more and more people will eventually be frustrated because expectations tend to increase faster than the opportunities required to migrate; especially in a world mired by vast demographic imbalances.

Remarkably, such a model fails to the extent that the essential causal mechanisms inducing or restricting migration take place within social relations among potential migrants and not within the migrants themselves. This concept cannot explain why so few people migrate from some regions in developing countries—or other parts of the South—while not from others and why so many return to the country of origin instead of settling once they have passed through the golden door. Take the example of Mexican–USA migration in which partial opening and closure policies of the frontier have applied for decades. In this case we find highly unequal rates of emigration when we look at different regions within Mexico (Massey et al. 1987). Also, the concept of relative frustration lacks concern for some of the most pivotal factors that enter the decision-making processes over exit, voice, and *in situ* adjustment, such as local assets of potential migrants to social units at the point of departure.

Insights Derived: Social Space and Time-Space Resolution

The various social-psychological models give us an idea of the social space by which actions of potential migrants are bounded. Space here does not only refer to physical features, but also to larger opportunity structures, the social life and the subjective images, values, and meanings that the specific and limited place represents to migrants (Hägerstrand 1975). Space is thus different from place in that it encompasses or spans various territorial locations. It includes two or more places. Space has a social meaning that extends beyond simple territoriality; only with concrete social or symbolic ties does it gain meaning for potential migrants. On a micro-level this has to be seen in conjunction with the use of time to form particular time-space strategies of potential migrants. Then space consists of the projects people are engaged in and the values they adhere to. Time is embedded in larger structures. The projects and events have a time duration, which sometimes is flexible but often is given, for example, in the individual life course or the pattern of recurrent migration. Interestingly, spatial movement necessarily implies temporal change but temporality in itself is not tied to spatial change. Therefore, migration always involves a spatial-temporal dimension. On the individual level, it can be mapped along the life course. Migration is thus a special instance of time-space resolution (Malmberg 1997). One of the main questions asked is thus: How are movements of people in temporal space limited by various opportunities and restrictions? Yet, following social-psychological theories, we do not learn much about the social embeddedness of the potential migrants' space. For example, in answering the question of why immigrants maintain ties to the country of origin, we certainly would like to know how the relationships between those migrating abroad and those who stayed in the country of origin have developed—altered, declined, or strengthened. If migrants maintain bonds in the course of migration, then we have the interesting case of a partial decoupling of territorial and social space.

Macro: The Gravity Model and the General Systems Approach

Research starting from structural opportunities has been abundant. Some of the more commonly held factors underlying economically motivated migration have already been mentioned, such as income and unemployment differentials and inequities in economic development between core and peripheral regions in the world economy. With respect to involuntary migration, international wars, especially World War Two, have caused substantial flows. Initially, the very formation of territorially bounded states in the South after decolonization resulted in migration and refugee flows. Moreover, in attendant processes of state formation and the rebuilding of states the persecution and expulsion of minority groups can achieve a high priority. External political and military intervention in less developed countries has been a common cause of refugee flows, for example in the South (Zolberg, Suhrke, and Aguayo 1989). Many of the more recent refugee flows have originated as a by-product of the formation of new states in the South, or upon social transformations such as revolutions and ethnic, tribal, religious, and other power conflicts in both old and new states.

The Pioneering Gravity Model: Countries as Communicating Tubes

The simplest and most powerful of macro-level models is the gravity approach (Ravenstein 1885 and 1889). It is concerned with the relation between distance and the propensity to move. The seven resulting 'laws' are:

(1) the majority migrate only short distances and thus establish 'currents of migration' towards larger centres;
(2) this causes displacement and development processes in connection with populations in emigration and destination regions;
(3) the processes of dispersion and absorption correspond with each other;
(4) migration chains develop over time;
(5) migration chains lead to exit movements towards centres of commerce and industry;
(6) urban residents are less prone to migrate than rural people;
(7) This last law is also true for the female population.

In short, the gravity model holds that the number of migrant events between two regions is directly proportional to the number of inhabitants in each region and indirectly proportional to the squared distance between the out-migration and the in-migration region. The model can be expressed in a simple equation:

$$M_{ij} = K \frac{P_i P_j}{D_{ij}^2}$$

where: M(ij) = number of migrants going from place i to place j
K = constant
P(i) = population of place i
P(j) = population of place j
D(ij) = distance between them

These observations are a useful starting point as empirical rules of thumb that may apply to certain regions of the world at specific time periods. More refined approaches found abundant evidence for the seven rules in mid-nineteenth century internal English migration and South–North migration (Lee 1964). The gravity model is useful as an empirical generalization about the relative volume of migration streams. However, the model cannot be used to explain why migration rates vary with the characteristics of migrants, from one country to another. More concretely, the gravity model predicts that some of the largest migration streams would be between India, China, and Russia because these are countries with large populations which are relatively close to one another. However, this has not been the case in the twentieth century. Also, in the nineteenth century when there were fewer barriers to international migration, the major flows were towards areas with low population density and not towards places where there were already large numbers of people. Quite the opposite of what the model predicts, there have been significant migration streams over the past decades between far remote areas, such as Pakistan and the United Kingdom. One could try to rescue the gravity model by introducing transportation costs and intervening obstacles as a factor—but that would already detract from the main claim and focus of the approach.

While rational choice theories of migration have evolved from the micro-level to introduce situational factors such as opportunity structures, system theorists have evolved the other way round: they first exclusively dealt with the macro-level—the migration systems consisting of several nation-states in a global economy, or regional variations—before they have gradually come to introduce lower aggregate level concepts such as migrant networks. At first, the analysts using this perspective spent time determining the macro-structural factors. Since then they have come to include analytical categories to explore the endogenous dynamics of migration.

General Systems Approaches

The earliest system theories assumed highly socialized actors. While they did not explicitly relate to migration, we can derive valuable insights. Let us start with the model of a social system in which—in a state of equilibrium—the agents behave according to their individual needs and the expectations of their interactive partners. These expectations and needs are regulated—among other things—by the internalization of common patterns of values and modes of behaviour and are social-structurally institutionalized (Parsons 1968).

This scheme of analytically differentiated descriptions of functions that have to be fulfiled in every society allows us to reconstruct some possible causes of migration (Eisenstadt 1954: 3). The four main functions are: adaptation (A), goal attainment (G), integration (I), and latent pattern maintenance (L), in short AGIL. Regarding adaptation, the emigration society does not provide enough facilities for this function. The potential migrant cannot maintain a given level of physical existence or ensure her family's survival within it. This would fit a variety of circumstances, for example, ranging from the persecution of ethnic minorities to the ecological flight of peasants. Looking at the second function, goal attainment, the potential migrant feels that certain goals, mainly instrumental in nature, cannot be attained within the institutional structure of society, especially regarding economic goals. Here, we could think of peasants engaging in domestic and international migration due to land scarcity in a system of inheritance based upon primogeniture. The third goal, integration, could mean that a potential migrant's aspiration to solidarity cannot be fully gratified in the emigration nation-state. He cannot fulfil the goal of complete mutual identification with other persons and with the society as a whole. In a very abstract way which does not explicitly consider the immediate threat to life and death, this seems to apply to political refugees; more concretely to what has been called anticipatory refugee movements of potential migrants before full-scale persecution sets in (Kunz 1973). Turning to the fourth function, latent pattern mainteance, the society of origin does not afford the potential migrant a chance of attaining a worthwhile and sincere pattern of life, or does so only partially. This function relates to the meaning a potential migrant sees in his social environment. This is somewhat hard to grasp and would need to be considered in conjunction with other functions. Perhaps this is the case with those who resign from their countries of origin for religious reasons, but without being actually persecuted openly.

Another conceptual framework that applies the general social systems theory to the phenomenon of international migration starts with the fundamental relation between power and prestige in a society. In essence, international migration constitutes an 'interaction between societal systems geared to transfer tensions and thus balancing power and prestige' (author's translation; Hoffmann-Nowotny 1973: 19). In this conceptual universe 'prestige' legitimizes 'power'. In any society there exists some sort of consensus about the value attributed to material and immaterial goods such as money, education, and merit. Power and prestige in a social system are determined by the position and by the status attributed to the positions. Structural tensions arise from inequalities and status inconsistencies in the emigration country. These structural tensions may generate anomic tendencies, an imbalance between power and status. Action directed to resolve these tensions may take forms such as social mobility, giving up the social position held, or emigration to a country where status aspirations can be attained (Hoffmann-Nowotny 1973: 11–14).

While these conceptualizations offer a typology for causes of migration and a theory of structural tensions, we need to go further to answer the puzzle of relative immobility and mass migration: How can we specify the social and institutional processes through which these dimensions of construction of social order are interwoven? While we derive some plausible, albeit incomplete, causes for migration, and by default, for non-migration, by using the AGIL scheme, this abstract deductionism leads us to the same problem already encountered in the discussion of the rational choice perspective. This is most visible with respect to the fourth function, latent pattern maintenance. Agents in this conceptual universe have been critically labelled as oversocialized (Granovetter 1985). And it really is a perspective that focuses on one of the possible end-products or outcomes of social relations—the thorough internalization of social norms. If we assume that potential movers have internalized dominant group values, this does indeed constitute a distinct possibility. But in a way it would only be an extreme case of a quite problematic and quasi-successful overadaptation. It would leave little or no room for bargaining and negotiation over the decision to move or to stay. However, even in so-called traditional societies individuals do have latitude to bargain in migration decision-making (Magnarella 1974). Moreover, in a Parsonian-inspired account internalized value imperatives constitute the decisive link between individual actors and communities or societies, at the expense of utility-maximizing behaviour emphasized by the rational choice perspective. In its own way, this approach is as lopsided as those rational choice approaches that do not explicitly take ties between people into account.

Multiple Levels—Migration Systems Approaches: Moving from the World System to Migrant Networks

Later migration systems approaches are best at explaining the direction of international migration and, when enriched with migration networks, the dynamics of migration, once it has started. These concepts have three main characteristics:

1. They assume that migration systems pose the context in which movement occurs and that these systems influence actions on whether to stay or to move. Basically, a migration system includes two or more places—most often nation-states—connected to each other by flows and counterflows of people. Extending dependency theories and world system approaches, migration systems theory has stressed the existence

of linkages between countries other than people, such as trade and security alliances, colonial ties (Portes and Walton 1981), and flows of goods, services, information, and ideas. These linkages often have existed before migration flows occurred. For example, in the case of European immigration countries such as France, the Netherlands, and the United Kingdom most movers come from former colonies. By the late 1980s, north-western European destination countries had accepted a total of about 12 million migrant workers with their families. Out of those about 6 million were from former colonies. Therefore, when we speak of emigration and immigration countries in the following, these terms refer to locations within migration systems. The country of origin may turn into an immigrant country again, especially in the light of usually high rates of return in international migration. An analysis of trade and security linkages and colonial ties helps to explain the direction of international movement between core and (semi-)peripheral states.

2. Migration systems theory focuses on processes within migration systems. Movement is not a one-time event but rather a dynamic process consisting of a sequence of events across time (Boyd 1989: 641). Theorizing the dynamics of migration moves from a consideration of movement as a linear, unidirectional, push-and-pull, cause–effect movement to notions that emphasize migration as circular, interdependent, progressively complex, and self-modifying systems in which the effect of changes in one part can be traced through the whole of the systems (Magobunje 1970: 4). For example, this hypothesis partly explains why, once it has started, international migration often turns into a self-feeding process. Pioneer migrants or groups set examples that can develop into a stream of what can be called mass migration (Petersen 1958: 263–4). Network-building pioneer migrants reduce both the direct monetary costs of movement, and the opportunity costs—the earnings forgone while moving, searching for work and housing, learning new skills—and also decrease the psychological costs of adjustment to a new environment in the destination country (Fawcett 1989).

3. Within the context of important factors such as economic inequalities between nation-states and the admission policies of the immigration states, individuals, households, and families develop strategies to cope with stay or go alternatives—exit, voice, and various forms of *in situ* adjustment. Lately, systems theorists have vigorously applied social network theory. A network is defined as a set of individual or collective actors—ranging from individuals, families, firms, and nation-states—and the relations that couple them. Networks consist of more or less homogeneous sets of ties among three or more positions. Social

networks encompass ties linking nodes in a social system—ties that connect persons, groups, organizations, or clusters of ties, as well as people. Network patterns of ties comprise social, economic, political networks of interaction, as well as collectives such as groups—kinship groups or communities—and private or public associations. Network is a concept or strategy to study how resources, goods, and ideas flow through particular configurations of social and symbolic ties. An analysis of networks allows statements about the possibility of people to interact. Indicators are size, density or connectedness, degree, centrality, and clustering of positions. An added benefit of network analysis is that positions can be included which are not part of formal and tightly bound groups. Descriptions and explanations based solely on bound groups sometimes overlook members' cross-cutting memberships in various circles (Simmel 1955).

To identify positions in a complete network and to determine which agents jointly occupy each position, there are two basic alternatives. The first is to use a criterion of social cohesion, as indicated by the degree to which agents are connected to each other by cohesive bonds. Positions so identified are called cliques if every actor is directly tied to every other actor in the position or are called social circles if less stringent connections are required. The second alternative is to identify network positions by using criteria of structural equivalence, according to which actors are aggregated into a jointly occupied position or role to the extent that they have linkages to a common set of other actors in the system. According to the latter approach, no requirement is imposed that the actors in a position must have direct ties to each other (Knoke and Kukliniski 1982). We will see later that structural equivalence captures best the significant role of brokers in providing resources such as social capital crystallizing in migrant networks.

Insights Derived: Multiple Levels of Analysis and Endogenous Dynamics

Migrant networks link the three main components of international migration systems: a flow of migrants from origin to destination area, an immigrant stock residing in the country of destination; and a flow of migrants who return from the immigration to the emigration country. Networks of migrants serve as channels through which migrants are transferred from origin to destination but also may encourage permanent settlement or foster return migration. And even in the case of solitary migration, migrants commonly draw information, financial assistance and other resources from pioneer migrants who have already gone to the destination; weak ties then play a role.

The main assumption is aptly summarized in the provocative phrase that it is 'not people who migrate but networks' (Tilly 1990: 65). Migrant networks then are sets of interpersonal ties that connect movers, former movers, and non-movers in countries of origin and destination through social ties, be they relations of kinship, friendship, or remote acquaintances (Choldin 1973). In international migration, networks are even more important than in domestic migration because there are more barriers to overcome, e.g. exit and entry permits, and if not available, costs for illegal border crossing. Migrant networks lead to chain migration, 'arranged by means of primary social relationships with previous migrants' (MacDonald and MacDonald 1964: 82). Chain migration is a social mechanism in which numerous persons leave one well-defined area of origin serially for another well-defined location. They rely on people from the same origin and brokers for information, informal aid, and various other resources. Many chain migrations begin as circular migration of seasonal or longer cycle movement in which constantly returning agricultural workers, craftsmen or petty merchants form a base from which pioneer migrants and brokers can be drawn. This mechanism is so important because this sort of continuously connected migration system accounts for the great bulk of the last centuries' immigration to Europe and the Americas (Morawska 1990). If so, then relational analyses of international movement become a must.

Migration systems theory very explicitly elucidates the macro- and micro-structural opportunities for migration causes and, especially, the dynamics of migration (Kritz and Zlotnik 1992). First, following this perspective, the migration volume would be very low—an indicator of relative immobility—if there is no migration system that encompasses at least an origin and a destination state. Second, if there are no strong linkages of political, economic, and cultural nature between the potential emigration and immigration countries, we also expect very little or no international migration. Third, chain migration occurs and may turn eventually into mass migration when migrant networks reduce the risks and costs for international geographic mobility. If there are no migrant networks that lower costs, potential migrants would probably think twice before migrating to another country. Also, feedback effect of other types, such as changes in the economic structure of emigration villages and regions may set in. The first two bundles of factors—migration systems and linkages—are best at explaining the direction of migration while the third—chain migration—leads us to give further thought to the endogenous dynamics of international migration.

Network analysis thus posits that a patterned web of ties and positions has a particular effect on the actions of certain potential migrants enmeshed in these networks existing in families, neighbourhood, and local communities. It mainly considers the form and pattern of ties but not their contents. The neglect of the contents of ties points towards a deeper problem with network analysis. Network analysts in general and those working on migration in particular have taken recourse to purely structural effects. They claim that we can understand the behaviour of potential and actual migrants by looking at their position within a network of agents. However, the question coming up then is whether it is feasible to assume that there are purely structural effects (for a general criticism, see Homans 1986: p. xxvi).

In Need of Further Conceptualization: The Contents of Ties

The weakness of a radical version becomes clearer when we choose a particularly helpful concept established by network theory, the so-called 'strength-of-weak-ties' argument (Granovetter 1973): although news is more quickly disseminated through strong than weak ties, strong ties will hardly ever bring you news that is really new. The reason for this is that—in a group bounded by strong social ties—friends of friends will be friends. To use the 'forbidden triangle': if A is connected to B and to C, it is then very likely that B also entertains relations to C. No strong tie is thus likely to be a bridge to other networks, a bridge through which information might flow that is really new and possibly relevant to the goals of a potential migrant. This is an important insight. Yet, weak social ties as such do not entice potential migrants to go or to stay, unless the contact persons have good resources themselves or have contacts to others with sufficient resources to make going or staying a viable option, respectively.

Therefore, we need to pay attention not only to the structure of ties—such as their strength and their density—but also to the contents. It certainly makes a difference whether a migrant who has no family members abroad, knows her employer and is able to pay her journey can partake in the reciprocity available in, say, a village community. Pioneer migrants offer help in travel, job, housing, and child-rearing. In exchange, the helped migrant provides similar services of referrals once she is abroad—and so on. And the content of ties also matters when we think of religiously persecuted minorities who experience the solidarity from symbolic kin abroad. Seen in this way, resources such as information emanate from more fundamental tenets inherent in ties. Also, ties are not simply social ones; they also rest on symbolic functions.

While network analysis offers a first valuable explanation of the 'why so few' and 'why so many' in general, the unequal and uneven access of potential migrants to migrant networks still haunts any explanation of the volume and the spatial specificity of migration. In particular, a systems' perspective and a network approach, cannot answer two important questions. First, how do we explain the formation of networks, a sort of collective action? Second, how do the processes of migrant selection work within these networks?

Although we will deal with it extensively at a later stage, an answer to the second puzzle of simultaneous transnational spaces and immigrant adaptation can also gain from enlarged network approaches. For example, we can extend earlier researches on developing country migrants from rural areas to cities. These migrants were no longer members of solidary village communities, and conventional modernization theory suggested that they would become rootless members of urban mass society. Network analysts demonstrated that many migrants continued to maintain ties to their ancestral villages and to form new urban ties. The migrants' complex networks, composed of both rural and urban ties, helped them to obtain resources from both the village and the city in order to cope with the demands of modern life (Mitchell 1969). Hence we do not need to accept the weakening of village solidarities as proof of the loss of community. Instead, by tracing ties and resource flows, it has been established that migrants are indeed able to maintain viable—though spatially and socially dispersed—network communities composed of rural and urban ties (Wellman 1983: 158–9).

Similar findings, albeit not couched in terms of network methodology, are available for transatlantic migrants from Europe to the Americas in the nineteenth and early twentieth centuries. Instead of 'uprooted' immigrant groups (Handlin 1973) who bear much similarity with the 'marginal man' (Park 1950), researchers found that persons 'transplanted' many of their customs (Bodnar 1985). And contemporary research finds not only transplantation but vivid cross-fertilization and cultural syncretism, such as composite cultural forms (Clifford 1994). Taking these findings as a lead, the maintenance of transnational ties among first- and second-generation immigrants, accompanied by well-known forms of immigrant adaptation, do not seem to be contradictory at a second look.

Theory Building and Empirical Evidence

Having completed this tour de force of migration theories and their potential to help us in answering above all the first puzzle, we now need to specify the procedure for dealing with theories and empirical evidence in the chapters to come. The goal of this study is to describe the two puzzles which need to be explained, identify the explanatory factors, construct models explaining the puzzles, and illustrate all these findings with a specific instance.

Theory-building without systematic examples is a futile exercise. This study presents empirical evidence in two forms. First, the conceptual parts draw on examples all around the world to illustrate migration decisions and dynamics. Second, there is a continued case study. As an illustration only one case is taken, migration from Turkey to the Federal Republic of Germany between 1960 and the mid-1990s. Turkey–Germany is an exemplary case for theoretical reasons but by no means a representative case. Therefore, the empirical analysis of the Turkish–German example comes close to a theoretical case study (Eckstein 1966: p. vi).

The study includes only enough material from research reports on this case to make the propositions set forth plausible. In our case, the data required to illustrate the proposed concepts does not readily exist. Perhaps if enough researchers become intrigued with the theory, systematic attempts to collect the relevant evidence may be made in order to test the hypotheses. Nevertheless, existing studies and my own empirical research provide ample evidence to continue engaging in the proposed analysis.

Of course, theories and concepts can be buttressed by applications to selected cases. An equally compelling counter-argument says that theory-building with examples runs the danger that such illustrations marshal only the evidence they like. Then case research hazards becoming an ad hoc art, risking makeshift redescription. Therefore, the case study material presented throughout the analysis is no pseudo-test of theoretical propositions in dressing up patchy empirical findings, as if they were suitable for examining a general hypothesis about the role of ties and social capital in international migration. It rather serves the purpose of illustration and further refinement of hypotheses.

Turkish–German migration is an exemplary case for five reasons:

1. It is convenient because Turkey was not a significant emigration country until the early 1960s, but during the following three decades more than 4 million Turks emigrated abroad for employment. We can trace these processes from their very beginning because the recruitment of Turkish workers in the 1960s and 1970s and the flow of refugees since the 1980s has not been based on any noteworthy previous international migration experience. This is very important because we want to focus

on the endogenous dynamics of migration processes. This international migration went hand in hand with rapid urbanization, indicating high rates of internal migration. In 1945 82% of the population still lived in the countryside but only 18% in urban areas; in 1960 the share of the urban population had increased to 26% and in 1992 to 50% (Steinbach 1993: 514). Also, a significant number of refugees who have claimed asylum in the Federal Republic since the early 1980s originated in the south-eastern provinces of Turkey.

2. The case is crucial and exemplary because we find a continuum from forced to voluntary migrants and, in terms of state regulation, both labour migrants and refugees from Turkey in Germany. About one-third of all immigrants resident in Germany originated in Turkey. Therefore, Turkey–Germany is an ideal case to analyse the similarities, differences, and interdependencies of migration movements characterized by varying degrees of freedom among migrants, or, depending on the perspective, between labour migrants and refugees.

3. Germany has been the main magnet for labour migrants and refugees from Turkey in Europe. About 50% to 75% of Turkish net migration to Europe between 1960 and 1994 went to Germany. The official number of emigrated workers from Turkey to Europe swelled from 66,000 in 1964 to 130,000 in 1970, and then peaked at 136,000 in 1973. Between 1961 and 1975 about 805,000 workers were sent abroad through the Turkish Employment Service—TES—and another estimated 120,000 to 150,000 entered originally illegally (Gitmez 1989: 17). Typical cycles of family reunification and marriage migration ensued. The situation for asylum seekers from Turkey has been similar: Throughout the 1980s and 1990s refugees from Turkey represented, year by year, the second-largest contingent of asylum seekers in Germany. By the mid-1990s, the 2 million Turks made up about one-third of all immigrants in the Federal Republic or 2.5% of the German population. If Germany had not been the main destination, we could not treat Turkey–Germany as a quasi-autonomous migration system. We would then need to include more cases which would unduly complicate our analysis.

4. In terms of the level of socio-economic development, Turkey belongs to those countries from which the proportion of international migrants should be especially high. The 'inverted U-curve' hypothesis says that countries nearing a certain income threshold that is not very low but has not yet reached the level of the most developed industrialized countries, the potential for migration is especially high (Faini and Venturini 1994). Therefore, Turkey is a good example to analyse the mechanisms of both immobility and mobility.

5. For the time being, chain migration from Turkey to Germany has run its course. Because of restrictive policies on the side of all European receivers after 1973, the migration cycle of those movers classified as labour migrants has significantly slowed; with family reunification and marriage migration having reduced to a trickle. Yet refugee migration, enabled by the right to asylum application and building upon earlier migrant networks, is still under way.

Conclusion: In Search of the Meso Link

The main problem with rational choice theories on the micro-level is their rigid micro–macro understanding of social processes and their insufficient attention to the mechanisms translating into migration decisions. Rational choice theory fails because it views the people as atomistic agents, be they individual potential migrants, groups, households, organizations, and nation-states. In order to bridge analytical levels, ties and linkages between the positions these agents take within these broader structures could then only be introduced in an ad hoc manner. And refined approaches that take into account collectives do not sufficiently pay attention to relations within these groups pertaining to migration decision-making. This means that interests and identities are not completely preconstituted and unproblematic. The attributes of parties in a transaction are not totally given. It is not possible to simply deduce migration behaviour from pre-given and innate characteristics or properties of the individual parties. The focus then is on how past transactions have shaped reciprocal relations and mutual trust. None the less, the idea that assets differ in view of their cross-national transferability is useful.

The main drawback of stress-awareness and relative frustration models is that the allegedly strong correlation between individual potential migrants' attitudes or normative beliefs and migrants' behaviour is actually weak. The existence of stress or frustration does not tell us which option potential migrants choose—exit, voice, or *in situ* adjustment. Nevertheless, social psychological models help us go one step beyond rational choice assumptions in allowing us to place local assets in relationally bounded awareness spaces. The idea of an awareness space points to the fact that there is a social space in which actors move. This space is different from place because it is socially structured.

Migration systems theory covering several levels of analysis accounts best for the direction of international migration and the dynamics of migration. It is by far the best though still unsatisfactory answer to 'why are there so many migrants out of so few places?' while it is not sufficient to tackle the first question of the first puzzle: 'why are there so few migrants out of most places?'. This theory tends to impute self-sustaining logic to social and political structures, again without sufficiently specifying the causal mechanisms, especially the type of resources needed to maintain processes such as chain migration. Therefore, migration systems theories have to be enriched to first connect mobility with the fact of high rates of relative immobility and, second, to explain the simultaneous occurrence of transnational ties and immigrant adaptation.

As a meso link, formal network theory provides an adequate underlay for the general argument on relative immobility and mass migration. It is important to treat it as a point of departure rather than one of arrival. Network theory in itself is a method and gives no substantive theory. And as to implicit theoretical assumptions, it simply posits that the position within a network guides action. However, it totally neglects the contents of ties connecting positions. For example, network theory cannot tell us how migrant networks come into being. Moreover, network theory says nothing about the characteristics of resources inherent in social and symbolic ties.

To provide a meso link, the conceptual ambush here is to pursue a systematic relational analysis of migration and post-migration processes on the meso level. This analysis conceives potential migrants as embedded in and constituted by relationships and relationality. To develop and present a cohesive analysis we have discussed more essentialist micro- and macro-level theories as the conceptual other, and started to enlarge relationally oriented meso-level analyses. From the vantage points of relational analysis, decisions of migration and adaptation cannot be derived from attributes characterizing stages of economic development or political system (such as 'South' or 'North'), but by potential and actual migrants' places or positions in the matrix of multiple social and symbolic ties, and the content of ties connecting people who do not exist in singular forms.

3

Situating the First Puzzle: Why So Few Migrants and Why So Many?

Before turning to how relative immobility and chain migration proceed, we need to explain how macro-conditions set the stage for 'Why so few out of most places?' and 'Why so many out of very few places?'. Only when we know in detail the starting conditions of migration processes and the set-up under which migrant networks form later, can we hope to unearth the endogenous dynamics of international South to North migration flows.

We can start with the three following propositions:

1. The overall volume of international migration is still relatively low because there is a high, albeit differing and uneven, capacity and willingness of nation-states and international institutions to control flows and domestic structures regarding initial entry. Concomitantly, there is no global and only two functioning regional labour migration regimes—the European Union (EU) and the Nordic Labour Union (since 1954)—which would allow for the free movement of labour. Also, only a partial global refugee regime exists that does not guarantee an individual right to asylum in the case of persecution. This state of affairs reflects broader sets of political-economic dependence of migrants and migrant-originating countries in the South from hegemonic nation-states in the North. Beyond the economic disparities and their perceptions by potential migrants, these policies shape the rate of mobility. Depending on the capacity to control and the willingness to receive newcomers from certain countries on the destination side, public policies are vital elements to explain: Why so few migrants? Why so many migrants?

2. International South–North migration occurs mainly within migration systems. Specific emigration countries are connected to selected destination countries. Only within migration systems can processes of chain migration unfold. This is an important contribution to answering the twofold first puzzle of 'why are there so few international migrants out of most places?' and 'why are there so many out of few places?'—provided that by places we mean whole countries.

3. While the states of immigration may be able to control relatively effectively first entries, this is different for migration flows that follow the first waves from a given origin. Once certain categories of migrants and refugees have settled and have achieved a status of permanent residence, then repatriation becomes almost impossible and, even more important, family unification and marriage migration have to be allowed. This is so because most liberal democratic immigration states adhere to international human rights law, democracies tend to respect civil rights of minorities, and welfare states grant the majority of social rights on the principle of residence and not nationality—all with the evident exception of the Arab Gulf states. These conditions set the stage for a future self-feeding dynamic of increasing migration and sometimes even refugee flows—chain migration. Yet, while this proposition sheds light on the question 'why are there so many migrants out of few countries?', it does not explain intra-country differences and does not tell us how the ubiquitous migrant networks form. The principles of modern rights bound to people–state relationships has experienced some expansion in favour of the individual person in both the international and the internal realm. Interestingly, the bond has widened. Now it includes not only citizen–state but resident–state relations. Both the canonized international language of human rights and the basic principles of modern welfare states have become the two pivotal imperatives in justifying rights and demanding rights. To start from the international level, international human rights apply even to non-nationals in national polities, as evidenced in (*a*) international courts issuing orders, (*b*) organizations active in the pursuit of human rights (e.g. Amnesty International and various UN organizations; see Boli and Thomas 1997), and (*c*) universal discourses of rights (Soysal 1994: 41–4). The most crucial fact is that liberal democracies adhere to human rights law set on the international level. The individual person, in addition to the state, has become the object of international law. State authorities must increasingly consider persons qua persons. This means that states not only face responsibilities towards their own citizens. International human rights law applies to all residents of a state (Held 1995: 101–7; see also D. Jacobson 1995: 9–10 for a stronger version of this argument). For instance, growing rights of non-citizen residents made it more difficult for liberal democracies to expel or deport unwanted migrants. No forced repatriation occurs unless criminal acts on the part of the immigrant are involved. The person then loses her permits and faces deportation.

Domestically, developments of law took a turn in reinforcing international human rights law, concerning the civil rights of long-term residents. This helped the international human rights regime to gain validity, although in itself it lacks sufficient implementation and enforcement powers. For example, the Civil Rights Movement in the USA has carried a more expansive immigration policy in its aftermath. Rights now apply to many more minorities and refugees; immigration has provoked constitutional debates on the rights of resident foreigners. Importantly, family reunification proved to be a claim that fuelled chain migration from South to North in the aftermath of European labour recruitment and North American labour and human capital immigration.

Yet the very principles of modern welfare states that grant rights to alien newcomers primarily according to the residence principle have proved most important on the domestic level. And prolonged residence usually helps to acquire permanent residence and, hence, claims to bring in close relatives and protection against expulsion.

The real change does not occur so much between nation-states but between immigration countries or accepting states and migrants. It is not the status as foreign citizens as such that is decisive: as long as potential migrants reside in their country of origin, they have no recourse to entitlements of the immigration state; as soon as they enter the territory, they acquire some—increasing with the length of residence and legal status. The immigration and accepting states do not in themselves produce chain or mass migration. But they set some of the necessary conditions: entitlements for resident migrants. These domestic and international, legal and institutional factors create the broad frame in which chain migration, networks of contact between kin, friends, villagers, and traffickers may give rise to continued and even increased migration.

Thus, the following discussion shows systematically how relations on the macro-level set the stage simultaneously for both relatively effective control of flows and for chain migration. First, this chapter outlines the functions of institutions in selecting categories of labour migrants and persecuted groups that end up as displaced persons or refugees. Second, the analysis turns to how international organizations and nation-states seek to regulate the flows of migrants and refugees in mostly bilateral labour migration systems and in the global refugee regime. It describes the functioning of legal norms that have inhibited the autonomy of immigration states to deal with migrants at will, especially with those who have found work and residence inside their territory. The third part analyses some factors found within the immigration states that contribute to the bewildering situation of why so few and why so many. Fourth, the analysis exemplifies the asymmetric relations between countries of emigration and immigration, using the example of Turkish–German migration flows from the early 1960s to the mid-1990s.

The Production and Selection of Labour Migrants and Refugees

State regulation can be interpreted to fulfil certain functions, *inter alia*, the production and selection of migrants or refugees, the adaptation in the immigration country such as finding housing, work, or participation in social and political organizations, and readaptation in the country of origin upon return. The production and selection of migrants, and refugees, the recruitment of labour migrants and expulsion of refugees in emigration countries and admission in countries of destination differs fundamentally: in the case of labour migrants, the immigration states are the main instigators. In the case of refugees, it is the producing states, respectively. In both instances, states operate in wider global and regional trade, political and migration or refugee systems.

The Political Economy of South–North Disparities

Labour migration reflects the inequality between core and periphery in the world economy, regional economies, and nation-state economies. A strong version of this argument says that international migration is predetermined by macro-system processes (Amin 1974). Common to all models is that spatial economic disparities create the conditions. These concepts carry the implicit assumption that these disparities underpin flows of labour migrants which, in turn, usually aggravate and perpetuate such inequalities (Myrdal 1957).

Depending on the vantage point, much migration can be seen as either demand-pull or supply-push, embedded in broader systems. The selection of migrants in the demand-pull dimension says that the post-war migrations to the North began, for the most part, in response to the demand of employers in high-growth industries to cheap and docile labour from the periphery—from Mexico and the Caribbean basin to North America and from the former colonies, such as the Caribbean islands and the Indian subcontinent, or from southern Europe, North Africa, and Turkey to Europe. The receivers implemented public policy instruments that regulated and legitimized these flows through instruments such as *Gastarbeiter* and *bracero* policies. The economically beneficial arrangements, mainly so for the immigration countries, corresponded to the liberal spirit of the post-war economy. Under the Bretton Woods system, international institutions like the International Monetary Fund (IMF), the General Agreement on Trade and Tariffs (GATT), the World Bank, as well as the Organization for Economic Cooperation and Development (OECD), aimed to promote international labour migration—as part of a broader strategy that included the expanded exchange of goods and financial flows.

The supply-push dimension gained political and public currency when the growth rates in the OECD countries slowed in the 1970s, in the aftermath of the first big post-war recession after 1973–4. As a response, Western European governments implemented curbs on the import of migrant labour. However, by that time, migrant networks promoting chain migration had become established, and it proved exceedingly difficult over the next two decades to stop further inflows, especially those related to family reunification, or to return settled migrant workers and their kin. This meant that the selection of migrants was much more restricted than before, because it had come to be increasingly governed by human rights and welfare state considerations. In sum, all kinds of demand-pull and supply-push factors can only operate if migrant networks link the respective countries within specific migration systems. This applies with equal force to the second main category of flows, refugee movements.

Accordingly, the research question concerning refugees is: Under what conditions do refugee-producing nation-states select certain categories of population as targets for persecution, expel them outright, and create conditions that push them into a risky flight? Concomitantly, under what conditions do accepting nation-states accept and recognize certain categories of migrants as refugees? Fundamentally, there must be a nation-state willing to accept refugees (Zolberg 1983: 27). Of course, a corollary to this claim is that in cases where no country of destination willing to accept victims exists, there is little outflow; and, in some cases, it may help the respective nation-state rulers to engage in policies bordering on extinction. Note that in contradistinction to South–North movements, some South–South refugee movements occur because some states of destination are simply not able to effectively police their borders.

In the post-war period, political transformations have undergirded refugee flows from South to North. The first has resulted from the reorganization of political communities, particularly the formation of new nation-states out of former, often colonial empires. The second contributed to refugee flows because of abrupt changes of political regime, particularly during social revolutions and upheavals, and the responses of incumbent rulers to revolutionary challenges. The main point is that a large number of states in the South have been affected by violent conflicts surrounding nation-state formation in the wake of independence; much fewer have experienced large-scale social revolutions.

Nation-State Formation

Some of the world's regions have been in the process of sorting themselves into independent nation-states. In the colonial and semi-colonial areas of Africa and Asia, a kind of self-determination emulating the European model soon followed imperial rule. This involved the destruction of old solidarities and the construction of new ones. But the intrinsic difficulties of this task have been compounded by socio-economic underdevelopment and internal mismanagement. Rulers in general believe that only a powerful state can afford them the leverage necessary for overcoming internal and external constraints, in order to maintain political power, to forge and solidify new collective identities, and to foster economic development. This kind of reliance on the centralization of power in a few hands has eventually exacerbated attempts to authoritarian rule. Yet the adoption of authoritarian strategies of nation-state formation has frequently entailed the political persecution of certain categories of the population along ethnic, national and religious lines (Zolberg 1983).

During decolonization, the process of refugee production usually started abruptly, triggered by a change of internal or external circumstances, such as struggles for political power in the newly formed nation-states, and the simultaneous intervention of global or regional powers. At the initial stage stood a generalized political crisis, in the course of which victim groups were especially likely to emerge. The production of refugees was not the only possible outcome, but has been a very likely one (Arendt 1973). The designation or evolution of one group or several groups as obstacles to the successful formation of a nation-state or the maintenance of power then frequently marks the onset of persecution along various lines such as race, ethnicity, nationality, religion, or political belonging. Particularly vulnerable in such processes are stranded minorities that straddle more than one nation-state such as Kurds in Northern Iraq during the Gulf War in 1991/2, middlemen groups, such as Indians in Africa, or religious minorities, such as in the civil wars in the successor states of former Yugoslavia.

There are self-reinforcing aspects of refugee production. Since the conflicts usually do not remain limited to one country only but affect a whole region, a heightened tension between states results. This often leads to international conflict, which in turn exacerbates refugee-producing conditions in each state of the region. For example, this happened in the aftermath of the Afghan regime change after 1978 when conflicts involved countries as diverse as the former USSR, Pakistan, India, Iran, and the USA. The frequent cases of active intervention of external powers is of particular relevance in separatist instances. These projects are rarely successful without foreign intervention.

The respective rulers in the South rarely achieved nation-building at one fell swoop. It has involved repeated tries. This has meant that political transformation into a consolidated nation-state often proves to be a protracted process. Each step towards it may result in a refugee-generating crisis. If the respective nation-state gains strength, it may be the end of the refugee-producing process by assimilation of remaining persecuted groups, and the expulsion of others. If the new states remain weak, rulers may drift to outright terrorism; take the Horn of Africa since the 1980s. Even a modicum of political stability is often precarious because rulers are generally drawn from specific ethnic and/or religious groups—as has been the case in Burundi and Rwanda.

Social Revolution

Refugees not only emerge in processes of nation-state building. They may also be a product of encompassing and sweeping revolutions accompanying a wholesale change of political regime and a fundamental restructuring of society and economy. In these cases not only political activists flee but also categories of people singled out by the new rulers as undesirable. Social revolutions have not only gripped developing states in the aftermath of colonial penetration and independence—take Cuba as a prominent example. They have also affected empires and states which never were under colonial rule such as Ethiopia and Afghanistan.

While the selective functions of nation-states differ markedly, depending on whether we deal with labour migration or refugee movements, it can only be adequately conceptualized in a broader framework that encompasses both regions of origin and destination. Most states in the South have undergone violent conflicts, accompanied by refugees. And stranded minorities such as the Kurds in Turkey, Syria, Iran, and Iraq figure prominently in international migration. But even in these cases most of these rather involuntary migrants have remained inside the countries as displaced persons or have moved to neighbouring states in the South. In order to move from 'why so many overall migrants?' to 'why so few international migrants out of most states?' and 'why so many out of very few?' we need to look at the interrelationships between nation-states in the South and in the North. The countries between which we observe large-scale South–North migration flows have all entertained significant historical, political, cultural, economic, and social linkages within specific migration systems. In other words, relations between these countries serve as the carriers for migrant flows.

The International Regulation of Labour Migration and Refugee Flows

Nation-states regulate South–North labour migration by bilateral agreements. This has profound implications for the structural dependence of countries of emigration upon countries of immigration: immigration countries can unilaterally terminate the import of foreign labour. Although refugee flows generally follow very similar directions as labour migration in South–North movements, international norms and international organizations matter more in its regulation than in the case of labour migrants. This points to different opportunities of nation-states to regulate the admission of labour migrants with respect to refugees.

Labour Migration: Migration Systems, their Regional Nature, and Bilateral Agreements

The core idea of the migration systems approach is that there is a more or less pronounced exchange of goods, capital, and people between a set of countries and a less intense exchange between others. These systems are characterized by relatively large flows of migrants between member countries compared to flows from outside the system (Bilsborrow and Zlotnik 1994). This view suggests that international migration systems are regionally limited, generally include a core immigration region, which may be a country or group of countries, and a set of specific emigration countries linked to it by unusually large flows.

We can differentiate the linkages between potential emigration and immigration countries along a continuum from weak to strong. Only the existence of strong linkages creates favourable conditions for the emergence of population flows among the countries. Strong linkages are those in which there are, first, frequent and routine interactions among nation-states. There is, second, a high density of interactions with respect to one or more of the following areas of exchange: economic, political, and security relationships, and cultural ties through common use of languages and the flow of information, such as the mass media. Third, strong linkages also require a basis in transnationally interactive civil societies, such as secondary associations exchanging goods, ideas, and persons. Weak linkages, on the other hand, are defined by less frequent interactions, there is less exchange in the political, economic, and cultural spheres among actors in the respective nation-states. In many cases strong linkages are a necessary, though not sufficient, basis for migration to emerge.

Migration systems analysis shows that individual nation-states are particularly receptive to immigrants originating from a select group of countries with which they have had strong linkages. By the same token, these same nation-states are much more restrictive towards immigrants from other emigration states in the South. For example, about 75% of the total ethnic minority population in Britain originates from the Commonwealth and Pakistan. In Germany, the majority of former contract workers—so-called guestworkers—are from former Yugoslavia, within Germany's former sphere of economic influence (International Labour Office 1945)—and from Turkey. In the latter case weak linkages evolved into stronger ones due to migration.

There are three initial situations out of which international migration flows develop: strong state linkages in (post-)colonial and hegemonic relations, one-issue linkages, and weak linkages but few alternatives for the country of immigration:

1. Recall that migration systems can be defined as two or more places or, more specifically, countries connected to each other by flows and counterflows of people. Besides flows of people, other flows link countries together in a system (Kritz and Zlotnik 1992). Indeed, past or current flows of goods and information and political relations compose one of the possible prerequisites for flows of people to emerge in the first place. These various inter- and transnational linkages appear in many guises, more specifically in the realms of security: defence treaties such as NATO, economics: trade and foreign investment, politics: influence of the more powerful country on the internal affairs of the dominated one, culture: common languages such as English, French, Portuguese, or Spanish, and a common religion. Colonial relationships encompass many of these forms of linkages. It is by no means coincidental that the most extensive flows of labour migrants and partly refugees have emerged out of previous colonial relationships between emigration and immigration countries. In Europe, for example, the overwhelming number of migrants after World War Two to countries

such as France and the United Kingdom have come from former colonies. Typical migration systems include France on the destination side and most of the West African countries on the emigration side, such as Senegal, Niger, Mali, Chad, and Central Africa (Nogle 1994). In the Americas, this applies to most of Latin America as a region of emigration, and the USA and Canada as the most important immigration states.

2. However, colonial encounters are not the only important relationships. Sometimes, earlier one-issue linkages proved potent enough to trigger migration in the case of immigration country input. An example are economic ties between Yugoslavia and Germany. Yugoslavia's mines and other extractive branches of industry made up a cheap source of raw material and foodstuffs for industrialized Germany (Chepulis 1984: 240).

3. In other cases, rather weak relationships prove instrumental when recruiting countries in search of foreign labour have few alternatives. A case in point is the Turkish–German migration flow since the 1960s. Although security relations between Turkey and Germany have existed since the early nineteenth century this does not explain the onset of large-scale migration. Lack of alternatives for the German recruiters does.

Labour migration flows can also be followed by refugee flows. The crucial prerequisite is existing migrant networks. Since 1980, for each year, refugees from Turkey have been among the three to four most numerous groups seeking asylum in Germany; in the early 1990s, refugees from the war-torn regions of the Balkans constituted the single largest group of asylum seekers.

Nation-state relations that range along a continuum from weak to strong linkages are asymmetric. It is one of the few undisputed findings of international migration research that the immigration countries in the North have initiated virtually all labour migration flows. Also, destination countries most often select emigration countries according to politico-economic criteria. For example, the German government did not sign a recruitment agreement with Yugoslavia until this country introduced some market principles in 1965 (Lohrmann and Manfrass 1974: 375). It is the recruiting country authorities who have a final say over the selection of the workers, not the authorities in the country of emigration. Within migration systems the pattern of recruitment is usually very similar. For example, in many European countries during the 1960s, the receivers meant to institute a guestworker system, i.e. temporary labour governed by a rotational principle. A somewhat different system of contract labour is still operative on a large scale in many of the oil-rich countries of the Middle East, importing labour from Asia, and on a smaller scale in virtually all countries of the North when it comes to seasonal and posted workers. While there are some general international norms set up by the International Labour Organization (ILO) guiding the employment of migrant labourers, the specific conditions are negotiated between receivers and senders—with an overwhelming dominance of the immigration countries.

The signing of supranational norms offers a first glimpse at the bi- and multilateral asymmetries. There are four main Conventions by the ILO that concern the rights of migrant workers. The first is the ILO 'Migration for Employment Convention' (Revised), 1949 (No. 97). It is aimed towards the recruitment, placement, and working conditions of recruited migrant workers. It foresees the equality of treatment principle, such as same wages for the same kind of work. The ILO 'Migrant Workers (Supplementary Provisions) Convention of 1975' (No. 143) aims to eliminate illicit migration and illegal employment and to promote a real policy of equality of opportunity and treatment; stipulating affirmative action clauses for discriminated groups in labour markets. Another two Conventions deal with social security (No. 118, 1962 and No. 157, 1982) and seek to ensure equality of treatment in this sphere (Böhning and Werquin 1989: 6–7). However, the ratification record of relevant ILO Conventions by the currently major immigration countries in Europe—some of them were still senders about 15 to 20 years ago—is rather low, as the overview in Figure 3.1 suggests.

International norms do not govern the bilateral relationships at the initial stages of labour migration. This asymmetric dependence reflects

ILO Convention	No. 97	No. 118	No. 143	No. 157
Ratified by	France Germany Belgium Italy The Netherlands Portugal Spain United Kingdom	Denmark France Germany Ireland Italy	Italy Portugal	Spain Sweden

FIG. 3.1. *Ratification record of major ILO Conventions concerning migrant workers by selected immigration countries*
Source: Böhning and Werquin (1989: 8).

the gross power differentials between the two sides that make unilateral decisions to start and stop active recruitment or immigration very likely. The control policies of the countries in the North decisively shape the onset, the direction, and the selection of migrants. One of the most crucial facts of state control of international flows of people is that the nation-states in the North largely determine first entries—the arrival of pioneer migrants and the first members of kinship groups. Sovereign nation-states have the capacity to open and close their borders to pioneer migrants.

Asymmetric Dependence between Countries of Emigration and Immigration

The question arises what kind of asymmetry can be found in the relationships between emigration and immigration states. To present the dilemma of cooperation in which collective actors, such as the governments of emigration and immigration states find themselves, Figure 3.2 is an appropriate starting point. It cannot be represented as a game because of the grave asymmetry between countries of origin and destination. None the less, the stylized representation of options for the nation-state involved helps to clarify the original expectations on the part of the collective actors involved.

Each government has two basic strategies: to allow migration, either immigration or emigration, or to forbid it. The first case (1) is basically a mutually beneficial situation. Actors in both countries perceive benefits and this makes governments on both sides agree: employers in the immigration countries benefit from young male or female workers, healthy and ready to work. For governments, banks and households in the countries of emigration foreign currency and remittances are

Emigration country *Immigration country*	emigration	stop emigration
immigration	+++, ++ (1: mutual benefit)	++, + (2: unrealistic)
stop immigration	+++, + (3: one-sided immigration country advantage)	++, + (4: no linkages)

FIG. 3.2. *Potential pay-offs for emigration and immigration countries in an asymmetric setup*

Note: The pay-off utils '+' are selected randomly to indicate the intensity of assumed preference for one of the four possible outcomes. The higher the number of '+', the higher the expected utility. The first set of each pair indicates the util attributed to the immigration country, the second one applies to the emigration country.

advantageous. But they lose young workers. However, this is compensated for by the function of international migration as a safety valve in the labour market. Therefore, the potential utils in the payoff can be put quite high.

In the second case (2), when immigration countries still allow immigration but the emigration side prohibits emigration, it is usually the state of origin that does not gain as much. Although there are generally other countries of destination available in the long view, the emigration countries usually cannot find alternatives in the short run. The immigration countries would not be very much affected because the prisoner's dilemma situation among the senders ensures that there is an abundant supply of potential emigration countries (Zolberg 1992). Emigration countries compete among each other for the immigration countries' most favoured status. Yet even if emigration countries agreed on a common policy towards the receivers, such as minimum standards of wages and working conditions and provisions combating brain drain, they would be faced with the danger of defection. Partly, this could be overcome by the implementation of international rules. However, one problem is the weak position of an enforcing third party, for example, international organizations such as the ILO. As we have already seen, the 'Migration for Employment Convention' (1949) and subsequent agreements have exceedingly few enforcement mechanisms; certain countries have not even signed it. Therefore, the pay-off matrix is slightly in favour of the immigration countries.

A very similar situation in terms of the pay-offs can be found in the third case (3), when the immigration country stops or severely curtails immigration. The country of destination, as discussed above, can deal with impacts upon labour markets and social standards, advance integration, or return of labour migrants, as in the first case, and later resume its import of immigrant workers. Again, it is the emigration country that suffers the most. It needs some time to find other countries to send its workers to. Needless to say that in the fourth case (4), a bilateral stop of immigrant and emigration on both sides, is most likely to hurt interests of actors in the emigration countries.

If we look at the four possible scenarios concerning the expectations of collective actors, it is obvious that cases (1) and (3) are most likely. A termination of labour emigration on the side of the economically less developed countries is very unlikely and has occurred only rarely: the Communist regimes in Eastern Europe until 1989, and a few dictatorships in developing countries. Moreover, Algeria did so in 1973, one year before the French recruitment stopped (Castles and Miller 1993: 113). The reason for this rare occurrence is obvious and needs only to be hinted at: labour migrants bring in foreign currency, although the impact on general economic development in the country of origin may be minimal. It is evident that the high likelihood of cases (1) and (3) and the unlikeliness of cases (2) and (4) is due to the asymmetric nature of relations between countries of origin and destination.

As international migration flows unfold, the asymmetric kind of linkages between states of emigration and immigration shades in the background. The relationship between migrants and the immigration state increasingly shapes the currents of endogenous dynamics. Once migration flows started into the economically more developed industrial democracies of the North, especially Europe, North America, and Australia, public policies did not succeed in cutting off the inflow immediately and totally. Instead, halts to labour recruitment were followed by vigorous and increased family reunification and curbs on family reunification encountered widespread resistance by entrenched interest groups of immigrants (LeMay 1985). This was not only due to domestic factors, such as employers wanting cheap and docile labour or domestic pressure groups demanding to uphold the right to asylum. It was also because of domestically guaranteed civil rights that corresponded to a set of international human rights rules. One of the most central issues is that many immigration states assent to a set of basic rights granted to migrants qua persons and not as citizens or permanent residents as, for example, the right to reunification of spouses and nuclear families. Migrants can use these civil rights to establish a foothold in liberal democracies.

We are now in a position to sum up some of the effects of macro-factors upon the volume and dynamics of international labour migration, notably on the destination side. First, the control efforts of nation-states are only partially limited or hampered by strong international regimes because of weak international regulation of labour migration. This is a clear instance of asymmetric dependence. Second, however, as migration unfolds, the selective function is increasingly restricted due to human and civil rights enabling migrants to bring in kin and dependents. Once labour migrants have achieved a permanent residency status, they can fetch their families.

Asymmetric interdependence grows over time, as migration processes intensify historically embedded and strong linkages. Once the migration process is underway, destination countries are somewhat less likely to take unilateral actions that disregard the interests of the emigration states completely. In short, liberal democratic states have not lost control over immigration and immigrant policies. Rather, their actions have been severely constrained by the rights of settled migrants, such as the prominent claims to human, civil, and social rights.

The International Regulation of Refugee Flows: Asylum Seekers vis-à-vis States

There are no bilateral agreements between producing and accepting countries in the case of refugees; yet the outcome regarding entitlements for settled movers is roughly the same. Producers and acceptors usually do not negotiate over the terms of asylum. Instead, it is the immigration country authorities with regards to the asylum seeker, and, less important, international organizations that impinge upon the chance to obtain refugee status. Because individual asylum seekers directly face the accepting state government, the prime purport of migrants' claims vis-à-vis the state emerges even more palpably. And the international dimension occupies centre stage: in contrast to the usually bilateral regulation of labour migration, rules applying to refugees suggest that a partial international coordination or a regime exists that implies certain impositions upon immigration states. This partial regime found its expression in the Geneva Convention and subsequent codifications.

After World War Two, the Geneva Convention (1951) and New York Protocol (1967) led to certain self-binding effects for the signatory nation-states. However, although the Geneva Convention entails obligations on the part of member states, these do not extend to admission itself. Also, in the case of refugees, for example, Article 14 of the Universal Declaration of Human Rights provides that 'everyone has the right to seek and enjoy in other countries asylum from persecution'. The aspirational nature of the Declaration and the pervasive principle of nation-state sovereignty have prevented Article 14 from being entrenched as a right of asylum seekers to enter the potential accepting countries. Since it is the prerogative of the sovereign nation-state authorities to grant asylum, there is no entitlement an individual can claim in relation to any potential accepting nation-state. Therefore, the fact that there are no clear-cut universal criteria of who is a refugee and who is not characterizes the uncertain prospects for refugees.

Despite this caveat, the partial refugee regime entails self-binding rules for immigration states that are much harder to circumvent than the mostly bilateral agreements on labour procurement. This may be partly so because the norm of admitting a person whose livelihood is endangered is much more powerful in a moral sense and as a foil for action than restricting entry to labour migrants who presumably look for better job opportunities. Overall, the question of whether the immigration states adhere to such regimes is really a function of the extent to which more powerful states in the system are willing to enforce the principles and norms of the regime. For example, the USA recognized refugees from Cuba in the 1960s while it did not certify those from various authoritarian regimes in Central and South America.

Like labour migration flows, South–North refugee streams follow established migration circuits mostly within migration systems, such as refugee flows from Turkey and former Yugoslavia to Germany, from Central America and the Caribbean states to the USA, and from Africa to France and the UK, and the Middle East to Sweden. All followed upon the contract worker flows. As in the case of movers categorized as labour migrants, historically evolved linkages between the respective nation-states form the main routes for refugees. However, the decisive difference is that in a considerable number of these cases refugee flows followed after labour migration.

External intervention into refugee-producing situations usually does not succeed in curbing flows. In the wake of failed or precarious nation-state projects and revolutions, members of minority groups often seek to widen their political influence over domestic affairs by relocating abroad and eventually form diasporas. Especially so, if their political activities are restricted. In more dramatic cases, civil war, politicide, or even genocide ensue. In most of these cases widespread flight is usually one of the consequences (Gurr 1994). This also raises difficult questions of whether the acceptors are interested, able and willing to intervene into the internal politics of the refugee-producing countries. First, political groups of refugees usually become active in the accepting countries along lines of client politics. This is especially so for those refugees who consider themselves as exiles and strive to return to their country of origin. For example, they seek to widen quotas, curb illegal inflows from their emigration countries, and demand government assistance for newcomers. It is not a foregone conclusion that they use the voice option for extended immigration. But in the case of refugee flows from the emigration countries they usually do.

Second, multilateral intervention, taking the form of humanitarian intervention, has only partial success in stopping refugee flows (Gillessen 1997). The reason can be nicely summarized in the old Talleyrand dictum that you can do a lot with guns—but one thing you cannot: rest upon them. In refugee-producing instances, most of the refugees do not reach the North but make it to neighbouring countries.

To summarize, accepting nation-state capacity has tended to be somewhat more restrained by international norms embedded in both historical-political linkages and international conventions or regimes than in the case of labour migration. This is so because of a partial global refugee regime to which many liberal democratic states adhere.

Nevertheless, there is no individual right to asylum. Yet concerning the capacity of states to restrict further admission of kin and dependents, the same considerations as in the case of labour migrants apply. Once refugees have a permanent status in the country, they can bring their dependents and family. Equally important, labour migrant and refugee flows are frequently following upon each other; suggesting that international migrants travel along familiar avenues, circumscribed by strong linkages within or evolving within migration systems and by the examples set by earlier movers and the support structures established by them.

The argument is that industrial democracies honouring civil rights (*Rechtsstaaten*) cannot effectively restrict immigration once it has taken off. The reasons can be found in both informal links through migrant networks and rights granted formally to immigrants. When immigrants have settled in an immigration country characterized by a modicum of civil and social rights, forced expulsion is not a viable option anymore. And once immigrants have permanent residence, nothing can stop them from bringing in spouses and family, and nothing short of police state methods could stop illicit immigration. This, in turn, at least in the first migrant generation, results in marriage migration when parents look for men and women as partners from the countries of origin for their children in the country of settlement.

Domestic Regulation in the Immigration or Accepting States

So far, the emphasis has been on how the linkages between nation-states, both informal and formalized by international norms, have impacted upon the selection of categories such as labour migrants and refugees in the countries of origin and their admission in the immigration or accepting countries. Because of asymmetric (inter-) dependence, the immigration or accepting countries play the pivotal role in the admission process. The restrictive capacities of destination states regarding labour migrants and the fact that asylum is not an entitlement for refugees start to explain 'why are there so few migrants out of most places?'. And, obviously, refugee-producing states capacities to consolidate their rule is one element for 'why so many?'. Yet this has to be seen in conjunction with the existence of migration systems and immigration-side willingness in liberal democracies to adhere to international norms. This sets the stage for 'so many out of so few countries'.

It is now possible to glimpse at the impact of domestic conditions on admission of migrants. Four reasons explain the shifts from more open policies to more restrictive ones—or vice versa: (1) threats to social and labour standards in the immigration welfare states, and the experiences that have led to learning among policy-makers since the 1960s; (2) conflicts over normative issues of who is entitled to what rights and provisions in the country of destination; (3) conflicts around perceived ethnic and racial homogeneity; and (4) an expansion of civil and social rights, the implication of which also extend to non-citizen immigrants. As we can see, the expansion of rights on the domestic level, promoted by universal human rights discourses, has had a significant feedback effect: via learning among policy-makers, it has contributed to further restrictions of first entries. For example, countries such as Germany admitted new labour migrants in the early 1990s on a strict rotational principle. In selected industries such as construction, German general contractors have hired foreign subcontractors to carry out building projects. The workers sent to Germany are not covered by German but by foreign labour and social security law. Because of the rotational principle and their extraterritorial legal status, these contract workers cannot establish legal claims to residency for themselves or their families in Germany (Faist et al. 1999).

A Swinging Pendulum: Restrictionist vs. Expansionist Immigration Policies

The fundamental issue of moving back and forth between expansive and restrictive immigration policies arises from the fact that benefits from migration are easily privatized—for example, by employers getting access to cheap and docile or extraordinarily qualified labour. However, the perceived costs of immigration tend to be collectivized—be they infrastructural in terms of education or social welfare, or sometimes cultural, regarding conflicts around multicultural demands (Freeman 1995). Policy-makers react to these collectivized costs in curbing immigration beyond a certain threshold. Nevertheless, there are usually more expansionist tendencies counterbalancing restrictionist tendencies in liberal democracies.

Whether restrictive or expansive policies win at one point in time depends on many contingent factors. But restrictionist and expansionist political coalitions face a number of conditions favourable and detrimental to their cause: those favouring restriction need to rally not only diverse groupings around the flag; this is also true of expansionist camps. The crucial difference is that it is relatively easy to lobby for clearly defined special interests—for example, those of employers seeking docile workers and those of immigrant groups favouring family reunification. Also, there are those pushing for the recognition of moral obligations, such as advocates of human rights trying to promote the implementation of international norms that realize and extend the internal constitutions of liberal democracies. By contrast, restrictionists constantly need to balance political forces with highly diffuse interests. For example, populists build up immigration as a meta-issue—tying immigration to fundamental problems of restructuring welfare states in globalizing economies, such as structural unemployment. And then there are always those concerned with the moral and ethnic composition of bounded nation-states. While such issues sometimes garner votes in election times, the corresponding catch-all coalitions across various political trench lines are extraordinarily fragile. Therefore, the manifold extensionist lobbies—consisting of employers, immigrant organizations, civil and human rights organizations—are likely to win almost as often as the more restrictionist camps.

What should be noted is that these dynamics of restrictionist and extensionist policies apply to those immigration countries characterized by controversial and adversarial politics and policy-making. There are cases of nation-states, such as Sweden, that have designed and implemented immigration policies in an unanimous way, bringing together bureaucracy, interest groups, and political parties. Such a policy style that intends decisions to be made after long internal debates among key institutions is usually embedded in a general consensus over goals specifying the 'national interest'. This leads to virtually no or very little politicization of public debates over immigration (Hammar 1985: 26, 44–6).

We have already seen that migration systems within a fundamental structure of asymmetry identify 'why are there so few out of most countries?' and 'why are there so many out of a few countries?' Restrictionist immigration policies contribute to explain 'Why so few international migrants?'. Taking into account the equally forceful reality of expansionist tendencies helps us to also consider answers to 'Why so many?'—as does the impact of rights available to migrants. In particular, the extension of human, civil, and social rights, especially individual entitlements within many national welfare states, encourages migrants to stay and bring in more friends and relatives. In addition to nationally guaranteed and internationally reinforced human and civil rights, social rights emerge out of nationally bounded welfare states—serving to ward off the detrimental impacts of a global competitive economy.

Depending on whether we deal with the so-called guestworker systems, post-colonial predicaments, or former white settler colonies, the mechanisms involved in the extension of immigrant rights is different.

Nevertheless, in all three different systems windows of opportunities for immigrant rights and migrant networks do emerge—all for the very same reason: extension of entitlements for foreign residents. In the former contract worker countries such as Germany and Belgium, the 'guests' invited to work and who nevertheless settled could not be expelled; albeit new entries are easy to prevent in cancelling existing agreements. In the wake of colonial empires, residents from former overseas territories could not be immediately denied entry; citizenship requirements and definitions had to be changed; consider the case of the UK in the early 1980s (Dummett 1994). And last, in classical immigration countries, there are manifold ways to get around the quota system; even illegally residing immigrants could legalize their status in the past, for example, through the Immigration Reform and Control Act (IRCA) of 1986 in the USA.

All of the liberal democracies, characterized by these three types of immigration systems, have strengthened personal rights vis-à-vis government agencies in the twentieth century, and immigrants with a secure residence status cannot be excluded from these achievements. Moreover, virtually all of the immigration countries in the North have signed international treaties such as the Geneva Convention which, for example, commit them to the powerful principle of *non-refoulement*: this means that these states cannot repatriate or expel those who have asked for shelter but were denied refugee status, if their life would be threatened or harmed in the country of origin. And once a migrant has lived in a country for several years, she gains a legal status that usually allows her to avoid deportation. This also happened because in liberal democratic regimes governments are constrained by constitutional norms and procedures. Anti-discrimination legislation in the labour market in many countries also helped to steady the legal position of immigrant workers (Böhning and de Beijl 1995: 22–46). And here we see how inextricably the domestic and international levels intermesh: rights based upon liberal values are embedded in democratic immigration states, as well as in the international system in which these nation-states interact (Hollifield 1992: 222–3, 230–1).

A Fundamental Difference: Liberal Democracies and Authoritarian Regimes

While we can establish a firm link between civil and human rights, expressed in claims to family reunification and *non-refoulement*, in eventually facilitating the formation of migrant networks, there are instances in which rights are only of secondary importance. This is the case in immigration country regimes characterized by authoritarian rule. The strategies of authoritarian governments to restrict immigration can be summarized as follows.

First, policy-makers can strictly enforce the rotation principle in order to avoid permanent settlement of temporary workers in the long run. In recent years, Asian countries such as Singapore have pioneered novel economic instruments to manage temporary labour migration, such as levying a tax on employers who hire contract workers and requiring these labourers to deposit 30% to 50% of their earnings in savings accounts that they can reclaim only in their country of origin.

Second, authoritarian states aim to disregard migrants' civil and social rights. Most immigration states outside Europe, North America, and Oceania are wealthy states and not welfare states and liberal democracies, such as Kuwait, Malaysia, Singapore, Nigeria, and Venezuela (Figure 3.3). For example, the Gulf states have been able to ignore the Arab League and international instruments from the ILO pertaining to international migration. During the Gulf War of 1990/1, hostile immigration countries such as Kuwait, Iraq, and Saudi Arabia evicted hundreds of thousands of Yemeni, Palestinian, and Egyptian migrant workers and their dependents, including many who had been long-term residents. This massive expulsion was possible because wealthy states have not cared much about human rights, and immigrants are devoid of guaranteed and fundamental civil and social rights. No matter how long immigrants stay, they have no legal recourse to permanent work and residence permits. The wealthy state of destination can re-export or oust manpower more at will than in liberal welfare states in which foreign residents with denizen status have social rights at a similar level to citizens. The threat of expulsion renders migrants in the Gulf states more compliant and makes it harder to organize than those in liberal democratic welfare states.

As we know by now, even under these more restrictive conditions, migrant networks have formed. In these cases they are not based on civil, human, and social rights and derivative mechanisms such as family reunifications, but on official recruitment bureaus, community networks, and the illicit trade of people by traffickers (Shah 1996). However, authoritarian immigration countries can truncate the flows of people across networks at will, and have repeatedly done so.

Degree of rights for migrants *Realm of adaptation*	High Western Europe and North America	Low Arab Gulf States
Access to labour markets	after a certain period granting of permanent work permit (despite for those groups for which rotational principle is enforced)	strict enforcement of rotational principle for all groups of labour migrants; if not: no legal claim to unlimited work permit
Civil rights	freedom of religious activities; human and civil rights more or less the same as for citizens	foreign citizens can be expelled at any time; public religious activities of non-Muslims are forbidden; foreigners are not allowed to acquire property; labour migrants are not allowed to bring family (unless their income surpasses a certain limit determined by the respective government)
Social rights	graded system; permanent residents (denizens) generally enjoy status close to citizens	no claims to social rights and benefits; yet sometimes right to run schools; health insurance on firm level
Political rights	rights to join unions; freedom to assemble	no right to join unions; no right to assemble
Citizenship	possible to acquire for permanent residents	not possible to acquire citizenship for migrants and their children

FIG. 3.3. *Degree of rights and realms of adaptation for (temporary) migrants*
Source: Weiner (1986: 53–5).

The Turkish–German Case: Asymmetric Dependence—and Expanding Rights of Resident Immigrants

The Turkish–German case study details the structure of asymmetric dependence in the course and after the demise of the contract worker system, succeeded by refugee flows. While it gives us an impression of 'Why so many migrants out of one country?'—when compared to other potential senders—it also presents us with arguments for effective immigration control on the immigration side. The emigration side set one major precondition: freedom to exit. The Turkish government granted this freedom to their citizens through the constitution in 1961. Only then did exit and re-entry become a basic right for Turkish citizens.

Periods of Turkish–German Migration

In the aftermath, Turkish–German labour migration can be divided into five major phases, of which each offered different opportunities for migrant workers:

1. In the first period, single male exodus dominated, and mostly husbands left their wives and children at home (1961–3). Pioneer migrants then came to Germany.

2. Thereafter, family reunion occurred under special conditions, implying a minimum term of two-year employment abroad (1963–5). The migration rate then steeply increased (Figures 3.4 and 3.5) because some migrant workers could bring along members of their families.

3. Employers and recruiting agents set a priority in the recruitment of women workers (1966–73). In this period, the migration of single women workers, often later joined by their husbands, reached a maximum. Also, when more and more male migrants took the route to enter Germany as tourists, outside the regular recruitment channels, they emigrated in the hope of regularizing their employment and residence status later on.

4. The termination of recruitment stop in 1973 brought about a consolidation of the number of migrant workers, encouraged family

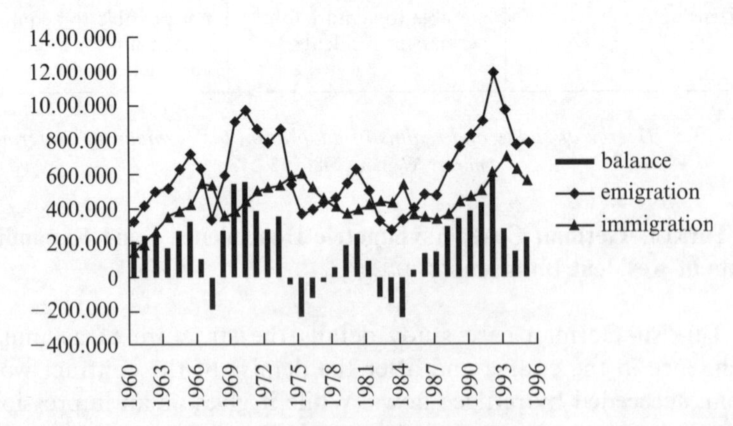

FIG. 3.4. *Total immigration to Germany and emigration from Germany abroad, 1961–96*

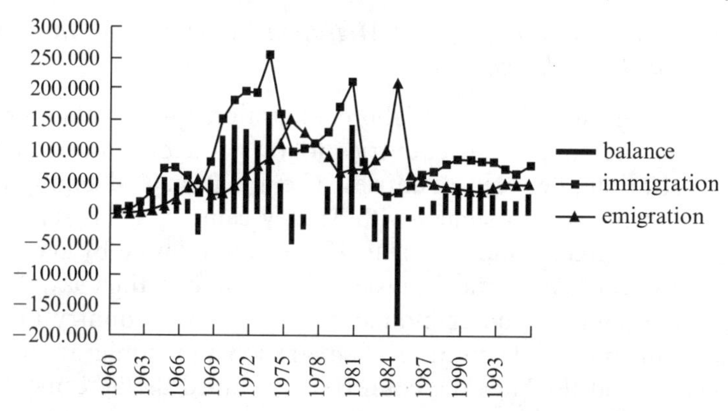

FIG. 3.5. *Immigration from Turkey to Germany and emigration from Germany to Turkey, 1961–96*

reunion and marriage migration, and opened work possibilities to women migrants. At the same time we find an acceleration of Turkish male migration to oil-rich Arab countries.

5. Refugee flows from Turkey to Germany built upon the avenues paved by labour migrants. In the mid-1980s, when fighting intensified between Turkish army and para-military forces, on the one hand, and PKK guerrillas, on the other hand, refugees from the south-eastern provinces or Kurdistan began to enter Germany as asylum seekers in larger numbers than ever before (Figure 3.6). Quite often, these refugees depended on close relatives and friends who had emigrated to Germany as labour migrants many years before.

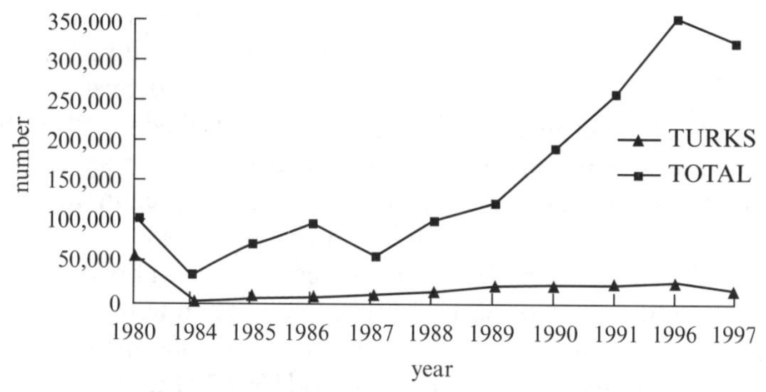

Year	1980	1984	1985	1986	1987	1988	1989	1990	1991	1996	1997
Turks	57,913	4,180	7,528	8,693	11,426	14,873	20,020	22,082	23,877	23,814	16,840
Total	107,818	35,278	73,832	99,650	57,379	103,076	121,318	193,063	256,112	350,000	320,000

FIG. 3.6. *Asylum seekers to Germany: overall numbers and Turkish citizens, 1980–97*

The Evolution of an International Migration System: Weak Inter-State Linkages but Few Alternatives

The chronological ordering of labour migration agreements Germany signed with the emigration countries follows roughly the strength of bilateral relations between countries of emigration and immigration. The recruitment accord signed with Turkey came in 1961—after Italy (1955), Spain, Greece, and Portugal (1960), and followed by agreements with Yugoslavia (1968) and Tunisia (1965). We can thus say that the stronger the political and economic inter- and cross-country linkages, the earlier the potential countries of emigration and immigration signed agreements. And the later the countries concluded the agreements, the weaker the linkages. Yugoslavia is the odd one out. Despite of stronger historical linkages to Yugoslavia than to Turkey, the East–West conflict delayed the signing of the accord.

No strong colonial or hegemonic linkages existed between Germany and Turkey. Nevertheless, Germany chose to recruit in Turkey after labour pools in other countries such as Spain, Portugal, Italy, and Greece had proved insufficient. There were basically two options left in the mid-1960s: Maghreb countries such as Tunisia and Morocco and south-eastern Europe, meaning Yugoslavia and Turkey. While Germany actually concluded agreements with Tunisia and Morocco, labour recruitment from these countries never got off the ground in substantial numbers; probably because they were already oriented towards France. The agreements with Yugoslavia and Turkey were successful. The two latter categories represented about half of all foreign labour in the early 1970s in Germany.

While no strong linkages existed between Germany and Turkey, recruitment proceeded between two friendly nation-states. Earlier, the German Reich and the Ottoman Empire, entertained over a hundred years of cordial governmental relations before the Federal Republic of Germany and the Republic of Turkey signed the labour agreements in the early 1960s, and before refugees from Turkey began to apply as asylum seekers in increasing numbers in the early 1980s. In the beginning, the linkages between Turkey and Germany had above all a security-military and an economic nature. In the nineteenth century, Prussian officers reformed and modernized the Turkish army. The ostentatious *Waffenbrüderschaft* in World War One followed. This could be found more in the memories of the Turks than the Germans which is another reminder of the asymmetric nature of the ties and linkages in the hearts and minds of those concerned. In the economic realm, the German empire had engaged in constructing the Baghdad railway before World War One. And when the major European powers including Greece tried to divide the remains of the collapsed Ottoman Empire among themselves after World War One, Germany—a fellow-loser, could not join the fray. Although relations in the inter-war period were much less intense, Germany and Turkey reached a friendship treaty in 1924. Moreover, during World War Two, Turkey remained neutral, almost up to the last minute. Not surprisingly, the two countries grew closer together again in the aftermath; military and economic relations resumed. Their common experiences as border-states found expression in a vigorous domestic anti-communism and membership in the NATO. Both Turkey and Germany figured prominently in US development schemes such as the Marshall Plan. And in the economic realm, Germany developed into Turkey's most important trade partner as early as the 1950s. In terms of development aid, Germany has been the most relevant donor country. Following India, Turkey has received the most German development aid of all countries since the 1960s.

A Typical Set-up: Asymmetric Relations on All Accounts

Regarding labour migration, it is plausible to treat German–Turkish government relations within a situation of asymmetry (see Figure 3.1 above). In the early 1960s, the collective actors and governments in particular perceived 'mutual benefit' (1). The German side expected cheap and docile labour. And the Turkish government still believed in the viability and success of at least one of the three R's—remittances; the potential other two being the return of labour migrants and the retransfer of skills through return migrants from Germany to Turkey. International labour emigration helped to reduce the unemployment rate in Turkey. In the absence of labour migration, and *ceteris paribus*, the number of unemployed would have increased more than 36% and would have reached about 23% instead of 17% during the 1960s. The terms of Turkish worker employment followed the pattern of restricted labour migration in a set-up of unequal authority: for example, Turkish authorities had no say in the selection of workers or in determining the level of qualifications (Akgündüz 1993: 179). The Federal Employment Office (Bundesanstalt für Arbeit) sent its officials to select. The Turkish Employment Service (TES) was left to screen the workers to be sent to the German recruitment bureaus in cities such as Istanbul and Izmir, before the German authorities took a look at them.

The situation gradually changed to 'one-sided immigration country advantage' (3), when the German government decided to stop recruitment in the early 1970s. Over time, actors on the German side had started to perceive a shifting cost-benefit matrix, such as follow-up costs regarding the infrastructure for the descendants of immigrants and housing. Yet the Turkish government had little reason to doubt the three R advantages on their side. Although the effect of labour migration on unemployment significantly dropped after the recruitment stopped—down from 31% in the 1962–7 and 69% in the 1967–73 period—labour migrants constituted 23% of the additional labour surplus from 1973 to 1986 (Barşık, Eraydın and Gedik 1990: 319). As to remittances, in 1964, three years after the migration stream from Turkey to Germany had begun, remittances constituted the largest source of foreign currency. In 1971, remittances amounted to 471 million dollars, which was more than the value of total imports (Kudat 1975: 15). The only disadvantage was the transfer of skills through labour migrants in the 1960s and 1970s: the empirical evidence suggested that Turkish returnees from Europe did not utilize skills acquired abroad for economic development in Turkey (Bulutay 1995: 37–9).

When the German government halted recruitment and hoped to curb the follow-up costs, Turkey could not greatly increase the flow of remittances and the export of labour surplus. At all times, the German side eventually curbed and controlled the flows quite successfully, despite unintended and sometimes undesired consequences, such as shortages in infrastructural provisions, or intensified family reunification after the end of recruitment. Of course, the higher the level of moral obligations, the more difficult one-sided cancellations became. As we would expect, in the case of refugee flows from densely Kurdish-populated areas in Turkey in particular and asylum seekers in general, this was quite impossible because Germany was bound to international norms embodied in the Geneva Convention and carried special and self-binding obligations from World War Two.

Both German employers who preferred loyal long-time workers to costly annual turnover, and human and civil rights considerations of politicians brought first an extension of the rotation to two years, and later to an indefinite period. When German authorities departed from the strict application of the rotation principle, it created the legal conditions for migrant networks as we know them. Overall, the labour migration rate was lower than it could have been until the recruitment stopped. This was due to the abolishment of the rotation principle. Those workers who stayed in Germany foreclosed an opportunity for new ones to arrive. Since labour migrants abroad proved to the single most important source of foreign currency, it would have been in the interest of the Turkish government to sustain the principle of mandatory rotation. Yet, neither did the Turkish government have a coherent migration policy, nor could it have effectively intervened in the domestic German policy debate (Abadan-Unat and Kemiksiz 1992: 18).

On the German side, the shift from an expansionist to a restrictive immigration policy showed the capacity to consolidate labour recruitment. Clearly, while the benefits were privatized—German employers accessing docile labour and German blue-collar workers moving upwards on the occupational status ladder—the costs were collectivized. In the long run, the conflict over who had to bear the costs could be solved through the termination of recruitment. Thus, the inherent consequences of the programmes account a great deal for the termination. Already before the oil-crisis in 1973/4, the Sociopolitical Discussion Group—made up of representatives from German unions, employers, church and welfare groups, federal and state ministries—agreed on a unilateral termination. The asymmetric character of the relationship is clear, the German government did not consult any of the emigration countries in this matter (Lohrmann and Manfrass 1974: 376). All other major foreign worker importers in Europe—the Netherlands, Belgium, and France—also suspended the official recruitment of foreign labour in the wake of the Oil Crisis. In Germany, the individual Länder and their interior ministers voiced strong calls to terminate the agreements in 1971. The Länder and individual cities—much more than the federal government—carried the burden of infrastructural follow-up costs; a scenario to be repeated later, when the number of asylum seekers reached new heights in the late 1980s and early 1990s (Münch 1992).

When labour migration to Germany subsided in the mid-1970s, more and more Turkish migrants went to Arab oil countries, especially Libya, Saudi Arabia, and Iraq. The Turkish government supported labour migration via Turkish construction companies in the Gulf states. Experts estimated that about 68% of the labour force of the six Gulf Cooperation Council (GCC) countries Bahrain, Kuwait, Oman, Saudi Arabia, Qatar, and the United Arab Emirates consisted of foreign citizens in 1990 (Shah 1994); about 10% of them were Turks. Similar to earlier experiences, the states of origin and destination signed bilateral agreements. Since the wealthy Middle East states of destination strictly enforced the rotation principle in sharp contrast to their European counterparts during the 1960s this kind of labour migration has been predominantly short term and without accompanying family members. Migrants could never claim human, civil, social, and political rights. Also, this new direction of migration meant that the share of female migrants substantially declined (Barşık, Eraydın and Gedik 1990: 305). Since the seminal changes in the former communist bloc, there has been a substantial flow into the republics of the former USSR, especially the Turkmenic regions (İçduygu, Sirekci, and Muradoğlu 1998).

The Political Consequence of Labour Migration on the International Level

Since the recruitment stopped in 1973, the supply of potential labour migrants in Turkey has not been reduced—given such fundamental facts as the growing disparity between the number of new labour force entrants and available jobs. Growing linkages to Germany and the EU led to the inclusion of migration into multilateral negotiations. Because of Turkey's partial integration into the process of European integration through an association agreement that later foresaw the freedom of movement for Turkish workers in 1986, the Republic of Turkey could negotiate over the compensation for the final non-implementation of this clause. In effect, this proviso would have provided for the integration of Turkey into the regional regime of free movement. Earlier, Turkish efforts to join the European Community and cordial relations with one of the most important Member States had resulted in the association treaty of 1963. But this very success weighed heavily upon inter-state relations because the EU—Germany leading this group, supported by obstinate Greece—proved unwilling to grant free mobility to Turkish labour. Freedom of movement gradually took root within the Common Market, whereas it remained a promise in the association treaty of the EU with Turkey. Since this promise remained unfulfiled, this also had repercussions for the Turkish–German relationship. In the 1980s, serious difficulties surged. For example, the protocols to the EU Association Agreement had assured freedom of movement to Turkish citizens beginning in December 1986. Yet the EU governments reneged. And when Turkey applied for full membership in 1987, the EU denied it in December 1989. Officially, the German government feared that Turkish workers—not least because of established migration pathways and migrant networks—would flood the German labour market in large numbers. In the ensuing negotiations over compensations, the German government pressured Turkey to renounce freedom of mobility in exchange for a package of financial and economic aid. Finally, Turkey accepted that the problem of freedom of mobility would only be solved in the context of a more comprehensive agreement between the EU and Turkey.

As in the case of labour migration, refugees from Turkey immediately turned into a highly politicized issue connected to the contested ascension of Turkey into the EU: there was a tight link to human rights issues. The production of refugees primarily originated in the effort of the Turkish government to complete the project of a nationally homogeneous state and the ever more recalcitrant responses of Kurdish opposition groups.

The Production of Kurdish Refugees in Turkey and the German Response

Because of the close relations in terms of common NATO membership and association in the European Community and strengthened by manifold migration experiences, the German public and the German government have become implicated in the most ferocious and violent domestic conflict in Turkey bordering on civil war—the 'Kurdish question'. In the 1980s, it turned into Turkey's single greatest domestic challenge with manifold international currents. The then Turkish president Türgut Özal wrote to his prime minister, Süleyman Demirel, in 1993: 'The Turkish Republic is facing its gravest threat yet. A social earthquake could cut one part of Turkey from the rest, and we could all be buried beneath it' (cit. in McDowall 1996: 1).

No precise or even reliable estimate of the Kurdish population exists. Today, there are probably in the order of 24 to 27 million Kurds living in the Middle East—mainly in Turkey, Iraq, Iran, but also in Syria and Armenia. The Kurds constitute by far the largest people in the world without a state of its own. About half of these, at least 12 million, live in Turkey, that is about 25% of the Turkish population (McDowall 1996: 3; see van Bruinessen 1978). Other estimates, closer to the Turkish government, give a much lower percentage, c.13% (Turkish Democracy Foundation 1996: 3). About one-fourth or 500,000 of the close to two million Turkish immigrants living in Germany in the mid-1990s are probably of Kurdish descent. Out of the Kurds living abroad, another estimated 60,000 reside in France, 10,000 in Sweden, 5,000 in Belgium, and others in the UK, the Netherlands, and Italy (Gunter 1990: 103). In addition to those from Turkey, there are also Kurds from Iran and Iraq that have been living in Germany since the 1980s.

The conflict has revolved around political and cultural autonomy of groups that call themselves Kurds. In a state with the Kemalist ideology of one nation only, Kurdish activists in the late twentieth century have been engaged in the project of simultaneous group-making and nation-state building. This has been a difficult task: with the exception of the seventeenth century poet, Ahmad-i Khani, there is virtually no evidence that any Kurds thought in terms of a whole Kurdish people until the later years of the nineteenth century. It was in the early years of the twentieth century that they acquired a sense of community as Kurds. Until the 1920s and 1930s, few urban Kurds would have described themselves as such. Until nationality became an issue after the founding of the Turkish Republic, townspeople would have defined themselves in terms of their *millet*, or religious community, and their urban status which lifted them, in their view, above the rough-cut peasantry, and ensured their antagonism to the tribes and their alien values. Moreover, Kurdish opposition to the Turkish state in the 1920s and 1930s rallied around religion and found no base in the claim to a distinct ethnicity. The fragmentation by religious and tribal affiliation, by socio-economic activity and by language, prevented effective opposition of Kurds towards the Turkish republic in the decades before World War Two. The non-identification with Turkey as a single and cohesive nation has been the most tremendous obstacle faced by Turkish nation-builders, above all Kemal Atatürk: 'Europe solved its problems concerning nationalism a century and a half ago. Are we in the same situation? Go to a village in Anatolia and ask a villager, 'Who are you?' His answer will be, "Thank God, I am a Moslem". He does not say "I am Turkish". This consciousness has not yet been awakened' (cited in Grothusen 1984: 177). In this way, the 'Kurdish question' revealed one of the main fissures in Turkish nation-building.

In sum, manifold problems concerning socio-economic underdevelopment, suppression of political representation, and denial of cultural expression in the public sphere have turned into a national problem with the strategies of annihilation and flight dominating the discourse over solutions such as (partial) political and cultural autonomy, embedded in processes within an authoritarian republic. For example, the *Yasakdiller Yasası* (1983–91; Law No. 2932 prohibiting the use of Kurdish in public) stipulated that Kurdish could not be used as a language in public. Thus, one could always speak Kurdish but native speakers could not use it in state institutions, private or public schools, and in print and other media. Even since the ban was lifted in the early 1990s, the repression of Kurdish language products in public has continued. The government has employed language policies as one major device to assimilate Kurds into the Turkish Republic since the 1920s. Those Kurds who publicly identify with Kurdish language and culture have risked persecution and are thus potential refugees (Chaliand *et al.* 1978: 122–33). The Turkish government has codified the denial of any language or culture that deems to be non-Turkish. Along with very broad definitions of terrorism, this provides state authorities with a carte blanche to prosecute activists who strive for political or cultural autonomy or separation. The Turkish security forces have stubbornly repressed even moderate Kurdish groups. This served the PKK to claim sole representation of the Kurdish cause.

The PKK (*Partiya Karkarên Kurdistan*)—founded in 1978—launched military operations that have led to an undeclared civil war since 1984. Since then successive Turkish governments have tried to stamp out 'Kurdish terrorism'. However, the argument that Kurdish aspirations threaten the territorial integrity of the Turkish state is only partially convincing. While public debates and media attention have focused on the role of the PKK, autonomists among Kurdish groups and organizations have always outnumbered separatists (Wiessner 1995: 162). Certainly, however, an authoritarian-cum-democratic Turkish government has seen its goal of a nationally homogeneous population threatened.

The so-called Kurdish question is a typical example of problems arising in the wake of nation-building in late-coming nation-states. The conflict has not remained limited to Turkey but affects the whole region including Syria, Iran and Iraq. It has also resulted in a heightened tension between these nation-states. In the course of international conflicts, such as between Iraq, and Kuwait, refugee-producing conditions exacerbated when some Kurdish groups actively engaged in fighting, or suffered as targets and victims. In particular, Turkey has repeatedly fought against PKK guerrillas in Iraq.

Nevertheless, because of earlier migration links most Kurdish refugees who went to Europe came from Turkey. The area in south-eastern Turkey called Kurdistan is populated by roughly 10 million persons, most of whom belong to various Kurdish tribes. According to Turkish government statistics, a massive build-up of weapons has taken place—in the mid-1990s about 50,000 PKK fighters and 375,000 supporters facing about 220,000 soldiers, 16,000 police and other civil representatives from the central government; helped by para-military village guards paid by the government, who are armed by security forces and meant to protect habitations from PKK attacks. Since the 1980s, more than 3,000 villages were evacuated and razed. The Turkish government spoke of about 2,700 villages destroyed and two million persons evicted in the south-eastern provinces until 1995 (Fact Sheet of the International Association for Human Rights in Kurdistan 1996: 2), that is about 15% of all habitations in south-eastern Turkey. Close to 12,000 persons died in the armed conflicts between the PKK and the Turkish army. The latter deployed two-thirds of the total force in Kurdistan during the 1980s and 1990s. More than 2 million displaced Kurds fled. Among the reasons given by surveyed refugees were: PKK attacks, military purges and pacification operations on the part of the security forces, reprisals for refusal to join the village guard system, the difficulty of feeding themselves because of war conditions, and lack of security under those conditions (Turkey Human Rights Report 1994; Ergil et al. 1995).

The fighting has caused major migration movements to nearby cities, especially of those caught in the crossfire of the conflict when security forces and PKK matched each other's ruthlessness. The immediate effect of fighting has produced large numbers of homeless people, driven into the towns and cities of Kurdistan. For example, the city of Diyarbakır had probably already had 500,000 inhabitants in late 1990, despite its official population of 350,000.

The Turkish state extended their emergency rule many times in the 1980s and 1990s for south-eastern provinces, such as Bitlis, Tunceli, Şirnak, Mardin, Van, Hakkari, Diyarbakır, Batman, Bingöl, and Siirt. People from razed hamlets moved to Diyarbakır, Van, Adana, and Mersin—and many moved further west. By the end of 1994, an estimated one million refugees from the countryside had sought shelter there, a pattern repeated town after town across provinces heavily inhabited by Kurds. Also, as some Kurds moved to western Turkey, the polarization grew between migrant Kurdish communities and their neighbours, particularly in areas of large concentration such as Istanbul, Ankara, and Izmir. Whereas in the 1960s migrant Kurds had been a noticeable but scattered phenomenon, by the mid-1990s coherent Kurdish districts and townships existed in many Turkish cities (McDowall 1996: 438–40). Yet, compared to the huge number of internally displaced victims, only a few thousand Kurds each year made it to European countries such as Germany (go back to Figure 3.5). Compared to the number of internally displaced persons, only about 2% of all refugees ended up in countries of the EU.

The German government, among many other non-governmental and supra-national actors, has repeatedly criticized the human rights record of the Turkish government. Yet, due to close security-military cooperation, this critique has repeatedly run into trouble. Although, in 1993, the German government followed the lead of other European governments, such as Sweden, and outlawed the PKK, relations between Turkey and Germany did not significantly improve. From the Turkish point of view, the curb came quite late. Long before, the PKK had carried its struggle into Western Europe and thus transnationalized the internal fighting. In addition to asylum seekers from the south-eastern provinces, the German government faced substantial political activity of Kurdish organizations in Germany. This development has contributed to asymmetric interdependence between these emigration and immigration states because governments on both sides have been led to control both movement of refugees and non-state military or guerrilla action. In decisions to permit or outlaw Kurdish organizations, the German authorities developed a keen interest in upholding internal security. The higher the number of Kurdish refugees climbed and the stronger the activities of all kinds of Kurdish groups in Germany grew, the less the German government was able to focus solely on recognition of refugees. It also became involved in monitoring and sanctioning activities of Kurdish activists in Germany.

As we would have expected, the largest percentage of asylum seekers from Turkey, about 50% from 1980 to 1995, went to Germany because of established networks and considerable settlements of Turkish immigrants. However, not only the size and established networks influenced the flow of asylum seekers to countries in Western Europe: policies seemed to have played a role as well. Although the Netherlands had the second largest Turkish community in Europe, only 1% of asylum seekers from Turkey went there. Similar considerations apply to Switzerland. It ranks sixth in the size of the Turkish immigrant communities in Europe but about 7% of all asylum seekers from Turkey applied there (see Table 3.1; Içduygu 1998: 29–30).

TABLE 3.1. *Number of Turkish asylum seekers by period of arrival in western Europe, 1983–94*

Country	1983–1994	1983–1985	1986–1988	1989–1991	1992–1994
Austria	12,000	800	2,000	5,400	3,800
Belgium	14,200	2,000	2,700	7,000	2,500
Denmark	2,000	1,500	300	100	100
France	66,600	4,900	15,400	39,000	7,300
Germany	205,900	21,900	35,000	66,000	83,000
Netherlands	2,300	200	500	500	1,100
Norway	800	100	200	400	100
Sweden	5,000	600	1,000	2,300	1,100
Switzerland	22,300	300	3,500	13,000	5,500
UK	11,900	100	500	5,700	5,600
Other West European	3,400	300	600	1,400	1,100
TOTAL WEST EUROPEAN	346,400	32,700	61,700	140,800	111,200

Source: Estimated by Ahmet İçduygu (1998) based on various reports of UNHCR, OECD, and EUROSTAT.

Conclusion: Effective Immigration Control and Expanding Immigrant Rights

The policies of origin and destination countries attest to the fact that South–North migratory and refugee movements, once underway, are neither akin to flights of locusts nor can they be controlled at will. Asymmetric dependence between emigration and immigration states forms the framework. This helps to explain the direction of international migration from few and selected senders to the immigration countries. Even more important, in liberal democratic immigration states, the presence of immigrant groups on their territory carries implications for human, civil, and social rights. These claims form the basis for subsequent migration from the same region, subverting the original intentions of policy-makers concerning temporary labour migration, the selective import of human capital migrants, or the limited recognition of refugees from a particular country during a specific conflict. Through international human rights discourses and domestic rights expansions niches of opportunity open for migrant networks that foster specific mechanisms such as family reunification.

It is striking that regardless of variations in the migration control capacity of immigration states, the type of entry—contract worker recruitment, post-colonial (re)migration, immigration via quota into the former white settler colonies—and various rules for access to rights, we find both effective immigration control and entitlements granted to immigrants by liberal democratic states to virtually all of its residents qua personhood, irrespective of nationality. This finding is not as contradictory as it seems at first sight: the former concerns the admission of newcomers, the latter the claims of migrants as human beings and, above all, the rights immigrants acquire by working and residing in the country of destination.

A macro-structural perspective gives us partial answers to both questions of the first puzzle. The 'why so few?' lies in effective control capacities of states for border regulation. The 'why so many?' is not explained—but the structural preconditions seem to allow for the formation of migrant networks. We get a first answer to 'why are there so many out of very few places?' if we restrict ourselves to nation-state entities. Migration systems theory follows migrant flows along strong linkages and those that evolve from weak to strong, linked to former colonial encounters and hegemonic penetrations of peripheral regions in the world economy and the international system of states. The 'why are there so few out of most places?' is a mirror image of the preceding question. Yet, the preliminary answers to 'out of most places' and 'out of very few places' only pertain to the nation-state and not to lower levels, such as vast within-country differences. And the mechanisms of expanding rights only set limiting conditions. They circumscribe parameters of the overall puzzle that is still in dire need of explanation.

4

The Crucial Meso Link: Social Capital in Social and Symbolic Ties

Once the broader opportunities are set, the familiar story about evolving migration dynamics goes like this: as migration flows develop, potential migrants who have stayed at home can move in increasing numbers. For this to occur, migrant networks need to form. With the existence of migration networks and the support they carry, it becomes easier to travel abroad, to find work and housing, to get adjusted to new types of work, to change jobs, to find child care, to keep in touch with the country of origin, and to consummate communal and spiritual needs. Information then flows through personal contacts, such as recurrent, transilient, and return migrants, and within immigrant clusters, such as manifold *Landsmannschaften*. In short, migrant networks reduce the economic and psychological risks and costs associated with international long-distance migration. The potential migrants also feel the feedback effects of international migration—such as growing scarcity of land bought by return migrants or lower social status associated with not migrating abroad. Feeling relatively frustrated or being actually dislocated, potential migrants then turn into actual ones. As these migration processes get underway, the opportunities to move and the mental maps of potential migrants change. Captivated by the allure of life abroad, migrants engage in chain migration.

Following this train of thought, a similar yet distinct process applies to more involuntary migration: refugees fleeing North also move to specific countries, those within given migration systems. But then it would not be recruitment policies but internal persecution or discrimination in their countries of origin and the prospect of finding asylum abroad that sets off chains of events leading to flight and more flight from South to North. Yet, because of low degrees of choice, the perpetuating and increasing endogenous go-aheads are less likely and forceful. Notably, even in the absence of direct persecution and repression, minority groups in nation-states could perhaps come to favour a relocation abroad in order to escape intolerable living conditions and even bring down the oppressive political regime from exile.

However, this short and widely accepted version of migration dynamics has to be further specified: if international migration is such a pervasive feature, why is it then that the majority of potential migrants remains relatively immobile? Why do the majority of refugees end up as displaced persons or why do most economically motivated migrants engage in seasonal and recurrent migration? Finally, why is it that there are so many international migrants out of a few places and so few out of most? Network theory claims that networks in themselves are the crucial mechanisms. However, this is a circuitous reasoning because it assumes what needs to be explained. Instead, we need to first examine more closely the content of social and symbolic network ties, and explore the functions of resources such as obligations, reciprocity, and solidarity. Therefore, before we turn to the question of how migration flows and sometimes even refugee movements turn into self-feeding events that, at times, engender even more migration, it is necessary to define more clearly the relational nature of migration. This applies not only to those migrants who follow established and well-trodden paths, but also to pioneer migrants. That is, we need to define more clearly the basic resources at the disposal of potential migrants.

Three propositions guide the analysis in this chapter:

1. Emphasis needs to be placed on how people take decisions on moving and staying in and between groups. This means to focus on webs of kinship clusters and various forms of larger communities. Decisions to move or to stay are not taken by isolated individuals for whom economic-political-cultural structures only represent external constraints and opportunities. In an interpersonal and inter-group perspective, decisions over moving and staying may be taken on different levels, by individuals and differently sized groups, or imposed upon these groups by outsiders, such as governments of nation-states. Yet the basic assumption is that potential migrants and groups always relate to their immediate surroundings along a continuum of degrees of freedom. Particular units such as households, kinship groups, and local communities therefore deserve special attention. Empirical studies muster up abundant evidence that these units have figured most prominently not only in earlier transatlantic migrations from Europe to the white settler colonies (Bodnar 1985) but also do so in contemporary movements from the South to the North, especially from rural areas in the South (Hugo 1995).

2. It would be naive to conceptualize all social units, such as kinship systems or households, as single-interest decision-making bodies. There is too much evidence on the importance of diverging interests and of

power relations within these units, as expressed in hierarchical and patriarchal decision-making, for example (see Chapter 2). A relational or meso-link perspective rather means that individual actors are not characterized by solipsistic existence and that the decisions of individuals or households are contingent upon their respective location or position within broader networks of persons or groups.

3. Social capital, the set of resources inherent in social and symbolic ties, forms the very cynosure of explanation. Various dimensions of social capital and benefits derived from it espouse an ambiguous quality. On the one hand, they constitute local assets and thus add to relative immobility of potential migrants through manifold attachments and ties to the immediate spatial surroundings. On the other hand, social and symbolic ties crystallize in migrant networks that are able to span geographically remote locations in two or more different nation-states. This means that expanding migration opportunities through decreasing costs and the changing desires of potential migrants are not automatically given because local assets cannot be transferred abroad easily. Among these assets we may find attachment to kin and friends, a language that is familiar, communities such as a church congregation that offers spiritual nourishment, and an ethnic group or a nation with a distinct cultural-ideological outlook. Certain assets remain local unless wrenched into motion not only by macro-structural factors such as recruitment or civil wars—but also by the evolution and presence of mechanisms inherent in the manifold ties connecting potential movers, stayers, and larger communities and organizations.

This chapter first introduces a pioneering exemplar of meso-level analysis, Thomas and Znaniecki's seminal study on *The Polish Peasant in America*. Second, it defines key concepts to be used: social and symbolic ties that link potential movers and stayers. Special emphasis rests on the specific resources that can be mobilized within groups and networks—social capital: obligations as a pattern of social exchange, reciprocity as a social norm, and solidarity; and the benefits derived from social capital: access to resources of others, information, and social control through authority. Third, the analysis moves to define social capital as both resources for individual actors, and as collective assets inherent in social and symbolic ties. Fourth, the analysis gauges the importance of social capital for migration. The specificity of resources under the heading of social capital shapes migration decisions and its volume because of their dual character as local assets and as readily transferable resources. The analysis of social capital provides a much-needed meso link between micro- and macro-levels of analysis: its various dimensions indicate that it serves as both a resource to people and as one of the devices integrating groups, organizations, and symbolic communities. In particular, social capital fulfils the functions of selecting potential migrants to move and to return and to diffuse this pattern of exit behaviour; generally, tightly coupled with voice and *in situ* adaptation. The benefits derived from social capital also function to bridge migratory spaces through flows of persons, ideas, information, and goods. We can also speak of an adaptive function that helps migrants to adjust to new environments. Immigrants not only adjust to and learn from the immigration society, but also alter it and produce their life from within.

A Pioneering Exemplar: *The Polish Peasant in Europe and America*

One exemplar that implicitly sketches theoretical considerations and empirical evidence along relational lines is William Thomas's and Florian Znaniecki's acknowledged masterpiece on *The Polish Peasant in Europe and America* (1927). It deals with transatlantic migration of peasants from Russian Congress Poland to the USA around the turn of the nineteenth and twentieth century. According to Thomas and Znaniecki, the decisions of movers and stayers resulted from the break-up of traditional agricultural society, and particularly of its extended family system. This was due to the marketization of economic life in the areas of origin. The dissolution of the peasant family created new possibilities, especially through the 'growing assertion of the personality' (ii. 217). This evolutionary determinism may be criticized, but the shift from affectual to purposive and rational forms of action is the most relevant aspect of *The Polish Peasant* for the study of the causes and dynamics of migration. People regroup in new forms of organization—groups in which at least one (set of) actor(s) has the right to speak authoritatively for the whole. Importantly, Thomas and Znaniecki argued that this development of more abstract, complex, and cognitive levels of social reorganization largely evolved out of the kinship groups. It did not entail the disappearance of primary group attitudes and values but a regrouping.

As we have seen, newer research has focused on migration not as an expression of societal disorganization but, for example, as an active strategy to diversify income in rural households dependent on crops. What kind of reorganization occurs and on what level it proceeds, depends on the context: in times of crises of traditional social organizations, we certainly have to deal with the disorganization of larger structures such as nation-states and their economies. These processes find their counterpart on lower levels of aggregation, such as the household or kinship level. The focus of Thomas and Znaniecki on household, communal, and other ties remains valuable because it helps to construct the meso link, whether we focus on disorganization such as the persecution of political refugees or organization, or on migration as a household strategy for economic survival and advancement.

Thomas and Znaniecki observed that potential migrants can re-organize both in the country of origin and in the new country of settlement. In the homeland, examples of collective action included the emergence of joint institutions, such as cooperative shops, loan and savings banks and agricultural improvement societies (iv. 178–304). Nowadays, we would add forms of political voice such as peasant protests (Scott 1976). Through these forms of collective action, potential migrants had alternatives to moving in improving the life situation in the country of origin, active *in situ* adaptation. Those who moved to the main country of destination, the United States, came to be members of various forms of communal life, ranging from mutual aid societies and parishes to cultural organizations. Typically, immigrants such as Poles used their investments in kinship and religious groups as resources to redefine their situation, such as workers, citizens, and members of household and religious congregations. Moreover, a vivid transatlantic exchange of ideas developed, often associated with periodic return migration. A parallel story could be told in many instances about political refugees. Although the root causes may differ and options to stay without endangering their lives may be minimal for refugees at the time of flight, the same principles of analysis can be applied.

This early exemplar illustrates some of the main principles of migration decision-making. The lesson is that no analysis can sufficiently describe and explain migration process without taking into account the ties within the social, economic, cultural, and political units potential migrants and their significant others are enmeshed.

The Main Elements of the Meso Link: Ties and Social Capital

Social relations, viz. ties in collectives and networks, constitute distinct sets of intermediate structures on the meso level. It is via these relations that actors relate their resources to opportunity structures. This insight connects two sets of approaches or aggregate levels; hence its function as a meso link: according to rational choice approaches, decisions to move or to stay are inevitably made by individual or collective actors such as households who weigh the costs and benefits involved. What migration-systems theories rightly emphasize is that these decisions are always made within specific economic, political, and cultural contexts, embedded in larger opportunity structures such as wage differentials, economic crises, wars, and persecution.

Social Ties

Social ties are a continuing series of interpersonal transactions to which participants attach shared interests, obligations, expectations, and norms. For example, social ties constitute themselves in talk, association such as participation in a meeting or membership in a club, formal transactions such as in authority relations, or relations based upon biological connections, as is evident in lineage kinship groups (see Wasserman and Faust 1994: 18). Social ties differ along several dimensions: they include the strength of ties, the size of group in which they are found, the density of ties in a network or a group which hints at the potential for information, and the centrality of actors. The latter signals authority and relevant orientations of action. In the broadest sense, transactions are bounded communications between one actor and others.

Fundamentally, social ties can be distinguished according to their strength. Strong ties are characterized by intensive transactions between the participants or members. They are enduring and involve obligations and often emotions. They can be frequently found in small, clearly defined institutions such as households, kinship groups, and communal organizations. Social capital as reciprocal obligations and expectations emerges above all in a web of strong ties. By contrast, weak ties are defined by mostly indirect relations. Weak ties imply only indirect or more superficial personal contact. Transactions between 'friends of friends' (Boissevain 1974) are a useful shorthand for weak ties. However, it would be fallacious to regard weak social ties as an inferior carrier of social resources. This is because weak ties often establish bridgeheads in getting access to important resources beyond the immediate sphere of intimate relations, such as jobs (Granovetter 1973); while strong ties, of course, can also fulfil such bridging functions. Regarding migration, something similar could be said about potential migrants who are able to establish ties to the immigration country through return migrants. It is therefore plausible to assume that weak social ties are useful above all for the diffusion of information, provided they establish links between more dense networks of persons or even groups. Strong social ties, on the other hand, are very important not only for information transfer but also when analysing decisions on international migration or flight.

Symbolic Ties

In contrast to social ties, symbolic ties are not necessarily a continuing series of transactions. For example, they can be mobilized even in the absence of earlier direct contact, based on presumed commonalties of the participants. Symbolic ties are perceived bonds, both face-to-face and indirect, to which participants attach shared meanings, memories, future expectations, and representations. Symbolic ties can go further on than direct relations, involving members of the same religious belief, language, ethnic, or national group. For example, 'imagined communities' such as nations (Anderson 1983) crucially depend on the existence of symbolic ties. One of the main functions of symbolic ties in such communities is to integrate an otherwise anonymous crowd of strangers.

Chains of migrants only tend to develop when information and other resources spill over to wider groups and networks. Within kinship groups, the potential for migrants is generally quickly exhausted because of limited size. Ties reaching beyond narrow kinship systems are necessary for chain migration to unfold. Frequently, the ties involved are not only social but also symbolic; especially between refugees and the receiving groups abroad.

Social Capital and Transaction Costs

Social and symbolic ties between actors carry important sets of resources that can be called social capital. Social capital is a prototypical meso link. Distilling the literature on social capital we find that some have understood it as a resource to be employed by persons (for many, see Bourdieu 1983), while others have insisted that social capital is embodied in networks of cooperation and the norm of reciprocity (for a prominent example, see Putnam 1993). Only when we bring these two meanings together can we use social capital as an analytical tool to establish the meso link: *Social capital are those resources that help people or groups to achieve their goals in ties and the assets inherent in patterned social and symbolic ties that allow actors to cooperate in networks and organizations, serving as a mechanism to integrate groups and symbolic communities.* Social capital therefore has two aspects. First, it is a resource for individual and collective actors. This means that social capital serves as a door opener to people who have specific and desired resources. Second, social capital relates to an aspect of social structure that facilitates cooperation. Social capital is a collective good, although the benefits can be consumed individually. Thus, social capital serves to connect people to networks, groups, and organizations through social and symbolic ties—allowing for the integration of groups through social and symbolic ties.

The term 'social capital' has two advantages over the notion of social resources. Social capital draws attention more directly to discounting, returns on investment—benefits—and to institutional influences on the value of social resources. Speaking loosely in economic terms, we can say that profit or the benefits derived from social capital equals the investment or stock (a question of production) times the rate of return (a question of opportunity). None the less, we should be careful about the terms 'investment' and 'production': social capital generally is an unintended by-product of transactions proceeding in social and symbolic ties.

From the point of view of collectives, the most important function of social capital is to reduce transaction costs and to facilitate cooperation. In institutional economics, transaction costs mean the costs of making an agreement, monitoring its terms, and enforcing it (Williamson 1981). These costs refer to the expenses of exchange itself, such as collecting information on transaction partners and on the commodity or action that is exchanged, the costs of negotiating an agreement or contract and of monitoring its implementation, and the actual enforcement costs of the agreement. Transaction costs exist because human beings' rationality is bounded, not least by the time and effort of collecting and processing information (Coase 1960). Also, people occasionally act opportunistically, and then violate trust. Or, they may take advantage of vulnerable transaction partners, if they can get away with it. As for international migration, for example, some migrants do not send home remittances, as agreed upon. Or, they may look for new spouses or partners in the country of destination. In general, transaction costs arise because real-life situations are complex and uncertain, making it unlikely to anticipate and explicitly consent to all the contingencies. Exit coupled with voice and *in situ* adaptation is a particularly interesting case for analysing transaction costs, because the process of moving in the contemporary South–North context reinforces the tendencies of weakening kinship, communal and manifold other ties. In principle, international movements threaten to cut or weaken social and symbolic ties.

Social Capital Investments: Facilitating Cooperation and Integration

The first aspect of social capital concerns the resources and mechanisms that facilitate cooperation and integrate groups. Here, we look at the content of social and symbolic ties. What kind of good is social capital? At the most basic level social capital is not a conscious investment but a by-product of transactions and of collective representations. If available, it can contribute to overcome free-rider problems because it lowers transaction costs. It is a collective good. A certain structure of transactions that crystallizes in networks of cooperation and their content helps to overcome serious problems of cooperation, as there are obligations as a pattern of social exchange, reciprocity as a norm, and solidarity as an outflow of symbolic representations.

We can analytically differentiate three mechanisms of social capital that lower transaction costs and facilitate cooperation: obligations as a result of social exchange, reciprocity as a norm, and solidarity. Although they refer to rational, norm-guided, and expressive realms of action, there is no simple opposition between these three realms of behaviour. Rather the triad alludes to different analytical aspects of action.

Mechanism No. 1: Obligations as a Pattern of Social Exchange

This includes mutual obligations and expectations of the actors, associated with specific social ties and based on exchanges and services rendered in the past. These obligations and expectations can be an outcome of instrumental activity, for example, the tit-for-tat principle (Axelrod 1984). Metaphorically, the principle of exchange in relations between people is best captured by market transactions. Prices, the allocation of scarce resources, and the distribution of outputs can be explained by rational maximization of utility by economic actors in relation to money outlay. However, it is disputed to what extent this approach can be applied to the wider subject matter of social life. The success of economic theory depends on there being a definite currency in the market exchange, available to both the potential migrant and the theorist. Diverse currencies such as happiness, prestige, influence, and power have been offered as functionally equivalent non-economic currencies (Bredemeier and Stephenson 1970). But these individual goals are also frequently in competition with each other and we need to know more about how such fundamental values are prioritized by the relevant actors. Moreover, the occurrence of exchange between individuals can also be seen as an effect rather than a cause of social order, because stable relationships of exchange depend on a pre-existing minimum of informal trust and formal law enforcement.

None the less, we can use the market imagery in a loose sense to describe the characteristics of exchange-based obligations: in the course of transactions between migrants, brokers, gatekeepers, and those left behind, all actors accumulate deposits of social capital that are based on past mutual services; within patterns of direct and strong social ties. They thus improve their stock of social capital. If A does something for B and trusts that B will reciprocate this in the future, this leads A to expect B to do something and B to an obligation finalizing this trust. This obligation can be interpreted as a sort of voucher that A has, in order to be redeemed by an act on the part of B in the future, such as a service. Often, there are a great many mutual vouchers. Three elements seem to be crucial for expectations and obligations to work as social capital: the degree of trust in the other actors, the actual number of obligations (Coleman 1990: 306), and the kind of services rendered in the past. We cannot imagine this kind of obligation and expectation to emerge without personal acquaintance of some sort.

People in a network or a group differ according to how many vouchers or obligations they draw. The higher the number of vouchers, the higher the amount of social capital available. Yet the vouchers A has from B and the vouchers B has from A do not seem to be as easily exchangeable as monetary vouchers. Also, the vouchers are not always used to balance each other; there is not necessarily a full *quid pro quo* (Stinchcombe 1986: 231–67).

Persons involved in aiding international migrants to travel, to find work and housing, such as brokers, can also expect to benefit through material profits, such as money, and immaterial gains, such as social status. Migrants, return migrants, and migration merchants exchange favours, information, approval, and other valued items. In the course of social transaction, the movers, stayers, and facilitators accumulate even more deposits based on previous favours by others.

Mechanism No. 2: Reciprocity as a Social Norm

It exists when what one party receives from the other requires some return. Reciprocity implies 'actions that are contingent on rewarding reactions from others and that cease when these expected reactions are not forthcoming' (Blau 1974: 6). In general, '(r)eciprocity refers to exchanges of roughly equivalent values in which the actions of each party are contingent on the prior actions of the others in such a way that good is returned for good, and bad for bad' (Keohane 1986: 8).

The norm of reciprocity is an important dimension and a mechanism associated with social capital because obligations are not always clear-cut, there may be situations in which multiple meanings can be attached: 'Being indeterminate, the norm can be applied to countless and ad hoc transactions, thus providing a flexible moral standard for transactions, which might not otherwise be regulated by specific obligations' (Gouldner 1960: 171). Reciprocity is a social norm when at least two sub-norms are adhered to: first, persons help those who have helped them, and second, persons should not harm those who helped them before. Reciprocity signifies trust between members of relevant collectives such as families or households—or the control of malfeasance. The tolerance of large outstanding balances signals the presence of trust or implicit threats (Ben-Porah 1980: 7).

While the norm of reciprocity tends to enhance cooperation, it can lead to exploitation, revenge, and retaliation. We then encounter sour social capital. Take the *guanxi* and *ganqing* ('sentiment') relations between Chinese businessmen. Usually they are viewed as positive mechanisms crucial to the trust and credit that make the overseas Chinese commercial world go round, provide them with access to inside information, and commercial contacts (Ong 1997). True enough, *guanxi* ties demarcate various relationships of comity and privilege with specific sorts of people, such as classmates, people from the same birthplace or 'brothers'. This means that conflicts with people and groups outside *guanxi* ties can easily get out of hand because reciprocity means collective action against a competing group. Also, the norm of reciprocity does not necessarily increase individual autonomy. It may make autonomous action much harder for people, for example, if some of the persons involved aim at self-realization.

Examining reciprocity, we have to distinguish five characteristics: the balance of accounts (specific and generalized reciprocity), the temporal sequence of transactions, the kind of service exchanged, benefactor-contributor relations, and power relations.

1. We can differentiate specific and generalized reciprocity. Specific reciprocity refers to situations in which specified partners exchange items of equivalent value in a strictly delimited sequence. If any obligations exist, they are clearly specified in terms of rights and duties of a particular actor. Specific reciprocity pertains to varied situations, for example, when migrants care for their elderly parents, either by returning to the country of emigration, or providing for family unification in the country of immigration. Generalized reciprocity means that equivalence is less precise, one's partners may be viewed as a group in

a community or a country, rather than as particular actors, and the sequence of events is less narrowly bounded. It involves conforming to generally accepted standards of behaviour. While specific reciprocity requires bilateral balancing between particular actors, generalized reciprocity emphasizes an overall balance within a group.

2. The temporal sequence of transactions ranges along a continuum. At the one end are cases where ego renders a service, and alter immediately returns the same service for ego. At the other end of the continuum are services that are returned much later, sometimes years after the first exchange took place. For example, ego helps a friend with information on migration opportunities and alter helps ego years later in doing the same for her after returning to the country of emigration.

3. The kind of service also matters. For example, one family helps the other during harvest season. The other family responds to this help in also supporting the first family in their work. This form of reciprocity is frequently found between households in farming villages. Or, ego may help a neighbour in building his house; alter returns this service in supporting ego's candidacy for a public office. In this case service and response are not of the same kind.

4. Reciprocity obligations must not be met by providing return directly to those who have provided benefit. We can imagine at least one alternative pattern: ego can reciprocate indirectly, to someone other than the original benefactor (Ekeh 1974). Reciprocity then has the potential to spread beyond narrowly bounded groups. An even more altruistic form of reciprocity is 'the gift' (Mauss 1954). The transfer then occurs at the possessor's discretion, without any prior stipulation on the receiver's consequent obligations.

5. It makes a lot of difference whether there is rough symmetry of power or authority between the actors or whether one of the actors can more or less unilaterally define the terms of the exchange contract. For example, in many cases the head of the kin group is responsible for the flow of the household income. Yet this does not mean that the head moves herself in order to supply cash. In this case reciprocity would mean that, on the one hand, the moving family members remain loyal and actually send money back home and, on the other hand, the immobile family members work in the fields.

To illustrate these five characteristics of reciprocity: someone from a village in Central Anatolia who has moved to Berlin in Germany turns up on the doorsteps of a fellow-villager to ask for job referrals. The same villager who has been helped by the established migrant may not return the favour to the same individual but to other newcomers from the same village who arrive even later; this time not in finding work but housing. This is a specific instance of generalized and not of specific reciprocity. Also, there is not a simultaneous reciprocity but months or perhaps years are in between. The services exchanged may not be the same: the first migrant helped his fellow-villager to find a job, the second one responded in providing housing. And the benefactor in the second case was not the original migrant who helped but a new one from the same village in Turkey. Also, there is no explicit balancing of the exchange in terms of a unit of account. The highly interdependent elements of the contract exist as a package. Prices cannot be used as weights for adding up all the various elements of the contract. Nevertheless, reciprocity as a mechanism of social capital reduces transaction costs through binding social norms.

The norm of reciprocity as social capital helps to maintain, renew, or forge fresh social and symbolic ties and is a prerequisite for the formation of kinship-based, religiously, ethnically or nationally grounded migrant networks. Thus, reciprocity as social capital lowers transaction costs within small units such as the family by reducing the need for bilateral relationships. We can speak loosely of transitivity here: the pairwise investment of each member with the centre—often the head of a household—links her or him to all the others. This means that structural equivalence and not the existence of circles or cliques are the essential precondition. Enforcement of norms occurs mostly internal, though some social control from the outside can usually be found, especially through neighbourhood groups or state agencies.

Mechanism No. 3: Solidarity Based on Collective Representations

A third dimension of social capital is solidarity with others in a group who share similar social and symbolic ties. Earlier, we have used the metaphor of a voucher to describe the transactions between participants. If we look at social capital as vouchers only, we miss the point that the identity of the partners often are non-negotiable and non-transferable. Solidarity signals affiliation of group members to the rest of the world. When viewed as money, vouchers reduce the role of individual or collective identity. The transactional facility, liquidity, and negotiability of purely instrumental social capital rest on the fact that its value is independent of the collective identity of the participants involved. In many contexts, however, despite increasing standardization of production and exchange in modernizing countries, identity plays a crucial role in kinship systems, communities, and even in symbolic communities—ranging from religious collectives such as the Catholic Church or the Islamic *umma* to labour unions and social movements.

At the root of solidarity we find a willingness to transcend immediate self-interest, grounded in emotional identification with others. This is a fellow-feeling. It is the ability to empathize, the willingness to see things through someone else's eyes, to commiserate, the capacity to rejoice in other person's joys and feel sad because of their sorrows. For example, solidarity with members of a collective can induce politically persecuted to decide against territorial exit and in favour of the voice option, or to support those left behind from the safe haven of exile.

Collective representations provide the common ground for identities—a group, organizational, or symbolic community consciousness that refers to a unity of wanting and action. It is important to realize that such identities cannot simply be imputed from classification into singular categories such as gender, race, religion, ethnicity, or class. The fact that a set of actors is distinguished by a single categorical criterion is not sufficient to talk about collective identity (Somers 1994: 616–18). Rather, in a relational perspective, identity is an actor's experience of categories such as gender, ethnicity, or class, of social and symbolic ties, groups or organizations or symbolic communities, coupled with a public representation of that experience. The public representation often takes the form of a shared story, a narrative (Tilly 1996: 7).

Solidarity, therefore, is an expressive form of social action. The most important basis of solidarity is collective representations. These are shared ideas, beliefs, evaluations, and symbols. Collective representations can be expressed in some sort of collective identity—'we'-feeling or 'we'-consciousness—and refer to a unit of action. Collective representations are richer than individual activities and thus come to be autonomous of the group from which they emerge. Collective representations come to lead a life of their own, 'once born, obey laws all their own' (Durkheim 1965: 471). Collective representations help to order and make sense of the world, but they also express, symbolize, and interpret social and symbolic ties.

As such, solidarity can be either focused, directed towards a narrow kin group, frequently bounded by household and blood lineage, or it can extend to more diffuse forms. Diffuse solidarity pertains to larger aggregates, such as territorial and symbolic community groupings and organizations in which participants and members largely lack face-to-face contact. What exactly differentiates kin groups from larger organizations is in flux. It should always be remembered that families or households are not social units with universal behaviour. The very meaning of the term 'family' and other basic, taken-for-granted cultural aspects of kinship, like who is considered a relative, varies among sundry cultures. For example, some immigrant groups such as the Vietnamese in the USA in the 1970s and 1980s, may even draw 'fictive kin' into the bosom of the family (Kibria 1993).

Solidarity can have negative consequences for the persons involved. Sometimes, it does not only encourage people to help each other in times of need, during migration. As a social mechanism, it also encourages envy. And there are plenty of cases showing that kinship solidarity stifles entrepreneurship as well as fostering it. For example, if benefits from entrepreneurial activities have to be split in a large kinship group, money for reinvestment becomes scarce and entrepreneurs have less incentive to toil.

Usually, transactions of the exchange type are characterized by weak social ties, while reciprocity as a norm and solidarity require strong social ties (Sahlins 1965). Yet solidarity goes with weak social ties when individual or collective actors feel closely bound to religious, ethnic, national, and other symbolic ties. Movers and stayers in networks and collectives can be connected through symbolic ties, characterized by transactions based on shared world-views, understandings, forecasts, and memories—in short, common collective representations. Symbolic ties which enable solidarity are not reducible to individual constituents. They are grounded in ideas and beliefs elaborated by a collectivity. Group-cohesion can transcend local ties and yet be thoroughly realistic and concrete (Simmel 1955: 143). This is true in two senses, spatially and group-wise.

First, symbolic ties function to bridge vast geographical distances that cross nation-state borders for members of kinship or ethnic migrant groups. Cultural communities, such as families, ethnic groups, national groups, religious parishes, professional congregations, and nations can live far apart, separated by many borders. Second, differentiating between social and symbolic ties helps us to recognize that action is not only directed towards agents as persons, but also as carriers of certain characteristics and roles. On the lowest aggregate level, symbolic ties could thus be interpreted as primordial ties that encompass common kinship (Shils 1957: 142). If symbolic ties are socially and politically mediated, they can refer to larger aggregates characterized by common language, religion, ethnicity, and nationality. This is directly relevant for international flows, especially for refugee movements. For example, in many African countries borders of nation-states are the result of drawing board exercises by the former colonial powers, and arbitrarily cut across ethnic and linguistic groups. Refugees that traverse international borders are often more generously received by groups with whom they share strong symbolic affinities. The existence of symbolic ties across nation-states and the fact that most refugees in the South are movers with few resources explain why some refugees end up in countries adjoining the state of origin. This is also part of the answer to why only a minority ever moves onward to countries in the North.

As other dimensions of social capital, solidarity can exist in non-institutionalized and institutionalized varieties. As for its institutionalized variants, citizenship in a nation-state constitutes an expression of full and formal membership. It forms a continuing series of transactions, between a citizen and a nation-state. Each bargaining side can claim a set of mutually enforceable rights and duties. Citizenship is the public representation of ties between members and corresponding nation-states. It is based on the perception of common belonging to a state—or a nation or both—and it confers the identity 'citizen' (Bröskamp 1993: 185–7). As an institutionalized form of solidarity, it is in short supply among virtually all newcomers to a polity and, in the long run, among those immigrants barred from naturalization.

Social Capital and the Rate of Return

The second aspect of social capital includes all those resources that people use to pursue their goals in groups or networks. It refers to the potential value that inheres in social relations: 'Social capital is the sum of the resources, actual or virtual, that accrue to an individual or a group by virtue of possessing a durable network of more or less institutionalized relationships of mutual acquaintance and recognition' (Bourdieu and Wacquant 1992: 11). Social capital constitutes a wealth of (in)tangible social resources. Such benefits derived from social capital include the information on jobs in a potential destination country, knowledge about means of transport, or loans to finance a journey to the country of destination, or contacts on the neighbourhood level, such as taking care of watching children playing in the streets.

In essence, this second analytical aspect of social capital describes the manner in which resources available to any one agent are contingent on the resources available to others socially proximate to the person. This meaning has been operationalized as the number of persons who are prepared to help you and the amount of economic and human capital that these persons can muster up to serve your goals. We can add: information derived from such contacts, and control over others in networks and organizations. Predicting the rate of return or benefits on investment in social capital depends on knowing the resources of a person's contacts. The results should be obvious: the more numerous the ties, the wider the range of the ego-centred network, the higher the resources of those other actors to whom the ties give access to, and the higher one's own capital, the more successful an agent should be in achieving her goals. For example, some researchers have found that people with larger contact networks obtain higher paying positions than people with small networks (Flap 1991). To simplify things, the following discussion is limited to individuals when talking of actors using social capital. In conclusion, individual and collective actors can derive three main benefits from social capital—access to other people's resources, improved information, and increased control over other people:

Benefit No. 1: Access to Resources of Others

Resources embedded in ties help members of networks or groups to get access to more financial (economic), human, and social capital. This crucially depends on the amount and kind of resources those people have, who can be reached via social and symbolic ties. Also, it is important to take into account the sheer number of persons in a network or collective which are prepared or obliged to help you when called upon to do—the number of social and symbolic ties (Bourdieu 1983: 190–5).

Benefit No. 2: Improved Information

Increased information is a specific benefit derived from social capital. *Ceteris paribus*, the information benefits of a large, diverse network are higher than those of a small, homogeneous network. The higher the density within a network, the higher the potential for the flow of information. In short, bigger is better. But size is a mixed blessing: more ties can mean more exposure of valuable information, early exposure, and more referrals. Yet increasing network size without considering diversity can cripple a network in significant ways. What matters is the number of non-redundant contacts. Contacts are redundant to the extent that they lead to the same people, and so provide the same information benefits. People who know each other tend to know about the same things at about the same time. Therefore, the more non-redundant ties one has and the more people reached through these primary contacts, the higher the potential to get new information—because the higher the number of social and symbolic ties, the more likely it is to find someone with ties outside the charmed circle of known friends and relatives. However, in emotionally loaded ties, increasing efficiency through non-redundant ties does not always matter. In emotionally important ties it makes more sense to optimize for saturation than for efficiency (see Burt 1992 for a somewhat different interpretation). The question of non-redundant ties becomes particularly important when we look at network structures that go beyond kinship groups. For example, migrants rely on others outside their kinship group for information on travel and destination, as is often the case with illicit migration.

Benefit No. 3: Control and Authority

The higher the stock of social capital, the more potential for control exists. Persons with authority can then monitor and sanction others. The basic idea is that the extent matters to which any particular person is an important link in the indirect ties to others in controlling the flow of information, authority, power, and other resources. This means that some positions in a network or a group mediate the flow of resources by virtue of their patterns of ties to other points. The subsequent centralization of links means that ties and resources are concentrated in a few people rather than being spread more evenly across the whole group. Centralization is a necessary but not sufficient prerequisite for exercising authority. For example, in many groups and organizations free-riding is an obstacle to sharing the costs of governance and is a component of transaction costs, the costs of policing the agreement on governance. Authority is one means to solve the free-rider problem (Olson 1965) if, say, a kinship group strives towards collective goals such as economic security. The head of a kin group decides who migrates and for what purposes the group spends the remittances. Authority relations are also important in enforcing the norm that individual interests must sometimes take a backseat with regard to the norms of the collective. This can be done by sanctions, by the internalization of norms, or by solidary action.

To illustrate the basic idea, Figure 4.1 represents 'A' exerting most control because of her central position. 'A' is directly connected to both 'H' and 'F'. Thus, 'A' can access directly (via strong ties) all actors in her network and indirectly (through weak ties), and those directly reached by 'H' and 'F'. Actors 'H' and 'F' have the second-best position in this network, they each have one tie to another network.

The incumbency of a structural position is itself a scarce resource and is important in understanding migration brokers. In migration pro-

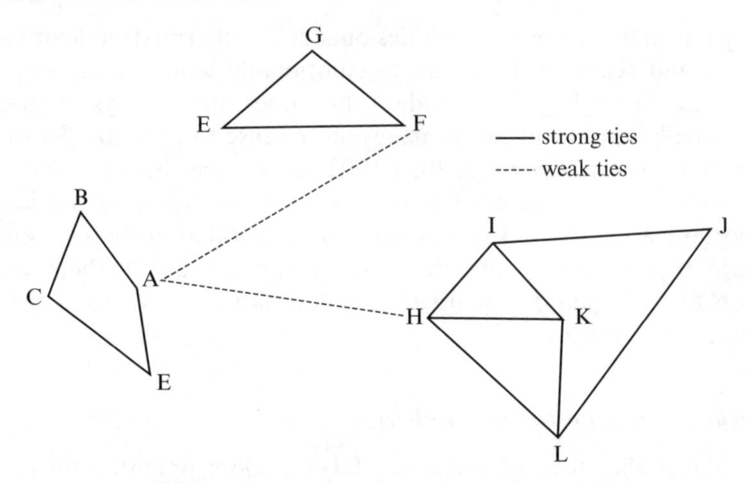

FIG. 4.1. *Opportunities for control in networks*

cesses, return migrants and others facilitate cooperation in migrant networks. Brokers determine access to other resources: they connect potential migrants to travel agencies and illegal guides in the case of undocumented migration, or they relate migrants to community members in far-distant places for job referrals. These members profit from their structural positions. A broker, linking two network clusters such as the emigration and the immigration community, takes a share of the resources passing through that position. Indeed, a canny broker can impede transitivity by working to prevent other people from forming direct links between these clusters. Brokers, by their very structural position, cannot be full members of any network cluster. Migration brokers are typical *tertius gaudens.* Often their marginal nature means they are not fully trusted because no single cluster can exercise social control over them (Wellman 1983: 177). This is especially true for brokers who are migration merchants and professionally ship migrants abroad. These merchants—Mexican *coyotes*, Ecuadorian *tramitadores*, Chinese 'snake heads'—are middlemen between potential migrants in the emigration countries, travel agencies in the countries of origin that supply visas and, at times, forged passports for countries en route to the final destination, and employers in the destination countries.

Social capital can be mobilized to pursue both individual and collective goals. Taking the distinction between self-orientation and collectivity-orientation as a point of departure (Parsons 1951: 60), we can distinguish between migration behaviour that is oriented towards the self and towards relevant collectives. Tensions can arise between, for example, occupational self-fulfilment, and the expectation to contribute to the sustenance of the family in the country of origin (W. I. Thomas and Znaniecki 1927). For example, movers at the onset of political persecution decide to further support their family, a sign of collectivity orientation, although imminent danger of being singled out as a target of violence strongly suggests that they move immediately, albeit individually. To complicate matters even further, potential movers are not only members of families but occupy various and sometimes conflicting roles—citizens of a nation-state, members of religious or ethnic and national groups.

We have considered the benefits derived from social capital from the view of those in control in groups and organizations. Regarding the second meaning of social capital—facilitating cooperation—it depends on the perspective of the respective actors whether social capital has positive or negative functions. For instance, social capital does not always work to increase individual autonomy. The affected individuals then regard this as negative social capital (Portes and Sensenbrenner 1993) or sour social capital. While social capital furnishes international migrants with resources beyond their individual reach—creating social connections and support for migrating—it also limits their possibilities of success because of the very obligations inherent in social capital. If these expectations and obligations are too demanding, they may limit not only individual autonomy but also economic success. Sour capital is embedded in social and symbolic ties that do not give the potential migrant or refugee a chance to achieve goals such as economic security or security of life. An example for sour capital is when control structures in families do not allow autonomous decisions over staying or going by each adult member.

Transactions clump into ties, and social and symbolic ties concatenate into networks. In other words, potential migrants use the resources available in and through ties. Furthermore, the various mechanisms of social capital help people to cooperate and thus facilitate collective action. Groups and organizations partly control the choices available to various problems that can be dealt with when migrating. This depends, among other things, on the specificity of various mechanisms of social capital—on how existing networks and groups enable and constrain migration and immobility.

The Characteristics of Social Capital as a Meso Link

Social capital allows us to look at both the properties of cooperation in networks and groups, and the resources and strategies of individual actors. Indeed, the two facets of social capital that can be analytically separated form a whole. We can interpret the three dimensions or mechanisms of social capital as a meso link when we look at the orientation of actors towards decisions—the micro-level, and larger social structures—the macro-level—Three dimensions are discernible on the macro-level that pre-form transactions between people and groups: functional prerequisites, normative expectations, and collective identity (Peters 1993). Taking these three types, we can identify three dimensions of meso-linking social capital: exchange-based obligations and expectations, the norm of reciprocity, and solidarity (Figure 4.2). Another typology distinguishes between exchange, reciprocity, and redistribution (Polanyi 1957: 250–6). It is only the third category that differs slightly from the distinction developed here. Crucially, solidarity is a central prerequisite for successful redistribution in both small groups, such as kinship systems, and large groups that are highly differentiated organizationally and in which solidarity has been successfully institutionalized, such as nationally bounded welfare states. On the micro-level of individual actors, we distinguish in ideal-typical manner between interest-related, norm-guided, and expressive action or behaviour.

Social capital thus has a dual thrust in lowering transaction costs: it helps and enables actors to achieve their goals by facilitating cooperation between individual actors in creating and using obligations, expectations, reciprocity, and solidarity. At the same time, it links individuals to social structures and helps to maintain them through cooperation. In turn, groups can also use social capital to monitor and sanction members.

This is an important qualification because individual and group action cannot be adequately understood independently of one another. With the concept of social capital we can emphasize the dualism of

micro-level orientation of actors	interest-related	norm-oriented	expressive
meso-link dimensions of social capital	obligations as a pattern of social exchange	reciprocity as a social norm	solidarity
macro-level integration	functional considerations	normative expectations	collective identity

FIG. 4.2. *Three aspects of social integration and three dimensions of social capital on the micro, meso, and macro level*

individual actors and groups. On the one hand, the transactions of the actors determine the nature of groups; by the social and symbolic ties of their members to one another as well as to other people and groups. On the other hand, the characteristics of the actors are shaped by the intersection of groups 'within' them, by their various group affiliations (Simmel 1955: 162–3). People constitute actions relationally. Actors who draw upon social capital are by definition required to be participants in networks or members in groups or organizations. In sum, social capital is therefore not simply an attribute of individual actors but also an attribute of groups and organizations. Analytically, it thus extends into both micro- and macro-level dimensions.

Specificities of Capital: Economic, Human, and Social

We can think of social capital having certain commonalties with other forms of capital but also specificities that distinguish it. Economic capital, human capital, and social capital have in common that they can, under certain circumstances, increase the autonomy of individuals, enlarge their freedom of choice. All forms of capital are created by spending time and effort in transformation and transaction activities. Economic capital is the arrangement of material resources to improve flows of future income. Human capital is the knowledge and skills that people bring to the solution of any problem (Ostrom 1995). Social capital, as we have defined it, is the arrangement of resources wielded by social and symbolic ties to reduce transaction costs, to improve cooperation, and to help people pursue their goals. In sum, people create capital by spending time and energy working with others to find ways of making possible the achievement of certain ends that in its absence would not be possible.

The linkage of economic, human, and social capital can be visualized like this (Figure 4.3): individual or collective actors have human and economic capital at their disposal. In network-analytic terms, the nodes or positions X, Y, and Z characterize the human capital available to the agents. People occupying network positions can also mobilize economic capital which is external to them and not inherent in ties. The agents are tied to each other by links. Social capital constitutes resources that can be accumulated, maintained, and mobilized through the social ties the actors have to each other. Economic capital can be mobilized both by human capital and social capital. In this way, various forms of capital not only function additively but also interactively.

Social capital is distinct in several respects:

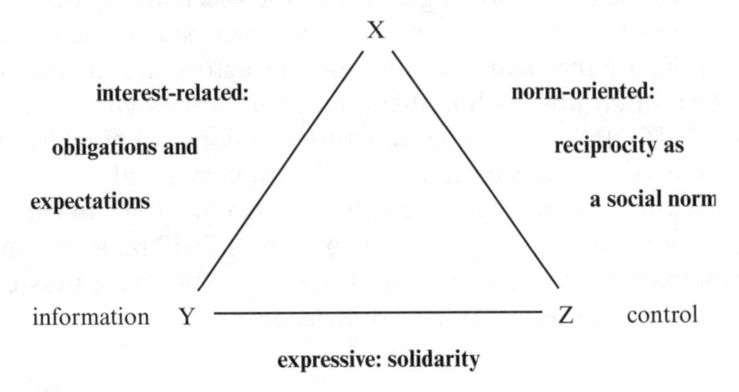

FIG. 4.3. *Social capital in networks and collectives*

1. People or a group can hold economic and human capital in whole or in part. But social capital is a thing owned jointly by the parties to a relationship. No one has exclusive ownership rights to social capital! If a partner in a relationship withdraws, the connection, with whatever social capital it contained, dissolves. This is why territorial exit, namely international migration, presents a potential threat to the stock of social capital. And it suggests that voice, when connected to loyalty, tends to uphold accumulated social capital.

2. Social capital mainly serves as a facilitator. It does not have the direct and simple goal specificity of economic and human capital. The main function of networks in processes of international migration is to reduce situations of complete uncertainty to those of mere risk to which, in principle, certain probabilities or expectancies can be attached. In effect, social networks and institutions perform insurance functions. Security is a precondition for all investment, as Adam Smith recognized a long time ago: when people are 'secure of enjoying the fruits of their industry, they naturally exert it to better their condition and to acquire not only the necessaries, but the conveniences and elegancies of life' (Smith 1961: 426). In situations of high risk, characteristic of the beginning stages of rather voluntary migration and even more in contexts of uncertainty that are characteristic of starkly involuntary flows, kinship systems and informal networks often provide support that cannot be provided by formal organizations. Social and symbolic ties in kinship systems and communities can often be better used to master events and tasks with high contingencies. If, however, situations are highly standardized by universally, locally, or contextually applicable laws and rules, the value of obligations, reciprocity,

solidarity, and various benefits shrink. Generally speaking, social capital resources are of most use in volatile and turbulent situations.

3. The reciprocal and solidary mechanisms of social capital are 'moral resources' (Hirschman 1984) that do not lose in value by using them. Quite on the contrary, by employing these resources, stocks can be accumulated. Most importantly, only then can benefits accrue, such as information and control. And the benefits derived from social capital function as an informal security or insurance system against the risks and uncertainties of the open market, power interchanges, and political struggles. To go further, by not wielding these resources, social capital may lose value. For example, migrants living abroad who are not connected to their significant others at home, lose some of the stock of their former social capital. It is in this sense that social capital is very fragile.

4. Organizations show the fundamental importance of social capital. When organizations grant its members formal rights, such as claims to time or money, they alter the role of social capital. Then, for example, informal networks of social help and control may be still important as a basis for national welfare states. But they then do not constitute the only device anymore. When institutionalized, social capital makes persons less dependent on one another—sometimes a prerequisite for more freedom of choice. Also, the pristine dimensions of reciprocity or solidarity are weakened by the exigencies of power and instrumental relations (Eisenstadt and Roniger 1984: 39). However, we should not forget that certain dimensions of social capital, such as generalized reciprocity and diffuse solidarity, enable organizations to emerge and to be effective in the first place.

There is one important effect of the degree of social capital institutionalization that impacts upon the volume of migration. For example, social policies in the emigration state, such as minimal welfare state guarantees that help to reduce the risk of economic insecurity, make international migration a less attractive option. Note that this argument is not the same as saying that welfare state securities in the countries of destination offer an incentive for migration. The latter is usually overrated: in most countries of origin informal networks of social help exist that fulfil some of the functions of social security in welfare states. To return to the emigration country: the development of social security such as pension systems do encourage internal migration and not international migration, they foster relative immobility such as *in situ* adaptation or internal migration over international mobility. In principle, a migrant's changing attitudes towards the kinship group, her orientation towards greater individual autonomy threatens established forms of specific reciprocity and focused solidarity. But these changes are partly compensated by formal insurance systems: in the first years after migration from rural villages to towns or cities, institutionalized social insurances of all kinds usually do not yet have the great significance they may have later. Yet this changes when the first migrants retire. This information is passed on to younger ones and, among them, the perceived importance of insurance greatly increases. Availability of formal insurance is one comparative advantage of living in the city as compared to the rural countryside. This is true especially in situations when all children have moved to the city and none remains to take care of the old parents.

5. The last specificity of social capital to be discussed here is of the most fundamental importance for solving our two puzzles. It concerns the spatial connectedness of social capital. Economic capital is easy to transfer nationally and transnationally. One subset, financial capital provides a good example. If we proceed to human capital, the description is less clear-cut. The benefits can be measured as the degree to which participants in markets increase their returns, such as salaries depending on educational credentials or professional experience. In the case of educational degrees as an important part of human capital, we immediately see that its transferability from one location to another and from one country to another is much more restricted than economic capital. Social capital is even harder to define, since it is to be found in the relations or more precisely, the social and symbolic ties, between people and groups. It facilitates action in favouring cooperation, coordination, or conflict. However, social capital cannot be exchanged as easily as economic capital, or legalized in work contracts as human capital. It cannot be sold.

Therefore, when it comes to migration, social capital has two important functions: first, without facilitating cross-border networks, it is very hard to transfer from one country to another. It is primarily a local asset. Thus, in addition to political regulations of international migration, it is one of the main causes for the relatively low rates of international mobility. However, if transnational networks and chain migration emerge in the course of migration, the transferability of social capital increases. Only when local assets become transferable across borders does a second characteristic come to the fore: social capital is necessary to help persons move and to mobilize other forms of capital, especially among those short of financial means. Social capital is a crucial mechanism for applying other resources. It operates as a transmission belt that bridges collectives and networks in distinct and separate nation-states and helps newcomers to adapt to the novel situation. Often, immigrants need social and symbolic ties to established immigrants or brokers to find work, to employ their human capital such as vocational skills and educational degrees in the immigration country. Social capital is also a sort of castor oil to establish a flourishing political and cultural life abroad.

The Four Functions of Social Capital in Migration Processes

Social capital fulfils various functions in international migration—selection of potential migrants; diffusion of migration via migrant networks and chain migration; bridging networks, groups, and organizations within migration systems; and adaptation of immigrants in the countries of immigration or readaptation in the country of emigration. The following oversimplified model sketches the obligations, reciprocity, and solidarity, and the benefits derived therefrom that fulfil decisive functions in migration systems (Figure 4.4). The functions refer to variously aggregated actors—people, groups, and organizations.

The Selective Function

Social capital has a selective function. The wealth of empirical evidence suggests that kinship, communal, and friendship ties heavily influence

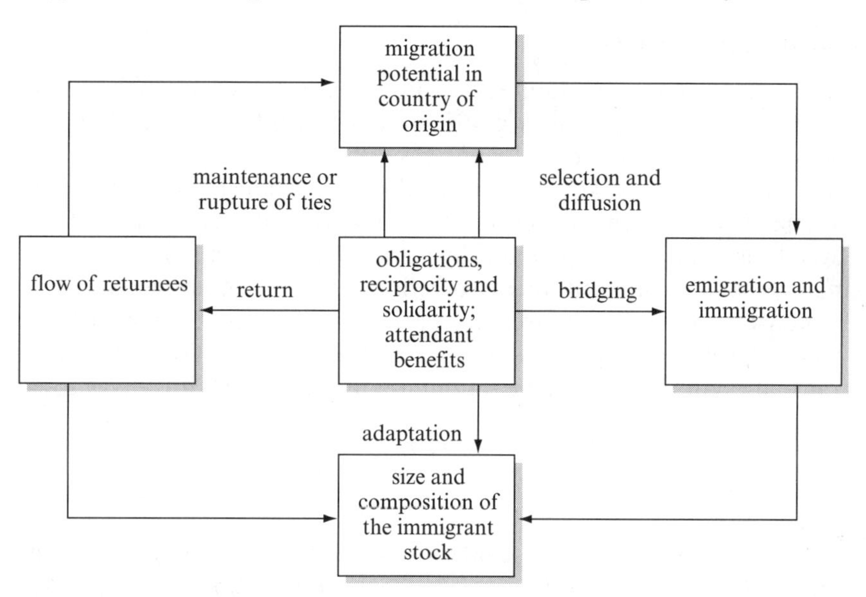

FIG. 4.4. *The functions of social capital in a migration system—a simplified model*

exit. The various incarnations of social capital and the returns to the persons and groups using them are pivotal resources that also move with or stay immobile with the people. It is necessary to explain both immobility and mobility. As to the latter, we need to know in detail how migrant networks of international movers and their relatively immobile significant others emerge, and how these migrant networks interact with institutions such as recruiting agencies, refugee organizations, and even nation-states in larger migration networks.

The Diffusion Function

In a further step we want to know whether successive exits accumulate into chain migration, and what kind of causal mechanisms operate: positive feedbacks that steadily increase migration streams up to a possible tipping point or negative feedbacks that keep the volume of migration relatively constant.

There is plenty of empirical evidence that the social and symbolic ties of migrants and refugees are not ruptured immediately after arrival in the country of destination. In addition to the legal possibilities and, in the case of refugees, freedom from persecution in the country of origin, these ties are a prerequisite for return. Returnees transform the network of ties from a unidirectional to a bi-directional system.

The Bridging Function

Migrants tend to maintain social and symbolic ties with significant others in the countries of origin; sometimes even beyond the first lineage generation. The most obvious case illustrating this bridging function are seasonal workers who move abroad periodically from South to North. These migrants recurrently transverse different nation-states. Even those who do not periodically move back and forth in a systematic manner send back remittances, sometimes travel back home during the holidays, want their children to learn their mother tongue, or help village development projects in the country of origin. Over time, such transnational ties may evolve into more durable forms of transnational spaces.

The Adaptation Function

The adaptation function includes various forms of insertion in the immigration or reintegration in the former emigration country in the economic, political, and cultural spheres. Once international migrants are in the respective country of destination, they face daily problems such as finding work and housing, childcare, and space for religious and political activities, and cultural expression. Reciprocity and solidarity embedded in kinship, friendship, and community networks, groups, and organizations often help migrants to adapt to the new environment—such as grandparents who mind the children while mother and father are out to work, relatives who enjoy the cheap and docile labour of remote cousins in sweatshops, or fellow-villagers who explain basic work rules to the newcomers. If migrants keep up transnational ties, the question comes up what role social capital has in guiding concomitant adaptation in the country of destination or readaptation in the country of origin and transnational activities.

Conclusion: Social Capital as a Local Asset and as a Transmission Belt

International geographical mobility is an especially interesting phenomenon for a relational meso-link analysis because the various dimensions of social capital are both local assets and transmission belts. Meso-link analysis places a potential migrant's actions within a larger web of opportunities and indicates the ties mediating people's desires. Not only the existence of social and symbolic ties matters, but also the specific content of these relations. Social capital is not a set of free-floating resources but has definite foundations in concrete social and symbolic ties between persons and within groups and organizations. Among other things, it is specific inasmuch as the returns materialize only in the exchange between specific parties, in that it cannot be owned by people or groups, and that the capital stock loses its value when the participants separate spatially—because of high costs of maintaining ties across borders. Nevertheless, in the case of international migration, new webs of ties and corresponding capital often crystallize in migrant networks. The uneven distribution of resources mobilized through ties helps to account for differential rates of migration out of various communities and within communities within the countries of origin.

5

The Selective Functions of Social Capital: Why Are There So Few Migrants Out of Most Places?

Social capital depends on continuous transactions establishing social ties or collective representations expressed in symbolic ties, or both. Exit of people or whole groups abroad potentially depletes the stock of social capital or at least changes its composition. Because the rate of migration not only varies along countries but is also highly unevenly distributed within developing countries, we need to look more closely at the selection process. This helps us to distinguish the role of social capital in relative immobility—internal migration and *in situ* adaptation—and international migration.

Three propositions guide the analysis in this chapter:

1. Social capital is primarily a set of local assets, not easily transferred abroad.
2. The principle of cumulative causation applies to immobility: the more often a person has decided not to migrate, the more likely she is to stay put.
3. Some dimensions of social capital—those that are used by and within smaller groups, e.g. specific reciprocity and focused solidarity—render themselves to reinforce relative immobility. By contrast, generalized reciprocity and diffuse solidarity have a greater potential to reduce the benefits of social capital beyond small groups and thus give rise to diffusion effects.

This chapter discusses first the costs of transferring social capital abroad. Moving capital incurs maintenance costs, such as keeping ties alive to home and adaptation costs that arise from at least partly adapting to a new environment. Second, the Turkish–German case study illustrates how the transferability of migrants' resources explains why there are relatively few migrants out of most places.

Social Capital as a Local Asset

In order to answer what contributes to migration or enhances immobility, we have to start from the fundamental insight that many resources are local assets. Local assets are tied to interests, norms, and expressions that often engage people more than do great national affairs (Tocqueville 1988: 162). Only under unusual but important conditions of national crises or change are people motivated to transfer local resources, not by routine everyday habits and interests.

There are two cases to be distinguished. First, for many people the transfer of social capital is not an issue. They cannot choose. For the majority of persons living in developing countries the question is not between *in situ* adaptation or migration. They are despondent: they completely lack all forms of capital for exit and voice, and are in a state of resignation in a hostile environment around them. Because of severe structural constraints, these persons cannot be considered potential migrants anymore. Given abysmally low degrees of freedom, they can only respond by moving physically, without carefully scheming. The by far greatest percentage of persons in the South is mired by absolute poverty which, again, prohibits planning on their part (see e.g. UNHCR 1995: 143–9).

Second, if people have resources to take across borders, the difficult issue of loyalty and transferability arises. In general, international migration raises three forms of transaction costs, loyalty, maintenance, and adaptation costs. Loyalty to a community makes people more likely to opt for *in situ* adaptation or voice instead of exit. By and large, transferring local assets to foreign countries and/or maintaining them involves high costs. Moreover, people's investments in social capital crucially depend upon the expectations of ties forged in the past and of future changes in conditions. This is because social capital lowers transaction costs. When some people of a kinship group live far away from home, perhaps in another country or even another continent, transaction costs tend to increase. As physical distance between members increases and as political-cultural contexts between emigration and immigration countries vary sharply, the attending expenses for monitoring, bookkeeping, and surveillance also increase, as does the incentive for dishonesty. In addition, the various forms of social capital fade away if no action is undertaken, that is, if people do not consistently communicate, or if they cannot uphold common representations.

Loyalty: Obligations out of Solidarity

People may feel loyal towards many groups—for example, families, local communities, religious congregations, or even a nation. Loyalty is tightly connected to the identity of a 'we'-group and often represents strong social but certainly symbolic ties to a given economic, political, or cultural unit. It is a specific instance of a sense of obligations arising from solidarity. Even if the monetary and social costs of moving abroad decline substantially, a strong sense of loyalty can counterbalance the exit option by making potential migrants search for alternatives to migration first.

Let us take two stylized bundles of motives, economic and political. Better opportunities to earn one's livelihood abroad or a sudden decline in the economic performance of a state's economy may not trigger emigration of a potential migrant because, say, he feels a strong desire to fulfil his duties towards older family members he is expected to take care of. While loyalty in this case could lead to internal or seasonal migration, international migration would be a less likely event. It would conflict timewise with the role to provide for family members. The other stylized case is a rapid decline in the performance of the political system. If in opposition and if the person feels a strong sense of loyalty towards her country, voice is a more likely response than territorial exit; at least in a first stage. Only if the voice option itself results in physical or psychological harm or threatens life, and if there is a state willing to take her in or is unable to prevent her immigration, do we expect the exit option to take over.

Maintenance Costs: Keeping in Touch

If a migrant leaves behind family, friends, and significant others, it involves high costs to maintain these ties while abroad. Many of these relationships are characterized by strong and affective social ties. Costs are economic such as return trips, social such as trying to sustain contacts to the circle of friends and relations, cultural in practising one's religion or other customs, and psychological in the costs of adapting to a new environment. The expenditures are especially high for pioneer migrants who cannot rely on established networks of movers to guide and facilitate their migration. This also explains why even pioneer migrants often do not venture out totally on their own, but are recruited by agencies or middlemen from the immigration countries. These costs tend to be lower if potential migrants choose internal migration.

Moreover, migration raises issues of social control. Transaction costs are high because physical distance and borders make it harder in the beginning stages of international migration to enforce norms. Migrants may reorient themselves while abroad. They may not fulfil obligations and the expectations of those left behind. And, of course, some pioneer migrants completely cut ties with home. The forms of social capital inherent in ties, such as obligations, reciprocity, and solidarity wither away if not regularly maintained and enforced through either continued social transactions and/or a strong attachment to the collective representations of (a) particular group(s).

Adaptation Costs: Establishing New Ties Abroad

Adaptation costs arise for pioneer migrants abroad, since it takes social capital to build new networks or even groups—and quite some resources are required. Of course, the need to do so crucially depends on the length of stay abroad. When entering and living in another country, international migrants become a minority group and lose, at least initially, communal networks based upon kinship, friendship, and neighbourhood which provided job and housing referrals, a social life, and assistance in raising children. It is quite consuming in terms of time and energy to construct or join new networks or organizations in the immigration country. This is especially so in those cases where significant others such as selected family members stay at home. It is even more difficult to establish and join new groups. Adaptation costs arise in the absence of social capital because it is often a prerequisite for the mobilization of human and economic capital. New social and sometimes even symbolic ties in the countries of destination have to be well established, before migrants can make use of their resources or those available to other migrants who support them. In particular, this applies to pioneer migrants and brokers who act as intermediaries for scarce resources. Yet even when migration networks exist, there are problems to be overcome: at the initial stages, migration through kin and friends is usually riskier than movement through recruitment agents (Shah 1996). This is somewhat different for migration merchants who offer services for illicit migration. Then trust is very low. The transaction pattern—safe guidance across borders in exchange for money paid in advance— cannot be enforced on the part of the migrant by either recourse to legal sanctions or the norm of reciprocity.

Moreover, without solidarity there is no basis for a rich cultural life in migrant communities. Again, this is especially so in the beginning stages of international migration. But, unless the immigrants remain exiles for the rest of their lives, they need to overcome cultural distance—such as learning a new language. Crossing such a cultural threshold calls for reassurances in commonalties of a new kind, not simply a continuation of country of origin cultural patterns. Similar things can be said about political participation. If migrants do not engage in collective action to voice their interests, they will not be able to fend off discrimination in the immigration countries. For political voice, they need to form associations.

Solidarity institutionalized in citizenship is usually not portable from South to North; albeit it is partly possible in regional migration systems such as the EU. And given the asymmetry of states in migration systems, emigration country governments usually cannot intervene effectively on behalf of their citizens abroad. If there is no citizenship tie to the new country of residence, immigrants face disadvantages vis-à-vis natives and citizens. This usually does not present a problem for short-term migrants who consider themselves as economic exiles. Yet it is more problematic if the stay turns out to be a prolonged one. It usually takes energy, time, and new bonds in the immigration country to acquire a new citizenship. For example, most immigration states require a fluency in the polity's main language, knowledge of basic civics such as the constitution, and a steady source of income.

High stocks of human and economic capital tend to facilitate the transfer of resources abroad. Immigration countries ease immigration for highly specialized professionals we could call human capital migrants (Salt 1997). Yet even in these cases, empirical observations indicate that the destinations are not simply chosen by the criteria of economic and human capital benefits only. Among human capital migrants, characteristics cluster around kinship group, professional discipline or academic institution, and year of graduation (Shah 1996). The same applies to those people willing to invest large sums of money in countries of immigration for productive purposes—economic capital migrants (Wong 1997). The majority of potential migrants in developing countries do not occupy such favourable positions. Nonetheless, while economic and human capital migrants do indeed have higher degrees of freedom through additional resources, social capital also plays a decisive role in shaping where they go and which positions in the labour, capital, and housing markets they find available.

In sum, local assets which are undergirded by sundry forms of capital can lead a potential mover to prefer *in situ* adaptation in the country of origin to moving abroad because maintenance and adaptation costs and risks are high. Therefore, we expect that potential migrants prefer those forms of exit that allow them to keep their ties intact, such as circular migration, to interrupt them only shortly such as seasonal migration, or to transfer the whole set of important ties abroad through migration with significant others. In cases of highly involuntary migration, however, refugees frequently do not have the opportunity to choose among these discrete options. This explains why we find the by far highest percentage of the world's refugees in the countries of South and not in those of the North.

Cumulative Causation and Immobility: Endogenous Dynamics

To conceptualize the internal or endogenous dynamics of immobility and migration, we need to highlight various aspects of cumulative causation with the two limiting cases of cumulative immobility and cumulative mobility. The idea is that decisions to remain immobile contribute to subsequent immobility or that rising emigration sets off structural changes which make additional migration more likely. In turn, immobility and additional migration or return migration affect various aspects of economic development and social, political, and cultural life. We can thus distinguish between causation leading to cumulative territorial inertia, viz. cumulative immobility, and to cumulative mobility. Virtually all research on international migration has focused on cumulative mobility, occluding the equally important facets of cumulative immobility. And while the feedback effects of migration on economic development have received most attention in the research and the literature at large, the migration process itself and the repercussions for social, cultural, and political change figure prominently among issues that demand our attention. Examples include the alteration of family and gender relations, a 'culture of migration', and migrants voicing their political dissent abroad. In mapping this road, we need to specify more clearly what kind of cumulative causation we are dealing with in specific instances. Concerning cumulative mobility, we can ask: Is it a self-reinforcing process which leads to more and more migration in positive feedback loops? Is it migration which leads to vigorous destination country restrictions and to its eventual decline in negative feedback loops? Do new social and political structures evolve in the course of migration that alter the nature altogether, such as transnational social spaces in multiple cause-effect-cause developments?

The effects of multiple decisions on whether to stay or to move internationally, culminate in processes of cumulative causation. The concept of cumulative causation is similar to the notion of path-dependence which has been linked to stable equilibrium concepts in economics. Unlike this latter concept which searches for the causes and ensuing dynamics of processes, locked into a certain pattern (North 1991), cumulative causation focuses on the very context that makes spiralling effects possible. And the concept of cumulative causation is a specific form of analysing presumed causalities. The presence of influences in both directions between two or more factors does not necessarily imply mutual or cumulative causation. There is no mutual causation if the size of influence in one direction is independent of the size of influence in the other direction, or if their apparent correlation is caused by a third factor (Maruyama 1963: 175). In the case of cumulative immobility, let us assume that landlessness is a major factor contributing to a pool of potential migrants in a rural area. We further observe that many peasants cluster in village cooperatives. They have chosen *in situ* adjustment over exit. In the case of cumulative mobility we expect the migrants in particular cities in the countries of immigration. There is no necessary mutual causation between the causes and the respective clustering. Only when we bring in what are commonly called intervening variables such as factors facilitating the flow of resources to enable cooperative activities or residential clustering can we start building a causal chain.

Basically, there are two main types of cumulative causation of interest for analysing the dynamics of international immobility and mobility. The first type is positive feedback cumulative causation: the cumulative effects propel a development to depart more and more from its origin. The second main type is negative feedback causation: the dynamics ensure that the system returns to the original point of departure. Negative feedbacks result in a return to the point of origin, and positive feedback situations describe a sort of escalation. In other words, positive feedback situations are deviation-amplifying systems and negative feedback situations are deviation-counteracting systems (Maruyama 1982). Positive feedbacks could lock actors into vicious or virtuous circles (Myrdal 1972: i. 75–8). In positive and negative loops therefore, each factor has an influence on all other factors either directly or indirectly, and each factor is influenced through other factors. There is no hierarchical causal priority in any of the elements.

Negative feedback causation implies feedback loops in which the system moves back to a prior state of affairs. It is best exemplified when thinking of temperature regulation via thermostat. In the case of international movement, it is of less importance. Yet the case of some refugee movements is instructive because it comes close. In the early stages of refugee flows, some accepting countries open their doors to asylum seekers. As long as there is only a trickle, the countries do take in refugees. However, the trickle may turn into a stream, when conditions in the refugee-producing country get worse. If the accepting country reneges on the norms of the Geneva Convention and closes its doors, further refugees will then be stuck in the emigration country, or worse: in transit, if there are no alternative destinations available. This situation for refugees was even worse before the Geneva Convention became operative in 1951. Historically, the fate of German Jews during the Nazi regime comes to mind: most potential immigration states in Europe and the Americas did not take in Jewish refugees (Wyman 1984). Jews were at the time not considered to be political refugees because they had not committed political 'crimes'. Nowadays, agreed-upon international refugee regimes make it somewhat more likely that states adhere to norms for asylum seekers.

Positive feedback loops imply processes that either bolster immobility or advance migration as a self-feeding effect in chain migration. In the first case, the more often potential migrants have decided to stay, the more likely it is that they remain relatively immobile and that significant others around them do the same. In the second case, later migrants emulate the example of pioneers. In a way, the more people migrate, the more are other potential migrants in the same place drawn into this behaviour, often as active movers.

As to relative immobility, we can see positive feedback loops at work. Over time, the decision to stay in the place of residence cumulatively increases the chance that potential migrants do not choose the exit option of international migration. Eventually, this leads to cumulative immobility. Given the three broad options of exit, voice, and *in situ* adaptation, potential migrants in a rural area get together and establish a village cooperative to market their produce. If successful, this cooperative will draw more and more of those potential migrants who have not already opted for exit. Over time, cooperation spins off activities which further improve production and distribution along a vertical axis, say, rainwater collection and the sale of handcrafted products in internal and international markets. This will make long-term international migration even less likely and encourage very short-term movement for business and educational purposes.

This outcome presents a specific variant of the rather general axiom of cumulative inertia: we find a rather robust positive linear correlation between the length of residence in one place and the probability to remain there (McGinnis 1968: 716). If we look at social capital as a set of local assets, we get at one crucial element that contributes to this relationship. The longer a potential migrant lives in a place and works there, the more she tends to acquire social and symbolic ties and corresponding resources. These location-specific advantages, sometimes called insider advantages, often outweigh adaptation and maintenance costs involved in international migration; especially at the beginning of chain migrations.

An Illustration of 'Why Are There So Few Migrants Out of Most Places?'—Contract Worker Movement from Turkey to Germany

For the sake of simplicity, this section deals exclusively with the selective functions of social capital in the absence of migrant networks in the beginning stages of large-scale international migrations and in the case of first-time, not return, movers. This helps to understand the characteristics of various forms of social capital as a local asset. It thus sheds light on the first question of our first puzzle: Why are there so few migrants out of most places in the South?

Loyalty: Beyond the Force of Tradition

A widespread argument for indicating the importance of loyalty is the 'force of tradition'. Before the onset of large-scale emigration out of Turkey in the 1960s, some theorists had claimed that migration was out of the question for much of the rural population: 'The constricted peasant can more easily imagine destroying the self than relocating it in an unknown, i.e. frightful, setting' (Lerner 1958: 24–5; see also Stirling 1965: 30 and 202–3). It is unsatisfactory, however, to propose tradition as a catch-all hindrance to geographical mobility because this essentialist reasoning cannot imagine how attachments change. Symbolic ties, for example, do indeed play an important role for older potential migrants in rationalizing their decision to stay. When asked by an anthropological fieldworker why they did not join their children in Germany, some proposed: 'Why should I commit a *günah*?' *Günah* is a sin in the religious sense. The underlying argument is that migration into another cultural context necessarily entails a partial adoption of customs and mores (Schiffauer 1987: 269). In a way, these are maintenance costs not of social but of symbolic ties that can extend beyond religion to kinship and ethnic groups and the nation. However, such ties usually are not so overwhelming that they overdetermine immobility, and these ties are not totally invariant.

Let us turn to allegiances that arise from solidarity to highly aggregated groups. Most of those not only in opposition to the Turkish government but actively resisting it, such as Kurdish activists in outlawed organizations, do remain within Turkey or adjoining countries. In this instance loyalty does not refer to the state at large but to a group: i.e. a nation, the Kurds and a nation-state desired, Kurdistan. Ironically, it is important to note that international migration of Kurdish activists in organizations such as the PKK often occurs as part of the strategy of an authoritarian organization actually limiting the freedom of choice among its members; compelling or forcing them to serve where the leadership has deemed it worthy. It is an instance of sour social capital, of solidarity turned to limit individual autonomy.

Maintenance Costs: The Importance of Home

International migration involves maintenance costs that are higher than in the case of internal migration. Often, entry regulations, especially into the German guestworker system (1961–73), allowed only one family member from Turkey to live and work abroad for a limited time. For Turkish migrants who left behind relationships which are characterized by strong and affective social ties, migration involved high outlays to maintain these ties while abroad; for example, the costs for return trips and psychological costs of adjusting to an overwhelmingly new urban and a different cultural environment. One solution to high maintenance costs of social capital was joint migration (which was hard to realize because of the recruitment system) or family reunification. The latter option also did not work in the beginning stages of migration because of legal restrictions. For families to unite in the country of destination, the migrant needed a residence permit, usually granted only after five years of residence, and gainful employment. This meant that family fragmentation became almost a rule, in stark difference to internal migration, where the whole family tended to move. In particular, the separation of spouses resulted in long absences, causing alienation within marital life (Nauck 1985*b*).

However, in the early stages, Turkish migrants not only faced high maintenance costs due to entry and residence regulations imposed upon them by the German government. Many of the migrant workers intended to stay only for a limited period of time in order to earn enough money to sponsor *in situ* adaptation of their family. They imagined their situation to be of a temporary and economically-motivated exile.

Transaction costs also increased because geographical distance in combination with borders made it harder to enforce norms of reciprocity. After all, migrants could reorient themselves while abroad. Some migrant men did cease to deliver upon reciprocal duties and to observe the expectations of those left behind. One well-known example refers to kinship cohesion in nuclear families. During long absences, some Turkish men married to Turkish women in Turkey entered into long-lasting relationships with German women, some married them—and some did not hesitate to bring them back with them to Turkey during their annual vacation (for an example, see Kleff 1984: 193). However, for younger contract workers who were not yet married, maintenance costs were usually much lower. The evidence shows that younger Turkish migrants, who settled abroad, did not totally break off family ties. They more often adapted successfully into German society, often as socially marginal persons.

The lower feasibility of return considerably slowed international migration from rural areas compared to migration within Turkey. Case studies on villages in Central Anatolia suggest that the rural population until the early 1950s predominantly engaged in seasonal migration (Struck 1984: 50–5). Later, internal rural–urban migration dominated international migration. The former pattern had the advantage that urban–rural households could be integrated. Those kinship members living in the city could come to help in harvest times. Domestic rural–urban migration then went hand in hand with slowly changing conceptions of household and economic production. Domestic rural–urban migration in Turkey gradually replaced more traditional orientations with a heavy emphasis towards security and a lesser focus upon profit and efficiency. This division of labour reflected the conception of a family as a social body and the structure of asymmetric reciprocity relationships (Schiffauer 1987: 103–7)—specific reciprocity as a norm in paternal-authoritarian households.

Initially, those migrants who already lived in urban centres showed much more willingness to shoulder the maintenance costs incurred by international migration than the rural population. In the first phase of labour migration, the cities in the economic centre sent most migrants abroad. For example, in 1961 and 1963 Ankara, Izmir, and Istanbul sent 80% and 50%, respectively, of recruited contract workers. Only as late as the early 1970s did the majority of international migrants come from rural areas. This is not surprising. Those living in the major industrial centres of Turkey traditionally had more information about job opportunities abroad; companies and other organizations linked transnationally (Lohrmann and Manfrass 1974: 34). These early migrants benefited from access to urban communication networks. Moreover, some urban dwellers had already experienced a migratory transition. They were step-migrants who had earlier moved from villages in the countryside to the urban centres (Struck 1988). Often, stepwise migration also meant that traditional kinship ties had been transformed during the process of migration and settlement in the urban centres. Ultimately, reconstituted social and symbolic ties within households who had experienced step-migration led them to engage more frequently in international migration than members from rural households.

We find differences similar to the urban–rural ones when we look at ties associated with religious differences. There seem to be striking ethnic-religious differences in migration rates, although they cannot be pinned down very exactly, because the Turkish government does not keep statistics on membership in religious groupings. Qualitative data suggests that Alevis much more heavily engaged in international migration than the majority-group Sunnites. The Alevis, most often erroneously labelled as a Turkish equivalent to Iranian Shi'ites, are a religious minority that mixes Turkoman-Shaman, Zoroastrian, pre-Islamic, and Shi'i ideas with a great deal of secular thought. There are several ways to explain this distinct pattern. It could be that the maintenance costs for Alevis were lower than for Sunnites. After all, in some areas in rural Turkey Alevis have constituted a minority and experienced a substantial degree of resentment and recrimination. On the whole, they interpreted their situation in some rural areas as precarious. For Alevis, the benefits of migration compensated for maintenance costs: there were few left at home. Therefore, it makes sense to assume that they constituted very closely knit communities, where reciprocity and solidarity reached beyond narrow kinship lines (Kehl-Bodroği 1988). In other words, Alevi pioneer migrants may have been better able to forge community-wide migration networks than their Sunnite counterparts. In turn, this facilitated high-risk international migration.

As we would expect, those potential migrants who had economic incentives were more willing to shoulder maintenance costs than those for whom it was not worthwhile to migrate in order to improve their economic condition. As a rule, the upper 10–20% of village workforces usually did not consider going to Europe or to the Gulf states as manual workers. This upper class included farmers—not peasants—and senior government officials. Correspondingly, most government employees did not migrate but poor schoolteachers did (own interviews, 1997). A substantial number of primary schoolteachers, the poorest-paid government workers assigned for three years to rural areas outside their areas of origin, did migrate for manual jobs in Europe. Groups such as schoolteachers actually formed the vanguard of labour migrants from Turkey to Germany in the early 1960s. Urban residence and knowledge of programmes gave them a headstart.

Maintenance costs somewhat decreased for many migrants when the labour recruitment process changed. The maintenance costs declined substantially when migrants relied on friends and relatives in Germany. Once a long queue of applicants had formed by the late 1960s (waiting lists included up to 1 million) some potential migrants who experienced relative frustration turned to family members and friends who already lived in Germany. These migrants from Turkey then came to Germany as tourists, and German employers—who were already employing other Turkish migrants—hired them. Experts estimate that about 20% to 40% of all contract workers came to Germany this way (Gitmez 1989: 7). With friends and acquaintances abroad, the value of reciprocal and solidary forms of social capital went up. Often, the pioneer migrants housed the newcomers for a period and helped them to adapt.

Many of the decisions on moving and staying occurred under authoritarian rule that limited the degrees of freedom of people involved, especially in the later stages, when most migrants came directly from villages in the countryside. This had implications for the gendered structure of decision-making. It delayed the arrival of female migrants as first movers. Nevertheless, there was a turning point in the mid-1960s. From the late 1960s until the recruitment ended in 1973, about as many women came to Germany before their husbands, as women who followed their men. In 1974, women constituted about 26% of all Turkish migrant workers in Germany (Akgündüz 1993: 181). This signalled new and changing preferences of German employers and gatekeepers who looked for women as contract workers, e.g. in workplaces requiring manual dexterity. Therefore, it was beneficial for men, who were on the long waiting lists, to send their women abroad first and to follow later on the ticket of family reunification. Sending women abroad first often meant authoritative and not consensual conjugal decision-making concerning international migration. However, in some instances, sons and daughters turned against this negative form of social capital and fled paternal authority that was exercised in planned marriages (Yurtdaş 1995). These people could then exercise much more individual autonomy concerning their lives (Akpınar and Mertens 1977: 23). In other instances of authoritarian decision-making, one of the most important sources of dispute among working spouses turned out to be the allocation and control of household income; often many years later, upon settlement in Germany (Abadan-Unat 1985*b*: 219). Nevertheless, there were indeed groups of migrants who decided consensually on migrating. This minority comes closest to the proposal made by the new economics of migration, claiming that not individuals but families took the decision to migrate. In sum, high maintenance costs of social capital speak for the greater likelihood of internal as opposed to international migration and for *in situ* adaptation.

Adaptation Costs: Economic, Political, and Cultural

Migrants abroad also face adaptation costs because it takes social capital to link with other migrants and natives. Since this is much less a problem after migration networks arise, let us focus on pioneer migrants. Living abroad, albeit intended most often for a few years only, meant that migrants had to at least partially learn a new language, conform to a new work regime, adjust to particular forms of housing, and deal with state authorities controlling their stay. For pioneer migrants it took months and years to master this unfamiliar environment (Kağıtçıbaşı 1983). This was made more difficult by the fact that both Turkish migrants and German natives perceived high degrees of cultural distance. While we observe similar phenomena also among and towards immigrants from Italy in the 1960s, the Turkish–German relationship had roots in a particular cultural conflation: for centuries, people in Western and Central Europe have considered Turks as the prototypical incarnation of Muslim culture. Moreover, in the past, the Turkish presence in Europe had constantly been associated with warfare which is not surprising in the light of the Ottoman conquest of much of south-eastern Europe and the sieges of Vienna in 1529 and 1683. These facts left an undelible imprint in the collective memory of a secularizing but nevertheless Christian Europe (cf. Tibi 1998: 200–6).

For early migrants who intended their stay in Germany to be an intermittent one, adaptation costs proved quite high. This was true even though many of them were satisfied with the makeshift character of collective and communal life, such as prayer halls in apartments or old factory halls or tea houses in store-front shops. Of course, this changed somewhat when the Turkish immigrant presence gradually lost its completely temporary character in later years. But then new migrants knew that they could rely on support networks already established by pioneer migrants.

An Example for the Selective Function of Social Capital: Specific Reciprocity and Focused Solidarity vs. Generalized Reciprocity and Diffuse Solidarity

How the various forms of social capital in kinship and communal systems shape migration—hinder and enhance it—and how they affect maintenance and adaptation costs, can be easily seen in one of the few case studies available that lends itself to a relational analysis. It is an example of the mechanisms underlying two specific forms of social capital: reciprocity and solidarity. It illustrates how benefits or disadvantages arise from social capital, looking at information flows, authority, and control in gender relations. It becomes obvious that the content of social and symbolic ties, and not just their very existence, makes a difference for migration rates. Engelbrektsson (1978) asked how we can explain very differential volumes of migration and different rates of female migrants in migration from two villages in the Konya region. In one village migrants came from virtually all households, in another one only from one of many kinship groups (see Table 5.1). The following is a reinterpretation of Engelbrektsson's seminal study. She does not use our terminology. Yet she is sensitive to the effects of ties and networks which makes it possible to use her results as an illustration.

Obviously, somewhat different macro-conditions explain why the inhabitants of Alihan enlisted as contract workers at higher rates than those from Yeniköy. Alihan used to be a relatively poor village with few land resources. As far back as the 1930s, many members of the poorest families engaged in seasonal work outside the village and later as unskilled workers in the provincial capital of Konya. They availed themselves of *gurbet*. When the first migrant left the village for

TABLE 5.1. *Population and migration rates from two selected villages in Central Anatolia*

	Alihan *c.*100 km south of Konya	Yeniköy *c.*150 km north of Konya
Population in 1965	*c.* 650	*c.* 900
Emigration to Europe, 1965–1975	– 135 emigrants	– 28 emigrants
	– 15 women (11%)	– 10 women (38%)
	– migrants from *all* families and kinship groups	– all migrants from the *same* kinship group

Source: Engelbrektsson 1978: 9–12, 19, 29–30.

Germany, it was clear that the agricultural land would not suffice for a rapidly growing population. Yeniköy, by contrast, was one of the richer and more prosperous villages in the whole region. There was plenty of soil which farmers could use more intensively and mechanize work through tractors. Some entrepreneurial villagers managed to even establish follow-up improvements, such as transport firms. Most resident households profited from the economic betterment. Therefore, at the initial stages, we would expect a somewhat greater percentage of Alihan than Yeniköy residents engaging in international migration. And this is indeed what happened.

Only very few, about 4%, of all emigrants from Alihan entered and worked in Sweden and Germany via the official channels of contract worker recruitment. All the others migrated when the chances were very low because of long waiting lists between 1970 and 1973, or after the immigration countries implemented the termination of contract worker recruitment. And, very importantly, there were quite a few residents in Yeniköy outside the one kinship group engaged in pioneer migration who wanted to go abroad. However, the efforts of most of the Yeniköy residents, who were not members of the one successful migrant group to enter and work in Europe failed miserably.

These different rates of international migration can be explained by the ability of villagers to recur to various mechanisms rooted in reciprocity and solidarity. The potential migrants in Alihan, who followed the first pioneer migrants, could resort to reciprocal and solidary ties that encompassed more than one kinship group. However, those interested in migrating out of Yeniköy could not, if they were not members of the one kinship group from whom the first migrant left for Europe. Alihan represented a village with a strong social cohesion, relatively few economic differences, and a community exhibiting a high degree of common collective representations, grounded in a common history that reaches back to the sixteenth century. All villagers considered themselves descendants of the original settlers and most families showed marital connections to other families in the village. The household patriarchs mostly arranged marriages within the village with few newcomers entering the resident kinship groups. Villagers could rely on specific and generalized reciprocity in times of need: 'in most cases the villagers had no one except fellow villagers to rely upon for help in times of need. It was pointed out, however, that every family in the village which came into real trouble could definitely count on assistance from all those who had something to spare, whether or not they were kin' (Engelbrektsson 1978: 45). Generalized and not only specific reciprocity in the form of mutual obligations thus extended beyond the narrow kinship group. Villagers experienced non-kin reciprocity, embedded in a diffuse, i.e. village-wide solidarity of a sense of common origin, shared history, and multiple bonds of kinship that certainly is not representative of all Anatolian villages.

When Alihan villagers sought to join the stream to Europe and failed to overcome official hurdles in a first effort, fellow-villagers who concentrated in a few immigration country cities readily furnished them information, accommodation, and job referrals: 'It could be done because fellow villagers both abroad and at home were willing and felt a moral obligation to extend practical assistance to those who opted for emigration. Thus in a social context ordered by norms and traditions of mutual assistance, personal lack of finances does not necessarily pose a greater obstacle for emigration' (ibid. 287). In other words, information and access to the capital of others, embedded in forms such as generalized reciprocity and diffuse solidarity, acted as a partial substitute for economic capital, such as money. There is also a marked difference to migrants from urban contexts. In these contexts, it was above all those with above average income who migrated—perhaps due to the initial absence of the forms of social capital available to Alihan residents.

By contrast, pioneer migrants from Yeniköy exclusively supported the members of their own kinship group. They clannishly engaged in specific reciprocity and focused solidarity. Other potential migrants could not rely on reciprocity, solidarity, and benefits such as information emanating from social and symbolic ties in this one kinship group. The village had existed for about a hundred years in the mid-1960s and fell into three sub-communities. First, many of the original settlers owned most of the arable and rich land. Second, Kurdish settlers had come after World War One and joined Islamic sects. Many members of this group shrewdly moved upward economically. Third, there were Turkish refugees from Greece and Bulgaria who had arrived after World War One and depended on government subsidies. They clearly formed the bottom of the socio-economic set-up. No bonds of generalized reciprocity or diffuse solidarity crossed the borders between these three communities, and few strong social and symbolic ties linked kin groups within the sub-groups—reciprocity was specific and solidarity focused on the respective families. Intermarriage across the three communities practically did not occur. The household heads commonly arranged marriages with partners from other villages. By the same token, blood feuds at times even exaggerated existing antagonisms. Reciprocity and solidarity were tied to recrimination and retaliation that eventually led to escalation. It is thus not surprising that the one kinship group engaging in international migration, located in the poor Turkish community, did not share its resources concerning migration with other villagers.

Another striking difference between the two villages concerns the rate of female migration. An explanation can be found in the communal policies of gender separation. The rate of female migration from Yeniköy was much higher than from Alihan. In Alihan, a strict separation of the sexes prevailed. Daily and festive activities of men differed from and were separate from those of women. Simply put, men associated with men and women with women, with intimacy between men and women restricted to the area of sexual intimacy (ibid. 164). In these arranged marriages men left their wives behind when exiting. Migrating husbands tended to rely on social control in the village that would enforce their *namus*, their honour related to gender roles. Because of this set-up of social and symbolic ties in the village, most men could not imagine taking their wives abroad with them. These symbolic gender ties had repercussions for economic considerations: it simply would have been very costly moneywise to take their wives with them because these men would not have allowed their wives to work. They would also have needed bigger and spacier apartments to uphold gender segregation in the destination country (ibid. 32, 165, 168). Moreover, patriarchs presided over most kinship groups in Alihan. The father of the bridegroom had to buy the bride at great material cost. This practice, in turn, strengthened the position of the patriarchs. One outcome was that the patriarch and his wife usually could claim the domestic services of the son's wife. It is not surprising, therefore, that only a few men from Alihan took their wives with them. The few women who accompanied their husbands came from households in which the patriarch was already deceased (ibid. 167).

Again, in Yeniköy, we find a much less pronounced gender separation in the public and private realms. Men and women often played together as children and did not experience much segregation during adolescence. Men and women engaged in more openly emotional and less formally regulated gender relations than in Alihan. Although tradition and *namus* played an important role as well, men considered women much more likely to be able to carry their own responsibility in upholding the *namus* of the family (ibid. 185–7). Because of much closer gender relations they also had much more say in making choices in general, and in marriage and migration in particular (ibid. 171, 181–2). This web of gender relations conduced the heads of household more frequently to take along spouses in Yeniköy than in Alihan. Moreover, men in Yeniköy practised conjugal migration. Internal conflicts and manifold cleavages in the village, not within the kinship groups, made it necessary to engage in special measures to protect *namus*, such as the rigid spatial separation of families belonging to particular groups. In addition, men allowed their spouses to accompany them because most of the migrants came out of the poorest group in an otherwise comparably well-off village. Since economic survival and betterment can be assumed to be one of the most significant motives for exit, migrant men had every cause to have their wives contribute to family income (ibid. 187); certainly aided by the fact that bridewealth prices were even higher in Yeniköy than in Alihan (ibid. 178). Also, villagers in Yeniköy paid much less attention to religious conceptions and symbolic ties as an indicator for social status than in Alihan. Instead, for them, secular and material orientations signalled social recognition (ibid. 188).

In sum, the differential rates of female migration also shows the overall usefulness of a social capital perspective. Neither economic-political structural factors nor characteristics of individual decision-makers can in themselves explain the differences. Rather, various collective representations of religion and gender in the two villages, based on differential mechanisms of social control, account for the fact that we find a higher rate of women migrants emerging from Yeniköy than from Alihan.

Conclusion: What Kind of Local Asset?

While the mechanisms of social capital constitute primarily a set of local assets, their functions in contributing to relative immobility differs. Clearly, specific reciprocity and focused solidarity usually strengthen *in situ* adaptation over exit, especially so in the absence of support networks. As soon as local assets are present in more extensive forms, such as generalized reciprocity and diffuse solidarity, potential migrants experience a much wider range of choices regarding exit, voice, and other kinds of *in situ* adaptation.

6

The Selective and Diffusion Functions of Social Capital: Why So Many Migrants Out of So Few Places?

Despite a high migration potential in most developing countries which send many migrants abroad, there is a high place selectivity. Typically, in the few places out of which many emigrate abroad, migration as a behavioural pattern rapidly diffuses. Understandably, propitious conditions such as labour recruitment will raise desires among potential migrants. Relative frustration ensues. Yet changing preferences concerning exit, voice, and *in situ* adaptation do not automatically translate into growing levels of migration. In contrast to changing macro-structural opportunities and increasing desires, access to information, control, and other people's resources do not immediately improve to the same extent. There is a lag between rising opportunities and expectations, on the one hand, and actual migration, on the other hand. The ties that bind people involved and the resources inherent in these ties play a crucial role in overcoming this lag and, consequently, lead to the self-feeding migration dynamics of chain migration. The mechanisms and benefits of social capital are central in processes of cumulative mobility.

We know from research on social movements that recruitment of participants in collective action usually proceeds by means of pre-existing social and symbolic ties. Thus, mobilization is more likely when the members of the beneficiary population are linked by such ties. Personal and organizational networks are important for recruiting participants, and a fair amount of empirical evidence supports this claim (McAdams, McCarthy, and Zald 1996). Although international migration rarely occurs as organized social movement, the mechanisms used to study mass collective action shed light on geographical mobility, in particular the actualization of migration potentials. We need to identify the features which account for endogenously induced chain migration out of very few places.

Four propositions guide the analysis in this chapter:

1. Migration processes only go beyond pioneer migration if brokers such as pioneer migrants succeed in mobilizing specific kinds of resources via social and symbolic ties, such as economic and human capital, reciprocity, and solidarity. In particular, specific reciprocity and focused solidarity do not suffice to stimulate chain migration. They merely foster migration in rather closed kinship circles. Instead, generalized reciprocity and diffuse solidarity beyond kinship groups is necessary. Only then do the various mechanisms of social capital reduce transferral costs, stimulate a critical mass of migrants and reach an ever-growing supply of potential migrants. Otherwise, migration quickly stagnates.
2. If migrant networks are available, migration tends to become self-perpetuating because each act of migration strengthens the necessary ties and creates additional resources that promote and sustain more migration in processes of cumulative mobility. The steady expansion of networks yields feedback loops that are particularly vigorous. Importantly, factors external to this dynamic become less relevant the more an international migration system matures. The endogenous dynamics of migration flows then become predominant.
3. Despite these cumulative effects, migration flows tend to reach turning points at which migration does not increase further. This is somewhat independent of factors outside these processes themselves, such as wage equalization between the country of emigration and immigration in the case of economically motivated migrants. In the long run, exogenous factors intertwine with endogenous ones: The immigration states are likely to implement restrictions that do effectively curb older patterns of flows but do not prohibit new flows along established migrant networks.
4. The first three propositions usually do not apply to the same extent to asylum seekers due to the overwhelming importance of external force in producing and halting flows of refugees.

The first part of this analysis explains the function of social capital in selecting potential migrants and the diffusion effects. Second, the analysis presents a stage model of international migration processes as diffusion, ranging from the ties mustered by pioneer migrants to the formation of migrant and migration networks, the diffusion of chain migration and cumulative mobility, and finally, to the decline of specific international migration flows. Third, the Turkish–German case study exemplifies the sequence of endogenous processes in international migration, constantly halted and modified by immigration state policies.

The Selective and Diffusion Functions of Social Capital in Migrant Networks

Selection of migrants comes in three forms: organizational recruitment, personal contact, and brute force or indirect violence. First, organizations recruit workers abroad. For example, this happened in the early stages of European contract worker recruitment in the 1960s when immigration country governments set up agencies abroad to select labour migrants in cooperation with emigration country institutions. Other cases are travel bureaus or smuggling organizations who arrange trips for those who cross borders illicitly. Second, personal contact of potential migrants or refugees perform decisive selections. For example, one member of the family works abroad and others join them as tourists and later legalize their status, if possible. Third, brute force or indirect violence act as a cause or a catalyst of refugee movements in cases of unrest, persecution of minorities, civil war, and ecological disaster. Then *force majeure* primarily propels migrants.

In all three situations, potential migrants and refugees do not choose in isolation from one another. They are usually not aware of what everyone else in the broader groups or in networks surrounding them is doing. Rather, they tend to take their cues from those in social proximity—friends, family members, neighbours, fellow-villagers, or colleagues. Each member of the group or network takes into account what others do before deciding to join in. Ties operate in all three situations. In the first one, formal ties matter: organizational recruitment offers pioneer migrants a chance venture abroad. In turn, many pioneer migrants later provide the ties for emergent migrant networks. Moreover, personal contacts are sometimes decisive to get on recruitment lists of organizations pursuing selection. The second type of selection through personal ties characterizes the overwhelming majority of migration after the initial start-up phase. Once pioneer migrants have established a migration road, more and more potential migrants are drawn into it by information from former migrants. Veritable migration avenues then sprout. The third type is a limiting one because it makes us aware of severe structural constraints in making choices whether to stay or to go, exercise exit, voice, or *in situ* adaptation. In all three situations ties in networks carry obligations, reciprocal patterns, and solidarity. Ties provided by networks reduce the risks associated with international migration because individuals can expect help from earlier migrants to find a job and housing.

Thus, resources may congeal in networks of cooperation. These mechanisms do help migrants to muster the benefits of social capital—

information, control, and scarce resources of others, such as money. Because of lack of information about the labour and housing market in the country of destination, pioneer migrants and early refugees experience even higher risks and costs than those who follow later. For refugees, information about reception centres in potential destination countries are valuable resources. Often, only informal agreements and not legal contracts undergird these kinds of transactions between movers and intermediaries. Migrants then tap the resources of pioneer migrants and brokers. Very often, movers know who awaits them and many probably already know their prospective employer (Tilly 1990). When migrants arrive in the country of destination on prepaid tickets, they are expected to pay back the expenses defrayed beforehand. In addition, migrant networks help those who stay behind. Eased access to work and housing abroad helps migrants to send back remittances. After the migration of the first individual, the monetary and psychological costs of migration are substantially lower for friends, relatives, and selected members of communities in the country of origin. Information is most valuable when there is little of it; and it is always worth more, the more heterogeneous the network is.

Only when brokers initiate migration can international South–North migration evolve on a larger scale. Brokers work very selectively and do not cover all places in any given nation-state in the South. Therefore, migration does not start from all places, and not at the same time. This is a preliminary answer to the second part of our question: Why so many international migrants out of so few places?

When the selection of migrants reaches a critical mass, the diffusion function of social capital comes to the fore. In general, as the stock of social capital resources increases in networks of cooperation, the self-feeding processes of migration strengthen. The network expansion affects both the magnitude and the composition of additional flows, and it supports the direction of migration already given by the structural linkages between emigration and immigration countries.

We can discern the following stages in migration processes in a schematic way:

Phase I: Start and acceleration	Phase II: Climax	Phase III: Deceleration
• thresholds: the effects of pioneer migration • formation of migrant and migration networks	• diffusion and chain migration • self-feeding effects: cumulative mobility	• culture of migration: migration as a way of life • the exhaustion of mass migration

Phase I: Start and Acceleration

Threshold Effects: The Importance of Ties in a Critical Mass

If we compare places of origin which are very similar regarding both people's desires to move or stay and the opportunity structures they face, we often find widely varying migration rates. It has been repeatedly observed that the number of people moving abroad from—in this regard—two most similar villages can be very different (Struck 1984). We have mentioned part of the answer: different stocks and forms of social capital. To start with, a threshold model of collective behaviour (see Granovetter 1978) gives situation-specific explanations of moving and staying that do not explain outcomes solely in terms of structures, desires, and expectancies of agents before the movements begin. Instead, applied to international migration, this model can be used to look at how migratory processes unfold. This means that migration is dependent upon the number or proportion of other potential movers who must make the decision before another agent does likewise.

Threshold models are a special instance of critical mass models. One of the fundamental assumptions is that as the rate of knowledge in a system increases up to a certain level, there is very little adoption, but once this threshold is passed, further increases in awareness lead to increases. As to migration, it will not start unless there is an initial number of aware potential migrants. In this way, the threshold model specifies the stress-awareness model discussed earlier. The threshold model is superior to game-theoretic models in which the players must choose in parallel, without knowledge of others' strategies; with the partial exception of iterative games. The threshold model imagines serial rather than parallel choices: serial choices mean, in essence, that each potential migrant looks around to see how many others are participating before deciding to join in. By contrast, parallel choices imply that all agents know what the respective others around them are doing (Macy 1991). In the case of parallel choice, actions are solely a by-product of an underlying interest in marginal utility. Following the more realistic assumption of serial choice, we need to focus on the distribution of thresholds and social and symbolic ties through which members learn about the actions of others. Hence threshold models are of particular importance in understanding situations where opportunities and desires are favourable to international migration but no movement occurs. Immobility in the face of favourable macro-structural opportunities are such cases.

There is a serious limitation to the threshold model that can be overcome with a relational analysis. It shares with game-theoretic models the assumption of rational agents with complete information. This means that all participants know what all those involved do. In this view, the analysis then proceeds in a classical rational choice fashion—the overall risk level determines the expectations of returns. In other words, the central question is: How much does a migrant or refugee risk when migrating, being the first person to do so? According to this model, responses to the actions of a small group in social proximity would not appear to make much sense by any reasonably demanding criterion for rationality. Given this generally unrealistic assumption of complete information, rational actors are concerned primarily with the overall risk level, and not with the actions of their immediate circle. However, cooperation depends not only on the level of risk and the strength of collective interests—for instance, the interest of a kinship group—but also on the network of social and symbolic ties that channel the necessary chain reactions.

Hence, threshold models need to be extended in order to understand how participation in migrant networks follows the contours of the social structure and the resources inherent in the ties: potential migrants usually do not choose in total isolation from each other, nor are they completely aware of what everyone else in the group is doing. If they are not first-time pioneer migrants, they rather take their cues from their ties with significant others, those in social and/or symbolic proximity—kin, friends, neighbours, or colleagues. Each member of the group or network takes into account the ties with others and what others are doing before deciding to join in serial transactions. Whether and how migration then takes place crucially depends on how the mechanisms of social capital operate and what benefits they generate. It follows that the spread of migration crucially depends on the properties of the network of the respective social and symbolic ties, linking the members of the relevant groups. Only when taking into account the web of ties, can we hope to trace how the responses of potential migrants might lead to a critical mass of migrants. However, the lower the degree of freedom of the people involved, the less applicable the threshold model becomes. At the extreme, very brute forces leave practically no choice to observe what other people do.

According to a critical mass model, the central issue in migrant network formation is the problem of overcoming the start-up costs. The ties mustered by brokers are important for overcoming these costs, viz. thresholds. Brokers are the third persons who benefit, the *tertius gaudens.* The broker position denotes the freedom a person derives from conflicting group affiliations on the basis of multiple ties reaching into various networks (Simmel 1995: 297). Brokers derive benefits from negotiating and facilitating ties between other players (Burt 1992: 30–4). Here, the term refers to being the third between two or more parties trying to use the same set of ties. Because of their positions in networks, brokers have a high degree of information and exert a great amount of control. Brokers can be recruiters who work for companies abroad or employment agencies in the emigration country. They can also be pioneer migrants who capitalize on their experience, and thus respected individuals in the emigration or immigration communities or professionals in organizations concerned with labour recruitment. Alternatively, they can be commercial migration merchants who transport undocumented or falsely documented migrants across nation-state borders. Another type of *tertius gaudens* are gatekeepers. These are persons—migrant or native—who provide new migrants with access to employers, landlords, or public authorities. They are intermediaries who enable contacts of potential and actual migrants to employers, legal authorities, and other institutions.

Many brokers act as transnational entrepreneurs supporting mechanisms which include exchange-based obligations and reciprocity. They benefit from money or social debts incurred to them during the process of migration—instances of exchange-based obligations. For example, villagers in developing countries are likely to reap the best results from international migration if they all agree to sponsor selected individuals for graduate studies at a university in the North. The individualized strategy would be illegal entry in the country of destination. Sometimes brokers are themselves constrained by social norms when responding to legitimate claims for assistance in reciprocal transactions. Of course, reciprocal ties do not matter for those migration merchants and their helpers who simply abandon their human cargo whenever feasible.

The Formation of Migrant Networks: The Ties of Brokers

Once the number of movers reaches a critical threshold, capable of sustaining an extensive network of social and symbolic ties, migrant networks can emerge. Migrant networks are important overall mechanisms for enabling exits because they are characterized by low jointness of supply. Jointness of supply or non-rivalry means that the benefit of a collective good such as a network of cooperation does not diminish by other people also sharing it. Low jointness of supply is a fundamental characteristic of reciprocity and solidarity. With reciprocity and solidarity, embedded in migrant networks, the transaction costs of movement become lower. It decreases maintenance and adaptation costs. The question then is how migrant and migration networks come into existence. Networks that extend beyond the nuclear family and tightly knit kinship groups are particularly interesting because they are needed for chain migration to unfold.

Two assumptions are necessary: first, a higher overall prevalence of social and symbolic ties and a higher density of such ties promotes collective action in migrant networks. Note that a crucial proviso has to be added: the content of these ties needs to extend beyond specific reciprocity and focused solidarity to include exchange-based obligations, generalized reciprocity, and diffuse solidarity. Otherwise, the benefits of social capital remain limited to the parochial few. Only then does migration reach people outside kin groups who have pioneer migrants. Second, network centralization through organizers such as brokers tends to have a positive effect: the concentration of ties around, say, pioneer migrants, has an accelerating effect on migration. Additionally, the value of centralization increases as the heterogeneity of benefits derived from social capital grows (for a micro-level formulation of the same thought, see Marwell and Oliver 1993: 122–3). This is important because resources necessary to migrate such as money, travel information, accommodation, work, and other necessities are unevenly distributed among members of kin groups, friendship circles, and communities. When resources are distributed heterogeneously among the group, limitations on the key broker or organizer—the one with the highest amount of social or symbolic ties, viz. the largest ego-centred network—set by the amount of resources she might devote to mobilizing become much less important. Instead of ties that eventually induce the whole large network into migrating, brokers in a group with heterogeneous resources usually serve to influence others in their decision to move or to stay by transacting with a selected subgroup of the larger network or collective. Such brokers with large networks are very likely to be in contact with the few key people in the group, such as a village community or a city neighbourhood; for example, teachers in villages usually are in contact with both pioneer migrants abroad and local persons who are multipliers, such as the village notables and others, often via indirect contact with their students. What mechanism of social capital is operative—obligations, reciprocity, or solidarity—depends on the structure and content of ties within groups. Note that the people reached by the brokers need not be tied to each other directly and thus form circles or cliques. All that is necessary for them to be reached by ties is their common position in a network—a structural equivalence to the positions of brokers.

Often, migrants consider personally-known brokers more trustworthy than anonymous agencies (for many, see Spaan 1994: 109). From the potential migrants' point of view, these intermediaries range in decreasing benevolence from relatives and friends in their own, ego-centred networks, through casual smugglers and border guides, to sophisticated organizational recruitment which organizes the whole process, purveys documents, and provides guidance abroad.

Broker-induced territorial exits are the rule rather than the exception (see the examples, albeit using a different terminology, in Castles and Miller 1993: chs. 4 and 5). In most instances, a relatively small cadre of highly interested and resourcefully tied people produces migrant networks. It is not the effort of the average member of the community. Central is the importance of a critical mass of large contributors—'large actors' (Olson 1965)—to the formation of emergent migrant networks. This small group of necessary inducers consists of pioneer migrants, recruiters, migration merchants, and other facilitators. The evolving networks of cooperation then give benefits such as information, they increase the awareness space of potential migrants and widen access to resources of pioneer migrants and brokers in the country of destination.

The question now is what kind of ties are necessary and what role they play in network formation. And it is important to point out that it is not only the strength of ties that matters but also their content. An influential argument is that strong ties tend to form cliques, while weak ties tend to bridge cliques and bring everyone into the same network (see Chapter 4). Therefore, weak ties can often be a better basis for collective action (Granovetter 1973). In our case, this concerns the formation of migrant networks. Here, the argument is that decentralized nets and centralized wheels of weak ties are equally effective network structures for migration.

The weak ties argument has to be qualified in two respects to be useful for our purposes. First, not weak ties per se are useful, but their tendency to be centralized. This is a plausible assumption because without a centralization of ties by pioneer migrants and brokers, many potential migrants could not leave their country, and new migrants abroad could not adjust because they lack referrals. Second, the exclusive focus on social ties, whether strong or weak, misses important connections between potential migrants, pioneer migrants, and brokers. We have repeatedly come across case studies showing that ties extend beyond kinship groups and friendship circles and involve the whole community (e.g., Klaver 1997). Symbolically tied collectives that matter range from small village communities to ethnic or even transnational religious communities. For example, symbolic ties such as a common understanding of a long history can form the basis of solidarity in village communities and, in strong cases, give access to migration networks to virtually all willing members of the village; while the absence of a shared history, ancestry, or otherwise shared understandings can indicate a low degree of symbolic cohesion and is indicative of the fact that only members of smaller groups have access to their own particular migration networks. Thus, symbolic ties can significantly enhance the effect of social ties. In addition, symbolic ties carry a role of their own. This becomes most obvious in the virtual absence of strong social ties. For example, on the basis of a shared understanding concerning regional origin, persons in the immigration community may act as substitutes for pioneer migrants or early refugees and contribute to both the selective and adaptive functions of social capital in networks.

Phase II: Climax

Chain Migration as a Diffusion Process

It is likely that migrant networks of cooperation, a regular circuit in which migrants retain claims and contacts and routinely return to the country of origin, brings in its wake the migration of related individuals or households. This is a typical 'friends and relatives effect'. When looking at the dynamics, this process is akin to snowballing: the more immigrants of a given place stay in the destination region, the more want to come. It takes time to develop the chain and this is the reason why we see it full-fledged only in later phases of international migration. When brokers and gatekeepers find worthwhile benefits in advising and channelling movers, when norms of reciprocity such as remitting money home can be enforced and when forms of mutual aid among migrants create broad commitments to other migrants, then networks of cooperation that encompass movers and stayers begin to diffuse rapidly.

In order to understand the importance of networks of cooperation for the diffusion process, let us first consider its opposite, namely migration in the context of atomistic structures. Banfield (1958), for example, reports on a town in Italy's Basilicata region where prospective emigrants could not leave because their numerous fellow-townspeople abroad had severed all ties with the country of origin. We can infer that social ties in this town must have been extremely fractured—even more than is the rule in Southern Italy. This fact made chain migration impossible and stopped the diffusion process after it had taken off haltingly a few decades before. The reasons can be found in the absence of networks of cooperation that could continue the migration process. Associations, community organizations, clans, or other forms of generalized solidarity and diffuse solidarity were conspicuous by their absence. Moreover, the nuclear family household, the multilateral kinship system, and dyadic patronage—the basic forms of social organization in this part of Italy in the first half of this century—were precarious. Therefore, chain migration to the United States in the late nineteenth and early twentieth century, based on a 'hometown' society of the Southern Italian type necessarily ran the risk of leaving some prospective emigrants out on a limb (Macdonald and Macdonald 1964: 90–1). In such a situation, a potential sponsor abroad may desert her family, friends, and clients, when she adapts to the immigration country without keeping up ties with home, or when the frequent conflicts in this kind of social organization rupture bonds. Mechanisms of control reaching beyond the territorially absent nuclear family are missing. Also, a brokering sponsor in the immigration country may fulfil her duties of focused solidarity to those few fellow-townsmen who are close relatives, friends, or clients, and not give any thought to the majority to whom she has no customary obligations. This behaviour prevents migrant networks from expanding and exit options only extend to family members. Consequently, no chain migration evolves.

The transmission or diffusion of migration can be conceptualized as a two-stage process. The first stage is awareness—as suggested by the threshold model—in which brokers send signals by means of social and symbolic ties; sometimes reinforced through mass media portrayals of immigration country conditions. The second stage is the readiness to migrate. The diffusion effect is the cumulatively increasing degree of availability of obligatory, reciprocal, and solidary ties to migrate, resulting from the activation of networks. Then the reduction of transaction costs is positively related to the rate of adoption of migration if brokers exist, and negatively related if social capital can only be transferred under conditions of great risk or uncertainty.

Typically, diffusion processes are characterized by a change from an accelerative to a decelerative pattern. In an accelerative pattern the rate of adoption is proportional both to those who have adopted an item and to those who have not. Decelerative means that the rate of adoption is proportional only to those who have not yet adopted an item (see also Coleman, Katz, and Menzel 1966).

It is most likely that accelerative processes operate in the middle stages of migration courses, including all those persons connected by existing networks of cooperation. Only when international migration starts to reach beyond the well-entrenched circle of relatives of pioneer migrants, do we expect accelerative diffusion to blossom into chain migration. Once the accelerative processes have reached the majority of the potential migrants, diffusion is likely to turn into a decelerative pattern. Migration keeps going on but slows down over time—until the supply of potential migrants is exhausted. Accelerative diffusion implies exponentially growing chain migration, decelerative diffusion steadily declining flows through migrant networks. Thus, the nature of the process is bound to change as the diffusion proceeds, accelerative diffusion being most operative in the middle and decelerative diffusion when migration is dropping off.

The facility with which chain reactions spread through networks of cooperation depends on the kind of social and symbolic ties that link people, groups, and organizations. While strong ties embody greater potential for influencing behaviour, weak ties may be more effective as diffusion channels (Rogers and Kincaid 1981). Chain migration then evolves from one reference group in a community, extends across communities, and even across the boundaries of isolated clusters. As mentioned above, diffusion processes require types or mechanisms of social capital that extend beyond narrow kinship clusters.

As the stock of social capital inherent in social and symbolic ties grows over time—and as international migrant experience increases—migration becomes progressively less selective and thus spreads, for instance, from the middle to the lower segments of the socio-economic hierarchy (Massey et al. 1987). The socio-economic distribution of migration is tightly interlinked with life-course patterns. Once networks have developed to the point where a foreign job is within easy reach, international migration becomes a preferred strategy among poor families seeking to alleviate pressing economic needs caused by many dependents and few workers (Balán 1988: 56).

Gender-specific networks add to the dynamic of international migration. Here, we can see how migration networks overlap with social support networks in the area of origin. It is not true for many cases of today's international migration that women are the ones 'left behind' while their husbands go abroad (Sassen 1988 and Fernández-Kelly 1994). In some cases, network diffusion gives relatively immobile women a chance for *in situ* adaptation in a gender-specific way. For instance, single mothers from Mexico leave their children with their mothers, sisters, or other relatives for varying lengths of time while they work in the USA (Chavez 1992: 122). Child-fostering provides a stable source of income for non-migrant women, and a woman who fosters the children of relatives and friends abroad may be able to increase her stock of ties. At some point in time she may draw upon them when sending her children, other relatives, or friends abroad (Simon and Bretell 1986: 45–6). This strategy is gender-specific because in many southern and northern countries women are known to be more active in support networks related to kin and friends (see also Bott 1957: 138).

Migration as a Self-Feeding Process: The Mechanism of Cumulative Mobility

The diffusion of migration is a typical instance of cumulative mobility as positive feedback causation. Once the number of network ties in migration flows reaches a certain level, migration becomes self-perpetuating, because it reinforces and augments the ties and social capital necessary to sustain it. Once migration processes are underway, they fuel themselves. At some point in international migratory processes, networks of cooperation sustain population flows quite independently of objective economic conditions in the areas of origin and destination (Hugo 1981). Existing research has described processes of cumulative mobility from a micro-level and a macro-level vantage point. Despite contrary claims, a meso link is still missing and is provided here.

(1) The Macro-Level Vantage Point

On the emigration side, migration originates in profound transformations of developing societies, involving processes of mechanization, capitalization, and commercialization in agriculture and mechanization and profound rationalization in industry. Over time this produces socio-economic changes that encourage these trends and make subsequent migration more likely. For example, the mechanization of agriculture that began in many developing countries during the 1950s displaced peasants and agricultural workers. Similar processes apply to industrialization. Given access to work in the former colonial centres, in former white settler colonies and foreign labour recruitment programmes during the 1960s, industrial workers who searched for economic betterment and, later on, displaced peasants from the countryside who sought informal insurance and economic survival took up international migration. When networks evolved during and after the open door or recruitment phase, they enabled migrants, their kin and significant others to use the gates of family reunification, marriage migration, and illicit entry to immigrate in increasing numbers.

Effects of these chain migrations in the areas of origin have been manifold. Particularly in small villages, some migrants invested in mechanization and used more intensive production methods so that other villagers were finally displaced. More households were able to invest in capital-intensive production methods, and more families withdrew from cultivation. In this way, migration exacerbated the falling demand for agricultural labour and accelerated the shift to commercial agriculture. Temporary migration has been a strategy of risk diversification in rural households. Foreign wages have sometimes led farmers and peasants to cultivate their land less intensively than before or even let it lie fallow. If these migrants buy land, the outcome might be that there is less land under intensive cultivation in the community, that local food production is reduced, the price of staple crops raised, and the demand for labour decreased. This, too, gives incentives to the remaining members of the community to move (see e.g. Cornelius 1991).

If, on the other hand, land is more intensively cultivated, as farmer migrants can now afford more capital, more emigration evolves since less manual labour is needed (Massey 1990). However, remittances spent on agriculture could actually increase agricultural profits. They can help to develop productivity and output, and migrant farmers will keep marginal land under production (Cornelius 1991: 48). In this latter case we could not expect economic feedback effects to encourage further migration. Instead, forms of familial obligations and specific reciprocity are kept alive and undergo *in situ* adaptation more slowly than under circumstances of large-scale emigration.

(2) The Micro-Level Vantage Point

There is much empirical evidence that a history of prior migration increases the likelihood of future migration. This is true in two ways: for the repeated migration of individuals and for new migrants who choose the exit option. First, in the case of ready transferability of social and other forms of capital, we would expect that, *ceteris paribus*, each trip to the immigration country increases the likelihood of subsequent trips (Massey et al. 1993). An economistic focus upon the sunk costs—costs that have been expended in any long-standing line of action—suggests that the more investments go into certain lines, the higher is the stake (Becker 1975). Migrants can be thought to invest time and energy in social and symbolic ties, as well as more tangible resources in pursuing migratory careers. The costs of exit from such a line of behaviour are thus substantial—such as costs of readapting completely to life in the country of origin. Second, for potential migrants to exit, their desires need to change. For example, role theory predicts that the process by which people learn any new role may evolve into a stable pattern (Dahrendorf 1960). If we apply this to the problem at hand, new migrants are gradually socialized into their role as international movers, emulating the behaviour of earlier migrants. Ultimately, the 'Tocqueville effect'—desires rising more rapidly than opportunities (Chapter 2)—makes more and more potential migrants choose the exit option, even if they have to resort to unauthorized migration.

(3) The Meso Link

The mechanisms of positive feedback cumulative mobility can be summarized as shown in Figure 6.1.

Recruitment policies of immigration countries do indeed induce pioneer migrants to exit and move from South to North. Many pioneer migrants who establish themselves abroad but return continuously or intermittently, maintain ties with people in their kin groups and (former) communities. Thus, potential migrants see the advantages of also moving abroad. The diffusion of migration beyond narrow and small groups occurs through transaction cost reducing migrant networks. The rate of migration keeps going up. After a while, the admission policies of the countries of destination do not allow the reception of as many immigrants as are willing to come, partly because the desires

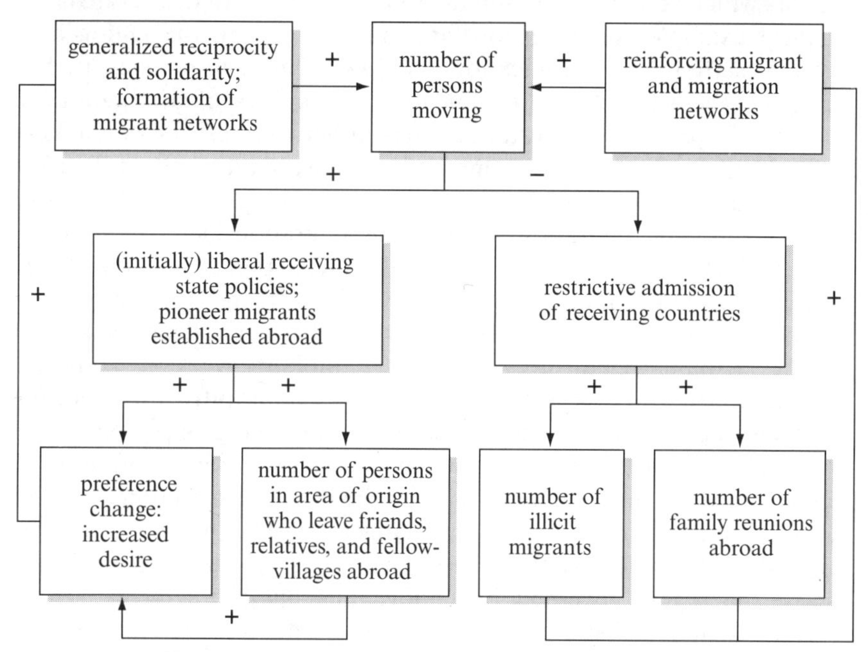

FIG. 6.1. *Cumulative mobility: positive feedback loops*

of potential migrants to exit grow faster than the opportunities foreseen by the legal admission channels. Migrant networks do not close this gap but widen it because they induce people to exit, providing even irregular forms of entry and stay.

This state of affairs gives rise to family reunification, marriage migration but also illicit entry. Family reunification is an avenue for those who enjoy intra-family reciprocity. Marriage migration is a strategy used by those, for example, who try to recur to obligations of friends and relatives in sending their son or daughter abroad. Migration occurring under weak ties in exchange-based obligations carries the highest risks for migrants. Especially so if migration merchants are involved. The migrants then have practically no chance to enforce social or legal norms should the migration merchant renege and break the informal contract to channel the migrant into the desired country of destination. Given this high level of risk, transaction costs can be exorbitant in the absence of trustworthy ties.

Once set in motion, migration flows develop under their own steam. In particular, generalized reciprocity and solidarity help to broaden the scope for actual migrants, driving up both emigration, immigration and the stock of immigrants in the places of destination. These endogenous processes are, at times, brought into being and altered by exogenous factors which contribute to initiate, to accelerate, or to decelerate flows. Typical examples of exogenous factors accelerating the endogenous dynamics are family reunification and *non-refoulement* policies. In general, they help to bring close kin into the country of destination, or entice refugees to select certain abodes rather than others as places of refuge. Stricter immigration controls have a decelerating effect. Because of generally efficient border controls and the high transaction costs involved in illicit migration regulated by migration merchants, organized and large-scale circumvention of official policies is unlikely to mushroom. Much more likely are new illicit channels via direct ties within webs of kin, friends, and fellow-members of collectives.

The various mechanisms of cumulative mobility work in a different manner for those whose personal freedom is significantly restricted. For example, persecuted activists, members of target groups, or simply victims of civil wars and environmental disasters are most often involuntary movers. Their exit occurs under the threat of sometimes massive physical and psychic violence and danger for their personal integrity and life itself. Hence, we then expect the process of cumulative mobility to be much less governed by endogenous but more by exogenous factors, such as a single event or a row of events that provoke or force an exodus. Therefore, the internal dynamics of flows of involuntary migrants tend to be less self-feeding than in the case of rather voluntary migration. Nevertheless, the distinction is often one of degree. The more migrants have active disposal over their fate, for example, in situations when they do not face acute persecution, the higher the chance that self-feeding processes operate, albeit within much more restricted bounds than in many cases of migration characterized by higher degrees of freedom for the potential migrants. The two limiting cases are countries with civil strife over decades that have either produced a trickle of refugees or forced expulsions of whole religious or ethnic groups at one point in time. Potential migrants in the former situation often tend to have a higher degree of freedom than those in the latter.

Phase III: Deceleration

Towards a Culture of Migration

In some instances of continued chain migration, a culture of migration develops which encompasses migration as an accepted and desirable way towards achieving social and economic mobility, a higher income, a lifestyle which could not be sustained by dependence on local resources only, or a way to challenge the political regime in the country of origin from exile abroad. For such cultures, the experience of geographical movement across nation-state borders and resettlement is formative. A culture of migration often spans several generations, as in the case of the Caribbean islands, where migration to North America and the British Isles has constituted an accepted lifestyle. The social and symbolic ties to the country of origin run on (for many, see Goulbourne 1991). This finding seriously challenges cherished conceptual distinctions, such as the one that migrants break off ties they entertain with these countries and regions after a certain period of time. They either remain sojourners and return to the emigration country—or another destination—or they become settlers and stay in the immigration country. Migration experiences such as the Caribbean islands–USA rarely conform to this dictum: there is, for example, abundant evidence on long-term circulators who work and invest abroad while their kinship base remains on the Caribbean islands (Pessar 1997: 2). This applies to groups among Puerto Ricans since the 1940s and Dominicans since the 1960s. In the West Indies, where the international migration experience dates back much further than in the rest of the Caribbean, people are calling such movers 'travellers'. In all these cases migration has not been decelerating but has proceeded on a stable and high level.

Decelerating International Migration Flows

So far, we have stressed that cumulative mobility—migration begetting more migration—works in a snowball fashion. The model of cumulative causation does not allow for the possibility of turning points, for reaching a maximum amount of migration, when migration stabilizes or falls, well before wages or job availability between the emigration and immigration countries equalize or political conditions in the countries of origin improve. The considerations pertaining to the decelerating stage of international migration processes are particularly difficult to ascertain because the empirical referents are tenuous. Very few of the migration flows induced after World War Two from South to North have reached their zenith. None the less, migration equilibria have evolved in some cases: emigration and (return) immigration have reached a rough balance. Examples include migration between Puerto Rico and the mainland USA—a sort of quasi-international migration, and between Portugal and Germany in the late 1960s, well before the termination of labour recruitment in 1973. Average wage differentials of a magnitude of 10 and 12 to 1 continued to exist between the mainland USA and Puerto Rico, and Germany and Portugal throughout the 1970s, 1980s, and 1990s. Puerto Ricans enjoyed freedom of movement, as did the Portuguese since 1986 in the EU. In addition, migration to alternative destinations did not grow. For example, the main destination of Portuguese workers, France, did not experience an increase in the immigration of Portuguese workers in the past thirty years. On the contrary, a decline occurred as well.

Economic arguments say that it is not the absolute differential between emigration and immigration country that matters. There are turning points that depend, among other things, on wage differentials. One of the key elements has been the so-called inverted U-curve thesis: economic development often first enhances and thereafter reduces the scope and incentives for migration (Faini and Venturini 1994). The thinking behind this hypothesis is as follows: there is usually very little emigration from countries with very low per capita incomes, where people work mostly in agriculture. If at all, there is internal migration. As soon as the per capita income reaches a higher level, we tend to find a higher percentage of persons who can afford the financial means to migrate abroad. The migration potential is highest at this stage. When a still higher income level is attained, the means to migrate increase but the actual emigration rates abroad are lower because wage differentials are not as stark any more (Figure 6.2). In this latter echelon, always to be thought along a continuum, human capital migrants are the most likely group to migrate abroad, since they could reap the highest relative profits (see Fischer et al. 1997*b*: 100).

However, such a view neglects a significant macro-level and a meso-level consideration. First, the inverted U-curve thesis is unsatisfactory because it assumes that a change in macro-structural conditions directly impinges on and translates into changing preferences of potential migrants. As the preceding analysis has shown, we need to take into account the intermediate structures and processes to complement the one-sided analysis of exogenous factors with decisive endogenous variables. Once a recognizable percentage of potential migrants starts moving, others will follow. And once the supply of potential migrants is exhausted, migration rates fall drastically. As usual, when the degree of freedom of choice declines, the applicability of the turning point model diminishes.

Second, the inverted U-curve argument does not include other determinants such as the endogenous dynamics of political regulation of exit and entry. For instance, more restrictive admission policies on the part of the immigration countries have tried to curb flows. Therefore, active labour recruitment has become rare. The more restrictive policies are usually part of post-migration developments. Large numbers of immigrants often raise the fear among the native and settled populations that the newcomers do not learn the mainstream language and practice religious beliefs that are alien to believers of the respective mainstream religions. Often, political parties evoke these dangers in election campaigns, followed—if successful among the populace—by

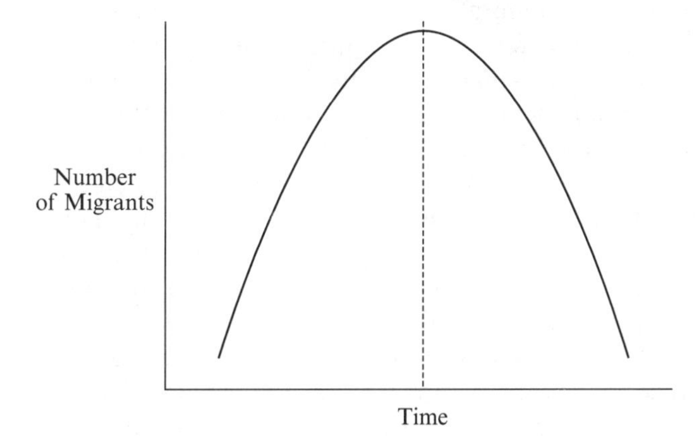

FIG. 6.2. *A stylized inverted U-curve*

the implementation of immigration control towards groups that have become unwelcome over time. However, as we have seen over and over again, even restrictionist policies cannot turn back the wheel to completely closed borders. The economistic argument totally depends on factors exogenous to migration movements and neglects not only the endogenous dynamics of migration but also of politics in immigration states. This becomes obvious in two realms of state regulation, welfare and security.

Deceleration and Restrictionist Policies: The Politicization of Welfare Provisions and Security

Restrictive immigration policies decisively shape decelerating migrations flows. Immigration states have employed both extensionist and restrictionist policies to regulate immigration and adaptation of labour migrants and asylum seekers. In turn, these policies have over time shaped political conflicts over welfare state provisions, external and internal security, and the fear of being culturally or politically overwhelmed by intruding newcomers. These conflicts have not endangered the consensus upon which nation-states are built but have increased the level of politicization of social rights and perceived security, and contributed to restrictionist immigration policies.

When dealing with perceived costs and benefits of immigration, it is of particular interest to look at the interplay of governments, political parties, interest groups, and voters. Politicians relate the shortages in the housing and labour markets, and problems of border control, among other things, to immigration. Although these problems may have other causes, they have become one of the prime targets for voicing dissent. Indeed, immigration has turned into a 'meta-issue' (Lasswell 1948): it can be referred to by intermediate organizations such as political parties in explaining many social and economic problems—such as unemployment, and housing shortages—without having to give concrete evidence because the effects of immigration are empirically hard to establish. In referring to these fears and in being responsive to the expectations of their constituency, especially politicians from populist parties have in fact introduced and reinforced xenophobic tendencies. This is not to say that threats to welfare and security in the immigration country are without any real-world foundation. However, through meta-politics low-level threats usually gain out-of-porportion significance. We cannot understand the saliency immigration has gained for public debates if we limit our discussion to the structural deficiencies of border control, internal policing, certain labour market segments characterized by a high representation of immigrant workers, and to certain social services in which we find a high proportion of immigrants. Instead, the broader question is how issues of material interest—border control, internal security, wage depression, job substitution, industrial relations, but also dependency of immigrants on social services—have fuelled debates over social justice, ethnic and national identity, and multiculturalism. Debates over identities and norms are generally much harder to resolve than conflicts over interests.

Sovereign states have crucial functions such as welfare, security, and the maintenance of national identity. Regarding welfare provisions, the standard argument for restriction is that continually high levels of immigration could lead to competition between immigrants and immigration country natives for jobs, housing, and social services and eventually even increase xenophobia (Ahfeldt 1993). More dispassionate observers have noted that high levels of immigration can be a factor leading to conflicts over scarce goods not simply because of direct competition between newcomers and the settled population. This version holds that high levels of immigration allow for the politicization of the immigration issue. Immigration can create an overabundance of cheap labour. This could threaten the balance of regulation of labour and housing markets that rests upon the cooperation of labour unions, employer associations, and state institutions. Given an abundant supply of labour willing to work under substandard conditions, individual employers, for example, would have more incentives to opt out of the regulation of labour markets. Unions, in turn, would lose economic and, finally, political power. Ultimately, this could lead not only to specific labour market segments for immigrants but to a levelling of social rights for all, immigrants and natives alike. And continuing high levels of immigration would not allow for the integration of immigrants who arrived earlier.

We could think of another version of this thesis. While the argument just made takes account of the importance of political conflicts as a driving force in the further development of immigration and integration policies, it does not consider immigration or immigrant policies themselves as a main factor contributing to the problems migration and the integration of immigrants pose for solidarity and social rights in receiving welfare states. It could be, for example, that restrictive immigration and integration policies entail a growing politicization of welfare state politics along immigrant-native lines. When potential immigrants from certain groups are rejected more often than others and migrants already present in the territory are barred from social rights, this could be interpreted to mean that even those who have gained entry have no legitimate claims to admission and membership. We thus have two versions of the argument, one concerning the effects of settlement, the other relating to very restrictive policies. In both cases we could find increasing levels of politicization over immigrant social rights. Both arguments are plausible, the first one regarding the adaptation of labour immigrants, and the second one with respect to restrictive policies towards labour migrants and asylum seekers.

The first version of the argument has been used to diagnose the 'Americanization of welfare state politics' in Europe. Mass migration of foreign labour 'reduced the political clout of those social strata that have traditionally been the chief source of support for welfare state development'. Specifically, the post-war mass migration 'diminished the power of organized labour by dividing the working class into national and immigrant camps, by easing the tight labour market conditions that would have enhanced labour's strategic resources and provoking a resurgence of right-wing and nativist political movements' (Freeman 1986: 83).

This thesis has the merit of linking immigration policies to the broader issue of welfare state integration. Yet there are two reasons to be sceptical about the claim that mass migration has undermined the consensus in European welfare states. First, although nationalist-populist parties in various European countries have run on anti-immigrant platforms, they usually do not attack the welfare state as such—in contrast to the neo-conservative rhetoric and onslaught during the 1980s. Rather, they demand strict restrictions on immigration and the repatriation of immigrants. Furthermore, there seems to be no conclusive empirical evidence that the political support for the welfare state as such has waned, despite various forms of 'welfare backlash' that have occurred since the 1980s. Contention has been limited to public assistance programmes while contributory insurance programmes still enjoy wide support among voters (Clayton and Pontusson 1998). Conflicts over immigrant social rights have been limited to tax-financed assistance programmes and benefits. Second, if the mass migrations since the 1960s had pitted the native working class against the immigrant working class we should see more signs of union opposition to continuing immigration. However, the latter has also not been the case (Faist 1995).

In order to explain how immigration and adaptation policies become contentious and lead to restrictionist measures, we have to analyse welfare state integration in three dimensions, functional, moral, and expressive (see also Figure 4.2). Temporary labour migrants are aliens hired to fill niches in the labour market for which employers cannot find domestic workers at prevailing wage rates and working conditions. Employers usually prefer to hire temporary labour, often on a rotational basis, i.e. migrants are supposed to return to the sending country after a fixed time period and an exchange of workers is supposed to take place. There are various reasons why temporary labour is hired, for example because it is assumed to be cheaper, more docile and because it may be used by employers in splitting the domestic workforce. Since temporary workers are mostly young, single, and healthy, costs to the welfare state are relatively low and benefits prevail in the eyes of the actors who initiated their recruitment, such as government bureaucracies, employers, and unions. In the course of the 1960s and 1970s migrant workers with secure residence and work permits have gradually lost their function as a 'conjuncture buffer' in Europe. Empirical studies show that in Western Europe they cannot simply be classified as part of secondary labour markets (Böhning 1984). And the native population started to perceive the costs of immigrant adaptation in areas such as housing, education, and health.

This is even more visible in the case of asylum seekers. The costs for asylum seekers and refugees to the coffers of receiving welfare states are visible in the short term. Their admission is justified on humanitarian and/or political grounds. Generally, asylum seekers are not allowed to work in the beginning stages and exclusively depend upon social provisions. Therefore, if the number of asylum seekers increases suddenly, we would expect political conflicts to focus on welfare provisions for this group. Indeed, while the numbers of asylum seekers sharply increased since the mid-1980s, recognition rates of refugees declined all over Europe (Joly, Kelly, and Nettleton 1997). The trend has been to grant proportionately more inferior categories of recognition to asylum seekers—for example, humanitarian status. These statuses confer considerably fewer social rights than full refugee status alienship and denizenship.

The important point is that once immigrants are in the territory they have access to a modicum of social rights and, unless a strict rotational principle is enforced, there is a high chance that they improve their legal status. In the post-1960 period there seems to have been a movement from alienship to denizenship among immigrants (Figure 6.3).

As to the security functions of immigration states, the control over external and internal borders can be interpreted as a sign of external and internal sovereignty of nation-states (Weiner 1995: ch. 6). Serious threats to the stability of states through migration are, however, exclusively limited to South–South migration. By contrast, the immigration countries in the North usually effectively control external borders and

Legal status	Immigrant categories
Alienship	– migrants with temporary residence and work permits (e.g. seasonal, contract, and postal workers) – asylum seekers, de facto refugees – undocumented aliens, illegal immigrants
Denizenship	– labour migrants with permanent residence status and their dependents – recognized refugees
Citizenship	– citizens of immigration nation-states – citizens of EU Member States

FIG. 6.3. *Alienship, denizenship and citizenship*

internal institutions, albeit with significant variations. In the North, the fear of concerned politicians, policy-makers, and parts of the public about a loss of both external and internal control and order in an age of intensified border-crossing exchanges of goods, information, ideas, symbols, and sometimes persons finds a ready expression in the focus in phenomena which are hard to capture with any certainty because of their largely undocumented nature, such as clandestine immigration, the alleged misuse of social services by asylum seekers, or unauthorized employment in low-paid services, agriculture, and the construction industry. Estimates of these phenomena usually vary widely (for example, on the estimates of clandestine migration into the USA, Borjas, Freeman and Lang 1991; on irregular employment in the European construction industry, Faist et al. 1999: ch. 4). As to the control over external borders, it is exceedingly hard to distinguish in practice between, say, checking clandestine migrants and drug trafficking.

Issues of external and internal control connect, among other things, through the welfare function of immigration states in the North. External control capacities of immigration states and the degree of internal regulation closely interlink. The lower the capacities and willingness for internal control, the higher the call for restrictive border control policies. By contrast, the higher internal control capacities of immigration states, the lower efforts to engage in very rigorous border control. This means that highly regulated welfare states tend to focus their activities on internal control, while less highly regulated welfare states are characterized by a partial absence of rigorous internal controls. For example, the increased efforts to control the Mexican–US border since the early 1990s is not simply a function of a long, contiguous, and therefore potentially porous border line. Anyway, such a border could only be sealed completely if the country of immigration was willing to use authoritarian police state methods. Institutions such as the Immigration and Naturalization Service (INS) and the Social Security Administration (SSA) do not exchange information on a regular and sustained basis. In Germany, by contrast, institutions such as health insurances, the German Employment Service (BA), and various institutions active in social security do indeed exchange information. It is therefore potentially much harder for undocumented immigrants to work in Germany with fraudulent papers than in the USA (for more examples, see, Vogel 1996).

The linkage of external and internal control is played out in the activities of interest groups. In less highly regulated welfare states, employer associations have a higher ability to consistently advocate special regulations for categories of workers. This leads to a constant balancing of restrictive and expansionist immigration policies. For example, part of the 1986 USA legalization programme—US Immigration Reform and Control Act (IRCA)—foresaw sanctioning employers for employing undocumented immigrants, and, at the same time, gave room for a Special Agricultural Workers (SAW) programme which brought in more workers from Mexico and the Caribbean. It attracted many first-time migrants from Mexico into the US labour force, and thus furthered more undocumented migration on the long run. The policies did not deter additional migration from within Mexico (Cornelius, Mertin, and Hollifield 1994: 34–5), simply because new migrant networks materialized and ran their course. Moreover, employer sanctions and the SAW programme furthered the fraudulent documents industry. This means that restrictive policies can be counterbalanced by measures that further more international migration in the long run. In more highly regulated welfare states consensus over immigration restrictions is usually easier to achieve because of more consensual policy-making (see Chapter 3).

It is no coincidence that—once migration flows have taken full speed—certain categories of international migrants become the object of intense debate over moral issues of acceptance into immigration states. Over the past decades two categories of international migrants have occupied the centre stage of restriction: asylum seekers and undocumented immigrants. Public debates about asylum seekers showed a clear-cut distinction between allegedly legitimate political refugees, on the one hand, and illegitimate economic refugees, on the other hand. In short, the claim of bogus asylum seekers has entered the debate over restrictions in all countries of immigration. Needless to say that such distinctions can rarely be established because the documentation of persecution is often hard to come by, given the irregular nature of refugee flights. Again, the connection of welfare and security figures prominently. This applies to demands to curtail the access of unauthorized immigrants to tax-supported public services, including education and health care. California's disputed Proposition 187 in the mid-1990s is just one prominent example.

In the expressive realm, migration can be seen as a threat to collective identity. This is not necessarily synonymous with threat to the immigration state (Huysmans 1995: 54–6). Rather, it concerns threats to religious and ethnic collectives. The nation involves the most complicated phenomena in this respect: while many countries of immigration base their collective self-conception on the basis of nationhood, the concept and understanding of nation in various states varies widely in its cultural-collective inclusiveness towards newcomers—ranging from states who regard themselves 'nations of immigrants', such as the former white settler colonies, to those who see themselves as 'not a country of immigration', such as some Central European states.

The expressive integration of ethnic, religious, and national collectives in 'we'-groups is certainly not simply constituted by identifying the 'other'. This would be a purely negative form of self-identification which could not integrate 'we'-groups in the long run. Nevertheless, responses to immigration tend to touch upon unfulfiled and problematic characteristics of self-identification. The paradigmatic case is the Chinese exclusion movement in California in the late nineteenth century (Saxton 1971). Considering the relatively minor role of actual economic competition between Chinese and European gold-diggers, and later, the Chinese enclave economy consisting of grocery stores, textile and cigar-making factories, and laundry businesses, the rabid and violent exclusionism directed at the Chinese, ranging from zero immigration (1880s until the end of World War Two) to segregation in all realms of life, calls for explanations going beyond economic competition. It is remarkable that the ideological justification of Chinese exclusion, over and over again, insisted upon their alleged status as contract or even slave labour. When we imagine the importance of the ideal of the small freeholder in the American West of the nineteenth century and the experience of slavery as a negative foil, we can start to comprehend the threat this group of immigrants presented to European settlers in California (Faist 1991).

Given all these inconsistencies in enforcing complete external and internal control in immigration states, but nevertheless overall effective external and internal control measures that do not threaten the integral security and welfare functions of immigration states, it is hard to escape the conclusion that the appearance of control is one of the principal goals of restrictive policies. This provides the fertile ground for the gardeners of meta-politics—populist intermediary organizations such as right-wing anti-immigrant parties. Overall, restrictive policies are not simply the result of hard-to-measure infrastructural limits to the intake capacity of immigration states. Since the transformation of welfare states, the end of the Cold War and the musings in public debates over a 'clash of civilizations', the welfarization and securitization of international migration have quickened. As a consequence, the meta-politics of immigration has created its own dynamics: the more restrictive policies have become, especially towards asylum seekers and undocumented immigrants, the more this has been seen to be proof of the illegitimacy of members of these immigrant categories to be admitted. As a consequence of these ratcheting effects, immigration legislation and practice has become more restrictive, partly counteracting chain migration.

Summing it all up: The S-Shaped Migration Curve

If we represent the inverted U-curve in a cumulative manner, we get an S-shaped curve (Figure 6.4). All steps of the processes so far can be visualized in the S-shaped migration curve. This general third-order curve indicates that there are accelerative and decelerative tendencies inherent in migration processes. The pattern of this curve depends upon factors that arise from the very process of migration itself, thus

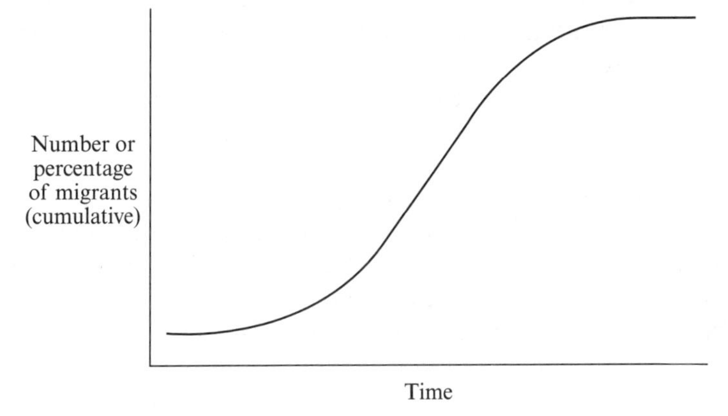

FIG. 6.4. *A stylized S-shaped migration curve*

constantly subverting the expressed original intentions of policy-makers for short-term employment of immigrants or low costs of control at the borders and inside the country although immigration control is quite effective in the long run.

When the process of migration diffusion runs for a sufficiently long time, the frequency of migration almost always follows an S-shaped curve. After pioneer migrants have sowed the seeds, the number of desired exits tends to increase quite rapidly, in fact almost exponentially. There follows an approximately linear increase, until the increase finally slows down and is barely perceptible. These are characteristics of the cumulative number of exits; the number of migrants per time unit—the rate of migration—is the derivative of the cumulative curve, and ordinarily increases to a maximum before decreasing considerably (see also Rogers 1983: 243–5 on general third-order diffusion in social and political life). The total number of migrants grows in a logistic fashion, whereas the temporal pattern of migrant flows follows a bell, i.e. inverted U-shaped curve.

Three phases can be distinguished. The first phase is dominated by the accelerative phase and the problem of start-up costs. The adoption rate is low at the beginning but accelerates as the network expands, and the costs and risks of migration decline due to the increased opportunities of transferability and deployment of various forms of social capital. The second phase, the middle phase, is the period of positive interdependence and growth. As the system develops its own momentum, migration becomes a widely imitated behaviour, and diffusion occurs. The third and last phase is dominated by optimization and self-limiting processes. Immigration flows diminish, as the system becomes saturated. It stops when all potential migrants who wished to move abroad have done so. A turning point is reached. Those with the strongest intentions have already migrated, and those who have not yet done so had weak desires. As a corollary, the composition of migrant flows becomes more heterogeneous over time because migrant networks increasingly encompass all segments of the population of origin. The social diversity, in most cases low at the initial stages of migration, usually increases strongly during the intermediate stages.

However, most international South–North migration flows have not reached their endogenously induced turning points. Instead, public policies of the countries of immigration have curbed flows significantly. As an analysis of two important state functions—welfare and security—suggests restrictive immigration is not simply an outgrowth of immigration reaching a maximum beyond which infrastructural problems arise and the adaptive capacity of the countries of settlement is exhausted. Even more obviously, intermediary organizations such as political parties, populist and nativist groups tie immigration and immigrant adaptation to serious political and policy problems in a globalizing world. While the politics of immigration does not exhaust itself in symbolic politics—collective agents trying to define the terms and images that serve above all strategic and tactical purposes of organizational competition—immigration control and immigrant adaptation serve as a meta-issue: intermediary organizations refer to them as causes of manifold problems in a context of persistent structural unemployment, welfare state retrenchment, and a perceived loss of external and internal security because of growing cross-border traffic (Faist 1994).

The Turkish–German Example: The Unfinished Yet Terminated Migration Curve

Processes of selection and diffusion in the Turkish–German case are of particular interest because the international migration curve has not yet run its full potential course. None the less, mass migration had been practically terminated by the mid-1970s through restrictive admission policies on the German side. Therefore, this case yields unusual insights in how endogenous and exogenous factors have intertwined in shaping the migration curve.

From 1961 to 1974, about 648,000 workers migrated to Germany by passing through German recruitment offices in Turkey—in total, more than 865,000 workers went to Germany. The German authorities estimate that about two-thirds of the legal, newly recruited Turks came under official auspices (1961–71). The balance came mostly as tourists who later legalized their status (Paine 1974: 59–60). In later stages of the migration process, during the 1970s and 1980s, family reunification and marriage migration became prominent, classic instances of how potential and actual migrants moved along social and symbolic ties. In yet a third period, family reunification and marriage migration continued at lower levels, while the number of refugees increased substantially after the military coup in Turkey in 1980. From the early 1980s until the late 1990s, asylum seekers from Turkey ranked year after year second or third in terms of total numbers applying for certified refugee status in Germany (see Figures 3.4 and 3.5).

The Selective and Diffusion Functions of Turkish Migrant Networks: Hemşeri *Ties*

All available evidence implies that urban migrants who dominated the very first phases of international mgration (1961–3) could rely on access to recruitment offices, while later-coming rural migrants heavily depended on kinship and communal ties. In the cases of rural–international migration, these important migrant networks did not arise *ex nihilo* but can be seen as continuations of existing village or neighbourhood networks, based on specific ties. In the villages, these networks lowered transaction costs in controlling the behaviour of villagers regarding the cultivation of land, communal tasks, and proved instrumental to arrange marriages. Generalized reciprocity and diffuse solidarity found in *hemşeri* ties undergirded chain migration.

Hemşerilik—Landsmannschaften in the old German sense of regional connotation, such as Saxons, Hessians, and Swabians—refers to networks of solidary social and symbolic ties that is based on communal or regional ties. Like kinship, it can be thought of as a primordial tie (Dubetsky 1973: 345), albeit in a symbolic way. The interpretation of the range of *hemşeri* ties varies among the people using it. Depending on context and usage, the term denotes fellow-villagers or people from the same region, viz. province.

Chain migration within Turkey, mostly rural–urban migrations, has always progressed within *hemşeri* ties. In the urban destinations of these rural migrants, the *gecekondus*—literally 'built overnight'—*hemşeri* networks provide accommodation and all sorts of material and psychological support to the migrants (Karpat 1976). In a country such as Turkey, where an extensive welfare state has been absent, *hemşeri* networks also offered welfare, mutual help, and support in the big cities—classical expressions of reciprocity and solidarity.

Most Turkish migrants considered friendship and *hemşerilik* on the same level. Interestingly, *hemşeri*, neighbourhood, and migration networks merge. The apogean case is when people of rural origin tend to marry *hemşeris.* In international migration, most migrants followed the footsteps of *hemşeri* pioneer migrants and depended on them: in a representative sample of recruited contract workers in the late 1960s, approximately two-thirds of the sample had either a relative or a friend in Germany before migrating. They received virtually all information from those already working in Germany. Only through the social capital benefit of information could the potential migrants compare their wages with those received for the same job in Germany and not to alternative jobs in Turkey (Aker 1972: 75–99). The reference being wage levels in Germany may explain why two-thirds of the respondent contract workers indicated that insufficient income was the cause of their emigration. However, their average income was more than that of 70% of the Turkish population. Wage differentials between Germany and Turkey were 2.1–5.6 to 1 in the period 1970–1, depending on the specific occupational group. Also, the proportion of the unemployed in this population was negligible. The unemployment rate among labour migrants prior to emigration was only 3%–14%, compared to more than one-third of the total working age population in Turkey (Gitmez 1984). Unemployment was not the main motive. Evidence from another survey among Turkish migrants in Berlin reinforces the image of the crucial role of pioneer migrants. Approximately 28% of labour migrants in Germany found their housing with the help of relatives and friends; another quarter used brokers in travel and interpreters' offices. 62% of Turkish migrants in a mid-1970s sample reported that their relatives, *hemşeris* and friends found jobs for them (Akpnar and Mertens 1977: 77). In other surveys, conducted in the same period, more than 40% of Turks disclosed that they found their apartment through a relative or *hemşeri* (Kleff 1984: 193). Beyond the selective and adaptive functions, *hemşeri* ties underwent a transformation in the city, be it in Turkish *gecekondus* or in German immigrant colonies. These ties lost their grip on people's behaviour and turned into more instrumental devices, both in Turkish (Ayata 1989; see also Magnarella 1972) and German urban contexts (Çağlar 1994). All in all, *hemşeri* ties are important for migration decision-making and timing, the selection at point of origin, the occupational and residential clustering of migrants in the immigration contexts, and finally, the internal organization of migrants' groups and their relations with immigration society in general. *Hemşeri* or similar networks foster international migration beyond narrow kinship groups.

Threshold Effects: Pioneers and Ties

Most of the first migrants destined for Germany left with little reliable information, yet subsequent migrants had much better knowledge of conditions abroad. Among the first migrants, the recruited persons were mainly men, usually 20 to 40 years old, with at least a primary school education. They possessed relatively high occupational skills when compared to the average skill level in Turkey. Many of them had worked as civil servants such as primary schoolteachers, but also as skilled industrial workers, shopkeepers, and some had been self-employed (Abadan-Unat 1964). They hailed from the economically more developed regions of the country (Keyder and Aksu-Koç 1988: 20). In this period, the proportion of urban-based migrants was much higher than that of rural migrants, more than 80% compared to 17% from villages. Migrant networks could barely be found.

Soon, loopholes emerged, increasing chances for network recruitment. The German government abolished the rotation principle, so that workers could stay more than one year in Germany, and fashion closer links to German employers and co-workers. Moreover, responding to an increasing demand by German employers, the German labour administration allowed the direct nomination of workers by German employers via Turkish workers. The selection committees in Turkey did not draw these workers from the official waiting lists. Instead, pioneer migrants—acting as both brokers in the villages of origin during vacation and as gatekeepers in German companies—nominated these workers, mostly activating their *hemşeri* ties if they came from villages in rural areas or were stepwise migrants who had earlier migrated from villages to big Turkish cities. These processes stimulated kinship migration and the migration of fellow-villagers and neighbourhood friends a few years after migration had started, in the mid-1960s. This meant that most contract workers interviewed immediately before departure were step-migrants (Paine 1974: 76, 187–8). They had migrated at least once before in their life but within Turkey (Krane 1975: 161).

In the case of rural emigration, international migration constituted an integral part of stepwise migration, first from rural Turkey to bigger cities and then abroad. Especially in the 1950s migration in Turkey occurred on the internal plane, seasonal pendular migration dominating the scene (Stirling 1974: 209–10). Many migrants left their villages and later on, after having consolidated economically, fetched their family members and settled in the rapidly growing cities (Akkayan 1979: 224). Some evidence suggests that an exploration phase preceded this early phase of massive seasonal migration (Struck 1988: 217). Once they had settled in towns and cities, the exploratory movers, viz. pioneer migrants, procured jobs, accommodation, and other daily necessities for the followers (Karpat 1976: 53–5).

The Formation of Networks: Official Recruitment and Nomination of Workers

Migrants and refugees from Turkey took five major routes entering and settling in Germany and in all of them resources inherent in social and symbolic ties proved important for migration: official recruitment, pioneer migrants giving names to German employers, illegal entry and regularization of status, family reunification and marriage migration, and asylum. In each of these cases broker-centred mobilization of social capital into networks proved essential, albeit in different ways.

Depending on the social and political structure of the emigration region within Turkey and the type of migration, migrant networks emerging during official recruitment and nomination took clientelist structures. Clientelism means that one partner is clearly superior to the other in his capacity to grant goods and services. This implies reciprocal rights and duties between patron and client. It is a clear instance of tightly controlled and centralized social capital. Clientelism is most useful where the formal institutional structure of society is weak and unable to deliver a sufficiently steady supply of goods and services. In south-eastern Anatolia, where Kurdish-speaking groups concentrate, relatively isolated groups who have poor access to power, prestige, or wealth establish a fertile ground for clientelism. The patron, often a wealthy and powerful *ağa*, provides economic aid and protection against both the legal and illegal executions of authority and the client in turn shows respect and loyalty to his patron (Kudat-Sertel 1972).

Emerging clientelist structures can be seen when patrons helped new arrivals to acquire residence and work permits, housing, and help with the tax authorities. We have seen earlier that the higher the stocks of social capital, the lower the transaction costs. Also, lower transaction costs usually favour the reproduction of existing organizational models in the immigration country. Established stocks of social capital and concomitant forms of groups and organization generally have the advantage over innovative solutions in the short term because transaction costs of devising, perfecting, and installing new solutions coming up during migration and post-migration processes exceed the costs of maintaining old ways. One interpretation would be that Turkish workers in Germany who were confronted with language barriers and the problem of getting access to housing and work, would use patrons—such as Turkish businessmen—as intermediaries (Kleff 1984: 244–60).

There are historical precedents: in the Italian *padrone* system, the powerholders had tasks such as financing migration, providing employment, and numerous other services which isolated new arrivals from the American society and kept them dependent. A *padrone* might have acted as a banker, landlord, foreman, scribe, interpreter, legal adviser, or ward boss. His clients bought continuing protection from a public figure who was somewhat subject to community pressure and dependent on its good will (Eisenstadt and Roniger 1984: 271). In Turkish *gecekondus*, political party activists have helped the new rural-born migrants to settle down, to deal with the authorities, to find employment, and even to marry. A particularly powerful weapon in the hands of the party controlling the municipal government has been to tolerate, or even legalize, the illegal squatter houses of the new urban migrants, or to demolish them by strictly implementing the laws. However, unlike the Italian *padrones* in the USA around the turn of the century or strongholders in Turkish *gecekondus*, the Turkish equivalents in Germany did not occupy key positions in the local German establishment. These transplanted networks were thus under constant pressure for readaptation in the country of destination.

Within these clientelist structures, the first two patterns mentioned above—official recruitment and nomination of workers—proved essential for the formation of migrant networks.

(1) Official Recruitment

During the peak of migration, in the late 1960s and early 1970s, the destination side, with the help of Turkish authorities, recruited most workers 'anonymously'. The waiting lists got longer in the mid-1960s as a result of relative frustration—it is estimated that more than one million workers had waiting times up to ten years in 1970 (Paine 1974: 67). The point of departure was the original policy criteria of the German government. German employers looking for Turkish workers applied to the German Employment Service (*Bundesanstalt für Arbeit*, in short: BA) for a specific number and type of worker. When no privileged workers—German citizens and EU nationals—could be found, the BA transmitted the employers' requests to the Turkish Employment Service (TES). TES maintained lists of workers wishing to go abroad for BA representatives in cities such as Istanbul, Izmir, and Ankara. At this stage ties to brokers did not yet prove instrumental and migrant networks were not widespread. This changed when TES altered as a reaction to the expansion of the lists from 500,000 in 1965 when 55,000 migrants were sent abroad, to over 1 million in 1970 when the TES sent 130,000 abroad.

Specifically, the TES decided to prefer applicants from the less developed regions of the country, members of Village Development Co-operatives, and persons from officially designated disaster areas. To achieve this end, they divided Turkey into three socio-economic development categories—developed, developing, and less developed. Persons from less developed regions formally had priority on the waiting lists. In addition, a rotation system supposedly assured that each year another province received priority. Natural disaster areas received special quota (Abadan-Unat 1974: 369–70). Turks interested in going abroad needed a residence certificate to register with TES. A local leader, a *muhtar*, could issue such a certificate, provided that the person had maintained residence for at least six months. Turks with relatives and friends in priority areas sometimes moved to the area just to obtain a second residence permit and thus to augment their chance of being among the chosen few. In these cases the *muhtars* served as brokers. Exchange-based obligations and reciprocal ties of all kinds proved instrumental. None the less, with this turbo chaser, migrant networks evolved in rural areas, based on kinship and communal ties. Because of the late start, workers from the poorest regions in Turkey, especially from villages and small towns, were least likely to have their family with them abroad when Germany stopped recruitment in late 1973 (Wilpert 1992: 179). They had the greatest potential for future entry into Germany because many family members still resided in Turkey. As a result of these policies, the percentage of unskilled workers with minimum education rose sharply, and emigration covered rural areas as well, such as central and south-east Anatolia (Gökdere 1978: 178).

(2) Nomination of Workers

When the German government abolished the rotation principle and allowed nomination of workers by German employers, networks surged. Instead of simply requesting a certain number of Turkish workers, an employer could name or nominate a particular Turkish worker to fill a vacant slot. Since these nominated workers obtained priority from the TES to emigrate, potential migrants asked their relatives already abroad to locate vacant jobs and persuade employers to nominate them. Thus, not only brokers in Turkey but also gatekeepers in Germany, mostly pioneer migrants, proved essential in providing help for later migrants. In the course of these transactions migrant networks evolved. In these cases mostly ties of reciprocity and solidarity were important. It is estimated that about one-third of the legally employed Turkish migrants, who came to Germany between 1967 and 1971, arrived through these channels (Gitmez 1989).

Chain Migration as a Diffusion Process: Tourism and Regularization

The route of entry via tourism, illegal stay, and regularization depended a lot on full-fledged migrant networks. The longer migration proceeded, forms other than recruitment via waiting lists and official referral of gatekeepers also evolved—tourism, illegal stay in Germany and regularization of the status in Turkey, and subsequent return to Germany. This avenue required substantial information, embedded in reciprocal and solidary ties of cooperative *hemşeri* networks. It worked in the following way: potential Turkish migrants obtained tourist passports, emigrated to seek employment, and then regularized their status or worked without authorization. They needed relatives or fellow-villagers to protect their illegal stay in Germany after their tourist visas had expired. When kin members helped them they depended on specific reciprocity or focused solidarity; when fellow-villagers extended a helping hand, they partook in generalized reciprocity or diffuse solidarity. The German *Länder* with the highest concentration of and demand for foreign labour—Hesse, North Rhine-Westphalia, and Baden-Württemberg—enacted legislation which permitted illegal alien Turks to return to Turkey, get proper work and residence documents, and then re-enter Germany. The number and share of such unofficial workers in the 1960s and 1970s is not known by the nature of the process, but one study reported that over 40% of a sample of migrants abroad in the mid-1970s had originally entered as tourists. Observers believe that about 20% of all Turkish migrants until the late 1970s went illegally, and that many of them eventually regularized their status (Martin 1991: 29).

The convertibility of social capital into other resources serves to explain why especially those migrants engaged in migrant networks who had access to only few resources in terms of formal criteria such as education, professional prestige, and money. Gendered variances illustrate this tendency.

Distinguishing along gender lines, we encounter three forms of migration: male, female, and joint migration in couples. In a mid-1980s representative sample drawn from contract workers in the Federal Republic, we find the following composition: male pioneer migrants (76.4%), female pioneer migrants (13.1%), and family migration (10.4%). Most family migrants actually came before the termination of recruitment in 1973 (Özel and Nauck 1987). In all these cases, extensive kinship networks played a crucial role. In most instances, the availability of a tight and extensive kinship system favoured male pioneer migrants. Moreover, the majority of male pioneer migrants came from very religious families, whereas most female pioneer migrants and joint couples came from nuclear and incomplete families. Interestingly, kinship lineage made a difference: if the kinship system of the wife was operative, we find more often female pioneer migrants, and vice versa. Each of these three types had its own climax: men in 1964–5 and 1968–9, women and couples in 1972–3.

Female pioneer migrants came overproportionately from urban centres in less developed provinces, while there is no stable correlation between modernity of province and male pioneer migrants. Most joint migrating couples departed from the urban metropoles. Furthermore, this data not only suggests that there was a continuous and substantial movement of pioneer migrant women, often overlooked. We also learn that most pioneer migrants, either men or women, were unmarried. This is an expected result when considered in the broader life course of persons: for young adults, social and symbolic ties with kinship groups tend to be somewhat weaker before the establishment of a family than thereafter.

As the end of recruitment approached, the pattern of diffusion had changed considerably because of the long waiting lists: conservative Turkish men in rural areas accepted migration of women and joint migration to a much higher degree than before (Abadan-Unat 1985*b*: 208). However, the numerical impact of this pattern should not be overestimated. Out of all female pioneer migrants, only a minority of women engaged in migration along this pattern.

Diffusion processes arose because social capital could substitute economic capital and individual human resources once pioneer migrants were established; this differed among various categories of movers. Pioneer migrants could act as brokers and gatekeepers and lower the amount of economic and human capital necessary for other potential migrants. In her study of two Anatolian villages Engelbrektsson (1978; see Chapter 5) found that from one of the villages—Alihan—migration mostly occurred after the end of recruitment: only one migrant left Alihan to go abroad during the official recruitment phase before 1973; all others came with the help of migrant gatekeepers. In 11 out of 13 cases, later migrants relied on support by pioneer migrants, *hemşeri* ties. For example, pioneer migrants provided the travel money necessary. Other mechanisms chosen included family reunification and marriage arrangements with Swedish women, or obtaining an employer's certification (ibid. 191–8, 221). At first sight, this somewhat contradicts the correct observation that mostly middle-income strata migrated. Yet, as the migration processes and networks matured, this allowed even those without the necessary economic means to migrate. Again, this shows that village and *hemşeri* network ties unfold dynamics not simply determined by larger structures and micro-motives. Here, fellow-villagers both abroad and at home were willing and felt a moral duty to grant practical assistance to those who opted for emigration. In this context, ordered by norms of reciprocity and traditions of solidarity and mutual assistance, personal lack of finances did not necessarily pose a great obstacle for emigration (ibid. 287).

A totally different pattern emerges among emigrants from the other village studied, Yeniköy: international migration did not diffuse. Pioneer migrants exclusively supported members of the their own kinship group. Therefore, non-members of the kinship group could not possibly convert the benefits from reciprocity and solidarity into economic capital. Not surprisingly, the number of migrants from non-kinship groups remained small (ibid. 109). The crucial difference in *hemşeri* ties was that the Alihan migrants considered their group identity abroad primarily in terms of their being members of the same Turkish village, while the Yeniköy migrants in Sweden reckoned their collective identity primarily in terms of being members of the same kinship unit (ibid. 194). The generalized reciprocity and communal solidarity of Alihan movers and stayers starkly contrasted to the specific reciprocity and family or household solidarity of their Yeniköy counterparts.

The diffusion of migration had implications for the pattern of domestic–international migration, too. Stepwise migration increased the likelihood of international migration. In the first years of migration, representative surveys indicate through a comparison of place of birth and place of residence before departure that cities which received most internal migration were also the ones overrepresented in international migration. From 1963 until 1973, the majority of international migrants came from the cities of Istanbul, Ankara, and Izmir (Leopold 1978: 150).

Once pioneer migrants had fostered intensive contacts, step-migration proved unnecessary. Nationwide data on Turkey confirms this claim: in the second half of the 1960s, the proportion of those who directly migrated from rural areas to urban places in Germany without intermediary steps in Turkey increased (Paine 1974: 75–6, 86). However, the proportion of those who directly moved from rural areas to Germany was lower than the proportion who engaged in step-migration before moving to Germany. This can be attributed to the termination of recruitment in 1973.

All of the evidence adduced points to occupational and residential clustering of Turkish immigrants in Germany. Since the evidence is well known by now, suffice it to say that these were the end points of migrant and migration networks. When pioneer migrants helped latecomers to gain admission to Germany, the brokers also catered for jobs. This is true for housing, too, hence the high degree of residential clustering in certain regions and cities in Germany (Jones 1990: 27), and within cities on the neighbourhood level (Esser, Hill, and van Oepen 1983; Wulf 1985).

Cumulative Mobility: The Climax of Endogenous Processes

The principle of cumulative mobility worked as follows in the Turkish case (1961–74): domestic and international migration originated in profound transformations of Turkish industry and agriculture. In the rural areas land was unequally distributed with vast differences between great landholders, on the one hand, and inefficient tenants and small holders engaging in subsistence economy, on the other. The land cultivated became smaller and smaller. Moreover, the number of landless peasants who had to work as labourers increased. Only great holdings had the means to engage in large-scale mechanization, starting in the late 1940s. They could increase productivity, purchasing mechanical power and yields. When the mechanization of agriculture picked up in Turkey during the 1950s, this process displaced peasants and agricultural workers. In addition, expanding great holders bought the land of tenants. All these processes speeded up the concentration of land. Domestic migration to big cities followed; built upon networks developed during seasonal migration since the 1940s (for a case study, see Struck 1984). Many rural villagers responded by migrating to big cities, processes that had gained momentum during the 1950s. Subsequently, in cities such as Istanbul and Izmir, rapid urbanization in the 1950s proceeded much faster than industrialization. In the industrial sectors import substitution ruled supreme and new industries concentrated in Western Turkey around Istanbul and Izmir. Yet its absorption capacity for the rural population proved to be much too low—in spite of a rapidly expanding service sector. In other parts of Turkey, mainly in the south-east, no industry developed (Leopold 1978: 154–63).

In the early 1960s when recruitment from Germany started, no new jobs were available in agriculture and employment elsewhere was scarce. Among those especially hard hit were small holders who were often highly indebted. Only when network diffusion reached deep into villages, did international chain migration emerge directly out of rural villages on a large scale. Before, primarily industrial workers and stepwise migrants from urban areas had participated. Increasingly, the income of those who neither engaged in internal nor international migration came to depend upon extra-village occupation and other sources, like the remittances of migrants.

For the regions of origin diverse effects can be observed, especially in the rural countryside. In the Turkish case, most of these feedback effects worked to increase domestic and international migration. First, in small villages, some return migrants invested in mechanization and used more intensive production methods so that other villagers finally gave up farming (Steinbach 1993: 522). By migrating relatively sooner than others in their system, pioneer migrants and early migrants achieved windfall profits, thereby tending to widen the socio-economic gap between these earlier adopting categories versus laggards. Thus, the early movers got richer, and the later migrants' economic profit was comparatively smaller. As migration became widespread, more households were able to invest in capital-intensive production methods and purchased tractors and farm machinery, partly because actual and potential migrants were reluctant to do farm work in the traditional manner. This prompted rapid agricultural mechanization in Turkey during the 1960s and 1970s (Martin 1991: 30). Nevertheless, many people withdrew from cultivation. In this way, migration exacerbated the falling demand for agricultural labour and accelerated the shift to commercial agriculture. In turn, it also increased permanent departure for Turkish and German cities. Yet these processes can only be observed in those cases when brokers of all kinds—pioneer migrants and, later on, kin and *hemşeri* in Germany—not only accumulated stocks of economic capital but also engaged in utilizing old ties back to their home communities and forged new ones in Germany to employers, bureaucrats, and landlords. The higher the density and strength of *hemşeri* ties, the higher the rate of emigration from particular communities and the higher the degree of residential clustering.

Most studies on the effects of remittances and return migration on the emigration communities agree that migrant income allowed households to improve their material standards of living dramatically but that earnings were spent in relatively unproductive ways. Remittances and savings generally went to current consumption rather than investment, such as the purchase and repair of homes and the acquisition of consumer goods. The little investment that occurred went to small commercial activities that generated little employment (Gitmez 1989). Nevertheless, migrants from rural areas did indeed buy farmland when they were able to do so. However, return migrants who had acquired land, often held it fallow. This was because some of them preferred to continue migrating or they retained this land as a source of security and prestige in the community. When farmland thus became even scarcer for those potential migrants who had remained, even more moved abroad.

Self-feeding effects operated relatively independent of economic factors. The example of successful migrants sometimes encouraged others to migrate as well. It created a sort of bandwagon effect, an example of positive feedback causation. It also increased in areas where farmland did not get scarcer. The interception and termination of recruitment then accelerated the flow of dependents from Turkey into Germany. The latter was a clear effect of the maturing Turkish–German migration system: network variables became an increasingly important reason for the attraction of immigrants, while the impact of economic and political factors in Germany declined (Waldorf 1996).

No Turkish–German Culture of Migration

In the Turkish–German case no veritable culture of migration emerged. Because of effective German admission policies that did not stop but curbed flows, exogenous opportunities for lifestyle migration did not exist for the *hoi polloi*. None the less, family reunification speeded up in later stages of the migration process, with an additional push after recruitment ended.

When family reunification had largely run its course and supply was exhausted in the mid-1980s, marriage migration became relatively more important. Often, this type of migration necessitated more generalized and diffuse ties. First-generation immigrants tried to arrange for the marriage of their offspring, their daughters in particular. Indeed, as late as the early 1990s, many first-generation Turkish immigrants all over Europe still preferred to marry their children to kin over non-kin. Among other things, they expected a relative to behave somewhat more loyal than an unrelated son- or daughter-in-law. Also, kin in rural areas of Turkey often anticipated their extended and remote family members to search for brides and bridegrooms within the wide kinship group first. A refusal on the part of immigrants in Europe was taken as evidence that they do no longer value kinship ties with home. In a study of a Dutch city in the late 1980s, for example, it turned out that half of the brides and bridegrooms of the second generation came from the kinship group in Turkey (Böcker 1994).

Understandably, the pressure of kin in Turkey to obtain a daughter-in-law in Europe increased after recruitment ended. In order to live and work in Europe, marrying the daughter of a migrant was one of the most attractive avenues for young men in their twenties and thirties, the major group of potential migrants. And this was not surprising because the demand for migration did not decrease during the 1980s. If at all, it probably increased in the 1980s as compared to the decade before because structural conditions did not change, this age cohort has numerically become stronger, and migrant networks still existed. However, transaction costs have gone up: over time, some second-generation women have grown more reluctant to be married to remote kin from Turkey. They increasingly want to choose their marriage partner on their own (Schmidt-Koddenberg 1989). Moreover, transnationally operative kinship and *hemşeri* ties grew weaker over the years.

While migration for family reunification can be interpreted as a straight continuation of earlier trends of transnational reciprocity, and marriage migration from Turkey to Germany as a result of continued symbolic and social ties to Turkey, the migration of asylum seekers bears similarities to these two kinds of migration but is yet different. It is similar in that certain political conditions, such as Turkey's unacknowledged civil war and Germany's comparatively liberal asylum laws, have to be seen in the context of mature migrant networks. Many of the asylum seekers already had relatives and friends in Germany. Among the two million Turkish immigrants in Germany in the 1980s, a fourth came from south-eastern Anatolia and can be considered from an ethnic point of view as Kurds. Network mechanisms provided access for activists who were persecuted, targets and victims of persecution, and those who used Germany's asylum regulations to improve their economic fortunes.

Decelerating Migration Flows: Effective Termination of Mass Migration

We can only speculate about the magnitude of migration flows from Turkey to Germany had they not been interrupted by the termination of recruitment and tightened asylum regulations. Based on all other known cases, it is safe to say that in the absence of restraints, migration would have continued on an even higher level than before. It could have been expected to continue snowballing because no endogenously derived turning point can be discerned. Turkish internal migration has still been substantial all through the 1990s. In the late 1980s, the country's population increased by more than 1 million annually, but the urban population grew about 1.5 million each year. This indicates that each year at least 400,000 rural Turks migrated annually to cities from 1980 until 1995. These internal migrants included both families and young men, the majority of which could not be absorbed into the industrial and service sectors (İçduygu 1998: 28). Given the existence of structural conditions conducive to migration, the relevant political and trade ties to Germany, and the preferred status as an associated country to the EU, but above all the mature and self-feeding nature of international migration observed in the Turkish case, it seems safe to speculate that international migration would have increased on an even larger scale than it did during the 1980s and 1990s. However, with the exception of refugee migration, all flows boiled down to a trickle when compared to Turkish-German flows from 1961 until 1973.

The three forms of migration have varying prospects. During the 1980s and 1990s, asylum migration has been of about the same size as family reunification. While it would be presumptuous to predict the future course of asylum migration, family reunification has tended to fall for obvious reasons. The same is true for marriage migration, albeit for somewhat more interesting causes. We have seen that many first-generation parents prefer arranged marriages for their children. However, this preference has slowly changed over the past years. Certainly, the children themselves are nowadays more likely to look for a spouse in Germany. Parent–children relations and thus reciprocal kinship ties have changed considerably from the early migrants to their children about 40 years after the first Turkish immigrants arrived in Germany.

In sum, despite the fact that the Turkish–German migration curve has not yet run its endogenously-patterned course, a decelerating period has been reached before the S-shaped curve had run its course and reached a decelerating stage under its own energy, mainly because of restrictionist policies on the German side (Figure 6.5).

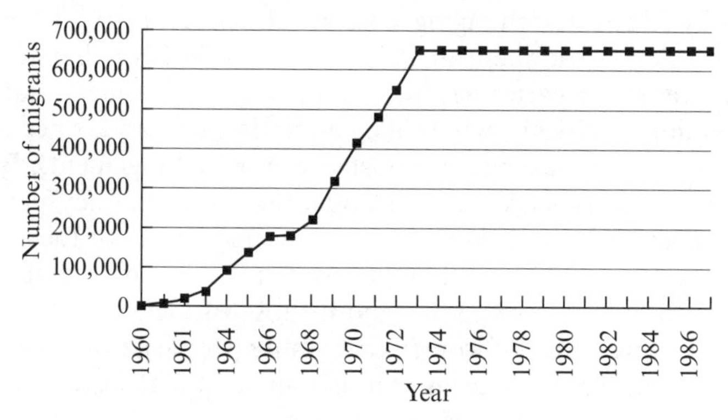

FIG. 6.5. *The unfinished yet terminated Turkish–German migration curve*

German Immigration Policies: Effective Termination of Labour Immigration

The Turkish case and much of contemporary South–North migration differs from the earlier transatlantic labour migration system in the nineteenth and early twentieth century that brought millions of Europeans to the Americas and Australia. Transatlantic mass migration was more migrant-friendly than the international migrations after World War One. The former took place in a world that allowed relatively free migration because white settler colonies looked for population to settle land deemed readily available and to power the production lines of emerging industries. However, World War One and the period after signalled a growing trend of protectionist food, trade, and labour policies. In many countries in Western Europe and in North America welfare state measures called for tighter protection of labour markets. Nowadays, labour recruitment and refugee reception, on the one hand,

and the stop of recruitment and curtailment of refugee inflows, on the other, occur on the basis of occupied land and a high level of social rights of the resident population when compared to the late nineteenth century. The scarcity of resources, potential and actual competition between the newcomers and the settled population, and meta-politics have contributed to a politicization of immigration. The main function of meta-politics has been to strengthen restrictive immigration policies. The impetus for restrictive immigration policies and thus the deceleration of international migration flows caused by exogenous macro-factors can be traced in three realms of state integration in welfare and security: functional cost-benefit calculations, moral questions of justice, and expressive considerations of solidarity and identity.

Viewed in the functional realm of societal integration, the German case vividly illustrates changing cost-benefit perceptions. The end of contract worker recruitment in 1973 marked a decisive change in that labour migrants thereafter had to use other entry channels—including family reunion, political asylum, illegal immigration and, since the late 1980s, increasingly seasonal and posted worker arrangements. Because some contract workers stayed on and others joined, they developed preferences and expectations which in turn made some of them remain in Germany for good. The characteristics relevant for social policies have come to resemble more and more those of German citizens. For example, the percentage of women and young people among the immigrant population has been rising, the labour force participation rate of men has decreased but has increased in the case of women, and employment in services and self-employment has been slowly rising. As the demographic, work and public services use patterns of former labour migrants and their children have adapted to those of German citizens, cost-benefit perceptions have been changing on the part of the latter.

Yet most empirical scholarship on costs-benefits associated with immigrant integration is inconclusive—making it a fertile field for meta-politics. Studies have consistently pointed out the overall beneficial aspects of immigrant employment for the native German population, such as increased mobility of German blue-collar workers into white-collar employment as a result of guestworker-recruitment and employment in the 1960s and 1970s (Heckmann 1981: 166). Numerous studies have confirmed that foreigners are net contributors to social insurance schemes such as pension funds. Moreover, some results suggest that during the late 1980s and early 1990s non-citizens have received much less in tax money than they contributed (Barabas 1992). A position favourable to immigration emphasizes the economic-demographic benefits immigrants provide for the host country. In regard to social security, it could be argued that declining birth rates in advanced industrial countries necessitate new immigration in order to pay for the pensions of retirees. Two arguments recur again and again: first, immigrants are a net benefit for public budgets because they pay more in taxes than they get in return in the form of services and social insurance. A typical calculation goes like this: In 1989 immigrant workers paid 12.8 billion Marks (8%) into pension funds, while immigrants only received pensions amounting to 3.7 billion (2%). Thus, immigrants pay about the amount that corresponds to their share in the total population, while they benefit much less (Rehfeld 1991). Second, contract workers and, later, ethnic Germans have stimulated the economy, especially in buying consumer goods, because they tend to be younger than the German population. A plausible conclusion derived from such arguments is that developed countries such as Germany need not fewer but perhaps even more immigrants (Hof 1993).

Costs to German taxpayers have been much more visible in the case of asylum seekers than contract workers. But even here it is hard to find conclusive evidence on costs and benefits. Research on labour market participation of recognized refugees and asylum seekers is too scarce to allow firm conclusions. Most of the debate focused on means-tested social assistance (*Sozialhilfe*) granted to asylum seekers. At first sight, if we look at total numbers, the percentage of non-citizens compared to German citizens receiving public assistance looks impressive. Although foreigners made up only 8.3% of the total population in 1991, their percentage of recipients of one type of means-tested public assistance, Aid to Subsistence (*Hilfe zum Lebensunterhalt*), was close to 15%. By comparison, about 5% of the German population received this type of assistance (Statistisches Bundesamt 1993: 513). Most of the non-citizens drawing assistance were asylum seekers. An unprecedented number of asylum seekers entered Germany during the late 1980s and early 1990s; in 1992, the number had reached a climax with 438,000 before it started receding. Therefore, the financial burden for the local communities who are responsible for housing and other services to asylum seekers rose drastically. Impressive as these numbers look at first sight, they exaggerate the dependence of non-citizens on welfare. Most of the non-citizen recipients were asylum seekers and since the mid-1990s ethnic Germans, not former contract workers. Also, in the early 1990s the government drastically cut benefits that accrued to asylum seekers. Since 1993 asylum seekers do not even have access to regular means-tested public assistance. They are only entitled to a limited set of social assistance benefits, such as a reduced form of Aid to Subsistence according to the *Asylbewerberleistungsgesetz* (*Deutsches Ausländerrecht* 1998: 263–9).

The second realm pertains to moral questions of social justice. An immigrant can be entitled to full social rights (denizen) without being a full member of the polity (citizen). This effectively means a decoupling of rights and duties, on the one hand, and nationality, on the other. This situation raises conflicts in the ethical and moral dimensions of welfare state integration. First, the dominant perception is that although there are universal human rights, social rights are ultimately tied to membership in the national polity. The increasing presence of non-citizens and their access to social rights thus raises the question of welfare state solidarity, of who is to be included. For example, in nationalist-populist views the foremost duty of the welfare state is to guarantee the decent livelihood of its own citizens before rights or claims are granted to non-members or those who aspire to become members. In effect, immigration and its consequences then become a question of social justice. In this view, migrants will be allowed to stay in the host country for only a short period of time. Accordingly, immigrants could claim only the most basic civil rights and certainly no political rights. Second, this immediately brings up another question: Whose rights are recognized?

The third realm concerns expressive considerations—collective representations—and involves the question of solidarity with whom? Debates over the effects of immigration on wages, unemployment, social security, education, and social services have increasingly been cast in 'we' vs. 'them' distinctions which fall along ethnic lines, albeit to varying degrees. There is a recurring argument that it is 'we', the taxpayers who pay for 'them', the immigrants of developing countries that are allegedly flooding welfare states in the West. Perceptions of increasing costs involved in recognizing social rights of newcomers tend to be associated with certain immigrant groups and not others. In particular, refugees from non-European developing countries seem to be seen as contributing to rising costs. 'We' vs. 'them' distinctions have long been a feature of the German national state and discrimination based on race a main feature of twentieth-century politics—of course, most explicitly so during the Nazi regime. However, political conflicts in the post-war welfare state were not demarcated along ethnic lines. Current debates thus have an expressive dimension that has been missing in post-war German welfare state politics.

What the national welfare state offers to its members, is not only a bundle of rights. The national welfare state also offers a sense of belonging. This belonging is located at the level of the nation-state.

While immigrants may seek to benefit and usually do at least partly so from individual rights of citizcnship, they may be excluded from this second meaning of citizenship. The main point is that the degree of perceived social distance in terms of nationality, religion, or ethnicity does serve as a criterion for informally evaluating the claims of immigrants for social rights and provisions. It is evident that in this sense ethical considerations have started to play an important role in welfare state politics once cost-benefit perceptions changed in the course of labour migrant employment, settlement, and the arrival of asylum seekers.

There is a probably changing rank ordering of national or ethnic groups which compete for admission, work, and settlement in the receiving welfare states. The most important question concerns the changing perceptions of social distance towards immigrant groups. They may be reinforced or weakened over time. They heavily depend upon the perception of costs and benefits of incorporating a particular group. Of particular importance are processes of the reproduction of social distance. In some cases, for example, social distance towards non-European labour migrants has been reproduced since the 1960s (e.g. Turks); in the case of workers from the southern European periphery (e.g. Italians), high degrees of social distance have been reduced (D. Fuchs, Gerhards, and Roller 1993). One of the main questions for empirical analysis is how perceptions of social distance change depending on different immigration policies. The reproduction of the rank ordering could depend upon the functions the receiving countries ascribe to migrants and the evolving ethnic and national solidarities of immigrant and immigration communities. For example, workers performing temporary work may come from countries or belong to groups that are placed very low on a scale of ethnic-national preference. At the opposite end of the spectrum are policies that give explicit preference to groups whose collective characteristics are seen, at least initially, as similar to the dominant group in the immigration country. This is the case with respect to immigrants considered to be permanent, like ethnic Germans from Eastern Europe.

In addition to these endogenous effects arising from immigration and integration, the changing scale of welfare state redistribution has contributed to a politicization of immigrant social rights. In welfare states citizens are not only integrated through political rights but also through social rights and benefits. Social rights entail claims to scarce resources such as social security, education, and social services. Political inclusion into the welfare state depends on the extent to which the distributional activities of the welfare state are considered to be legitimate and are accepted by the populace (Bommes and Halfmann 1998). In times of sluggish economic growth or recession, distributional struggles about scarce redistributional resources intensify. Immigration can serve as a rallying point around which the issues of redistribution and political inclusion in the welfare state crystallize. Indeed, the experience of the settlement of labour migrants and refugees, and very high levels of immigration give more opportunities for political actors to voice dissatisfaction and demands with welfare state politics and policies because the effects of immigration on natives in areas such as work, housing, social services, education, and health care are far from clear-cut.

The security function of states and its ramifications for restrictive immigration policies has recently nicely converged in the 'Fortress Europe' metaphor. It summarizes the security fears of politicians, policy-makers, and the populace. Generally, there is a widespread argument that border controls in the EU before abolishing many frontiers were effective. But in a borderless internal market Europe will be swamped by migrants unless tough measures are taken. In this view, functionally, the link between immigration and illegal activities such as crime—including smuggling of human cargo—is a prime question (for evidence on the activities of the transnational mafia in exploiting unauthorized migrants, see Thamm and Freiberg 1998). In the normative realm, the possibility that immigrants—and here especially asylum seekers and unauthorized immigrants—exploit social services and welfare is seen as a grave threat. Finally, in the expressive realm, the discussion focuses on the link between immigration and instability caused by xenophobia and racism which presumably is on the rise because of high numbers of immigrants. In the absence of direct borders with the South, the EU borders—especially towards the Mediterranean—have become important for German policy.

The loss of border controls between selected EU Member States, for example through the Schengen agreement, has led law enforcement authorities to partially suspend their traditional reliance on the filter function of border controls. As compensation, EU authorities determined to introduce a series of compensatory measures capable of minimizing the risk of a growing 'internal security gap'. Among other things, we can observe a plethoric development of working groups in the EU and on the European Council. For instance, the so-called Trevi group originally only covered terrorism. Later on it added concern over illegal immigration. This change has been symptomatic for the linkage between diverse aspects of a security problem internal to the EU: drugs, terrorism, and migration connect to each other. However, it is doubtful whether these many uncoordinated working groups have contributed to effectively coordinated policing of borders and internal territories of Member States.

In the absence of a common European migration policy, national and supranational institutions have engaged mostly in ad hoc security strategies. There has been no transfer of authority to regulate labour migration to the supranational level. Intergovernmentalism continues to be the dominant mode of coordination, as Member States have remained the major players in this game (Collinson 1994). Nevertheless, supranational institutions have made some efforts at a common policy, which can be perceived as an important agenda-setting. The European Community measures regarding immigration are included in each of the three 'pillars' of the Maastricht Treaty (1991). The first pillar, the treaty provisions concerning Community matters, include an article (100c) stating that the Council of Ministers 'shall determine the third countries whose nationals must be in possession of a visa when crossing the external borders of the member states'. The second pillar (foreign and security issues) touches, albeit indirectly, upon migration questions because the document relates security issues to the spatial movement of persons. The third pillar (intergovernmental cooperation in justice and home affairs) lists the areas that 'member states shall regard . . . as matters of common interest'. These matters include asylum policy, rules governing the crossing of external borders, immigration policy; policy regarding nationals of third countries, more specifically conditions of entry and movement, residence, family reunion and access to employment; and unauthorized immigration. The development of a common migration policy in Europe concentrates on three main policy lines: (1) action on the causes of migration pressure; (2) action on controlling immigration flows; and (3) action to strengthen the integration policies for legal immigrants (EC Communication 1994: 1b–1c). Overall, then, policy-makers on the nation-state level have accepted the free movement of labour and services under the umbrella of enhanced economic liberalism and eased the barriers of migration to EU citizen-workers. However, nation-states have not lost their sovereignty concerning the conditions of admission and employment of third country people.

To the extent that within the EU nation-state borders have diminished in importance because of agreements such as Schengen, the emphasis on internal controls has grown. For example, police forces have significantly stepped up capacities for internal control, such as increased checks in border regions: German border security police forces can now patrol a larger section of territory near the borders. Overall, there has been a slow shift from border and community policing to policing using more sophisticated criminal intelligence services. Other internal controls include measures such as intensified inter-agency cooperation and the exchange of information and the introduction of identity cards for non-citizen and citizen workers.

As to normative issues of justice and crime, no hard data exists to show that migrants threaten the lawful fabric of immigration states. Indeed, the two main categories of migrants charged with crime—asylum seekers and illegal immigrants—are unlikely candidates. Indeed, it is more feasible to assume that illegal immigrants who seek illicit employment and/or residence are less likely to commit crimes, so that they can avoid contact with the police (Bovenkerk 1992: 89, cited in den Boer 1995: 102). However, we would expect that members of these two categories are more likely to engage in offences only foreigners can commit, such as labouring without working permits, or working without a residence permit. And this is indeed what can be gleaned from the official statistics in Germany in the 1970s and 1980s. While crime rates of non-citizens have gone up comparing German citizens and foreigners between 1970 and 1989, there is a remarkable trend. More than 80% of the crimes committed by foreigners concerned asylum and residence permit offences. Certainly, German citizens could not commit those crimes. Moreover, when controlling for socio-economic status, the crime rate of foreigners is not higher than among Germans (Piehler 1991).

Concerning the expressive realm of security, there are two recurrent arguments in public debates, the control-adaptation thesis and the control-racism proposition. First, one justification for stricter border controls has emerged in the debate over resident *extracommunitari* in the EU. This policy proposition—forcefully argued not only by nation-state governments but also by the EU Commission and the European Parliament—is that strict oversight of new immigration is necessary in order to advance and secure the integration of these (foreign) immigrant populations and avoid the formation of ethnic ghettos. In short, the proponents claim that a successful immigrant adaptation, viz. integration policy, depends on strict entry control. Adaptation can be most easily defined in terms of labour market integration, using statistical indicators such as unemployment rates, income, and labour force participation. Full adaptation, then, would be said to have occurred if immigrants were to have rates of labour force participation, unemployment levels, and average incomes close to those of natives. According to these indicators, however, it appears that immigrant populations in the EU are disadvantaged, albeit with significant cross-country variations and differences between various immigrant groups (Werner 1994).

Second, there is the claim of a causal link between tight border and internal controls, on the one hand, and the absence or low rate of racist and xenophobic attacks, on the other hand. However, this link cannot be established empirically. For example, in the early 1990s, racist violence in Britain was at levels similar to Germany, although the UK had a much tighter regime of immigration control (Thränhardt 1993: 338).

All these selected examples suggest that international migration does not pose a grave security threat to the immigration states. Nevertheless, the issues are real in the sense of average increases to be expected in any kind of broder-crossing transactions—but they also become exaggerated in the meta-politics linking international migration to a host of domestic problems such as rising crime rates and a wider array of transnational exchanges crossing nation-state borders.

Conclusion: International Migration as Metamorphosis

Once begun, migration eventually develops an infrastructure that enables movement on a mass basis. Migrants transfer local assets internationally by means of networks of cooperation. Over time, the number of social and symbolic ties between areas of origin and destination grows, establishing migrant networks. All of them progressively reduce the risks and costs of international movement. People from the same kinship group and community are enmeshed in a web of reciprocal obligations upon which new migrants draw to enter and find shelter and work in the immigration society.

The application of the principle of positive feedback cumulative causation on the meso level has increased our understanding of the first puzzle of simultaneously and relatively little international migration yet massive chain migration within certain regions. Increased opportunities for migration abroad immediately raise expectations among potential migrants. But a change in the level of information, control, and access to other resources is achieved more slowly, and its effects on the other factors are delayed, so that there is a lag in the whole process of cumulation. Of special importance for these metamorphic developments is generalized reciprocity and diffuse solidarity. They are responsible for the rapid diffusion effects in modern international migration. Regarding future empirical studies, this evidence calls for a closer consideration of ties which reach beyond ties of narrow kinship groups.

These ties and corresponding networks eventually crystallize as new transnational linkages. It is a sort of ratcheting effect because one of the prerequisites for migration is usually pre-existing linkages between emigration and immigration states. Migrant networks emerge, maintained and sustained by ongoing processes of return whereby migrants and sometimes even refugees move back and forth between countries of origin and destination. Even settled migrants remigrate back to the emigration countries. While nation-states are not pusillanimous when it comes to the regulation of migration, the very policies that are meant to restrict additional migration often turn out to stimulate new forms of migration, although they effectively curb older patterns. All of this suggests that it is useful to analytically separate the endogenous dynamics of migration from macro-level structures and micro-level desires.

Most often, the endogenous dynamics of migration flows do not reach their internally induced turning point. They are primarily affected by welfare and security policies in the immigration countries. The welfare and security functions of the state do not only form a backdrop for restrictive policies. They also tie in with the symbolic politics of migration and immigrant adaptation which are amenable to immigration as a meta-issue.

7

The Bridging Function of Social Capital: Transnational Social Spaces

> *The people who first built a path between two places performed one of the greatest human achievements. (. . .) This achievement reaches its zenith in the construction of a bridge. Here the human will to connection seems to be confronted not only by the passive resistance of spatial separation but also by the active resistance of a special configuration. By overcoming this obstacle, the bridge symbolizes the extension of our volitional sphere over space. Only for us are the banks of a river not just apart but 'separated'; if we did not first connect them in our practical thoughts, in our needs and in our fantasy, then the concept of separation would have no meaning. But natural form here approaches this concept as if with a positive intention; here the separation seems imposed between the elements in and of themselves, over which the spirit now prevails, reconciling and uniting.*
>
> (Georg Simmel, 'Bridge and Door', in *Spatial and Urban Culture*, 171)

The interests, passions, and ideas undergirding and the resources inherent in social and symbolic ties can traverse nation-state borders for decades. As we have seen, migrant and migration networks help sustain international migration, even superseding initiating factors. They explain the quantitative leap from 'why so few out of so many places?' to 'why so many out of so few places?' These processes of critical mass also induce a qualitative leap: transnational networks precipitate full-fledged transnationalization, predisposing locally bound social spaces to further border-crossing transitions.

Examples are plentiful: Muslims from Morocco and Algeria who reside in France exchange religious instructors with the countries of origin. These imams contribute to a pluralization of the French religious landscape (Wihtol de Wenden 1997). Kurdish organizations in Germany, the Netherlands, and Sweden are trying to influence Turkish politics. Politicians from Mexico, the Dominican Republic, and Haiti campaign in Los Angeles and New York City for national elections (Guarnizo 1994). Their prospective voters are permanent residents or citizens of the USA. And quite tellingly, some migrant groups engage in recurrent international migration. Nurses from Jamaica work in New York City hospitals while their mothers rear the children in the Caribbean. The children, in turn, spend some of their childhood in the Big Apple (Brown 1997). Moreover, the second generation sometimes traverses borders to transfer their syncretist practices. The German-based and now disbanded rap group 'Cartel', made up of children of Turkish contract workers in Germany, toured Turkey in the summer of 1995 and replaced Michael Jackson as number 1 in the Turkish hit charts.

All these examples point towards circular, regular, and sustained flows of persons, goods, information, and symbols that has been triggered and reinforced by international labour migration and refugee movements. These spaces of flows include not only the bodily circulation of people but also multiple transactions of ideas, monetary resources, goods, symbols, and cultural practices (M. Smith and Guarnizo 1998: 19). In a first step, we need to establish the reality of transnational social spaces. The question is how such transnational phenomena can be described and categorized, and how their emergence is to be explained. A further question is whether these phenomena are limited to the first generation of migrants. Or, have the 1.5, second and third generations developed their own forms of transnational linkages? If this is the case, then transnational spaces are of utmost importance when considering long-term processes of migrant adaptation. The analysis of transnational social spaces then raises the questions of how durable the bridging effects of transnational linkages and ties are, how these bridges come about, and what their effects are on the congruence of places, viz. territories, peoples, the politics of membership and cultures—all time-honoured assumptions of political and social theorists. This makes it necessary to dissect the interstices between local, nation-state, and global elements in economic, political, and cultural activities of migrants.

In particular, territoriality as geographical propinquity can be thought—among other factors, such as a shared common interest and a common language—to be conducive to the formation of groups and communities. For example, English trade unions first organized along patterns such as location, e.g. cities. Later, trades such as carpenters replaced location as an organizing principle (Simmel 1955: 128–30). Therefore, transnational social spaces present an unexpected puzzle: general findings in social network research suggest that geographic distance and infrequent contact increase the difficulty of maintaining strong social ties (Wellman and Wortley 1990). Social theorists have relentlessly emphasized that to constitute social life morally, social transactions must be the conduit where norms, values, and standards come to be common or shared in nature. Transactions must be regular, frequent, and meaningful. The respective social and symbolic ties have to be intimately enough in contact to act and react (Durkheim 1964: 262). The development of transnational social spaces thus offers a unique opportunity to look into the formation of groups that span at least two nation-states.

International migrants living in transnational social spaces form networks, groups, and 'communities without propinquity' (Webber 1963). From an even larger view, the process of separation of space from place is essential to modernization. The advent of modernity has increasingly torn away space from place by fostering relations between absent others, locationally distant from any given situation of face-to-face interaction. Some analysts interpret large collectives such as nation-states not only as a social structure with distinctly defined borders, but also as a particular form, level, and moment of a continuing 'time space distanciation' (Giddens 1991: 14–19), in which rule evolved from direct face-to-face forms to bureaucratic oversight. One of the questions is by what principles geographical propinquity, the embeddedness of ties in place, is supplemented in modern phenomena such as transnational social spaces. What are significant relations, like being dis-embedded from one particular locality and re-embedded in distanciated relationships? It seems that physical location and geographical distance are not the only grid upon which migrants map collective political action, cultural codes, and economic cooperation.

These questions point towards our second puzzle, concomitant transnational social spaces and immigrant adaptation in immigration countries, and lead us to two propositions guiding the analysis in this chapter:

1. Transnational social spaces consist of combinations of ties and their contents, positions in networks and organizations, and networks of organizations that can be found in at least two geographically and internationally distinct places. The reality of transnational exchanges indicates that migration and return migration are not definite, irrevocable, and irreversible decisions; transnational lives in themselves may become a strategy of survival and betterment. We then speak of transmigrants. And even those migrants who have settled for a considerable time in the immigration country can entertain strong transnational links and may thus participate in transnational social spaces.

2. Over time, transnational links can concatenate in various forms of

transnational social spaces—transnational reciprocity in kinship groups, transnational circuits in exchange-based networks, and transnational communities such as diasporas, characterized by high degrees of diffuse solidarity. Among the prerequisites for durable transnational social spaces such as transnational communities are regular and sustained long-distance communication and travel, contentious minority politics in the countries of emigration, perceived discrimination on the part of the migrants in the countries of immigration, helped by the absence of forced assimilation and perhaps even generous multicultural policies.

The first part of this chapter defines transnational social spaces and establishes a typology. The second outlines some causal macro-factors that have opened up opportunities for migrants to build transnational spaces to a greater extent than before the 1970s. Third, the discussion presents some causal chains leading from migration to transnational reciprocity and transnational circuits further on to transnational communities. Three forays into the empirical realm serve to sketch the lineaments of transnational social spaces, focusing on the German and neglecting the Turkish end: the emergence of Turkish business niches in Germany and transnational businesses spanning both countries; efforts of some Kurdish groups to establish a homeland called Kurdistan; and collective identity in the religious realm, involving Islamic thought and organizations, but also secular forms of everyday culture. Fourth, the chapter concludes with a discussion of factors that may limit the future growth of transnational social spaces.

The Concept of Transnational Social Spaces

In conceptualizing transnational social spaces, we connect two essential aspects of transnational phenomena, using Georg Simmel's metaphor as a point of departure (see the quadripartite typology in Figure 7.1): on the one hand, there are issues related to the blocking or permitting aspects of external borders of nation-states and their internal gates, such as access to rights and services. These are the doors. They connote formal aspects of nation-state policies, for instance, exit and entry visas, immigration regulations, integration policies such as rules of citizenship acquisition and informal aspects, social distance (Bogardus 1959) in ethnic, racial, religious, regional, or cultural dispositions, opinions, and stereotypes. Many of these issues regularly become contentious during the process of settlement. On the other hand, we find phenomena

Spatial dimensions of analysis *Degree of policy formalization*	Doors blocking or permitting exit, admission and (re-) adaptation	Bridges attraction and linkages traversing nation-state borders
Institutionalized	exit and entry visas, immigration regulations, passport laws, asylum and refugee regulations, access to citizenship; in general: hostile, receptive, or indifferent government policies	labour recruitment; regional labour migration regimes; international social and labour standards; partial international regime for asylum seekers
Informal	expressions of social distance: negative or positive ethnic, racial, religious, cultural, regional stereotypes; (non-) prejudiced reception of newcomers; ties to brokers and gatekeepers	migrant networks of social and symbolic ties; migration networks; economic, cultural, and social linkages between groups and non-governmental organizations within regional migration systems

FIG. 7.1. *Bridges and doors in international migration*

connecting organizations, groups, and networks in and between nation-states by bridges. Viewed from a formal institutional vantage point, these include binational labour recruitment, partial international regimes dealing with refugees but also informal dimensions, such as the omnipresent migrant and migration networks. Pre-migration linkages and ties fostered by migration congeal in emergent economic, political, and cultural patterns—transnational social spaces.

The examples mentioned above attest to the ability of migrants to creatively pattern their personal and collective experience. We need to develop concepts that can be applied not only in either the emigration or the immigration regions but also refer to emerging transnational linkages, such as those between Algeria–France, India–the United Kingdom, Turkey–Germany, and Mexico and the Caribbean–USA (see e.g. Basch, Schiller, and Blanc 1994: 8; Smith and Guarnizo 1998; and Pries 1996). Transnational social spaces consist of combinations of sustained social and symbolic ties, their contents, positions in networks and organizations, and networks of organizations that can be found in multiple states. These spaces denote dynamic processes, not static notions of ties and positions. Cultural, political, and economic processes in transnational social spaces involve the accumulation, use, and effects of various sorts of capital, their volume and convertibility: economic capital, human capital, such as educational credentials, skills and know-how, and social capital, mainly resources inherent in or transmitted through social and symbolic ties.

The reality of transnational social spaces indicates, first, that migration and re-migration are not definite, irrevocable, and irreversible decisions. Transnational lives in themselves may become a strategy of survival and betterment. Second, even those migrants and refugees who have settled for a considerable time outside the country of origin frequently entertain strong transnational links. Third, to varying degrees activities in transnational spaces escape the control of the nation-states involved (see the earlier analyses dealing with transnational companies, Keohane and Nye 1977).

The transnational social spaces inhabited by immigrants and refugees and immobile residents in both countries thus supplement the international space of sovereign nation-states. Transnational social spaces are constituted by the various forms of resources or capital of spatially mobile and immobile persons, on the one hand, and the regulations imposed by nation-states and various other opportunities and constraints, on the other; for example, state-controlled immigration and refugee policies, and institutions in ethnic communities. Transnational social spaces consist of pentagonic relationships between the government of the immigration state, civil society organizations in the country of immigration, the rulers of the country of emigration (sometimes viewed as an external homeland), civil society groups in the emigration state, and the transnational group—migrants and/or refugee groups, or national, religious, and ethnic minorities. For example, quite a few countries of emigration have recently reacted to transnationalization and the wishes of immigrants for border-crossing recognition in adapting their citizenship rules and allowing for dual citizenship, and trying to sustain the flow of remittances and create investment avenues for citizens and their children from abroad. This has forced governments and publics in the immigration states to consider whether or not to tolerate dual citizenship.

To recall, the various forms of social capital have two important characteristics: first, they are very hard to transfer from one country to another, they are primarily local assets. However, if transnational networks and chain migration emerge in the course of migration, the transferability of ties enabling obligations, reciprocity, solidarity, and carrying the potential for information flows and control increases.

Second, the various forms of social capital provide transmission belts that link groups and networks in separate nation-states—if migrant and migration networks are available. They can do so because they are crucial mechanisms for applying other forms of capital. Resources inherent in social and symbolic ties are necessary to mobilize economic and human capital, not only among those short of financial capital. And frequently, immigrants need social ties to established immigrants or brokers to find work—to employ their human capital such as vocational skills and educational degrees in the immigration country. When transnational social spaces emerge out of migratory flows, even the return to the country of emigration may not be permanent, as many older migrants temporarily migrate in the opposite direction in order to secure their medical needs in the countries in which they once worked and some of their children or other kin still live. These forms of recurrent migration or transmigration would not be possible without intra-kinship obligations and reciprocity. Thus, social capital is crucial in the formation of an enduring and circular flow of people, information, and goods between countries and hence fulfils a bridging function.

Transnational social spaces develop in two stages. In a first phase they are a by-product of international migration and seem to be basically limited to the first generation of migrants. Migration does not simply involve a transfer from one place to another with few social and material links. Moreover, migrants do not automatically sever their ties with the emigration countries. Rather, pre-migration linkages such as post-colonial and hegemonic relations abound and, in turn, migration processes themselves usually generate continual exchanges between geographically distant communities. Only by the creation and reproduction of networks of migrants do migration flows turn into chain migration and thus become mass phenomena. Migrant networks, interacting with groups and institutions in the areas of destination and origin, form the raw material for the formation of new ethnic communities. Furthermore, international migrations result in continual processes of return migration, where recurrent migrants regularly go home for varying periods each year, or migrants return for good to their communities of origin.

In a second phase—the emphasis of this chapter—transnational social spaces go beyond strictly migratory chains of the first generation of migrants and develop a life of their own. This should be seen in the context of generational succession. Even among first-generation migrants we may be able to see a shift of transnational ties from sending home remittances to building businesses engaged in emigration–immigration country trade. And second- and plus generations can continue transnational ties and develop new forms of border-crossing links. For example, migrants might combine cultural practices from both or even additional countries, such as special brands of hip-hop among Turkish youth raised in Germany, or those of Algerian descent in France.

An adequate explanation of the formation of transnational social spaces has to start from the cumulation of migration processes, the maintenance of ties to the country of origin, and the adaptation of immigrants in the immigration country. A qualitative leap occurs when transnational social spaces come to be characterized by self-feeding processes, above all positive feedback mechanisms. As Gunnar Myrdal has pointed out, the direction of the initial kick is very important in all processes of cumulation (Myrdal 1957: 14). It determines the direction of the further development of transnational social spaces. In our case, the original push has been the onset of international South–North migration, transnational ties and migration in both directions. One of the effects has been the transnationalization in the economic, political, and cultural realms for migrants and immobiles in migration systems.

Three Forms of Transnational Social Spaces

What needs to be described is the formation of transnational social spaces, ranging from rather short-lived exchange relationships to long-lived transnational communities. Transnational social spaces are responses which start from dispersion in the wake of violent conflicts and repression, or the expansion of labour and trade. Taking the density of ties and linkages as a point of departure, we can identify three forms of transnational social spaces: transnational reciprocity in small groups, transnational exchange in circuits, and diffuse solidarity within transnational communities (see Figure 7.2).

(1) Transnational Kinship Groups

Reciprocity in transnational kinship groups is typical for many first-generation labour migrants and refugees. Reciprocity can be seen, for example, in remitters sending back money to members of his or her kinship group in the country of origin; especially in those cases when territorial exit is part of a strategy including economic survival or betterment among migrants and those who stay behind—migration as a sort of informal risk insurance. In those cases the migrants remit money to those who run household affairs in the sending place. Often,

Types of transnational social spaces	Primary resources in ties	Main characteristic	Typical examples
Transnational kinship groups	*reciprocity* what one party receives from the other requires some return	upholding the *social norm* of equivalence; control over members of small groups	*remittances* of household or family members from country of immigration to country of emigration: e.g. contract workers
Transnational circuits	*exchange* mutual obligations and expectations of the actors; outcome of instrumental activity (e.g. the tit-for-tat principle)	exploitation of *insider advantages*: language; strong and weak social ties in peer networks	*trading networks*, e.g. Chinese, Lebanese, and Indian business people
Transnational communities	*solidarity* shared ideas, beliefs, evaluations and symbols; expressed in some sort of collective identity	mobilization of *collective representations* within (abstract) symbolic ties: e.g. religion, nationality, ethnicity	*diasporas*: e.g. Jews, Armenians, Palestinians, Kurds

FIG. 7.2. *Three types of transnational social spaces arising from international migration and flight*

seasonal, recurrent, and eventual return migration are part of these strategies.

Transnational families are a specific expression of transnational ties, with relations not only between dispersed family members back home but also among each other. Thus, for example, transnational families can be found among human capital migrants (Gunatilleke 1997). They differ from labour migrant households in several respects. The persons involved generally have high occupational skills, an advanced educational degree and proficiency in an international language such as English. This high amount of human capital eases movement between countries, and increases the prospects of being accepted as permanent residents. After all, desirable immigration countries such as Canada and

Australia have based their admission policies for immigrants on point systems that accord priority to skills and funds to be invested. None the less, social capital is crucial: it is usually the kin network that establishes exemplary niches in the international labour market. Once a member of the family has migrated, others follow to emulate the example. This is different, however, from labour migrants who tend to congregate in one place abroad or cluster in one destination country.

A widespread phenomenon are multilocal families in two nation-states, with parents and children distributed in households across nation-state borders. It can take two forms. First, parents may live abroad with some or none of their children while other offspring reside in the emigration countries in households headed by relatives or non-relatives. This is common among Caribbean migrants (Guarnizo 1994). Another case is the international commuter marriage among professionals with husbands returning from the USA to Korea for a lucrative job while wife and children remain in the United States to take advantage of the educational opportunities there. The family members visit each other several times a year and communicate via fax, phone, and internet (Min 1998). Second, there are older migrants who return to the country of origin while their adult children and grandchildren stay in the immigration country (see e.g. Dietzel-Papakyriakou 1993: 81–5)—these are processes which can be observed all over the world. Over time, kinship ties stunningly cross national boundaries. For example, by the end of the 1980s, about half of all adult Mexicans were related to someone living in the USA (Rumbaut 1997*a*).

The transnational characteristic of specific reciprocity comes to the fore when observing international return migration. Only when reciprocity survives geographical separation over time and international migrants maintain ties to the country of origin does return migration occur on a wide scale. Many studies have consistently concluded that feelings of loyalty or allegiance to the country of origin is an important consideration among many migrants (Gmelch 1980: 150). Indeed, return rates have been impressive: The relatively high magnitude of return in international migration has been consistently observed for over a hundred years. While differences in return rates are substantial when compared across groups and conditions—such as economic crisis and boom or war—return rates have been significant. Return flows from the so-called classical immigration countries of North America and Australia have been considerable and unexpected. While overall estimates vary and most records of immigration are imprecise, return rates probably ranged from 25% to 60% for European immigrants in the USA in the early twentieth century (Wyman 1993: 25). Other estimates conjecture that 30% of all immigrants to the USA returned home between 1821 and 1924. Sometimes, even permanent migrants retained strong ties with their rural regions of origin. They bought land, build houses, and contributed to village and city projects (Isaac 1947). Overall, in the first decade of the twentieth century, about one-third of all immigrants who entered the USA left again; although it fell to about one-fourth in the restrictionist 1920s (Ueda 1994: 26). The return rate proved substantial even among Russian Jews who faced political repression and virulent anti-Semitism in the country of origin. Between 1880 and 1900, perhaps as many as 15% to 20% of those who entered the USA returned to Eastern Europe (Sarna 1981). This proportion fell to about 5% when repression in Russia intensified after 1900 (Wyman 1993: 11). From 1908 until 1957—the latest year when the USA kept records of both arrivals and departures—4.8 of 15.7 million immigrants re-migrated. This is overall about one-third of those admitted as legal immigrants (US Department of Commerce 1960). We do not know whether all these persons returned to the country of origin but we surmise that many of them did so. In the 1970s and 1980s, when the bulk of immigrants had shifted to those from developing countries in Latin America and Asia, about one-fifth of all migrants left the USA again (Barkan 1996). Studies in Mexican–USA labour migration, for example, found that 31% can be expected to return to Mexico within ten years of settlement, 54% within twenty years, and 67% return within thirty years of settlement; with settlement defined as a migrant who has been in the United States for three continuous years (Massey et al. 1987: 310).

The importance of social and symbolic ties seems obvious, since plenty of evidence suggests that actual return has entailed a continuing commitment to reciprocal and even solidary relations in the country of origin. Many of these returnees, now and then, have depended on kinship or household members in the countries of origin. For example, from 1870 until 1910, nearly 80% of Italian immigrants to the USA were Italian men who left behind wives, children, and parents. Some of these *ritornati* even re-migrated to the Americas, engaging in recurrent migration; as much as one-third. Many of these 'birds of passage' commuted back to their villages seasonally or after a few years in America (Wyman 1993: 79).

Similar trends can be discerned for the European experience after World War Two. As in earlier transatlantic migrations, the decision to permanently remain in the immigration country or to return hangs in the balance for a long time. Indeed, many more did eventually return than was commonly held (Kubat 1984: 2). In the time period 1960 until

1993 out of an estimated total of 12 million contract workers and dependents from the Mediterranean countries of Southern Europe and North Africa, 9.3 million returned to their countries of origin from Germany (this presentation does not take into consideration the fact that individuals repeated migration several times; own calculations, based upon Statistisches Bundesamt, 1955–95). The increase in the contract worker population in Germany can be explained by family reunification during the later 1970s and 1980s after the termination of contract worker recruitment. This suggests that migrants did not break the ties to the country of origin but that they sometimes maintained them in various ways. They developed a dual frame of spatial reference. In short, settlement in the immigration country and return to the emigration country are not mutually exclusive strategies.

Continued obligations and reciprocal relations that result in return migration are most easily observed in kinship systems, particularly in families. We can capture this phenomenon by speaking of a shadow group. It includes all persons whose principal commitments and obligations are to a particular group but who are not presently co-residing in that household (Caces et al. 1985: 8 speak of shadow households). The intensity of the members' commitments or obligations can be operationalized as indicators of group affiliation, such as sending back remittances, and emotional ties. Of course, the strength of ties differs from one culture to another, and depends on the closeness of kinship and other social or symbolic ties that bind units, such as nuclear or extended families together. Specific reciprocity shows when ailing or elderly parents obligate some migrants, particularly the eldest children, to return in order to keep up a family tradition, such as continuing a farm or a business.

(2) Transnational Circuits

Transnational circuits are characterized by a constant circulation of goods, people, and information transversing the borders of sending and receiving states (Rouse 1991) along the principle of exchange, viz. instrumental reciprocity. Often, economic entrepreneurs use insider advantages such as knowledge of the language, knowing friends and acquaintances abroad to establish a foothold. They also typically develop in a context in which we find often rather successful socio-economic adaptation to the conditions in the receiving country, or sucessful reintegration in the sending country. Extreme examples of circularity are hypermobile Chinese businessmen in North America in the late twentieth century. For example, these astronauts establish a business in (say) Singapore, yet locate their families in Los Angeles,

New York, or Toronto to maximize educational opportunities for their children or as a safe haven in the event of political instability. The astronauts constantly move between the two places (Cohen 1997: 93). Other entrepreneurs and their dependants are firmly rooted in either the emigration or the immigration or yet another country, and use it as a sort of base from which to carry out entrepreneurial activities in others.

Transnational circuits can also arise beyond the first generation when children of return migrants keep in touch with the country of origin. For example, upon return, some parents have tried to give their children a German- or American-style education. In Turkey, the number of schools—middle school and high school, equivalent to the German *Gymnasium* and French *lycée*—in which German is the main language of instruction grew from three in the school year 1955–6 to over fifteen in 1987–8. Only English-language schools experienced a higher growth rate in the same time period. It is evident that the greatest increase in German-language schools occurred from five schools in 1980–1 to twelve in 1984–5 (Demircan 1988: 119): In 1983, the German government officially sponsored return migration, and many of those who had intended to return took advantage of the financial sponsoring. The greater interest of Turkish parents—mostly return migrants—and the increase of the number of German-language schools can be attributed to the efforts of parents to increase the human capital assets of their children. It also speaks for the efforts to convert economic capital—eight of the fifteen schools were private and thus required substantial tuition—into benefits derived from social capital: social prestige and social status for the parents and their offspring. Furthermore, we find children of return migrants in transnationally-oriented sectors such as the tourism industry (Yüce 1997).

(3) Transnational Communities

Transnational communities characterize situations in which international movers and stayers are connected by dense and strong social and symbolic ties over time and across space to patterns of networks and circuits in two countries. Community (that is, *Gemeinschaft*) 'encompasses all forms of relationship which are characterized by a high degree of personal intimacy, emotional depth, moral commitment, social cohesion and continuity in time' (Nisbet 1966: 47). For transnational communities to emerge, solidarity has to reach beyond narrow kinship systems. Such communities without propinquity do not necessarily require individual persons living in two worlds simultaneously or between cultures in a total 'global village' of de-territorialized space. What is required, however, is that communities without propinquity link through exchange, reciprocity, and solidarity to achieve a high degree of social cohesion, and a common repertoire of symbolic and collective representations.

Transnational communities can emerge on different levels of aggregation. The most fundamental are village communities in emigration and immigration countries that connect through extensive forms of solidarity over longer periods of time. Frequently, investment of those abroad or of returnees in private and public projects exemplifies this kind of support (see e.g. Goldring 1996*b*). Transnational communities can also be of a larger kind, primarily held together by symbolic ties of common ethnicity or even nationhood. For example, refugees who have pursued nation-building or political opposition projects in their home countries typically try to develop and entertain dense transnational ties.

Transnational communities are characterized by a continuous involvement in a pentagonic relationship with state and non-state entities in the countries of emigration and immigration. If they pursue nationalistic projects they could evoke solidarities that may be inconsistent and sometimes even contradicting the allegiances demanded by the territorial nation-states involved. Especially in cases of war between the countries of emigration and immigration, the charge of dual loyalty and disloyalty has come up (Sheffer 1986: 8). This is most often the case with diasporas. History is chock full of examples for diasporas. The Jewish experience usually first comes to mind as a prototype for diaspora formation; and could be extended to include African-Americans, Armenians, and Palestinians. In diasporas, a group has suffered some kind of traumatic event which leads to the dispersal of its members, and there is a vision and remembrance of a lost homeland to be restored or an imagined homeland still to be established, often accompanied by a refusal of the receiving society to fully recognize the cultural distinctiveness of the immigrants (for a fuller list of characteristics, see Safran 1991). It is not useful to apply the term 'diaspora' to settlers and labour migrants because they did not experience traumatic experiences and it cannot be said that most of the members of these groups yearn to return to their lost homeland.

Diasporas can only be called transnational communities, if the members also develop some significant social and symbolic ties to the receiving country. If they do not, we can speak of exile. For instance, the political exile is a person who yearns to return to his home country after persecution and flight. Some temporary labour migrants with a clear intention to return home can also be regarded as exiles. Exile communities are single-mindedly drawn to the former homeland; albeit the intentions, especially among labour migrants may change. This goal is so overriding that no substantial ties to the new and supposedly temporary country of settlement develops.

To prosper, diasporas do not necessarily need concrete social ties. It is possible that the memory of a homeland manifests itself primarily in symbolic ties. This has been the case for the Jewish diaspora for centuries after the destruction of the Second Temple. More than a thousand years later, some authors have characterized the relationship of diasporic Jews with those in Israel as *mishpachah*, literally meaning 'family' (Jacobson 1995: 236). The difference between diasporas and other forms of transnational communities becomes clear when we compare the Jewish diaspora before the establishment of the state of Israel with global communities such as Chinese entrepreneurs and traders in many countries of South-East Asia, Africa, and the two Americas. Jews experienced dispersal in a traumatic fashion, and—at a time when assimilation seemed to be inevitable in many European countries—the horrors of the Holocaust rekindled their consciousness of kind. The Chinese went abroad as settlers, and later experienced xenophobia. The vision of the Chinese was, at first, much less oriented towards the ancestral homeland, and lacked components of exile. It was only later that Chinese in South-East Asia became united by discrimination. In addition, they gained increasing awareness of unity as a consequence of the revolution against Manchu rule and the resistance of the Japanese invasion of their homeland. The still later rise of nationalism throughout South-East Asia and the attacks against their economic position by the longer established ethnic groups further intensified their collective identity of being Chinese abroad.

Another distinct form of, in this case emerging, transnational communities are groups with collective identities in frontier regions. In the South–North context we can think of groups and networks in spaces characterized but not delimited by contiguous nation-state borders. Around and along these borders regular and sustained interstitial transactions arise. Prominent examples are the US–Mexican frontier region, with nowadays intensified economic transactions through NAFTA (Albert 1998) and the Western Mediterranean zone of the Iberian Peninsula, France, and Italy, on the one hand, and North African states such as Morocco, Tunisia, and Algeria, on the other hand. While we do not yet see a particular and unique collective identity of frontier peoples in the North American or the Euro-Mediterranean region, both border spaces carry the potential for sustained transactions going beyond economic links to political co-operation and cultural commonalities. If the more than thousand year old experiences of the frontier regions of the former Holy Roman

Empire offer any guide to the future—think of the Oberrhein region (Alsace-Baden-Switzerland)—it is that the common history gains new momentum through efforts at supranational economic integration.

Transnationalization and Globalization

The concept of transnational social spaces complements the views of world-systems theory and concepts of globalization. Similar to world-systems theory that starts from core–periphery differences, transnationalization emphasizes the axis between the country of origin and destination within migration systems. But the core can consist of several original destinations, such as Germany, Netherlands, Belgium, and Sweden in the case of Turkish migrants. It is thus possible that Turks in all these countries are interconnected in a network fashion, a main tenet of the globalization paradigm. The concept of transnational social spaces also shares with the concept of globalization a focus on the fact that space and time are more and more differentiated or distanciated, such as singular events happening and interacting at the same time in different spaces.

Yet, there is a marked difference between the concepts of globalization and transnationalization. The most radical thinker in the globalist vein was Karl Marx who described the advent of full-fledged capitalism in the economic realm as the 'annihilation of space and time' (Marx 1973: 423). Those who have interpreted globalization as a 'space of flows' (Harvey 1989), largely independent of territoriality, have taken up this thread again, albeit in a less radical way. However, we do not get very far when we define transnational or global communication as not only and sometimes not even primarily an actual process but certainly a potential one (Luhmann 1975). The only advantage this conceptualization has is that the very potentiality increases the perception of transnationality and globality even among those not spatially mobile. But it does not help us to analyse actual border-crossing processes.

It is important to note that—in contrast to a branch of globalization studies—transnational social spaces cannot be conceptualized as deterritorialized spaces of flows. Some globalization scholars have already pronounced the detached nature of cultural representations in global flows. They posit that flows 'occur in and through the growing disjunctures among ethnoscapes, technoscapes, financescapes, mediascapes, and ideoscapes' (Appadurai 1996: 37). The ethnoscapes relate to persons such as tourists, migrants, refugees, exiles, contract workers and other geographically mobile categories who influence the politics in and between nation-states to a degree not known before. To see transmigrants embodying the contemporary form of affluent homelessness is a tempting proposition. Transmigrants then appear as the first to live out the transnational condition in its most complete form. Transmigration reaches its very limits, when we look at persons living quasi-simultaneously in two places, an expression of modern-day ubiquity. But, as we have seen, this is true of only few migrants. Our analysis suggests that ethnoscapes are not magic carpets but fulfil contingent bridging functions between nation-states, demarcated by doors at the territorial borders and gates inside the nation-states. Aspects of the lives of transmigrants remain highly localized, albeit characterized by a profound bi- or sometimes even multifocality. This is so because the main resources involved are local assets that nevertheless function as a transnational bridge.

By contrast, transnationalization overlaps with globalization but typically has a more limited purview. Whereas global processes are largely decentred from specific nation-state territories and take place in a world context, transnational processes are anchored in and span two or more nation-states, involving actors from the spheres of both state and civil society (see R. Meyers 1979: 311–27). Transnationalization differs from denationalization, too. The latter term denotes the fact that the stateless and many minorities in post-World War One Europe had no recourse to governments to represent and protect them (Arendt 1973: 269).

Factors Conducive to the Formation of Transnational Social Spaces

Lest there be a misunderstanding, let us make one point very clear from the outset: transnational life among immigrants is not a 'new' phenomenon, at least when seen in the perspective over the past one hundred years. Multilocal and transnational families with members scattered across borders have been a feature of most international migration. And putting away money to buy land or build houses in the emigration country is another characteristic habit, at least among labour migrants. One indicator of continuing ties to the country of origin—return rates—have been substantial even at the turn of the century among European immigrants in the USA. Perceived social distance and thus problems of acceptance and discrimination, now and then, may have contributed to a desire to return home. Political life has always remained tied to the politics of the old country in many ways, not least through the immigrant press. And even before the mass distribution of newspapers, migrants originating in Europe have used letters to communicate transnationally on a large scale since the sixteenth century (see e.g. Fertig 1994 and Brinks 1995). Moreover, long-distance commuting of recurrent migrants who worked summers in the immigration country and spend the long winters in the countries of origin, is not a new feature.

A Necessary Prerequisite: Long-Distance Communication and Travel

What is novel is the magnitude and the nature of transnational opportunities available to migrants. Budding processes and dynamics have cropped up. One noteworthy macro-structural trend has accelerated the emergence of transnational social spaces. The technological breakthrough in long-distance communication and travel that occurred in the nineteenth century with transoceanic steamship passages and telegraph communication considerably decreased costs for bridging long geographical distances. Already around the turn of the century, Italian newspapers in the American city of Buffalo could advertise $30 round trips to Italy over Christmas (Yans-McLaughlin 1977: 76–7). This trend sharply accelerated after World War Two, and especially since the 1970s (for a variety of indicators, see Beisheim et al. 1998: 43–68). One may speculate that the full breakthrough of factors enabling long-distance communication and travel was significantly delayed by the two World Wars and the period in between, in which isolationism, immigration restriction to a level not known before and after, and the economic depression of the 1930s restricted transnational exchange. Combined with increased levels of labour migration and refugee flows after World War Two, improved methods of communication and travel set the necessary but not sufficient stage for the development of modern transnational ties. Transnational commuting is now possible to a higher extent than during the 1960s and 1970s. To give one example out of many: in 1979, about 1.3 million Turkish citizens travelled abroad, about 2.5% of the total population. By 1990, the figure had more than doubled and reached 2.9 million, amounting to 5% of the population. In turn, whereas the number of foreign tourists travelling to Turkey was 1.1 million in 1979, it climbed steeply to 5.4 million in 1990 (Toprak 1996: 103). In sum, a variety of structural and technological developments has liberated communities from the confines of territorially restricted neighbourhoods.

Economic, Political, and Cultural Transnationalization: Different Dynamics

We now have to distinguish processes of transnationalization in the economic sphere, from those in the political and cultural realm, on the other. In the economic realm the prototypical transnational spaces are transnational circuits. They require beneficial conditions for investing all sorts of capital in the original emigration country, such as lower production costs, connected to distribution in the countries of immigration. Although transnational entrepreneurs obviously benefit from social and symbolic ties between emigration and immigration countries, for example ties of friends and kinship systems, economic activities do not need to be strongly embedded in these systems over extended periods of time by mechanisms such as solidarity. Exchange- and reciprocity-based resources are sufficient.

This situation differs from the formation of transnational communities built around political or religious projects. Here, the main catalysts are, first, strong ties of migrants and refugees to the country of origin over an extended period of time. Social ties and symbolic ties need to flourish through vivid and border-crossing social connections, language, religion, and cultural norms. Second, these ties and corresponding resources are not only embedded in migration flows but in other linkages as well, such as political and economic inter-state linkages—characteristics of migration systems. Third, juridical and political regulations, such as domestic and international regimes, allow to varying degrees for the movement of people and tolerate political and religious activities of former migrants. In short, the stronger the manifold social and symbolic ties of migrants and refugees between the two or more countries in migration systems, the more numerous linkages other than migration and the more favourable the conditions for public political and cultural activities—the more propitious the conditions for the emergence of transnational spaces in the form of transnational communities.

We now need to specify some of the *ceteris paribus* conditions within the countries of immigration and emigration. First, the factor most conducive to transnationalization of politics and culture in the sending countries has been contentious minority politics relating to ethnicity, nationality, language, and religion, often associated with the building of fledgling nation-states. These sending country conflicts tend to be exported to the countries of immigration. Examples abound, ranging from Indian Sikhs in Great Britain, Canada, and the United States, Algerians in France to Kurds in Germany, the Netherlands, Belgium, and Sweden.

Second, in the country of immigration, serious obstacles to socio-economic integration and/or a denial of acculturation or cultural recognition is extremely conducive to the transnationalization of political and cultural activities. The two difficulties, economic and cultural, may go hand in hand, or may proceed separately. For example, some groups may be denied opportunities for cultural assimilation or recognition while they are well-integrated socio-economically. This used to be true for Chinese in the white settler colonies, until the 1940s. In other cases, partial socio-economic exclusion and a perception on the part of substantial groups among the newcomers that their cultural recognition is blocked, can go hand in hand, as the examples of some labour migrant groups in Western Europe suggest; for example, Surinamese in the Netherlands or Caribbeans in the United Kingdom.

Third, if the countries of immigration are liberal democracies that do not assimilate immigrants by force, immigrant minorities have greater chances to uphold cultural distinctiveness and ties to the countries of origin. This represents a specific 'political opportunity structure' (Tarrow 1994) for immigrants. In particular, multicultural policies of the countries of settlement are conducive to upholding immigrants' transnational ties. An example are Caribbeans in the UK (Goulbourne 1991). Put otherwise, not only repressive policies and discrimination advance immigrant transnationalization but also the opposite, windows for multicultural rights and activities.

Economic Transnationalization: Entrepreneurs Moving from the Ethnic Niche to Transnational Businesses

In the German-Turkish case we find that intra-kinship exchange, reciprocity, and solidarity has been complemented at later stages by partial transnational circuits that include families, but also larger groups such as ethnic communities. Three forms of economic transnationalization developed sequentially: first, remittances of labour migrants from Germany to Turkey; second, the inception and growth of immigrant businesses in Germany; and third, transnational production, distribution, and sale.

Specific Reciprocity and Remittances

In the first period from the early 1960s until the 1970s and 1980s labour migrant remitters transferred money to Turkey, and returning migrants invested in housing and consumer products. These actions were usually an instance of obligations and specific reciprocity: remittances were given in exchange for continuing household or reproduction work in Turkey. In the 1980s and 1990s, the share of remittances from Germany to Turkey as a percentage of foreign trade has decreased slightly, probably due to family reunification. While two-thirds of all migrants still transferred money back home in 1971, this share decreased to about 43% in 1980 (Pagenstecher 1996: 154). Partly, remittances from the Gulf states compensated for this decline. Nonetheless, if migrants' participation in the tourist and housing industries and their investments in other sectors are added to the family remittances, international migrants have become the single most important source of hard currency in Turkey.

The Growth of Immigrant Businesses: Transnational Reciprocity

In the second period, Turkish immigrants reached a higher scale of economic activity in Germany, with migrants investing in housing. Thus, the importance of an immigrant economy in Germany grew. The number of self-employed Turks in Germany tripled from 1983 to 1992, from about 10,000 to 35,000. The share of self-employed immigrants increased to about 8%; with Turkish immigrants coming closer to the higher rates of Greeks and Italians. This overall rate of immigrant self-employment now corresponds to the rate of self-employment among German citizens (*Bericht der Beauftragten* 1994: II.2.10). Migrant groups started in the entrepreneurial sector from a somewhat disadvantageous position compared to natives because their initial large-scale entrance into the manufacturing sector slowed down the accumulation of the assets necessary to establish businesses. However, this has been compensated by relatively strong ties in kinship groups running small shops. The typical activities of Turkish migrants have included grocery shops, craftspersons, travel agencies, and restaurants (Duymaz 1988). These are all endeavours necessitating reciprocal relations and focused solidarity for keeping down (social) wage costs and retaining profits inside the narrow nuclear family circle. Among Turkish immigrants about 65% of all these companies are family-owned and employ usually the owner and family members (Zentrum für Türkeistudien 1989: 177–8).

The supply of new labour for these businesses, serving an immigrant niche and a small but growing German clientele, has often come from the respective kinship group in Turkey. Therefore, many Turkish companies in Germany capitalize on kinship groups as a recruiting pool (A. Goldberg 1992). The mechanisms are clear: sponsored kinship migration—if need be, as asylum seekers—and marriage migration have enabled Turkish entrepreneurs in Germany to tap this pool of cheap and docile labour. This is a joint outcome of liberalized labour migration policies and ubiquitous migrant networks. Therefore, many Turkish companies in Germany use kin-based reciprocity. This form of reciprocity is often accompanied by a well-known dark side: excessive social control over new labour from Turkey. For example, a young female relative from Turkey is bound informally to work for a fixed time in Germany with the shopowner. She cannot choose at will. However, costs may also arise for the entrepreneurs. If there is a strong kinship solidarity, they are often required to employ relatives.

Transnational Businesses: Exchange-Based Obligations and Insider Advantages

More recently, a transition has occurred from the second to a third period, the immigrant niche has begun to be complemented by a fledgling transnational coordination of business activities. Some Turkish entrepreneurs have entered fields in which they found themselves competing with German businesses, such as software development and textile production (ATIAD 1996: 11–13). Especially in the latter sector production costs are much lower in Turkey than in Germany. This induced textile companies to move production to Turkey, while retaining their sales and distribution centres in Germany. A small group of Turkish entrepreneur immigrants based in Germany could exploit insider advantages, built upon information in transnational networks: they have used language skills, social and symbolic ties with friends and acquaintances in Turkey in order to gain a foothold in the transnational market. Especially exchange-based and mutual obligations in networks are of utmost importance because they help to lower transaction costs. For example, informal give-and-take arrangements cover the dealings with German and Turkish authorities.

This latest stage of business development is restricted to privileged entrepreneurs with relatively high amounts of financial capital; such as the textile entrepreneurs just mentioned. It is certainly important to emphasize that the majority of migrants have remained proletarian or—a small but growing minority—modestly self-employed such as shopkeepers. Yet small-scale export–import businesses and mid-sized textile firms both benefit from the same set of innovations in communications and transport that underlie larger-scale industrial relocations in textile, steel, and automobile production. Put more broadly, these grass-roots economic initiatives do not arise in opposition to more general trends of transnational relocation of production and trade, but are partly driven by them (Portes 1996). Petty transnational migrant entrepreneurs and mid-sized companies occupy specific niches in the international division of commerce and production. And in doing so, some migrant labourers who become self-employed have succeeded because they could partly convert social for economic capital.

A Case Study: Small Actors' Transnational Activities

Once again, the Alihan–Yeniköy case study helps to illustrate the evolution of transnational spaces involving smaller economic actors riding the crest of transnationalization (Engelbrektsson 1978). It shows the embeddedness of migrants' economic activities in social and symbolic ties. Generalized reciprocity and diffuse solidarity enabled Alihan men to be very ingenious in the economic realm. They were much more heavily involved in import–export business than Yeniköy men. For the Alihan villagers, international migration was indeed a part of a household survival and improvement strategy. As a by-product, most families in the village improved their living standard significantly, when measured by Turkish standards. Alihan men often went into joint-ownership projects with Turks outside their village, whereas their Yeniköy counterparts made no attempts to invest together with anyone outside their own group, inside or outside the village. Yeniköy migrants mostly returned to their village and tried to fit savings and investments into the local economic structure of the village. One of the reasons for their higher rate of return to the village of origin was that they had initially faced better economic opportunities at home than their Alihan counterparts.

The migrants from Alihan who followed the pioneers could resort to strong and dense ties that encompassed more than one kinship group, whereas those interested in migrating from Yeniköy could not, unless they belonged to a single kinship group from whom the first migrant left for Europe. Alihan represented a village with a strong social cohesion, relatively few economic differences, and a sense of collective communal identity. The collective representation of the village as a cohesive unit was pervasive. All villagers considered themselves descendants of the original settlers and most families showed marital connections to other families in the village. Help was present in times of need. Generalized reciprocity in the form of mutual obligations thus extended beyond the kinship group. In other words, various benefits, such as information and control of family members, could be derived from reciprocity, and village solidarity acted as a partial substitute for financial capital. By contrast, migrants from Yeniköy exclusively supported the members of their own kinship group. Potential migrants could not rely on the valuable reciprocity and information flowing from this or other kinship groups. The village that had existed for about 100 years in the mid-1960s was grouped into various communities—Turks from Anatolia, Turkish refugees from Bulgaria, Kurds—that had little contact with each other.

In sum, when migrants from both villages found themselves abroad, the Alihan community with higher amounts of generalized reciprocity, diffuse solidarity, information, and control exploited the new opportunities transnational social spaces offered to them more successfully than those migrants from Yeniköy who kept very close ties with only their own kinship group. We conclude that the transnational ties in the Yeniköy case existed for the duration of actual migration only; based on a narrow focus of reciprocity and solidarity in a single kinship group. Transnational economic activities in the Yeniköy case effectively stopped when the migrants returned from Europe to Turkey, whereas it continued in the Alihan case. For more than a dozen years, the Alihan villagers effectively functioned as a transnational community. Yet, while communal reciprocity undoubtedly furthered economic success of Alihan residents, it also cemented gender relations controlled by the patriarchs of extended families. After all, relatively immobile women, most of whom stayed behind in Turkey, shouldered the transnational lifestyle of Alihan men.

Political Transnationalization: Kurds between Exile and Adaptation

In the public realm transnational social and symbolic ties and linkages have gained particular currency for migrants who mobilize and struggle for political change in the countries of origin and destination. The vision of a homeland that is yet to be created and an eventual return to it is a powerful and crucial ingredient of diaspora formation in the case of large-scale ethnic and national transstate communities. Many politically active Kurds are engaged simultaneously in a group-making and a state-making project. Some Kurdish organizations have the very creation of a nation as a goal—be it an autonomous nation-state or, more modestly, increased cultural and political autonomy of the regions inhabited mainly by Kurds in south-eastern Turkey. Kurds, as a relatively coherent social, political, and cultural group and their homeland Kurdistan clearly are *ex post facto* constructions (Behrendt 1993). This is typical for new challenger groups in diasporas and akin, for example, to the Sikhs' intentions to form Khalistan. Kurdistan is largely a rhetorical feat because there is no nationalist movement encompassing Kurds in all the Middle Eastern states.

It is certain that politically active Kurds in Germany form a sort of stranded minority: a prior state never existed before they started to fight for national autonomy. Yet, the victorious *entente* powers partitioned the territory now claimed by nationalist Kurds into several territories when the Ottoman Empire, allied with the German Reich, was finally torn asunder in the aftermath of military defeat in World War One. Some Kurdish migrants from Turkey exemplify this tendency. They live in Germany and demand political and cultural autonomy in the Republic of Turkey. Various organizations direct their demands to both Turkish and German governments. PKK/Yek-Kom—founded in 1994 and the successor of Feyka-Kurdistan of 1984—mainly propagates separatist goals and pursues an independent Kurdish state. This PKK-led group has engaged in civil war in Turkey, in bombings, public demonstrations, and violent extortion in Germany. When the strategy of brutal assaults failed in the early 1990s and the German government outlawed the PKK and its subsidiaries, the leadership opted for less violent means. Yek-Kom claims to speak for all Kurds. The PKK affiliates are organized in a dense web of workers' organizations, sports clubs, cultural centres and migrants' organizations. By contrast, SPKT/Komkar, established in 1979, advocates a federalist solution in Turkey, ties Kurdish autonomy to wider issues of Turkish democracy, and is also engaged in combating racism and discrimination and establishing equality of opportunity for Kurds in Germany. There are also two smaller organizations. PPKK/Hevkar—established in 1982—aims to reform Turkish society and the Turkish state and calls for class solidarity between the Kurdish and the German working class. It cooperates with German solidarity groups. Instead of class, the KIP/Kurdische Gemeinde in Deutschland—founded in 1991 and successor of KKDK of 1982—rallies its followers around a common ethnicity, tries to achieve public recognition of a separate Kurdish identity in Germany, and also seeks to involve German solidarity groups. The three latter organizations have all called for boycotting German tourism to and in Turkey (for more details, see Falk 1998: 169–78). Some of these organizations maintain intense cross-national ties to Kurdish organizations in various other European countries, *inter alia*, Netherlands, Sweden, and Belgium (Nielsen 1992: 123) and, of course, to Turkey itself. Political transnationalization has to be analysed primarily as a multiple relationship between destination states such as Germany and other immigration countries, the emigration state Turkey, and the refugee or exiled minorities.

Numerically speaking, the Kurdish group constitutes the second strongest self-defined immigrant group after the Turks in Germany. Most Kurds either arrived as contract workers or asylum seekers. First, Kurds migrated to Germany as contract workers in the late 1960s and early 1970s; according to estimates of experts they form about 85% of all Turkish citizens of Kurdish descent in Germany in the mid-1990s. By the end of the contract worker recruitment period, very few Turkish citizens in Germany called themselves Kurds (Leggewie 1996: 81). Second, some Kurdish refugees arrived after the military coups in 1971 and 1980 as activists, victims, or targets of the fighting between the so-called state security forces and the PKK in the 1990s; comprising about 15% of the total. Compared to labour migrants who conceive of themselves as ethnic and national Turks, probably very little remigration has occurred among migrants and refugees who are Kurds. This suggests that ongoing military conflicts, resulting ecological devastation, poor economic prospects, and continuing persecution of the civilian population from either the state forces or the guerrilla PKK trigger outmigration and emigratory flight but prevent sizable return migration. Two periods mark the development of this particular transnational social space.

Contract Workers and Early Refugees: Emergent Kurdish Solidarity

In the 1960s and 1970s contract workers of the south-eastern Turkish provinces arrived in Germany. No significant political mobilization around Kurdish questions took place. In a first period of transnationalization, tension and violence escalated since the 1980s between Turkish army and police forces in south-eastern Turkey, on one side, and Kurdish armed groups, mainly the PKK, on the other. Since then more or less open warfare between the two sides with massive destruction of the environment led to high rates of displaced persons who mostly move towards the major cities in Western Turkey such as Istanbul, Izmir, and Ankara, but also big cities surrounding the south-eastern provinces such as Adana. As expected, only few of these refugees ever arrived in Germany. Martial law has been in use in many south-eastern provinces. While the activities by the PKK have not undermined the territorial integrity of the Turkish state, they have nevertheless been a formidable military threat.

Beyond the guerrilla warfare in the south-eastern provinces—many of which are inhabited by a Kurdish majority while others are ethnically heavily mixed—state forces have repressed various kinds of democratic forces in civil society. Kurds are among both the challengers and the victims. Much of the state repression has been motivated by an authoritarian form of central and dirigistic nationalism in the Kemalist sense, directed at all democratic opposition forces and thus including politically active Kurds. Examples for this suppression are the persecution of Kurdish journalists and Kurdish language media reporting on events in the south-eastern provinces. Other events concerned the incarceration of Kurdish deputies in the national grand assembly. These members belonged to the Kurdish political party HEP-Workers' Party of the People—founded in 1991 and later reconstituted as DEP-Democracy Party and HADEP-Democracy Party of the People. There have been linkages between PKK activists and members of these Kurdish parties (Çürükkaya 1997: 76).

Understandably, the severe repressive measures of the government have alienated a growing proportion of the Kurdish population, causing the PKK gradually to gain widespread support in spite of its reputation for brutal violence. Certainly, the armed conflict did not help to shift allegiances to the Turkish government. Nevertheless, the PKK has severe difficulties in recruiting supporters and fighters. The PKK is most successful among Kurds not espousing strong collective identities based on the tribal-kinship system and those who do not have strong loyalties to their leaders, the aghas. Tribal loyalties and deep-seated religious ties have made it very difficult for the PKK to recruit supporters and fighters for a pan-tribal, Kurdish national ideology (Wiessner 1995: 169–70). The PKK recruits guerrilla primarily out of groups who are willing to rate tribal consciousness lower than a Kurdish identity. Thus, we cannot speak of one Kurdish solidarity but competing solidarities, linked to various tribal, religious, and political projects.

In the face of immense conflict, we can hypothesize that among refugees who struggle with adaptation in their new environments, the acceptance of radical organizations is higher than among those who stayed. This means that symbolic ties can be mobilized more efficiently among refugees. There is some indirect evidence for this thesis. In a survey in the mid-1990s respondents in two main centres of refugees within Turkey—Adana and Mersin—had a higher acceptance of the PKK than those living in cities with higher rates of out-migration—Diyarbakır, Batman, and Mardin. Moreover, a newspaper close to PKK, *Özgür Ülke*, is more widely read in the in-migration than in the out-migration cities (Ergil 1995: 26 and 16–17).

Transnationalizing Political Conflict: Transplanting Diffuse Solidarity and Control

In a second period, both the PKK and the Turkish government moved the conflict abroad, particularly to Germany. The German government, a NATO ally and host to a large Turkish and Kurdish population, became the target for demands from the PKK who threatened to use Germany as a scene for warfare. In turn, the Turkish government intervened and demanded that Germany outlaw the PKK; the German Ministry of the Interior finally followed in 1993 as had other states such as Sweden before. This conflict has not simply involved militant organizations such as the PKK. The Turkish side also asked the German government not to grant official status to other Kurdish organizations. In 1985, for example, the German federal government did not recognize Kurdish and Armenian organizations as ethnic groups, the *Volksgruppen*. This status is a necessary condition for organizations to be eligible for government moneys in order to undertake immigrant adaptation measures, such as social work and language instruction.

Intensifying conflicts in Turkey and the neighbouring countries that also involved the German government and public have certainly added to the very high rate of mobilization of Kurds. In the mid-1990s, the German police estimated about 9,000 PKK activists and 50,000 sympathizers (Leggewie 1996: 82). One of the crucial results of mobilization on all sides involved has been an increasing transnationalization not only of major actors such as the PKK. Also, there is a close exchange of information and persons between migrated or exiled Kurds and those left behind in the south-eastern provinces or living in the Western parts of Turkey. The density of social ties is continuously increasing. Among some of the means used are newspapers, telephone, video and music cassettes.

Overall, the conflict spurred the efforts of Kurdish organizations in Germany advancing interests of Kurdish immigrants. Among the demands of organizations such as Komkar have been radio and TV programmes in Kurdish; counselling centres for Kurds; recognition of Kurdish names at German registrar's offices, public moneys for Kurdish self-help groups and additional instruction of Kurdish schoolchildren in their mother tongue(s) in public schools. Mother-tongue instruction in schools has only been offered in Turkish; with a few exceptions such as in Bremen and Hesse, where Kurdish is taught. When these Länder governments gave some room for Kurdish language instruction, the Turkish government considered this as interference in its internal affairs.

All these events did not only contribute to the mobilization of the Kurdish population in Germany but also sparked debates in the German public on whether to send back to Turkey those Kurdish asylum seekers whose claims were rejected by German authorities. For example, one position advocated by German authorities has been that there are alternatives to Germany as a safe haven, above all the western provinces of Turkey, in which no open civil strife has taken place. A veritable train of delegations from all walks of life in Germany to Turkey followed, including members of parliament, government, unions, and NGOs (Hocker and Liebe-Harkort 1996: 338–63).

Solidarity extended by the Kurdish activists and their Kurdish and German supporters to activists in Turkey makes the feedback loop complete: the armed conflict in Turkey has produced many refugees, some of them international. The ensuing social and symbolic ties span places in Germany, other EU states, and the EU itself in the form of a Kurdish parliament in exile founded in 1995. In addition, Turkey and adjoining countries such as Iran, Iraq, and Syria are the basis of support for PKK warriors and those sympathetic to this organization. But the contending Kurdish groups and organizations have not managed to unite transnationally across the space they call Kurdistan. Kurdish nationalist movements have not transcended nation-state boundaries in the Middle East. Part of the reason are insufficient commonalties as to language, religion, and culture but also ferocious power struggles between the Kurdish warlords within and across the nation-states involved. The focus of the individual movements has been on attaining autonomy or achieving independence in the individual nation-states. And even within states such as Turkey, Kurds are divided along familiar schisms, for example Sunni, Shi'ite, and Alevis. Nevertheless, in the Turkish case, the material resources originating from neighbouring countries—especially Syria—have intensified the armed conflict in the south-eastern provinces of Turkey up until the mid-1990s. One of the consequences has been that the flow of displaced persons and international refugees is steadily replenished. Some of the refugees moved to Germany and have mobilized into various Kurdish organizations, some of whom claim that life in Germany is only a temporary exile to be followed by the establishment of an independent Kurdistan.

The fascinating aspect is that organizations such as the PKK have virtually transplanted mechanisms of social control from Turkey to Germany. Temporarily high rates of mobilization attest to the encapsulated quality of a certain Kurdish political milieu in Germany. With its sectarian guerrilla ideology the PKK represents only a small fraction of the Kurdish population in the Federal Republic. Yet it has succeeded in presenting itself as the most prominent voice of the Kurdish people outside the Middle East. It managed to seize the lead from Kurdish intellectuals in exile and self-help groups. Nevertheless, judging the long-term prospects of mobilization, there is a low degree of fit between the mechanisms of control and mobilization exercised by the PKK, and those in other realms of German life experienced by activists or those sympathetic to their goals. The PKK is not organized as a party but as a secret society. Among other things, the PKK has ruthlessly extorted protection money from Kurdish businesses and has repeatedly executed 'defectors' and 'traitors'. As a result, a number of PKK activists quit the organization. In recent years, German courts have cracked down on criminal methods of the PKK, such as extorting money from Kurdish businesses in Germany. This is important because transnational communities have to cope with demands in both settings in the long run, not just in a temporary manner. If the PKK does not constantly replenish its personnel and supporters from Turkey through ongoing transnationalization, the prospects of continuing the despotic style will be dire because of the low degree of fit between an extremely authoritarian organization and the German political environment.

Social control used in the process of mobilization and challenge to state authorities has to be closely differentiated according to its effects, too. For example, the authoritarian leadership of the PKK has used symbolic ties with the Kurdish people in order to centralize control. The enhanced capacity to monitor and control members through violent extortion and threats is a negative benefit derived from diffuse solidarity. It helps to advance the cause of an authoritarian organization involved in a separatist or autonomous Kurdish project but has sacrificed individual autonomy and many lives. Interestingly, centralized control has been exerted not in one hierarchical organization but through a maze of formally independent groups—ranging from culture and sports to migrants' affairs.

We can certainly discern diaspora elements among the Kurdish population in Germany because some seek to establish a homeland or cultural autonomy and try to adapt to the German environment in advancing socio-economic integration. But the variety of positions taken on all these issues is fairly wide and too diffuse to speak of coherent trends going either way. Moreover, the shared cultural expressions are still rare; aside from folkloristic phenomena such as the *Newroz* festival. It is likely that activist refugees form the main basis of the groups building a diaspora. However, there are significant differences: activists and supporters of the PKK and their German intellectual allies are trying to build a sort of 'refugee warrior diaspora' akin to the Palestinian example. They insist on the exile aspect of the diaspora and are busy affirming an emerging Kurdish identity. They clearly see Kurds in Turkey and Europe as forming a temporary transnational community pursuing a national project. By contrast, organizations such as Komkar have developed transnational networks, seek autonomy instead of independence in Kurdistan, and encourage adaptation of Kurds in Germany. They demand both more rights to cultural and political autonomy for Kurds in Turkey and the integration of Kurdish settlers in Germany on an ethnically self-conscious basis. In short, the positions within this large 'we'-group in the making are full of unresolved tensions.

These tensions among Kurds in Germany can be tentatively seen in self-descriptions of collective identity. Comparing two representative samples from the mid-1980s and early 1990s, we find that the percentage of Kurds in Germany who feel 'Turkish' went down significantly, both among the first and second generation, from about 40% to about zero (Brieden 1996: 41). This research also indicates that there is very little social contact between Kurds and Turks living in Germany. The frequency of contact primarily depends upon the attitude towards the 'Kurdish question'. There is an attenuating trend concerning the general re-ethnicization, however: the renationalization is much stronger among the first than among the second generation of Turks and Kurds. Among both Kurds and Turks is a significant percentage saying that they are neither Kurdish, Turkish, or German but European, cosmopolitan, or simply 'human beings'. This is reminiscent of the 'cosmopolitan stranger', an ideal type who would show no collective identification, except when pressured to claim identity (Park 1950).

Cultural Transnationalization: Young Muslims between Disintegration, Syncretism, and Segmentation

To emphasize the transnational aspect in the development of collective identity is not the same as saying that labour migrants and refugees live between two cultures. Collective identity denotes two dimensions: first, a common core of shared beliefs, ideas, the memory of a common history, aspirations, the identification with certain projects—in short, a core of collective representations—and second, ascription by others concerning the collective character, certain dispositions and memories. Identity can refer to roles, ties, groups, and organizations. Early attempts have sought to interpret the experience of the 1.5 and second-generation Turkish immigrants as being uprooted from Turkish cultures and not having been inserted in German culture. (Further refinements are possible, '1.75' generation for 0–5 year olds and '1.25' for 13–17 year olds; see Rumbaut 1994.) Additionally, one finds the assumption that to become uprooted and removed from a nation-state community is automatically to lose one's identity, traditions, and culture (Stein 1981: 325). This view not only implies a transformation but a loss of culture and identity. It reflects an essentialist understanding of culture. A transnational approach shifts the emphasis from the question of whether international migrants 'lose' or 'retain' culture to how they experience ties, groups, and organizations in transnational social spaces, a trans-cultural mélange.

Empirical evidence generated by ethnic and national self-description gives a first impression of the complicated collective identity set-up. In the survey mentioned above, we gather that the percentage of Turks and Kurds who feel totally German is close to zero; even among the children of immigrants (Brieden 1996: 43). The reasons given by the respondents fall into two sets: first, a subjective feeling of rejection by the German majority culture, and second, the fact of discrimination by native German citizens. Yet, the percentage of those who also feel German was already 29% among Turks and 12% among Kurds in the early 1990s; an indication towards a sort of syncretist or at least dual self-classification that includes both German, Turkish or Kurdish elements of collective identity.

We can now phrase the question more precisely as to what kind of syncretism exists regarding collective identity: Is this the sort of transitory syncretism observed by scholars among immigrants of European descent who arrived in the United States in the late nineteenth and early twentieth centuries—the almost proverbial Italian-Americans and Irish-Americans—finally leading to cultural assimilation of the *sujets mixtes* in generations following the original migrants? Or, do these syncretist identities indicate a more sustained and uneasy coexistence of various ethnic and national identities and cultural practices which are not brought together successfully in an integrative synthesis, because cultural segregation develops that isolates these communities? Yet a third alternative would be that syncretist collective identities develop which successfully occupy a cultural space in between emigration and immigration states at least temporarily—this is the claim advanced here.

Temporary Exile, Enclave Religion, and Triadic Culture

Transnational social and symbolic ties and the development of collective identities in the realms of religion, nation, and ethnicity can be interpreted as a process of cumulative causation. Again, various periods of transnationalization can be distinguished. In the first phase, Turkish labour migrants, sometimes joined by family members, intended to spend a few years earning money and then return to Turkey. In this period, they confined their cultural practices mostly to the private sphere; the perceived transitional nature of religious affairs found its expression in factory rooms or apartments that served as prayer halls. While the Turkish government certainly did everything to increase the flow of remittances, it did nothing to organize religious life. This changed completely in the second period when various aspects of Turkish culture began to flourish more visibly in Germany in the 1970s and 1980s. For example, believers built mosques and founded cultural organizations. Cultural affairs became confined to religious enclaves; yet the internal differentiation along ethnic, religious, and political lines increased.

In a third period, immigrants have come to use more and more elements found in both countries of origin and destination to cope with discrimination they encounter in the immigration countries, to participate in events back in the emigration countries, and to take advantage of an increasingly multicultural environment in the immigration polities which recognize cultural difference and ethnic diversity. The pentagonic nature of the relationship has come to the fore when the German government also got involved in dealing with religious and cultural organizations. Many of the Islamic organizations competing for official recognition as religious institutions in Germany are outposts of the Turkish government, Turkish political parties and other intermediate organizations.

Disintegration Against Syncretism

The emergence of a transnational social space and concomitant feedback loops in the cultural realm can be exemplified when looking at young Muslims. Some authors have interpreted the experience of many Turkish youth in Germany to be one of disintegration (Heitmeyer, Müller, and Schröder 1997: 44): The underlying hypothesis is that issues of collective identity surfaced among the descendants of Turkish immigrants. Nationalist and religious 'we'-groups have grown more important because universally valid mechanisms such as access to the labour market and the educational system have not provided the basis needed for the formation of a satisfactory individual identity. According to this view, many young Turks suffer from the effects of modernization such as the ever-increasing demands for educational credentials or higher than average rates of unemployment compared to German youth, xenophobic violence, and a denial of cultural recognition on the part of the German majority society. These tendencies then contribute to the retreat of Turkish youth into ethnically organized 'we'-groups that offer a collective identity along nationalist and religious lines. Importantly, these youth are seen as deracinated in both the German and the Turkish society. Many descendants of Turkish migrants are Turks in Germany and *Almancılar* or *Deutschländer* in Turkey. In short, this view holds that the experience of disintegration and manifold fears are the fertile breeding ground for Islamic and Turkish chauvinist orientations among a growing part of Turkish youth because they are threatened to become a liminal people. The stronger discrimination is felt and the higher the propensity that 'traditional values' are passed on from parents to youth in Turkish migrant families, the greater the likelihood that these youth espouse positions such as support of *Qur'an* courses and schools, of Islamic superiority and of religiously legitimized readiness to use force as a means of politics.

Taking this partial explication and extending it forwardly, we interpret the tendency among some descendants of Turkish immigrants to adhere to Islamic organizations as a stimulus for certain German groups: they take it as a sign that these young men and women of Turkish descent are unwilling to assimilate. Again, populist and xenophobic groups in Germany feel justified in their prejudices. The feedback loop is complete when manifestations of racism cause new sources of apprehension and further inclinations to clannishness and endogamy on the Turkish side. For example, a substantial number of 1.5 and second-generation Turks in Germany marry imported partners from Turkey. This kind of behaviour could be thought to breed further hostility and estrangement on both sides.

While the idea of a spiraling feedback loop is a plausible one, this particular interpretation of Islamic youth as the victims of both German xenophobia and rejection on the part of German society is flawed for at least three reasons.

(1) Tolerance in Immigration Country Furthers Multiculturalism and Transnationalization

The transnationalization in the cultural realm is readily advanced by discourses and even public policies favouring multiculturalist tendencies, a mix of demands and efforts to grant specific individual and group rights to minorities, so that they may express cultural distinctiveness, develop political organization and engage in economic betterment. The demands of the certainly not coherent multiculturalist agenda include voting rights for permanent residents who are not citizens; affirmative action programmes that aim to increase the representation of visible minorities in major educational and economic institutions; revising work schedules so as to accommodate the religious holidays of immigrant groups; providing bilingual education programmes for the children of immigrants, so that their earliest years of education are conducted partly in their mother tongue, this is meant to be a transitional phase to secondary and post-secondary education in German. In the 1980s and 1990s these tendencies have been publicized above all by German academics and many a politician. Also, Turkish interest groups who do not share any of the premisses of the German organizations have taken up many of these demands and made them part of their own agenda. Islamic groups demand recognition as a religious group on a basis similar to the main Christian denominations and establish primary schools. To the extent that multiculturalist policies agree with the agenda of Muslim organizations, or that these organizations seize upon these demands, we observe efforts on their part to maintain, change, and build symbolically cohesive collectives based on religious, ethnic, and national representations. In itself, this is a sign of immigrant adaptation, albeit we may want to interpret the behaviour of Islamic organizations in a purely instrumental manner. To conclude, integration, viz. adaptation of immigrants, is not synonymous with melting into the majority core of the destination state. Assimilation is not another word for adaptation, it is simply one possible outcome among several (see Chapter 8).

(2) Transplanted Ties Undergo Changes in Germany

The activities of Islamic organizations in Germany are partly an outgrowth of an ever-increasing re-Islamization of public life in Turkey. For these organizations, Turkish migrants in Germany are primarily of political interest. Over the course of time, however, these groups have lost control over shaping the symbolic ties for their German-based clients. Islamic groups have tried to gain power in Turkish domestic politics. Since the 1950s Islam has become an extremely contested current in Turkey. For example, Islamic groups have tried to present Islam as the new bond for Turkish nationalism; thus challenging the legacy of Kemalist nationalism. These developments among Turkish migrants in Germany cannot be understood without the new policies of the Turkish government towards Islam. It has accelerated mobilization around religion among the most numerous religious groups, the Sunnis and Alevis. Since the early 1990s, the Turkish government has departed from the Kemalist tradition, at times actively fostering a Turkish–Islamic synthesis. For instance, the government made religious education, once an optional subject in primary and secondary schools, mandatory. It strengthened the Directorate of Religious Affairs, built numerous new mosques and appointed imams. What once started out as a confused right-wing doctrine to address the spread of socialism during the 1970s in Turkey—combining fervent Turkish nationalism and Islamism—has virtually come to be elevated to a quasi-official state policy (Toprak 1996: 108).

In Germany, the DİTİB (*Diyanet İşleri Türk İslam Birliği*), a branch of the Turkish Directorate of Religious Affairs (*Diyanet İşleri Başkanlığı*, DİB), has been active in Germany since 1985, but only after Islamist organizations such the Association of the New World View in Europe (AMGT/*Avrupa Milli Görüş Teşikatları*; nowadays IGMG or *Milli Görüş*) and the Association of Islamic Cultural Centers (VIKZ/*İslam Kültür Merkezleri Birliği*) had recruited members and built mosques. As virtually all emigration states during the 1960s, Turkey took an attitude of indifference towards her migrants abroad. This changed, however, in the 1980s when the implications of expatriate political and religious groups became visible. The Turkish government then developed a high degree of involvement in the internal affairs of its citizens abroad. It had every reason to assume that *Milli Görüş* supported the electoral campaigns of the former Prosperity Party (*Refah*) in Turkey (*Informationsdienst zur Ausländerarbeit* 1/1994: 6).

While the activities of Islamic organizations in Turkey and Germany may have strengthened Turkish nationalism and Muslim transnational representations, the messages of the organizations involved have contradictory implications. On the one hand, Islamic propaganda emphasizes in-group social and symbolic ties and thus segregation from German society (Gür 1993: 45–9). On the other hand, the overwhelming majority of the 1.5, the second, and third generations will stay in Germany. While permanent residence in Germany does not necessarily lead to increased contacts with Germans and vice versa, a one-sided orientation to Turkey gradually transfigures into a bi- or transnational focus. For example, issues of education and employment are practical questions to be solved in Germany, and so is cultural recognition for all those following the first generation. Even nationalist and religious organizations wooing young Turks grown up in Germany deliver a double message: 'Wir, wir, wir sind von hier, sind Einheimische' (We, we, we are from here, we are indigenous) and 'Wir sind Türken, sind Muslime, sind zivilisiert' (We are Turks, we are Muslims, we are civilized; cited in Karakaşoğlu-Aydin 1997: 37). Very different organizations extend this double message to young Turks in Germany, ranging from the now nationalist-cum-Islamic Grey Wolves and the Islamic

Milli Görüş to the religious organizations directed by the Turkish Directory of Religious Affairs with its German branch DİTİB. In short, in an effort to control young Muslims' social and symbolic ties in Germany, religious organizations inadvertently relinquish a one-sided emigration country orientation. They have not successfully connected their projects to implant Islamic politics in Turkey, on the one hand, with widespread control over Turkish youth in Germany, on the other.

Organizations such as IGMG, VIKZ, and the state-controlled DİTİB have also realized that in order to work meaningfully with young Turkish adults in Germany, they require a sustained and legally secured presence in Germany. This is one of the reasons why the three major Islamic players in Germany have tried to achieve recognition as a religious body, a *Religionsgemeinschaft* in the sense of a *Körperschaft des öffentlichen Rechts.* This would elevate their status beyond a simple lawful association to an organization authorized to impose taxes, to fill free time on TV and other mass media, to instruct Muslim children in German public schools, to cater officially for inmates in hospitals and prisons, to receive subsidies for their work with the young—to name only a few of the benefits involved. At the same time, the struggle to achieve official recognition has incited discussions within these organizations about their future direction. Clearly, a Turkey-centred agenda of Islamic revival does not suffice anymore. Instead, organizations such as *Milli Görüş* nowadays grapple with dual citizenship, juvenile crime, and social work. Not surprisingly, the internal differentiation of opinions has increased. In short, Islamic organizations in Germany are not simply outposts of Turkish domestic politics anymore, if they ever were. And their positions on the value of liberal democracy have diversified.

(3) Translation Instead of Transplantation

The victim angle emphasizing disintegration and the instrumentalization of young Turks by religious and nationalist organization seriously underrates the fertile potentials of young Turks living in Germany. The conceptualization of collective action based on essentialist categories underlying the disintegration thesis is seriously flawed. The disintegration thesis rests on a simplistic understanding of Durkheim's *The Division of Labour* (1964): the advancing differentiation of society—read: increasing division of labour or modernization—threatens the shared consciousness based on the essential similarity of individual immigrants. Into the gap arising between the level of differentiation, on the one side, and the level of shared consciousness, on the other, moves anomie. Yet, leaving the account at that, we learn nothing about why and how immigrant youth mobilize and organize. Again, they are simply victims of fundamentalist zealots.

We need to reformulate the problem of discrimination and non-recognition to arrive at a more satisfactory interpretation of cultural activities of young German Turks. Collective representations cannot be simply imputed from classification into singular categories such as loser of modernization processes, nationality, immigrant, religion, or ethnicity. Rather, in a relational perspective, we need to specify the mechanisms through which mobilization proceeds in social and symbolic ties.

The victim angle, for example, neglects all those youth who understand themselves as practising Muslims, yet not as Islamists. Moreover, in three consecutive surveys among young Turks in Berlin (1989, 1991, 1997), about 24% to 27% of the young people said they had a close tie to religion, while between 36% and 50% responded that theirs was a somewhat distant attitude (Senatsverwaltung für Gesundheit und Soziales 1997: 3). The concept of disintegration is flawed because it tends to emphasize the idea of either uprootedness or transplantation. It is here that the term 'translated people' is apt to enrich existing images. This term, borrowed from the novelist Salman Rushdie (1989), is different from 'uprooted' (Handlin 1973), i.e. immigrants seeking to acculturate to a majority core, and 'transplanted' (Bodnar 1985), i.e. newcomers who transfer their cultural baggage from the country of origin to their new homesteads. Immigrants continually engage in translating languages, culture, norms, and social and symbolic ties. Note that the term 'translated' does not aim to criticize Handlin's and Bodnar's analyses. Their work dealt with European migrants in the United States around the turn of the century. Migration and adaptation occurred under different circumstances than today.

Since we know that people usually do not fly around on magic carpets but cross bridges and open or walk through doors, the spatial embeddedness of locally specific yet internationally transferrable resources places a limit to the free-floating symbolic representations and attachments. There are limits to translation in that strong ties cannot easily exist to many groups, organizations, and networks. However, relating to more than one collective identity does not necessarily result in a cognitive and emotional overload.

The vibrant energy freed by translations can materialize in the adaptation of musical styles. Music groups export hip hop and rap to Turkey. A preliminary ethnographic analysis of some texts by Turkish youth suggests that empirical research would do well to extend its one-sided focus on discrimination, alienation, and sympathy to religiously

Islamic and nationalist organizations. One young Germany-Turkish man (*Deutschland-Türke*) put it succinctly:

'Ich bin, der ich bin. Diese scheiße mit den zwei kulturen steht mir bis hier, was soll das, was bringt mir'n kluger schnack mit zwei fellen, auf denen mein arsch kein platz hat, 'n fell streck ich mir über'n leib, damit mir nich bange wird, aber unter'n arsch brauch ich verdammich bloß festen boden, wo ich kauer und ende. Die wollen mir weismachen, daß ich wie ne vertrackte rumheul an muttern ihr zipfel und, auch wenn's hell is, bibber vor angst, weil mich das mit innen und außen plagt.' (Zaimoglu 1995: 96).*

This is not the double consciousness in the sense of W. E. B. DuBois (1989: 1–9) which divides the space of consciousness with a veil. Quite contrary, it is partly a self-conscious search for individual and collective identity, navigating the unsteady waters of both Germany and Turkey. 1.5 and second-generation Turkish youth in Germany have not become exactly like Germans. Nor are they any longer just like Turks in the former country of origin. These expressions of identity are transnational, embedded in more encompassing youth subcultures.

The Core of Cultural Transnationalization: Syncretist Symbolic Ties

What the discussion of the transnationalization of politics already indicated, comes to the fore when looking at collective identity related to religion and nation: underlying this extension is a recognition that lively transnational social spaces not only require concrete social ties but also symbolic ties involving acts of imagination. In the age of instantaneous telecommunication, not to forget on-the-spot social science and theology, religious communities such as the *umma* can foster global images of spiritual imagination. These communities have local roots, sometimes in two or more countries, while symbolic ties act as bridges between different nation-state contexts.

The *umma* is a particularly interesting case of imagined transnational space because the claim extends to a truly transnational Muslim community of believers transcending nation-state borders and the domestic politics of the countries covered. While there is certainly no one *umma*, many Turkish-German organizations entertain close formal links to counterparts not only in Turkey but also in other European countries.

* 'I am who I am. This shit with the two cultures—I am fed up to the back teeth with it, what about it; why would I need clever chat on two hides, on which my ass does not fit. I dress myself with a hide so that I am not afraid anymore. But under my ass I very much need solid ground, where I crouch and wind up. They are trying to tell me that I cling like a leech to my mothers strings; when it is daylight, I shiver because I am afraid because I am tormented on the inside and the outside' (Zaimoglu 1995: 96).

For example, IGMG entertains close links to the former Turkish *Refah Partisi*. Even more transnational is the Association of Islamic Cultural Centers (VIKZ), since it constitutes the German branch of a worldwide enterprise with representations in countries such as Poland, the Czech Republic, Russia, USA, Argentina, and Brazil (see Feindt-Riggers and Steinbach 1997: 44–6 for a gloomy evaluation). While Muslim organizations are not structured in the same worldwide way as the Catholic church, transnational ties foster networks that go beyond bilateral linkages.

In sum, the positive feedback processes concern a declining legitimacy of cultural assimilation as a shared vision, the extension of multicultural rights, the denial of political rights, and the experiences of cultural discrimination and socio-economic exclusion, the translation of cultural and political conflicts from Turkey to Germany and back, and the entrepreneurial and creative use of collective representations taken from various contexts. All these have contributed to an increasing transnationalization (see Figure 7.3).

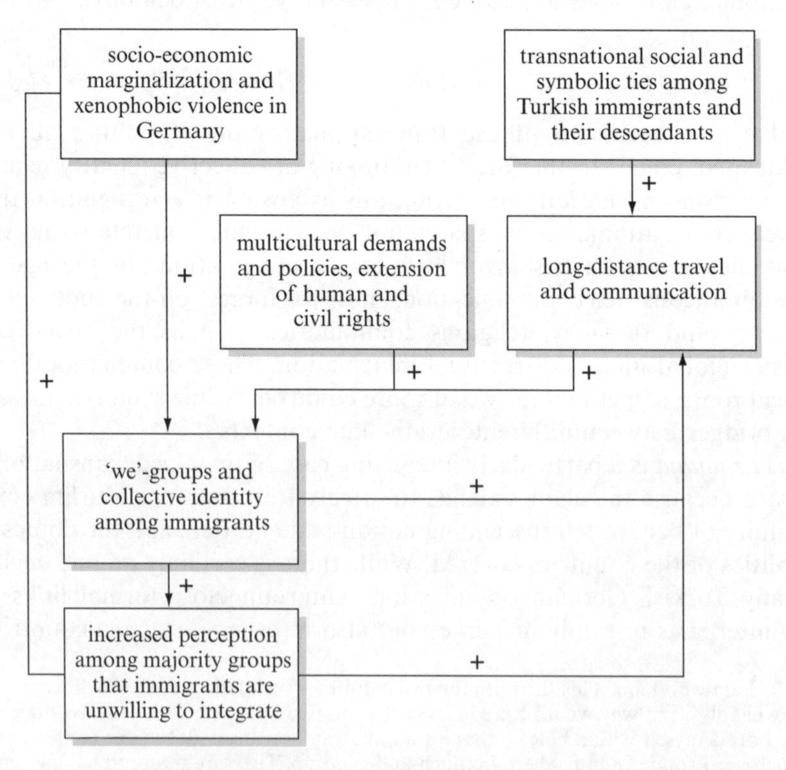

FIG. 7.3. *Cumulative causation in transnational spaces: positive feedback effects in the German-Turkish transnational space*

The Many Faces of Cultural Syncretism

Looking at similar phenomena, some observers have peremptorily coined the concept of hybrid identity, individual and collective. The social space of hybrid identities are then thought to be diasporas, especially in the British case with the experience of Afro-Caribbeans (Clifford 1994). However, this hypothesis has to be qualified, when looking at the experience of migrants and refugees from Turkey who have lived in Germany—not only because 'hybrid' connotes offspring not able to reproduce itself. The empirical material available suggests that there is no utopia of a Turkish homeland among second-generation Turks; which is somewhat different for members of some Kurdish groups.

Instead of stretching the term 'diaspora' beyond its limits, it is more meaningful to speak of a segmented and transnationalized cultural space, characterized by syncretist identities and populated by sundry ethnic, national, religious, and subcultural groups: transnational means that cultural elements from both the countries of origin and destination have found entry in the cultural repertoire of the descendants of migrants, aided by constant border-crossing communication. In addition, it is sometimes part of an international or global culture, as in the youth subculture. Collective representations can be thought to be syncretist to emphasize the active role of the immigrants themselves.

Segmented cultural space means, first, that there could be a significant dichotomy between cultural expressions and identity in the public realm, on the one hand, and in the private sphere, on the other. So far, most of the discussion of cultural practices and collective identity has focused on the highly contested public realm, revolving around Islamism, cultural (non-) recognition, and multicultural policies. However, it would be premature to conclude from highly contested and symbolic political debates and answers of respondents to such items—Islamic conceptions of law and order vs. laicism and democracy—that non-adaptation of Turkish migrants in Germany is deepening. By contrast, we know very little about adaptation to cultural practices and everyday life in the private or small-group realm (Yalçın-Heckmann 1994).

Second, cultural segmentation characterizes the world of Turkish migrants along ethnic and religious differences. For example, not only Sunni but also Alevi groups have begun to act collectively. The internal and cross-cutting ethnic and religious differentiation among Turkish immigrants in Germany are varied and complicated. If we take the three most numerous both self- and other-defined national and ethnic groups among Turkish citizens and their descendants as a point of departure—Turks, Kurds, and Arabs among others—we can differentiate the following groups in a rough and preliminary way: among Turks and Arabs we find mostly Sunnis, Alevis, and atheists; among Kurds we find all these groups and very small Shi'ite groups such as the Yezidis (see Spuler-Stegmann 1996 and Aydin 1997). A recent study identified 47 distinct ethnic groups in Turkey (Andrews 1989). Current processes of positive feedback causation suggest that groups other than Sunnis and Alevis are waiting in the wings to join the multicultural fray. This is a typical 'Tocqueville effect': a move from very repressive to somewhat attenuated policies towards non-Turkish cultural practices has led to even higher hopes and desires among ethnic and religious groups. And mobilization has surged. With the Turkish government's relaxation of bans on associations and non-Turkish languages, culture and identity politics among ethnic groups in Turkey have revived, e.g. among Alevis, Circassians, and Laz. As has been the case among Kurds and Sunni Islamists discussed above, we could expect this new mobilization to translate from Turkey to Germany. Alevis in Turkey, for instance, have founded a political party (*Bariş Partisi*), closely tied to supporting Alevi groups all over Europe (own interviews, 1998).

This mobilization has been underway among Alevis in Turkey and Germany, involving a politicization of religion in both contexts, mutually reinforcing each other. In Turkey, a state obligated to a laicist model, the rulers have shown tendencies to elevate the Sunni version of Islam to a quasi-official religion in the early 1990s, which was later renounced by the military. In turn, the PKK also jumped the train by incorporating Islamic rhetoric into their programme and official proclamations. This has had severe consequences for some PKK adherents and supporters. For example, Alevis as a whole have been a rather secular group. During the 1970s and 1980s they formed a good-sized support group for militant left operations; and the PKK recruited a sizable portion of fighters from this milieu. However, estranged by Islamic declarations by the PKK's leader, some Alevis have turned to ethnic symbols, thereby claiming an own collective identity. One way of doing this has been by the adoption of Zaza, a Kurdish language spoken around Dersim, a majority Alevi city in south-eastern Anatolia (Roy 1996: 101).

Generally, transnational bridges helped to transfer the conflicts between Sunnis and Alevis to Germany. Religious and political entrepreneurs—the descendants of migration brokers—are clearly more transnational than their followers in moving between the two worlds. Up until now, most active Alevis participated in the German political realm, for example, in the Social-Democratic Party (SPD). Trying to reach members of the second generation, more and more Alevi entrepreneurs organize religious groups and try to mobilize their clients around the cultural symbols of Alevidom. In turn, this has feedback effects for conflicts between Sunnis and Alevis in Turkey; financial, human, and social resources flow from Germany to Turkey to support the development of an organizational infrastructure among Alevis.

Without a close analysis of actual patterns of adaptation and, possibly, syncretism in both the public and private realms and the manifold variations and trench lines in the religious world, we risk dramatic and unsubstantiated conclusions such as the portrayal of a more or less coherent Turkish transnational community or diaspora. Syncretist identities in this case do not signal a full-fledged diaspora consciousness, on the one hand, nor does it necessarily denote a successful stage in the transition from one collective identity to another, on the other. We do not find overwhelming evidence for a collective identity carrying elements of both Turkish or Kurdish and German but with a strong dominance of the former element due to an aspired homeland or collective religious community. Also we have not yet encountered the ideal-typical collective identity succession from Italian to Italian-American, and further on to simply American. Rather, we detect transnational ties and often segmented cultural practices that do refer to a successful synthesis in some cases—such as hip-hop musicians among the cultural elite—but also to an unintegrated existence of both German and Turkish elements next to each other. The latter is sometimes thought to apply to young Islamists. However, their painting gear contains more than replicas of faded Turkish sketches. Above all, they are what the author Zafer Şenocak calls *Deutschland-Türken* (Germany-Turks).

Prospects for the Further Development and the Possible Demise of Transnational Social Spaces

Although transnational social spaces are by and large neither intermittent nor serendipitous developments, two caveats relating to their continued feasibility are in order. Politicians, administrators, and members of civil society in fairly liberal nation-states may attenuate the casualness they currently show towards ethnically-based political, religious, and cultural formations which entertain strong transnational linkages. The conditions for the existence of transnational spaces are mercurial. In times of war, nationalism in the country of immigration can induce factors under which self-proclaimed guardians of the state accuse groups with transnational linkages of disloyalty and test them about whether they are patriots or traitors.

Consider the *cause célèbre* of German Americans or native-born Americans of German descent for a moment. For most of the latter part of the nineteenth century and until World War One, many of the ties this chapter described for Germany-Turks characterized German-Americans in the USA. The revolution of 1848–9 triggered a significant part of the German flow and, subsequently, German political radicals of the era and the reform wing of the Republican Party in the USA cross-fertilized each other, as the distinguished career of Carl Schurz indicates. Economic ties can be found in the development of the American economy by firms such as Anheiser Busch, Steinway pianos, and all of the American optical industry. Moreover, German-language schools and a rich *Vereinsleben* signalled the buoyant symbolic ties of *Landsmannschaften*. Despite that, in the wake of war between the USA and Germany, almost all of these linkages sundered, and in fact most German-Americans gave up their native language as well as their *Gesangvereine* and other distinctive cultural forms. For example, the legislatures forbade German as a language of instruction in high schools in 26 US states. And church congregations switched from German to English. Germanness lived on only in certain sects of the Lutheran Church, and even there in hidden forms. Not only did transnational ties disappear, but for all intents and purposes so did America's largest white ethnic group vanish from the public scene.

Transnationalization can also demise when seen in the longer historical perspective for reasons other than the domestic repercussions of international conditions. What nowadays seems like a comparative advantage at one point—for example, Kurdish exiles having a secure political basis to struggle for more autonomy or even independence in the south-eastern provinces of Turkey, or Turkish Muslims of various religious groups using Germany as a base to fight against secularism and laicism in Turkey—may be a springboard to a certified religious group status for some, while it becomes a ghettoized trap for others, preventing them from making more successful moves within the nation-state that has become their new home. It is only when these immigrants find an additional basis for their political and cultural activities other than the affairs of the country of origin that elements of transnationalization can remain beneficial to them in the long run (see Modood and Berthoud 1997 for more examples). In short, we should not lose sight of the ever-present lures of cultural adaptation, on the one hand,

and the vicissitudes of socio-economic and cultural segregation in the immigration countries, on the other.

All these examples suggest that it is too early to say whether these forms of transnational spaces are enduring or rather temporary phenomena lasting for little more than one or two generations. What is certain, is that the development of transnational social spaces populated by migrants is part of a larger phenomenon of transnationalization and globalization. Migrant organizations ride the crest of an unprecedented growth of International Non-Governmental Organizations (INGOs): in the period from 1970 to 1994, a total of 544 ethnic organizations registered with the Union of International Organizations. Transnational communities of faith have doubled since 1970, to a total of more than 3,000 (Boulding 1997: p. x). Not only are there transnational spaces populated by migrant and refugees but also by birdwatchers, business-persons, soccer hooligans, political parties with international branches, devoted members of religious sects, and new social movements (Tarrow 1996)—this list could go on almost endlessly. Some of these are organized in INGOs, out of which the business associations (BINGOs) occupy a substantial part, but in which unspectacular groups such as meteorologists and ophthalmologists are the majority (Boli and Thomas 1997).

Conclusion: From Places and Essences to Spaces and Ties

Various forms of cumulative causation in international migration start with migration as a set of self-feeding processes, typically producing migration flows that may last several decades with a clearly defined beginning and end. This is a necessary but not a sufficient hallmark for more transnational social spaces. More enduring forms of sustained border-crossing transactions involve a growing transnational expansion of migrants' activities, encompassing all spheres of life. International migrants partake in a more general process of transnationalization, albeit not as large 'global players'. This does not mean, however, that migrants engaged in transnational exchanges and reciprocity already form transnational communities (as implied by Portes, Guarnizo, and Landolt 1999), or that they are the prototypes of a global lifestyle (Beck 1996: 55–61). And we do not know whether they are part of an ethnic 'global contagion' (Gurr 1993) in advancing collective identities that are often no less essentialized than the completed nation-building projects of their immigration states. Moreover, the sustained transnationalization of migrant ties is often called 'transnationalism'—as if migrants engaged in border-crossing activities held a separate and distinct ideology that counters capitalism and imperialism (see, for example, Basch, Schiller, and Blanc 1994 and Smith and Guarnizo 1998). These hortatory and alarmist, celebratory and dystopian tones are unwarranted. Whether lasting forms of transnational social spaces have developed that will reach beyond the second generation of immigrants is too early to say. However, these phenomena have turned out to be a worthy subject of study in their own right. Transmigrants have occupied economic niches in the changing division of labour and political entrepreneurs are busy building highways carrying conflicts across borders. Above all, transnationality functions for immigrants to search for and designate acceptable labels for self-designation among immigrant groups. It thus facilitates the establishment of a consciousness of kind, a crucial part of collective identity. Transnational bridges are one element to reduce social distance within immigrant groups, to facilitate communication, and they may eventually result in the formation of a common culture, or a culture shared by both immigrants and natives.

The dynamics driving the formation of transnational spaces are of utmost importance. Underlying the accumulation of local assets and their transnational transmission among migrants is a seminal tendency in liberal democratic nation-states. They are increasingly unable or unwilling to enforce assimilation, yet they are not entirely ready to recognize cultural diversity. A unique brew of experienced discrimination and greater tolerance towards multiculturalism fuels cumulative border-crossing activities in the political and economic dimensions.

The problems arising in this second period of transnationalization are much more far-reaching than in the first one. One challenge has often been noted: nation-states controlling international migration and the activities of migrants are not simply faced with checking borders or with granting specific legal status up to citizenship. The civil rights revolution for immigrants, the internalization of international human rights norms in nation-state regulations and social rights available in nationally bounded welfare states—such as the residency principle—have limited the sovereignty of democratic nation-states not so much in admitting but in expelling non-citizens and cutting spill-over flows at will.

Yet the challenges to nation-state policies in emigration and immigration contexts are much broader once transnational social spaces in the guise of transnational communities have unfolded. They question cherished notions of place-bound attributes of groups and organizations, and direct our attention to the relational mechanisms of communities without geographical propinquity. Although the relationship between countries of origin and destination is still asymmetric in terms of power, the interdependence is stronger due to migrants living in both contexts, either practically, when migrants commute back and forth and exchange goods and information, or symbolically, when cultural representations span two or more countries. It is here that further questions emerge such as: What happens to kinship systems and their traditional living together in one place when economic reproduction, risk diversification and betterment encompass various countries? What happens to notions of nationalism and nation-state unity when citizens move abroad and seek to establish a new homeland, carved out of the old one? What happens to notions of cultural uniqueness when persons acquire cultural repertoires which are transnational?

We have raised the question of the durability of transnational links: Does transnationalization entail new forms of immigrant adaptation? It is doubtful whether the either-or logic, such as either eventual adaptation or transnational spaces, is sufficient to grasp the importance of transnational social and symbolic ties. True, scholars have mostly approached the terrain of what we have called here transnational social spaces when studying nationalism among immigrants as a matter of divided loyalty. Such research looks at moments when the country of origin and the country of destination came into direct conflict—World War One for German-Americans or World War Two for Japanese-Americans, for instance. But why should we assume that immigrants can only entertain one brand of loyalty to one country only? Since immigrant adaptation and the maintenance of transnational ties are not necessarily linked in a linear and reciprocal fashion, then much more complex constellations of cultural identity, economic participation, and political membership open up for research.

8

The Adaptive Functions of Social Capital: Transnationalization and Nation-State Membership

The empirical evidence we have encountered suggests that transnational ties do indeed coexist with continuing immigrant adaptation. Initially, this has led us to the second puzzle guiding this study: How can we explain that the formation of transnational social spaces and unfolding immigrant adaptation proceed simultaneously? Our findings, crystallizing in this puzzle, flatly contradict known theories of immigrant adaptation. The objection regarding concomitant transnationalization and immigrant adaptation is: the more transnational or multifocal ties immigrants entertain, the greater their ambivalence towards the immigration polity, the weaker the roots in the nation-state of settlement, the stronger the incentives to form a transnational community, the bolder the claim to a diaspora, the greater the tendency on the part of natives to question the allegiance of the newcomers, and, finally, the weaker the inclination of immigrants to adapt in the country of destination. In order to understand why the empirical evidence clashes at times with this chain of assumptions, we need to relate conceptually migrant border-crossing links to the well-established theoretical frameworks for immigrant adaptation—assimilation and ethnic pluralism.

A preliminary answer to the second puzzle has significant implications for a sophisticated understanding of the economic, political, and cultural sequel to large-scale international migration. The transnational nature of many ties evolving out of international migration, reinforcing and altering pre-migration linkages, concern membership in groups and organizations, such as nation-state citizenship, and informal membership, such as participation in networks that find their expression in cross-national business and cultural representations. Therefore, the debates on immigrant participation in business and labour markets, their political rights and civic duties, their sense of belonging and cultures, cannot be understood without explicit reference and consideration of both local and transnational ties in the places of origin and destination. These various mechanisms and forms of social capital have adaptive functions. It helps newcomers to adjust both to the demands and requirements of the immigration societies, and enables transmigrants to productively redevelop and forge links within migration systems.

This chapter discusses the plausibility of two propositions:

1. The trajectories of immigrant adaptation envisaged by the canonical concepts of assimilation and ethnic pluralism theories hold in certain cases. Other phenomena, such as continuing transnational ties and linkages, need to be categorized in a new and separate conceptual niche. Assimilation and ethnic pluralism are insufficient because they espouse a container concept of space—adaptation of immigrants within nation-states is considered to be a process not significantly influenced by border-crossing transactions. However, since growing transnationalization contributes to the plurality of avenues open to labour migrants and refugees in various nation-states, but is nevertheless always tied to specific places, the concept of border-crossing expansion of space enriches our understanding of adaptation.

2. There is an elective affinity between the three broad concepts to explain and describe immigrant adaptation: assimilation, ethnic pluralism, and border-crossing expansion of social space, on the one hand, and the concepts used to describe and explain economic activities, politics (citizenship), and culture, on the other hand. In the economic sphere the concepts are socio-economic parity with the majority groups, enclaves and niches, and transnational entrepreneurship; in the political realm: national, multicultural, and transnational citizenship, and in the culture sphere: acculturation, cultural retention, and transnational syncretism. Treated as ideal-typical concepts each of the concepts captures an important part of political membership.

First, the discussion focuses on how contemporary international migration processes differ from those at the beginning of this century in several respects. Second, the analysis moves on to the canonical concepts of immigrant adaptation: assimilation, ethnic pluralism, enriched by border-crossing expanse of social space. The discussion refers to the economic, political and cultural adjustment of immigrants in the countries of immigration. Third, the three ideal-typical models serve to sketch how the different forms of transnational social spaces—transnational reciprocity in small groups, transnational circuits, and transnational communities—can be linked in chronological sequence to the modes of adaptation predicted by assimilation and ethnic pluralism. Fourth, the analysis dives into three realms of immigrant adaptation—economic, political, and cultural, and—in using manifold examples from the migratory world—shows that each concept describes important aspects.

Changing Immigration and Adaptation Patterns in the Contemporary World

Virtually all researches on present-day migration adaptation attempt to use assimilation and ethnic pluralism, dating from the effort to make sense of mass migration into the USA in the early parts of this century. Today's discussion of immigrant adaptation is rife with comparisons to what we assume to know about the experience of pre-1924 immigrants in the USA. So is this chapter. Yet nothing is more deceitful than historical resemblances and alleged similarities between now and then. We have to retain awareness that in different contexts outwardly and even basically similar phenomena may have different causes and effects. To deal with it meaningfully, it is necessary to make these implicit comparisons explicit, and point out where such comparisons are appropriate and where the contemporary period radically differs.

The 'new immigration' in both Europe and the United States is only about thirty to forty years old. This is not a long time regarding processes of immigrant adaptation that can be evaluated in their totality only after three to four generations. But most of the data available on either side of the Atlantic Ocean is built on the experiences of the first and the 1.5 generations. And even if we have systematic evidence for the second generation, it is on teenagers and very young adults. On a more sanguine note, it is also true that the path-breaking concepts of assimilation and ethnic pluralism emerged in the late 1910s and early 1920s—again about thirty years after immigrants to the USA had started to hail from Europe in ever-increasing numbers, until this virtually stopped from 1924 until the 1960s.

In the past decades, processes of admission to membership, participation of immigrants, and the willingness of newcomers and natives to adapt have not changed entirely, but the processes involved have become more plural and multilayered. While this could be read as advancing the trend towards the build-up of new social spaces via transnational circuits and communities, we cannot draw hard and fast conclusions peremptorily. Looking at evidence from the wealth of research on immigrant group experiences in the West European, Australian, Japanese, and North American contexts in recent years, there is an unmistakable trend towards assimilation in the political and economic sphere; albeit signs towards the marginalization of substantial minorities within selected immigrant groups clearly exist as well. Economic integration and socio-economic marginalization frequently co-exist. What has to be taken into account are the following four seminal changes in international migration:

(1) Ongoing Migration Flows under Graded Restrictions

We can expect the ongoing flows since the 1960s to sustain themselves for quite some time (OECD: SOPEMI, various years). Processes of cumulative mobility occur in a period of unprecedented population growth, although cumulative immobility is even more widespread, taking into account indicators such as migration flows and stocks of foreign-born over the past 150 years. While this is not the end of international migration history as we know it, it is likely that this makes the immigration states spaces of continuous immigration rather than states of periodic entry. The continuity here does not refer to one and the same immigrant group but to successive flows from different emigration countries. Continued inflows bring new recruits who enrich and replenish immigrant communities and build new ones, compete with selected natives and sometimes threaten their cherished perceptions of relative cultural homogeneity. In addition, these probable newcomers include substantial numbers with still close ties to the country of origin.

By contrast, periodic entry had been characteristic for virtually all nation-states in the North-Western hemisphere since the early nineteenth century. There were great pauses in between. Upon the great inflow of Europeans into the USA from the 1880s to the 1910s followed a period from roughly the 1920s until the 1960s, when the flow fell to the functional equivalent of zero. In Europe and Australia, the 1920s and 1930s also constituted a period of only minor immigration. Indeed, in this particular inter-war period, almost all European countries experienced a hiatus in large-scale immigration—with the exception of the then outlier France who has experienced demographic shortages for centuries. And if acculturation, naturalization, and economic integration in the national economy had not already worked their way, the two World Wars violently ruptured existing transnational spaces. After the millions of downtrodden forced labour for the German war machinery and the refugee turmoil following World War Two another decisive pause set in. But very soon, foreign labour recruitment jump-started again in the late 1950s on a major scale (for historical statistics, see Moch 1992 on Europe and Segal 1993 on the whole world). All the moratorium periods mentioned here in passing made sure that domestic factors would prove essential in inserting new immigrants into the immigration states, minimizing transnational influences.

It would therefore be highly misleading to take this pattern of immigration from the 1920s until the 1960s as a proxy for current and future developments because it occurred in a glasshouse virtually excluding durable transnationalization.

We now see a more perpetual pattern of immigration on the horizon. On the demand side, it includes more than one generation that progressed as a single cohort through the following periods, as European immigrants did in the United States around the turn of the nineteenth to the twentieth century. Nowadays, in the USA and Australia, the immigration levels of the 1960s and 1970s show no signs of abiding (Barkan 1996). The trend is steady. In Europe as a whole, despite restrictive labour import policies and tightened admission procedures for refugees, immigration flows have even increased over the past decades (Table 8.1).

On the supply side, in most of the developing countries, the factors causing, precipitating, and favouring migration such as wage differentials, high risks upon economic activities in the country of origin, civil wars in regional conflicts, and the penetration of markets show no signs of abiding.

Once processes of international migration have proceeded, we find closure movements on the demand side going beyond the usual cycle of open-restrictive immigration policy. However, the post-World War Two experience of expanding human and civil rights regimes on the national

TABLE 8.1. *Annual migration into the EU (in thousands)*

Year	Regular immigration of non-citizens	Asylum seekers and refugees	Ethnic Germans (Aussiedler, Germany only)	Total
1986	1189	217	43	1449
1987	1218	187	79	1484
1988	1500	253	203	1956
1989	2185	334	377	2896
1990	2445	460	397	3302
1991	1944	593	222	2759
1992	2134	719	231	3084
1993	1989	591	219	2799
1994	1643	334	223	2200
1995	1674	288	218	2180

Source: Eurostat, Statistisches Amt der Europäischen Gemeinschaften, Amt für Veröffentlichungen der EU, Reihe A, Jahrbücher und jährliche Statistiken, Luxemburg 1997.

Statistisches Bundesamt 1994 & 1997: Statistisches Jahrbuch für die Bundesrepublik Deutschland, Berlin.

and international level indicates that zero immigration in the North is a highly unlikely feature of the contemporary world, despite more restrictive policies in the European context. All this means that, for immigration states, periodic entry has probably been replaced by continuous entry and much shorter time intervals in between major flows of immigrant categories.

(2) The Communications and Transport Revolution

As emphasized in the preceding chapter, the technological breakthroughs in long-distance communication and travel over the past 150 years have considerably decreased costs for bridging long geographical distances. Improved methods of communication such as satellite dishes that transmit emigration country affairs and products, telephone, fax, internet, and other electronic means have set the necessary stage for the development of transnational ties. And transnational commuting is now possible to an ever-increasing extent. These technological developments have liberated kinship groups, religious and political organizations, and assorted communities from the confines of one specific territorial place. Increased information makes international long-distance migration more likely, even for shorter periods of time.

(3) A Paradoxical Trend: Increasing Clustering and Dispersion of Immigrants

If this rendition is plausible, then geographic clustering of some immigrant categories—a time-proven effect of migrant and migration networks—is not going to dissolve that easily, at least as long as the same migrant group is concerned. Clustering is a trend especially among those migrants who convert to a large extent social capital into economic capital in order to establish themselves in the countries of immigration. This applies best to labour migrants. There is even some empirical evidence—at least pertaining to the USA—that the geographic clustering of the new immigrants is even more concentrated than anytime before in modern history (Massey 1995). In other words, this is a variation of the second half of our first puzzle of 'why so many migrants *out of* so few places' further on '*to* so few places'. This could have consequences for language retention and syncretist cultural practices. Ongoing international migration, the transfer of associations from emigration to immigration countries and the spatial clustering help to shift the balance somewhat from the still dominant immigration country influences to emigration country impacts and new syncretist forms. The 'so many out of so few places' effect inherent in any international migration strengthens this pattern. Eventually, this means that immigrants' social capital gains added value because country of origin and syncretist forms, such as employment with compatriots, country of origin political activities and *mélange* cultural practices figure more prominently in their new lives. Qualitatively new stages such as transnational social spaces develop out of densely knit networks of exchange and cooperation. This implies that the range of opportunities for migrants expands as a result of transnational transactions *sui generis*. One caveat is in order. Long-term geographical clustering works in those cases where we observe the continued immigration of the same immigrant group. Take Mexicans in the USA.

Paradoxically, processes in contemporary migration also foster a trend opposite to clustering, dispersion. It best applies to what we have called human and economic capital migrants in transnational families (Gunatilleke 1997). Labour markets for highly skilled professionals have become more transnationalized—Indian computer specialists in the USA and Europe represent just one prominent example. Human capital migrants in selected fields with universally applicable skills often have more than one option for destination. Their movement is concentrated to urban conglomerations with 'global city' functions in the financial and service sectors, often proceeds within multinational companies, and the stay in one particular place abroad tends to be more short term when compared to lower occupational- and social-status migrants (Wolter 1996; see Glebe 1997 for a case study on Frankfurt). Although they also show distinct patterns of spatial concentration on the city level, their dispersion on the country level tends to be higher than among migrants who have been recruited into industrial sectors during the 1960s and 1970s. For example, while the bulk of Turkish labour migrants went to Germany, Turkish professionals have established themselves in virtually all countries in the OECD world, including Australia, Canada, and the USA (see İçduygu 1991 for an example).

(4) Diversifying Economic Opportunities for Immigrants

The economic opportunity structure for immigrants has changed radically and has diversified. Seen from the demand side, European immigrants around the turn of the century in the USA entered at the time of an economic boom and long-term expansion of the American economy. Because of many factors, contemporary immigrants and refugees have entered not only highly stratified economies characterized by substantial income inequalities but have also experienced growing labour market obstacles to traditional careers for blue-collar immigrants.

As to the supply side, new immigrants to the USA who hail mostly from Latin America and South-East and South Asia, as well as newcomers to Europe who departed from North Africa, the Middle East, and the Indian subcontinent, usually are highly differentiated groups right from the start and enter economies with extremely stratified or segmented sectors. The scope ranges from illegal immigrants in American agriculture or European construction business to upwardly mobile middle-class academics in research labouratories (Stalker 1994: 196).

In the period of contemporary massive economic restructuring, various forms of social capital yield additional benefits for both natives and newcomers. Existing social ties, exclusively connecting immigrants to jobs in the manufacturing and agricultural sector, may lead to socio-economic marginalization. This is exactly the opposite for symbol and knowledge workers, business administrators, and economic entrepreneuers. In sum, the diversity of contemporary immigration into the USA, for example, is such that different immigrant groups account at once for the highest and lowest rates of education, self-employment, home ownership, poverty, welfare-dependency, and fertility (see Rumbaut 1997*b*: 507). Increasingly, this is also the European experience (Salt 1997).

In a trend towards an 'hourglass' economy, with knowledge-intensive, high-paying jobs at one end and labour-intensive, low-paying jobs at the other, the socio-economic opportunity structure for immigrants has changed fundamentally. It has taken away several rungs of the mobility ladder that have been crucial for enabling immigrants, especially those with little education and few job skills, who started to climb up from the bottom. Therefore, the issue of divergent destinies of immigrant groups comes to the fore even more than in the past and has to be dealt with conceptually.

Transmigrant Examples: Mexicans in the USA and Turks around the Globe

There are two groups that allow us a glimpse at the impact of changing demand- and supply-side factors and ongoing migration upon assimilation, ethnic pluralism, and the border-crossing expansion of social space, that is Mexican-Americans in the USA and Turkish migrants abroad. In the Mexican case, a contiguous frontier—a geographically diffuse border zone—between South and North has resulted over the past 100 years in some of the very same effects that have been observable only in the last few decades around the globe over larger geographical distances. Practically all Mexican-Americans living in the USA nowadays are immigrants who entered after the United States annexed the former Mexican territories in 1848. They came mainly between 1890 when Mexican hands became of interest for the railroads and agriculture, through the 1920s when they were first recruited for the industrial hubs such as Chicago—until today, when new arrivals occupy slots in a broader range of activities. With the exception of a very short time period during the Great Depression in the 1930s, this group thus had a continuous immigration to and return migration from the United States. Since the 1960s, the flow has not been interrupted. Instead, numbers have been continually increasing. Subsequently, the stock of immigrants from Mexico who have established permanent residence in the USA has gone up continually:

1960–1970	260,000–290,000
1970–1980	1,200,000–1,550,000
1980–1990	2,100,000–2,600,000

Source: Estimates based on US Commission on Immigration Reform 1998: 8.

A contiguous border and improved means of communication and travel have made border-crossings relatively easy. Clustering of Mexican immigrants has speeded up over the past decades. They concentrate in the major metropolitan areas where job opportunities are and to which migrant networks connect them. This development has been fostered by changes in the US economy, which concentrates the majority of both high-paying and low-paying jobs in selected metropolitan centres. Yet in terms of agricultural work immigrants have spread more widely in recent years, ranging from the traditional ones in the American South-West, the North-West, the Midwest and Florida to areas such as New Jersey.

Since the late nineteenth century, some Mexican-Americans have followed the footsteps of migrants from Europe, especially in the American Midwest (Cardenas 1976)—a prime example of melting into the core, as predicted by assimilation theory in all spheres of life. However, we also encounter large pockets of Mexican-American third-generation immigrants in the South-West who have experienced downward mobility; the very opposite of successful socio-economic adaptation (Featherman and Hauser 1978: 461–78). Also, the few indigenous Mexican- Americans in states such as Arizona and New Mexico struggle to reclaim ownership rights of land which belonged to their ancestors. The category Mexican immigrants—when viewed over successive generations—ranges widely concerning the spread of income, residence, education, and political views (HPDP 1990; Skerry 1993). Migrant networks and the spreading of enforceable civil and human rights for migrants have turned processes of cumulative international mobility in a perpetuum mobile; with flows sometimes decreasing but not totally ceasing during economic depression.

In addition to these well-known trends, transnational ties carry ever more political ramifications. For example, in order to capture the electoral vote abroad and to maintain the economic remittances, the Mexican government adjusted and finally passed a dual nationality law in 1997. Nevertheless, and this is of major importance, this amendment to the Mexican constitution also cuts off citizenship *jure sanguinis* after the first generation born overseas. This suggests that the governance of nation-state membership has changed as a result of the border-crossing expansion of social space. The Mexican government is now interested in using its citizens abroad for internal purposes such as remittances and investments and as external representatives—using measures such as the Program for Mexican Communities Living Abroad (PMCLFC) (Smith 1999). One explicit reason for now encouraging Mexican immigrants to take US citizenship is that the Mexican government hopes that they will lobby on behalf of Mexico in the USA. This is vital because of the North American Free Trade Agreement (NAFTA).

One can easily argue that the Mexican case is exceptionally conducive to transnationalization because a long and contiguous South–North land frontier offers many opportunities for circular international migration and thus to establishing transnational social spaces—with the specific phenomenon of a border region, populated by competitive and mostly US-financed companies on the Mexican side (*maquiladoras*), security forces, and border-crossers on both sides. Nevertheless, the four characteristics mentioned above—ongoing emigration, communication and transport revolution, clustering and dispersion, and diversifying economic opportunities—are also operative in a very different case, that of Turkish international migrants; albeit with somewhat different results. While high levels of international migration from Turkey to Germany have effectively been slowed by the termination of recruitment in 1973, marriage and family migration have continued at lower but nevertheless rather stable levels throughout the 1980s and 1990s. And established migrant networks and transnationally operating organizations have played a role in channelling asylum seekers from Turkey to Germany at stable levels in the past twenty years (see also Chapter 3). Yet since the 1970s migration opportunities for Turkish professionals have clearly been better than for labour migrants. As mentioned above, they have dispersed to many countries.

In a significant way, the communications revolution has contributed to inter-state conflicts on the integration of Turkish migrants abroad. For example, the German government has repeatedly charged that the

Turkish counterpart inhibits the adaptation of Turkish immigrants to German life through various measures such as Turkish-language television that reports extensively on discrimination of Turks in Germany (own interviews in Turkey 1998). Whether there is any hard evidence for this claim of non-adaptation is open for empirical investigation (Karacabey 1996). What is clear, however, is that the Turkish government has a keen interest in migrants' remittances, investments, and tourism in Turkey.

While it would be presumptuous to use these neither unique nor representative but exemplary experiences as a guide to the future, they are nevertheless indicative in that we cannot treat immigrant categories of national or ethnic descent in contemporary migration as if they constituted a single age cohort. In most instances, there is continuous immigration of ever new cohorts from the countries of emigration in the South, a trend favouring the ever-increasing transnationalization of ties and capital for immigrant adaptation.

The Canonical Concepts of Assimilation and Ethnic Pluralism and an Apocryphal Extension: The Border-Crossing Expansion of Social Space

Like the gospels validated by the church, the models of assimilation and ethnic pluralism have occupied centre stage. In the contemporary period, a still apocryphal model, border-crossing expansion of social space, is needed. We can then differentiate three concepts to describe and categorize immigrant adaptation, covering the economic, political, and cultural realms (Figure 8.1).

Assimilation: Melting into the Core

The first concept, assimilation in the country of destination, still offers the most complete theory of adaptation. Essentially, immigrant adaptation means melting into the majority core in virtually all respects of life. In this view, the course of adaptation features an orderly progression from the poverty and discrimination often endured by the first generation to the rapid acculturation of the second generation and gradual economic advancement. By the third generation, the loss of ethnic linguistic and cultural traits, as well as the disappearance of earlier labour market disadvantages, could be virtually complete.

This model aptly applies best to the American situation in a specific period. One could argue that one of the main factors that contributed to the success of its predictions was a long period of extremely low

Approach / *Realms of adaptation*	Assimilation	Ethnic pluralism	Border-crossing expansion of social space
Main prediction	melting into the core	pluralization	transnationalization
Economic: social status and occupational mobility	socio-economic parity with autochthonous population; in the case of failure: socio-economic marginality	niches and enclaves; middleman minorities: groups specializing in trade and concentrating in the petite bourgeoisie	transnational entrepreneurship in kinship- and community-based groups and in transnational circuits
Political: state–citizen ties	national citizenship: unitary national political culture	multicultural citizenship: recognition of cultural differences	dual citizenship: elements from various states can be complementary
Cultural: language and collective identity	acculturation: melting into values and behaviour of the nation-state's core	cultural retention: practices and identities transplanted into a new context	syncretism: diffusion and emergence of new types—mixed identities

FIG. 8.1. *Three concepts for the analysis of immigrant adaptation in the immigration countries*

immigration—from World War One until the 1960s. During this phase assimilationist tendencies could work.

Terms such as 'assimilation' evoke the historical baggage of questionable ideological assumptions. Actually, most criticisms pertain to the obvious ideological content of assimilation theory that have been masqueraded as empirically observable facts. For example, in the original conceptualization (Park and Burgess 1969), it carried the assumption of a unified and 'non-ethnic' core culture to which immigrants adapted. This idea lost sight of the very cultural heterogeneity of the native-settled people. However, this criticism seems to be more convincing when applied to the contemporary period of sprouting subcultures than to the early part of the twentieth century.

The pioneers of assimilation theory, Park and Burgess, defined assimilation as 'a process of interpenetration and fusion in which persons and groups acquire the memories, sentiments, and attitudes of other persons and groups and, by sharing their experience and history, are incorporated with them in a common cultural life' (Park and Burgess 1969: 735). This does not mean that assimilation requires the erasure of all signs of ethnic origins, of previous political ideologies, or religious beliefs. Folkloristic elements present no problems to assimilation theory.

Instead, the model implies the adjustment of immigrants into the mainstream of the life of the immigration country. Indeed, assimilation theory is compatible with the outcome that even mainstream culture changes as a result of immigrant adaptation. In its original meaning, assimilation can be thought to be operative mainly during the socialization of immigrants:

> Assimilation takes place not so much as a result of changes in the organization as in the content, i.e., the memories, of the personality. The individual units, as a result of intimate association, interpenetrate, so to speak, and come in this way into possession of a common experience and a common tradition. The permanence and solidarity of the group rest finally upon this body of common experience and tradition.
>
> (Park and Burgess 1969: 510)

Assimilation is also not necessarily a linear process but can travel along a 'bumpy-line' (Gans 1992).

Not only are interpersonal ties of crucial importance; assimilation is also a slow process of immigrant adaptation that is usually realized in the second generation only—if the overall conditions are appropriate, such as low social distance between immigrants and majority groups, and the decline of widespread discrimination. We should therefore be very careful to claim that assimilation among immigrants of the first generation is a feasible goal. As to this category, we can only speak of partial adaptation, namely accommodation.

In its most sophisticated variant (Gordon 1964), we encounter a typology of assimilation to capture the complexity of the process, ranging from cultural, structural, marital, identificational, attitude-receptional, behaviour-receptional, to civic assimilation. Gordon distinguished two meanings of assimilation—melting pot: A + B + C = D and 'Anglo conformity': A + B + C = A. He focused on the latter type which meant, in essence, the melting of new arrivals (B, C) into the Anglo-Saxon core culture (A). The Parsonian distinction between cultural assimilation, viz. acculturation, and structural assimilation allows us to divide the staged process of adaptation. Cultural assimilation means that immigrants change their patterns of language, norms and ideals, and finally accept those found in the country of immigration. Structural assimilation refers to the process of migrants entering the social institutions of the immigration society in large numbers. It is the pivotal step, it is the 'keystone of the arch of assimilation'. Once this is achieved, all other forms of assimilation follow quasi-automatically: marital assimilation, that is intermarriage between hosts and newcomers; identificational assimilation through the development of a

sense of common peoplehood with the natives; ...
behaviour-receptional assimilation, enabled by the ...
and discrimination, respectively, on the part of the ...
final step is civic assimilation, indicating the absence of ...
conflicts between immigrants and natives. Indeed, this ...
most plausible renditions of what happened to some maj...
groups of European descent over four to five generations ...
the USA in the early part of this century.

Without necessarily adhering to the stage-conception ...
models—for example, cultural assimilation as a necessary but n...
cient step towards economic integration—we could take some o...
main tenets to describe this pattern: it implies in the socio-econ...
realm that immigrants and refugees reach at least rough socio-econo...
parity with the prevailing occupational, residential, and behaviou...
patterns shown by representative groups of the native population. In
the political realm, a specific dimension of structural assimilation, we
expect immigrants or at least their descendants to acquire the citizenship of the country of settlement and express loyalty in the case of war. Furthermore, assimilation means that acculturation is especially prevalent among the second generation. Such developments may be accompanied by a mutual exchange of norms, values, and behavioural patterns between the migrant and native groups.

Ethnic Pluralism: Malevolent and Benevolent Pluralization

Ethnic pluralism constitutes the second main concept of immigrant adaptation. It emphasizes those experiences which distinguish immigrants from natives, on the basis of economic, political, and cultural pluralization, sometimes involving ethnic and religious separation. Largely disregarding the experience of forced migrants such as African Americans in slavery and partly conquered minorities such as Mexican Americans in the USA, the stage model of ethnic pluralists focuses on a pluralization of groups, world-views, and institutions beneficial to immigrants. The earliest mode conceives of four ideal-typical stages (Kallen 1996: 82, 87). First, immigrants try to adjust economically and seek upward mobility. Second, as a reaction to immigration country conditions, such as the experience of discrimination, the group begins to search for its past. This results, third, in a process opposite to assimilation, called dissimilation. In a fourth phase, true pluralism will emerge. The claim is that unison in a nation-state can be best achieved by each ethnic, i.e. cultural group, expressing their 'nationality'. Programmatically, there is no contradiction between immigrants' desire to adjust and cultural pluralism. Speaking about Jewish immigrants in nineteenth-century America, Kallen summarizes that 'the most early American of the immigrant groups are also the most autonomous and self-conscious in spirit and culture' (Kallen 1996: 88). This short and crude characterization suggests that ethnic pluralists are above all concerned with cultural pluralism. Therefore, this early position is a direct forerunner of contemporary multicultural visions.

The formation of ethnic niches and enclaves is part and parcel of this understanding because they entail separate or parallel economies that require labour power, economic and social capital, and even consumers in distinct immigrant communities. A specific variant of this pattern are middleman minorities (Bonacich 1979). They consist of groups specializing in trade and concentrating in the petite bourgeoisie. Usually, they experience a high degree of hostility in times of economic depression and war; for example, Chinese migrants in mid- to late nineteenth-century America. Some economically successful middleman minorities connect different ethnic groups (see also Weber 1980: 536–7). Occupying a mediating space, these minorities can be seen as a sort of collective and nodal *tertius gaudens*. They mediate, for instance, between native workers and employers. For example, in the late nineteenth century Chinese migrants in the white settler colonies of the Pacific Rim, such as Australia, New Zealand, California and British Columbia, and South American countries, such as Peru and Columbia, took up niches in sweatshops in the garment industry which were not particularly wanted by other groups. While European settlers pursued the dream of the independent landholder averse to wage labour, Chinese immigrants toiled in industries with abominable working conditions. Other groups linked the colonial powers and the native population, such as Indians in Africa. They established non-redundant social ties, thus acting as a bridge since the native population and the colonial powers did not communicate directly with each other. Both sides used the Indian intermediaries employed in the colonial administration. This formed one of the key mechanisms integrating 'plural societies' (Furnivall 1948).

In the political sphere, the claim towards political autonomy is the strategy built into ethnic pluralism. This could even go as far as efforts to secede, as demanded by some African-American groups during the 1930s who strove to establish a black state in the American South. There is, however, no known example among other immigrant groups. This already suggests that political autonomy is a rare demand among immigrants and that American blacks are exceptional in this respect. They are domestic migrants with a history of forced labour and slavery.

And even among them, black nationalism usually lost out, despite periodical resurgence. Nevertheless, the adequate strategy among immigrants is to advance multicultural rights geared towards, among other things, the preservation of the mother tongue or, even more powerful, religious organizations and rituals.

In the third dimension of adaptation, cultural retention essentially means that immigrants transfer cultural practices and collective identities from the emigration to the immigration country and that these identities develop in relative isolation from the immigration context. Extreme examples include Hutterite religionists from Russia who settled in sparsely populated regions of the USA and Canada. This example refers to the far end of a continuum. Ethnic pluralism theory mainly claims that, even if second- or third-generation groups can be seen to have acculturated, they still retain a significant number of so-called ethnic social ties, particularly familial and communal ones (Kallen 1996). Cultural retention converges with the third ideal-typical concept of border-crossing expansion of space. Both assume that immigrant groups, then often conceptually reduced to ethnics, retain social and symbolic ties with fellow-commoners. However, in contrast to the latter concept, ethnic pluralism focuses on ethnic social ties within the immigration country and not on transnational ties.

Border-Crossing Expansion of Social Space: Syncretism at Work

While the concept of border-crossing expansion of social space denotes by no means a totally new development emerging out of migration processes, the spread and magnitude of its empirical referent—transnationalization and transnational social spaces—have grown over the past decades, when compared to earlier transatlantic migration flows. Economically, it means that kinship- and community-based transnational reciprocity in the form of migrant remittances to significant others in country of origin kinship groups are gradually replaced by transnational circuits. The latter entail a high degree of transnational exchange, meaning that high-density trade and traffic characterize the transnational flows of goods, money, and information between the original emigration and immigration contexts.

On a more informal political plane, transnational political ties and linkages connect immigrants in various immigration countries, normally also the country of origin. As usual, the Greeks had a word for it, *politeuma*, select rights of partial autonomy for diaspora groups. Correspondingly, the formal political sphere contains dual or even multiple forms of institutionalized symbolic ties: citizenship not only pertains to one nation-state but as dual citizenship to two nation-states, with various forms possible, such as membership and rights always pertaining to the country where the respective migrant resides at the very moment. In the cultural realm, social and symbolic ties crystallize in 'communities without propinquity' that are durable for at least one lineage generation. Being very dense, socially coherent and symbolically integrated transnational social spaces—transnational communities—have the highest potential for syncretist cultural practices and collective identities, such as the by now often described *mélange* and creolized cultures of Caribbean transmigrants in the Americas and the United Kingdom after World War Two. The main cases remain religious-ethnic diasporas of Jews all over the world and trading communities of Chinese in South-East Asia.

Three Stages of International Migration and Transnationalization

Stage 1: Migration and Flight

The first stage following international migration and cumulative mobility are the many ways of transnational reciprocity, and, in the case of some refugees, sometimes an abrupt severing of transnational ties. Since the majority of migration occurs in kinship groups along community networks, the maintenance of transnational ties has been by far the most frequent. Following this stage, immigrants and refugees in the immigration countries could take three distinct paths, depending both on the opportunities available in the immigration country and their own resources: melting into the core, pluralization, and transnational circuits (Figure 8.2).

Stage 2: Melt into the Core, Separate, Transnationalize

For the second stage, assimilation theory predicts that immigrants and refugees become firmly embedded in the immigration countries while transnational social and symbolic ties are short-lived: melting into the core society. This implies that immigrants—in the absence of grave structural impediments such as severe discrimination—eventually acculturate into the immigration society within one to three generations. Nevertheless, symbolic ties still exist and a form of 'symbolic' or 'optional' ethnicity could emerge that refers to ethnic collective identity, without having a strong organizational basis among those who consider themselves belonging to an ethnic group. The case of 'white ethnics' in

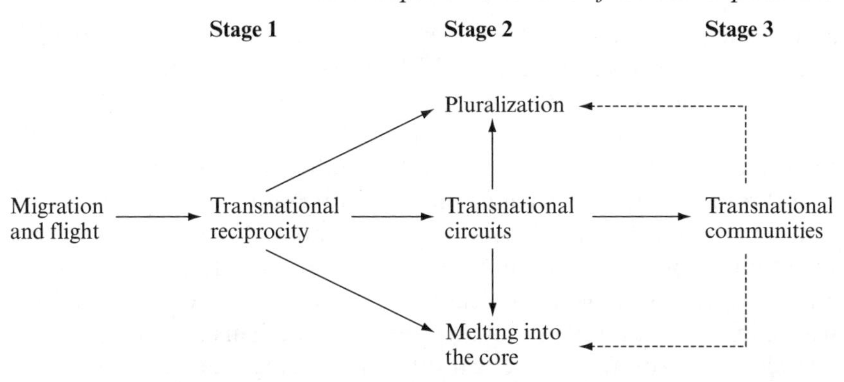

FIG. 8.2. *Stylized stages of melting into the core, pluralization and three forms of transnational social spaces*

Note: The dotted arrows indicate that the transition is a very difficult and somewhat unlikely process.

the USA, the descendants of European immigrants who arrived before the First World War, is a case in point (Gans 1979). Adaptation beyond acculturation is clearly impossible when the immigration society severely discriminates against the newcomers economically, culturally, and politically and when these groups cannot rely on strong transnational ties and linkages. The case of the descendants of slave labour in the Americas comes to mind; for example, African-Americans in the USA from 1865 until the mid-1960s. In this instance, manifold forms of spatial, occupational, and organizational segregation prevent the frequent and mutually beneficial exchange of goods, information, persons, and ideas even within the boundaries of ethnic groups, e.g. between different social classes.

The concept of ethnic pluralism is at its strongest when we look at varieties of pluralization between immigrants and natives and, less dramatically, at the social ties of present-day immigrants in the first and second generation. Social ties within families, immigrant, religious and ethnic groups, immigrant colonies, and corresponding immigrant self-help and grass-roots organizations abound. Immigrant ethnics retain social ties although acculturation proceeds through language acquisition. The ultimate theoretical contention does not relate to adaptation in the economic and political sphere, but makes claims about what is called acculturation or cultural retention, viz. multiculturalism, respectively.

But note that the assimilation and ethnic pluralism perspectives do not radically differ when it comes to symbolic ties, expressed in dimensions such as collective identity. Interestingly, both adherents of assimilation and ethnic pluralism theories present the USA as their main model (see e.g. Gordon 1964 and Glazer and Moynihan 1963). Both perspectives emphasize the expressive capacity of such identities beyond the first generation. But the two place their emphasis differently. Let us take language as an example: while assimilation theorists measure acculturation through indicators such as immigration country language acquisition—a proxy for symbolic ties to the country of destination—ethnic retentionists place a premium on emigration country language retention and interpret those as an indicator for active symbolic and social ties within immigrant families and their descendants. This is, as usual, much ado about overblown theoretical differences: language acquisition and retention are usually processes that occur simultaneously. For example, it depends very much on the strength of intra-familial ties, such as degrees of emotional attachment and parental authority, to what extent children engage in one or both activities at the same time (for many, see Fishman 1966 and Veltman 1988). This means that language acquisition can be used as an indicator of adaptation. However, language retention is not automatically measuring non-acculturation, especially if both the languages of the new home and the ancestral ones are learned simultaneously. What is important is that language provides a medium for the establishment and negotiation of the experience of ties, roles, groups, organizations, and the public representation of these understandings in commonly accessible narratives, usually called collective identities. In short, while assimilation and ethnic pluralism concepts are worthwhile perspectives in their own right, they only compete partly. At other times, they are simply looking at different issues.

This is, of course, also true for the third ideal-typical perspective, the border-traversing expansion of social space. For the second stage of immigrant adaptation, this concept suggests that transnational circuits develop, characterized by a constant and regular circulation of goods, people, and information crossing the borders within migration systems over a considerable period of time. There are alternative paths back to melting into the core and pluralization. Successful economic, political, and cultural entrepreneurs in transnational circuits can finally adapt to the immigration society. Among other things, a move from transnational circuits to melting into the core requires that 'immigrant jobs' or slots for immigrant entrepreneurs are filled by successive groups in a sort of queue: the latest arrivals enter at the bottom of the hierarchy, while the earlier entrants move up into more prestigious occupational positions. Or, self-employed immigrants and their children have the opportunity to open shops. Also, there is no massive political, ethnic, or religious conflict import from the emigration to the immigration country, and the descendants of immigrants do not experience continued discrimination. Looking at another end of the spectrum of possibilities, we can see that it is possible that marginalized descendants of immigrants and refugees develop syncretist identities which eventually function in a culturally segregate and separatist way, a sort of self-imposed multiculturalist segregation of the socio-economically excluded.

Stage 3: Transnationalization and Adaptation

In a third stage, melting into the core and pluralization may continue. Also, transnational ties can evolve from transnational circuits to fully-fledged transnational communities. In these communities, international movers in the immigration country and stayers in the country of origin connect through dense and strong social and symbolic ties over time and across space. This means that, in addition to social exchange and reciprocity, diffuse solidarity pertaining to larger collectives is necessary for the functioning of transnational communities. In contrast to transnational circuits, transnational communities are much less likely to change their adaptive trajectory into melting into the core. One prominent form of a transnational community—the diaspora—refers to stable equilibria with social and symbolic equidistance to the former emigration country and to the country of settlement. But even transnational communities vanish when we see gradual acculturation, or a forced rupture of material, social, and symbolic ties to the country of common origin during war times—or both. However, good-value-for-money long-distance communication and transportation, global economic niches for certain products produced by family businesses, and the continued quest for political autonomy among minorities in many nation-states in the 'South' with subsequent and continued refugee movements are likely to enhance the durability of transnational communities. It would seem that frontier regions between North and South, such as along the US–Mexican border and the European–Mediterranean rim of Southern Europe and Northern Africa face especially good prospects for hosting transnational communities because of ever-increasing economic integration in NAFTA and the EU, respectively.

Economic Participation and Membership: Socio-Economic Parity and Marginalization, Niche Entrepreneurship, and Transnationalization

Conceptually we can distinguish three broad patterns of immigrant adaptation in the economic life of the immigration countries.

Socio-Economic Parity with the Core Groups

The first is that the newcomers and their children attain occupational patterns similar to natives and majority groups. This avenue sometimes but not necessarily implies that employers hire immigrants for certain slots, or that natives or earlier immigrants move up the occupational prestige ladder and vacate slots for newcomers. Historically, this pattern applied to American immigration history around the turn of the nineteenth to the twentieth century and in post-World War Two Europe until the early 1970s. A burgeoning economic expansion demanded ever-increasing additional manual labour for the new or expanding smokestack industries. When domestic supplies—such as youth, women, and peasants—slowed to a trickle, employers generally recruited workers from abroad. Industries based on coal, steel, and iron radically changed the economic landscape in the Ruhr area in Germany, where Polish workers dug out the black gold, followed by Turks. Many of the descendants of the first-generation immigrants became part of a blue-collar working class. Vacating slots for newcomers also belong to this pattern. It is a game of musical chairs or a job queue, when newcomers or minorities find favourable entry positions in the course of upward job mobility among natives or majorities. A well-known example are public service jobs: many Irish have been replaced by African Americans since the 1960s in New York City; Americans of Irish descent moved out of the public sector and, moreover, the administration offered additional jobs for entering cohorts (Waldinger 1986/7).

Several decades later, researchers still ask questions of whether new immigrants such as Turks in Western Europe or Mexican Americans in North America will experience a trajectory similar to earlier immigrant generations that entered in periods of rapid capitalist expansion. These are truly very odd questions: while these latter groups also came in periods of economic boom after World War Two, the situation has changed dramatically since the 1970s, which was particularly relevant for the shrinking pool of blue-collar jobs available to newcomers. This trend has been more visible in Western Europe where the service sector did not grow as fast as in the USA.

Failed structural adaptation in the socio-economic sphere results in segregation through marginalization or even underclass formation among immigrants, mostly among their descendants. The question has been raised whether we find extreme forms of cumulative marginalization among newer immigrant groups, akin to a part of the African-American population in selected regions of large urban agglomerations in the USA (Myrdal 1972: i. 75–8). While the empirical evidence is mixed and murky (Wacquant 1997), it seems clear that first-generation immigrants usually do not form a group of extremely marginalized persons in immigration polities and economies. After all, they are mostly recruited to perform certain tasks. It is among their children that such processes can be observed.

Social capital in these unsuccessful cases then functions to channel the descendants of immigrant workers in declining sectors: for instance, if the educational credentials among the second lineage generation do not suffice to enter tertiary institutions of higher education, they are relegated to social ties of relatives and friends who typically cluster in certain industries. But only ties connecting entrants to positions in non-declining and well-paying industries are helpful. Exactly these positions are getting rarer.

Immigrant Niches and Enclaves

A second conceptual approach has tried to capture a small and distinct avenue in Europe and North America through immigrant niche economies. When these economies are spatially concentrated, we speak of enclaves. This approach proves useful when immigrants have engaged themselves in creating new occupational positions, or when there is a process of ethnic succession and replacement in self-employment proceeds. The move of former Chinese gold diggers into service-oriented businesses in California during the late nineteenth century illustrates the first type. Driven by their European competitors from the gold fields, they moved into a distinct niche made up mainly of laundry shops, cigar-making, groceries, and, above all, businesses catering to their compatriots. Enhanced by migrant and migration networks' *modus operandi*, group members hoarded access to economic and social capital needed to establish such businesses (Light 1972: Ch. 4). However, there have been entrepreneurs who cater beyond the enclave, such as Koreans in the United States and African Indians in the UK.

These middlemen minorities occupy positions in between groups in the dominant society. One of the mechanisms for building niche economies are rotating credit associations, an institution found in almost all parts of the world and a mechanism usually transplanted from emigration to immigration countries. These associations reduce risk by restricting their membership to established groups. Transaction costs such as monitoring fall and the costs of exclusion to defaulting members rise. This requires that strong and reciprocally-shaped social and symbolic ties of immigrants remain confined to in-groups; even ties in the economic sphere to the outside world are very much restricted in contrast to non-niche economies.

Niche economies contribute their share to increasing stocks and returns on a sense of group identity expressed in solidarity and mutual aid. And if the niche is one of the salient traits that group members share in common, it also becomes an interest that helps to define who they are. For example, we can observe this on a very small scale when tracing the formation of Turkish business associations in Germany. From the very start, these secondary groups have been very conscious of their obligations towards Turkish compatriots, supporting a wide range of social, academic, and cultural undertakings—giving themselves a distinct identity of an immigrant business association.

The second type of niche economy typifies contexts more favourable to economic activities of immigrants: ethnic succession. The metaphoric image that comes closest to this pattern is again that of a queue: when older groups of former immigrants leave certain sectors, such as garments, newer groups enter. An example is the garment industry in New York where in the 1970s and 1980s the older generation of manufacturers and contractors, mainly Jews, was succeeded by new Chinese immigrants (Waldinger 1986). It then depends on the prestige and remuneration of these jobs, and the use of social ties bridging towards the outside job market, whether it will be a dead end or a further step towards parity with natives, or even superseding them.

While insertion into labour markets at low occupational levels and return migration with a small-shop or *rentier* experience is an apt description for most international migrants of the 1960s and 1970s, this pattern has become more varied. The growing importance of the second pattern of dual or niche economies in the contemporary period is closely related to changes in the economies that also have an impact upon the forms of social capital available to immigrants. Changing labour markets in the countries of immigration have altered certain possibilities to access blue-collar manufacturing jobs. Social ties available for first-generation immigrants which led to good-paying blue-collar jobs now constitute a dead end for their descendants.

Various subforms of reciprocity and solidarity act as a substitute for welfare state provisions—and vice versa. Over the past years, changes in welfare state redistribution certainly have had an impact: social rights have become more restricted for some new immigrant groups, for example for asylum seekers. Focused solidarity within kinship and diffuse solidarity in religious and ethnic groups has thus become a more important feature of economic survival and improvement. This is even more true for undocumented migrants. After their status improved in the 1970s, the welfare backlash of the 1990s eliminated some of these claims *de jure*. Also, depending on the opportunity to legalize illicit residence, undocumented immigrants tend to extend their stay as long as documented ones. In times of economic boom, it is relatively easy for undocumented migrants to legalize their unauthorized status when employers clamoured for cheap and docile labour. This usually changes in more restrictive periods. Solidarity and state control play an even stronger role for undocumented than for documented migrants, when accessing the bare necessities of life.

Transnational Entrepreneurship

The third pattern overlaps with niche economies. Transnational entrepreneurship in immigrant or ethnic communities has grown increasingly important in the 1980s and 1990s, although it has not offered a viable alternative for dependent wage-work for the vast majority of immigrants. It is part of a highly stratified pattern of economic activities. Not all migrants engaged in transnational moves are capitalists. Among diverse groups, such as Chinese or Turkish migrants, these activities range from the sojourns of manual workers, to extended stays of members of professional salariats or students in major centres of knowledge and services, and 'bosses' commuting between business centres. To reduce the pool concerned even further: numerically speaking, only a small fraction of self-employed immigrants participates in it; although there is evidence of a large informal sector in which transnational economic activities play a role (Rath 1998). Take garment sweatshops in the Netherlands: Turkish entrepreneurs produce jeans for flea-markets in Germany. When discovered by the police, they quickly relocate their production, if not workforce, back to Turkey. Only by tapping a docile workforce, entrepreneurs can engage in this extreme form of capital flexibility and labour mobility.

One of the factors conducive to the formation of transnational links and economic niches could have been the changing economies of scale in the world economy. These conditions partly favour small-scale production, spatial dispersion, and the pursuit of highly specialized niches in unstable competitive markets, such as certain forms of flexible production. For the first time in history, relatively small family enterprises can enter into a truly global arena, once the exclusive preserve of large corporations (Harvey 1989: 147–59). In these cases, economies of scale have been replaced by—to create a new term—economies of scope, such as small-batch production 'just in time'. Therefore, in addition to economic restructuring and limited access to the labour market, changing global conditions have helped to make migrant and ethnic entrepreneurship more viable for parts of selected immigrant groups with high stocks of economic, human, and social capital. Tracing these changes, we need to look at altered structural opportunities, such as blocked occupational mobility, and relatively low entry barriers in some sectors of self-employment, for example, grocery shops and garment factories—many of those located in the informal economy. This is not to say, however, that it has been mostly unemployed former contract workers who went into self-employment, instead of those who were in secure positions. Yet exchange relationships have become more varied: networks not only pertain to job searches but also to establishing businesses. For example, information flowing through kin and communal reciprocal ties and mutual obligations help to mobilize much-needed financial credits and collateral.

An Exemplary Case: Economies of Scope in the Textile Industry

A sector such as the clothing industry vividly illustrates how the changing economies of scope create new opportunities for the use of social capital; a field that has traditionally been characterized by ethnic succession in the USA but that has also become a field of employment and entrepreneurship for immigrants in Europe.

(1) Stable Production Relationships

The clothing business always had relatively short production runs and relative design intensity. Therefore, it offers room for flexible production. The dominant three-tiered pattern of production—manufacturer, contractor, and workers—has been stable for decades. There is a cleavage between manufacturers and contractors. The manufacturer typically takes on the responsibility for design, the purchase of cloth, and merchandising. The contractor carries out the real production. She needs access to a ready supply of pliant labourers. Social capital in this set-up crystallizes, among other things, in the form of kinship and ethnic networks not demarcated by clear patterns of employer–employee relationships but by complex patterns of familial, clan, and ethnic solidarity among contractors and employees, on the one hand,

and the manufacturer, on the other. For example, in the USA around the turn of the century, many recent Jewish immigrants from Eastern Europe filled positions as contractors and resorted to their compatriots to labour long hours in the needle trades. All the contractors needed were sewing machines and willing ethnic labour. Since the 1970s, one finds many recent Chinese immigrants in similar positions (Waldinger 1986).

This situation changed somewhat when a shift towards more Taylorist production occurred in two stages after World War Two. The partial relocation of mass production into the developing countries involved two processes. First, retailers in advanced countries could purchase long production-run items from firms based in regions such as South Asia. Second, in search of cheap and docile labour, manufacturers in the advanced countries built factories, preferably in the export-processing zones of Third World countries (Fröbel, Heinrichs, and Kreye 1977: part 2, ch. 4). Overall, these imports from developing into developed countries worked for the less fashion-sensitive lines which excluded women's fashion for the most part. These manufacturing strategies set into motion larger-scale migration of labour from developing countries to developed ones. This can be seen as one of the unintended consequences of the build-up of textile factories in developing countries such as the Philippines because mostly women workers, who had migrated from the countryside to urban areas in the South, adapted to Western production and consumption patterns. In turn, these preference changes among the women workers induced migration from the Pacific islands to the USA (Sassen 1990: 12–25)—migrant networks then turned into travelled avenues.

(2) Niches for Family and Small Network Companies

In yet another and newer phase, the developing world has moved to Paris, Berlin, London, New York—in addition to many smaller conglomerates. Such cities have gained renewed prominence in the garment industry. The firm structure in the garment industry transformed: manufacturers began to outsource much more work, and production runs have become shorter, especially in women's fashion (Phizacklea 1980: 37–52). As a result, spot markets mushroom, in which rapid fashion changes and short runs predominate. The link to small immigrant businesses is that the latter tend to thrive, where techniques of mass production do not apply (Morokvasic, Waldinger, and Phizacklea 1990: 159). Thus, subcontracting articulates smoothly with chain migration. The contractor usually has access to an almost inexhaustible supply of cheap and willing workers from abroad, over whom she exercises great control. Ethnically segregated monopolies then appear.

In developed welfare states, insurance and tax-financed systems of social security such as pension plans and health-care systems cover a lot of the risks arising from labour market participation of workers in the formal economy. This is different in the informal economy in the urban fringes; often characterized by small-batch production and haphazard working conditions. Tight family structures and kinship systems need to shoulder risks and costs of work. A very close system of reciprocity and solidarity in kinship groups is necessary because contractors need to rely on workers at short notice, and for long and excessive hours. It is also obvious that it is a very informal economic activity available only for the peak months during the calendar year and thus without formal insurance regulations. Yet the degree of economic and social informality is, of course, dependent on the degree of labour market regulation. For example, it is higher in countries such as Germany than in France. This means that it is easier for immigrants to get access to small businesses in garment industries in Paris than in Berlin. In Germany, first-generation immigrants—although they have solid qualifications in tailoring—would not be able to set up business as easily. For them, the field of alterations remains because it is relatively easy to get permits for tailor shops.

There is one implication of this informality in the garment production process that reinforces the use of kinship or ethnically based social capital. Often, class lines are fluid because both the contractor and her variable term employees depend on a single manufacturer. The contractor then easily persuades her employees that they are all in the same boat vis-à-vis the manufacturer. Sometimes the contractor is in a position similar to her workers, meaning a year worker or unemployed person for part of the year (Morokvasic 1991). Thus, the specific pattern of manufacturer–contractor–worker relationship makes ethnic or kinship solidarity much more important than class solidarity within each of the three tiers.

The rapid extension of relatively privileged groups of international movers accelerates this development, among them human capital and economic capital migrants. One prototypical example are highly skilled and professional labour and businessmen from South-East Asia and the Indian subcontinent who settle on the American west coast (M. Goldberg 1985). We have already encountered a small subgroup thereof, the hypermobile Chinese astronauts. Many of the Chinese businessmen interviewed in a representative sample in Vancouver in the early 1990s gave as one of the most important reasons for their relocation to Canada the existence of an ethnic community with supple labour-supply and direct links to Hong Kong and Taiwan. Indeed, the subsequent empirical analysis confirmed that co-ethnic employment constituted a major feature of their business operation. In this case, recent capitalist transmigrants fully profited from the well-developed migrant networks of more recent labourer arrivals, and the symbolic ties of all involved to common strands of nationality (Wong 1997: 344–5), differentiated by regional attachments.

Diverse phenomena such as the reconceived importance of family businesses and the revival of sweatshop forms of production have very different implications for sections within one and the same ethnic group. For the very successful among them, such as transnational Chinese entrepreneurs in the Pacific Rim states, transnationality signifies entry into the upper echelon of business. In a nutshell, immigrant entrepreneurs floating in transnational circuits can employ their assets to melt into the majority core of domestic entrepreneurs. And even for some Turkish grocery or fast-food businesses in colonies in German cities of the Ruhr area transnationality may mean that they have access to a willing labour pool in Turkey. These businesses sometimes depend on labour transfer from Turkey to Germany (see Chapter 7). The existence of sour social capital is obvious when we view employment relationships in this sector from the point of view of transmigrating family labour. Stories abound of migrants whose relatives paid for the journey abroad and who were then expected to return their debts to their alleged benefactors; working under less than satisfactory conditions.

In sum, changing economies of scope help to understand why parts of some immigrant groups engage their capital in transnational activities. Frequently, transnational ventures supplement economic activities of immigrants in the immigration countries. They do not replace them. Overall, the notion of a uniform economic trajectory for immigrants has to be given up. The idea of a single location is an extrapolation of American experience around the turn of the century and the European experience until the 1970s. In those times, melting into the core for the majority and ethnic niches for a few entrepreneurs well described the dominant patterns. Nowadays, because of continuing chain migration, ongoing refugee flows despite more restrictive laws, and the rights accorded to non-citizen migrants, such as family reunification, international migration streams tend to be much more varied along categories such as age, gender, education, and wealth. Contextualized in a changing global economy, this has contributed to the third trajectory of economic adaptation, transnational entrepreneurship. The second and third concept, ethnic enclaves/niches and transnational entrepreneurship, are similar, yet diverge in one significant respect. Ethnic pluralist perspectives see the immigrant community as a captive market (ethnic enclaves), while it could also be a support for conducting business outside (ethnic niches). A transnational perspective emphasizes that both enclaves and niches can reach beyond the nation-state economic container.

A word of caution is in order. Transnational entrepreneurs do not operate in a deterritorialized space of exchange. In many cases, successful entrance of immigrant entrepreneurs into a transnational market hinges on having a solid base in one or several specific cultural territories. Of special importance in this respect is the 'size' of the cultural base for a specific industry; a special form of economies of scope. The notion of size does not correspond to a population strictly bounded by political borders, but rather to audiences and consumers that have an analogous linguistic-cultural universe. For instance, this makes the Turkic peoples in Minor and Central Asia so attractive for Turkish immigrant entrepreneurs in Germany, extending binational into multinational enterprises.

All three ideal-typical models are useful for explaining the experiences of contemporary migrants. Assimilation theory still captures very well the situation of many human capital migrants, highly skilled professionals and managers. None the less, some of them have become more mobile transnationally. Concepts focusing on economic niches cover a great deal of upwardly mobile working class but also economic (business) migrants. Such niches, however, do not exclusively cover markets in the destination countries. They sometimes extend transnationally to emigration country communities and circles.

Membership in Polities: Citizenship and *Politeuma*

Citizenship has been historically closely linked with the evolution of nation-states. The collective of citizens, a people, is often based on perceptions of a nation or a *Volk*. Modern states are based on state sovereignty, which—in the domestic sphere—means the priority over all other political institutions ensconced within the demarcated territory. Moreover, borders define the congruity of a state territory, recognized by neighbouring states and other members of the international system of states. Within this purview, residents have citizenship status when they are accepted with all rights and duties.

Citizenship in a state constitutes an expression of full and formal membership. Fundamentally, it is an institutionalized form of solidarity. Citizenship forms a continuing series of transactions, between a citizen and a state—whether or not we derive it from a contract between a state and citizens (Hobbes), or between citizens who are authors of their constitutions (Rousseau and Kant). States and citizens can claim a set of mutually enforceable rights and duties. Citizenship also connotes the public representation of ties between members and corresponding nation-states. It is based on the perception of common belonging to a state—or a nation or both—and it confers the identity 'citizen'. Citizenship is in short supply among virtually all newcomers to a polity and, in the long run, among those immigrants barred from naturalization.

Each of the three concepts of immigrant adaptation corresponds to distinct, albeit at times overlapping, understandings of citizenship—assimilation to exclusive citizenship in a single nation-state, ethnic pluralism to multicultural citizenship, based on the recognition of varied cultural heritage and representations, and border-crossing expansion of social space to dual citizenship and dual nationality.* These three forms of formal citizenship relate somewhat differently to the congruity assumption of one people to one territory and one cultural space. Also, forms of political membership in and between nation-states are to be observed, such as participation in associations oriented towards the emigration country, or truly transnational organizations that connect countries of origin with several immigration countries; nowadays exemplified by Muslim organizations in Europe, Australia, and North America, or diaspora communities striving to establish nation-states, carved out of their country of origin. Again, the question is whether it is possible to speak of one trajectory for newcomers, for example, in one polity with one citizenship, or whether membership in polities should better be thought multi-stranded when translating adaptation of contemporary immigrants into polities.

Dual state membership comes in two forms. The first is dual citizenship: a person holds passports of two nation-states and has full rights and duties in both—although one citizenship is usually resting. Only the citizenship of the actual country of residence is operative. The second is dual nationality. Dual nationality is different from dual citizenship in that the rights under the former are more restricted than under the latter. For example, holders of Declaration of Mexican Nationality IDs are not able to vote or hold political office in Mexico, or to serve in the Mexican Armed Forces. The benefits of Mexican nationality include

* I would like to thank Jürgen Gerdes for calling my attention to the elective affinities between the three forms of adaptation and various concepts of citizenship.

the right to buy and sell land free of the restrictions imposed on aliens and to receive better treatment under investment and inheritance laws in Mexico, to attend public schools and universities as Mexicans, and to access other Mexican government services and jobs. Other major countries of immigration also changed their laws to allow for dual citizenship, and increased the rights of expatriates (Cebecioğlu 1995). Pressured by the German government, the Turkish side had to relinquish granting dual citizenship and introduced a sort of dual nationality with the so-called 'pink card' in late 1997.

Assimilation and National Citizenship

Assimilation is akin to the idea of rather exclusive citizenship in a single nation-state, national citizenship. Assimilation theory sees a gradual adaptation of immigrants not only socio-economically but also culturally and behaviourally. Gradually, immigrants do away with the cultural baggage transported from the emigration country. As immigrants continue to embark upon the member-ships of the perhaps multiple rivers and riverains of the immigration country, the logical end point is single nation-state citizenship. It does not really matter here that assimilation theorists have not envisaged the political realm explicitly. What is important is that they did not see the necessity to consider the implications of transnational ties beyond the first generation, with exceptions pertaining mainly to folkloristic expressions. Rather, it might well be questioned how a person could develop the appropriate level of commitment and loyalty to two separate polities.

The best known and still most prevalent pattern of full membership acquisition by newcomers is insertion into the citizenship of a single nation-state which is the state of settlement. States regulate access to a single citizenship by various procedures. Two obvious juxtapositional modes are *ius sanguinis* vs. *ius soli* (legal notions) and *ius imperium* vs. *ius republica* (not legal notions). First, in some immigration countries, the Empire had a national as well as a global reference. Take Britain and the Netherlands. All subjects were theoretically free to travel to any other part of the Empire. As a consequence of this *ius imperium*, in the early periods of large-scale immigration after World War Two, these colonial powers admitted considerable numbers of immigrants, nominally with equal rights as the domestic citizens. This stood in marked contrast to *ius republica*, where in countries such as the USA, naturalization proceeded on the basis of the constitution. Needless to say that many in the latter countries found themselves outside the charmed circle of the republic's citizenship, as African Americans until the 1960s attest. A second venerable distinction ranges from the ideal types of *ius soli* (territory principle: citizenship accorded upon birth in a country, independent of the parents' citizenship) combined with *ius sanguinis* (blood principle: citizenship granted as a result of parents' or ancestral citizenship), on the one hand, to *ius sanguinis* without *ius soli*, on the other hand (de Rahm 1990). The USA is probably the case with the strongest elements of *ius soli*, followed by countries such as France. Germany, Greece, and Italy typify cases in which *ius sanguinis* rules supreme. The unique religious-national narrative in Israel, embodied in the 'Law of Return', represents the clearest case of this form of descent-based citizenship.

In order to complement the picture of access to citizenship we need a third principle, not a legal concept such as *ius sanguinis* and *ius soli*, but nevertheless a useful distinction. Virtually all countries have regulations which we could call a sort of *ius domicili*—that allows aliens and denizens to finally acquire full citizenship. Based on social and symbolic ties immigrants have developed since their arrival and their economic contributions, *ius domicili* specifies the conditions that newcomers have to fulfil when applying for citizenship, after having lived for periods of mostly two to eight years in the country of residence. Among the most common criteria for the admission of newcomers are uninterrupted residence and work history for some years, a regular income, sufficient living space, no criminal records, and mastery of the dominant language in the nation-state.

In recent years, some countries have altered their regulations somewhat, so that some of the dimensions just mentioned have begun to blur. For example, Germany has complemented her dominant *ius sanguinis* with *ius domicili*—since 1991 foreign citizens who have lived and went to school in Germany may claim a German passport between the age 16 to 21 years. And elements of *ius soli* have also found entry: probably beginning in 2000 children whose parents were born in Germany or have arrived before age 14 also automatically receive German citizenship. By contrast, the 1981 British Nationality Act changed access to citizenship to being mainly a matter of descent. This Act abolished *ius soli* whereby individuals acquired citizenship simply by the fact of birth on British soil, and promulgated *ius sanguinis.*

Yet there are some common elements which apply to all these cases. Liberal democratic nation-states as welfare states, characterized by high degrees of regulation and redistribution which require institutionalized solidarity, organize their political order on the basis of an egalitarian and homogenized citizenship, including—among other things—free and universal suffrage and access to social rights. The first to recognize this pattern, T. H. Marshall, ingeniously analysed membership in terms of rights accorded to members of a nation-state who share a sense of belonging. For him, citizenship connotes a bundle of rights and a few duties. The device of bundling entitlements is the territorially delimited state in which most permanent residents share a common nationality. In Marshall's words '(c)itizenship requires . . . a direct sense of community membership based on loyalty to a civilization which is a common possession' (Marshall 1964: 92).

The notion that solidary policies of redistribution and regulation demand a common understanding of who is a member and who is eligible for rights and services carries a lot of weight. Migration then raises a distinct challenge to this state of affairs because the world economy tends to favour open exchange, while the notion of citizenship demands certain territorial and communal protections. This is most clearly the case when we look at those nation-states that are highly developed welfare states, in which citizens have something to lose. These states usually have stricter external and internal controls but also relatively easy access to rights once inside. A comparison of Sweden and the USA bears out this claim. Researchers who have taken up Marshall's approach are mostly concerned with how immigration is changing the notion of citizenship in which rights, duties, and a sense of belonging have hitherto been inextricably linked to some sort of common culture (Brubaker 1992).

Marshall's reference to some sort of common bondings and shared customs as a basis for the recognition of equal status for all members remains valid. The questions then are: How much of a common consensus is necessary in multi-ethnic and multi-religious polities and what are the decisive elements of such a commonality? What kind of rights and how many should be granted to non-citizens? It is clear that immigration tends to further the unbundling of rights tied to formal citizenship in liberal democratic welfare states: even non-citizens are entitled not only to civil but also to certain social rights in national welfare states; and in some countries, such as the Netherlands and Sweden, permanent residents who are non-citizens are even allowed to exercise political rights, such as voting in local elections.

There is also an international extension of the national model, post-national membership (Soysal 1994). It is part of the academic musings that we are witnessing the dawning of a post-national era. It deals with international influences upon single nation-state citizenship rights. Basically, it tries to show that human rights have indeed come closer to citizen rights. While it was still possible to claim in the late 1940s that the right to citizenship transcended the rights of citizens because the persons without statehood found themselves without any recourse to legal claims (see the cogent analysis by Arendt 1949), post-nationals assert that liberal democratic nation-states have come to increasingly respect human rights of persons, irrespective of citizenship over the past few decades.

Unfortunately, if we extend the term membership to citizenship, we face difficult problems. There are virtually no supranational institutions conferring the status of citizenship—except the EU in a weak, albeit not totally declamatory, but steadily expanding form. Yet, EU citizenship does not cover third-country citizens. What post-national citizenship suggests is that supranational institutions and discourses have an impact on nation-state citizenship (Jacobson 1995). According to this view, the life-chances of immigrants in Western democracies have been primarily shaped not by belonging to a specific national community and the corresponding citizenship. Rather, human, civil, and social rights are governed by universal discourses, embedded both in international agreements, consensus, and nation-state constitutions. Human rights can be interpreted as a part of world culture (Meyer et al. 1997). Migrants take advantage of opportunities created by the growing prevalence of human and civil rights world polity discourse to move around and settle.

One obvious problem with this approach is that we do not know exactly *how* universal norms and discourses shape policy and practices on the ground. A competing explanation would simply say that virtually all nation-states have enshrined civil rights in their constitution. And as we know, the inclusion of immigrants into welfare states does not mainly depend on nationhood, at least not in their legal form. Access to full social rights is primarily tied to residence and not to nationality or citizenship. Therefore, the observation that membership and life-chances of immigrants do not so much depend on full citizenship can easily be explained as a consequence of welfare state principles when border-crossing and settlement of persons occur.

The point made by the post-nationals is more accurate when related to wider notions of membership, not to citizenship in the nation-state. Membership in nation-state polities is less often tied to formal citizenship but to rights arising from settlement and socialization. And the granting of citizens' rights is not coterminous with formal membership in the nation-state: take the concept of denizenship as located in between alien status and full citizenship (Hammar 1990). Denizens are permanent residents who practically hold the full set of rights accorded to citizens, except voting rights on the national level. It is the recognition of social ties and economic contributions of long-term resident aliens. In sum, the tie between denizens and the state is not as thick as that between citizens and the state, but not as thin as between aliens and the state. In essence, the triad citizen–denizen–alien partly reflects the old Greek distinction between *politai*–citizen, *katoikoi*–resident alien, now called denizen, and *xenoi*–foreigner. In contrast to the Greek concept *katoikoi*, the term 'denizen' suggests that permanent residency, i.e. denizenship, is a sort of social contract. Importantly, it included a promise by the state towards the denizen that full citizenship will be available on some conditions at a later time (Hammar 1990). Yet, to speak meaningfully about the membership of persons we could call transmigrants, we have to go beyond nation-states and institutions of international society such as INGOs, and allow for significant transnational ties.

Ethnic Pluralism and Multicultural Citizenship

In essence, the proponents of multicultural citizenship have revived the notion of ethnic pluralism in the political sphere. Like the proponents of assimilation theory, they regard adaptation exclusively in the container space of nation-states. This is also true for modern-day ethnic pluralists, usually referred to as multiculturalists. There are basically two types of multiculturalism, a passive and an active one. Passive multiculturalism means that immigrants and minorities can express their cultural difference in the private realm. However, the public realm is organized along principles of universalism and equal rights for all (Rex 1991). Here, only active multiculturalism is relevant: active multiculturalists argue that, taking freedom and equality seriously as preconditions for participation in public life, individuals need to be assured of a secure cultural background. The supportive framework of cultural groups constitutes such a 'context of choice' (Kymlicka 1995). Drawing normative and policy implications, the active multiculturalists then go on to postulate that this context can only be maintained by granting special rights to ethnic and religious groups; an assumption that engenders Herculean tasks to defend, both intellectually and policywise. Special rights necessary range from rights to political autonomy for indigenous groups to comparatively uncontroversial assurances for religious practices. Proponents of multiculturalism propose cultural rights to accommodate the cultural identities and practices of immigrant groups. These rights are meant to keep alive and strengthen the intra-group social and symbolic ties. Among these rights are the following: (1) voting rights for permanent immigrant residents; (2) affirmative action programmes that aim to increase the representation of visible minorities in major educational and economic institutions; (3) revised work schedules so as to accommodate the religious holidays of immigrant groups; (4) bilingual education programmes for the children of immigrants, so that their earliest years of education are conducted partly in their mother-tongue, as a transitional phase to secondary and post-secondary education in the dominant receiving country language; and (5) minority group schools such as Muslim schools. In this view, reciprocity and solidarity provide the basis for collective identities that foster common and publicly declared narratives.

What is noteworthy about all these conceptions of citizenship so far—the Marshallian and the multicultural types—is that they clearly point out the central role of nation-state institutions in the process of conferring membership status. After all, only nation-states can grant formal and institutional status. However, there are serious shortcomings. First, while some ground-breaking normative work has been done, the concept of transnational citizenship is not grounded in an empirical analysis of actually existing transnational ties and linkages. We need to examine more systematically the actual situations pertaining to transnational social spaces, before drawing conclusions about the nature of membership in such spaces and the desired congruity of social and political spaces. Second, the discussion on membership has focused on aspects of formal citizenship and corresponding claims individuals can make vis-à-vis a particular nation-state. This has been a valuable contribution to the general membership issues. The theoretical and empirical analysis of transnational spaces suggests that there is another layer to be added, namely the occluded memberships of associations contributing to transnationalizing civil societies. This perspective supplements the decisive role formal citizenship plays, and avoids the predominant focus on the attenuation of sovereignty for nation-states. After all, participation in public debates and conflicts in civil society can help to transform formal citizenship rights into substantive realities.

Border-Crossing Expansion of Social Space and Dual State Membership

Activities in transnational social spaces suggest that membership is multilayered. The natural equivalent to political activities and identities spanning nation-state borders in the formal political sphere is dual state membership. This form of transnational citizenship does not deny the existence or relevance of borders and nation-states. It simply recognizes the increasing possibility of membership in two states. Dual state membership refers to the fact of being a citizen in two states; less fully-fledged forms could mean being a citizen in one state and a settled immigrant with a sort of denizenship status in another. At a minimum it tolerates immigrants' close ties with the country of emigration.

The features of dual state membership become clear when we introduce the emigration country governments' interests, attitudes and policies towards their expatriates. All emigration countries are interested in economic benefits such as remittances and investments, and in political control of emigrants abroad. Two patterns emerge: some governments have used their expatriates abroad as a captive group to exercise maximum control. For example, the mainland Chinese government has insisted upon *ius sanguinis* for its citizens in South-East Asia since the 1950s. This meant to move from 'overseas Chinese' to 'Chinese living overseas' (Nonini and Ong 1997: 9). The People's Republic of China made a statement about controlling her citizens abroad. After all, there has been a competition between Taiwan and mainland China for overseas Chinese. But the People's Republic has gradually lost control. Quite contrary to this stance, other sending country governments, e.g. Mexico, have used the instrument of dual state membership to keep the ties of expatriates alive. The Mexican government has been using their immigrants as a support for conducting business at home and abroad (R. Smith 1999). In Europe, the Italian government opted for a homeland-oriented approach for its guestworkers during the 1960s and 1970s in Germany, led by expectations of returning migrants who would re-establish themselves in the Italian South and contribute to the development of this economically backward region (Schmitter Heisler 1984).

Given the asymmetric relationships between countries of emigration and immigration, the position of the latter proves decisive. If it allows dual citizenship or dual nationality, the sending states usually allow it as well. This has been a seminal trend. Earlier in this century, a new US citizen forfeited her citizenship if she voted in foreign elections, or held public office in another nation-state. Nowadays, the laws have not changed but the USA does not check upon dual state membership, and many emigration countries have rushed to allow it. Other countries such as the UK, France, and The Netherlands have tolerated dual citizenship. Indeed, in many countries of settlement a significant proportion of newcomers who get naturalized nowadays keep their former citizenship as well. Around half of the world's countries nowadays recognize dual citizenship or dual nationality (*Traces*, No. 3, 1998). From the immigrants' point of view, dual state membership constitutes a deliberate strategy to protect various rights in multiple states. This strategy has become more prominent, not least because many nation-states have liberalized their citizenship laws. Also, from a legal point of view, this development finds support. While in 1963 European nation-states still overwhelmingly supported the Convention to avoid multiple nationality, a majority of European nation-states now support a new 1997 Convention that explicitly allows dual citizenship. Even in a country such as Germany that has not signed the Convention, there are about 2 million Germans with a second passport (*Migration und Bevölkerung*, 1/1998: 2).

Politeuma: *Towards Limited Political Autonomy of Transnationally-Oriented Immigrants*

Membership in the political realm is not restricted to states. In other words, not all polities are states. The term *politeuma* described situations such as the Mediterranean Jewish polity when, after the fourth century BC until the second century, some Jewish groups in the Hellenistic world exercised a limited autonomy over religious and judicial affairs, intimately connected to financial transactions for the temple in Jerusalem. *Politeuma* constituted a tenuously recognized corporation of aliens enjoying the right of domicile in a foreign city and forming a separate, semi-autonomous civic body governing certain internal affairs of the respective community (Barclay 1996: 25 n. 18). What we nowadays would call multicultural rights were strongly related to support of the religious centre in Jerusalem because religious tax monies flowed from Egypt to Judea. The Jewish *politeuma* in Alexandria, for example, was independent of the Greek *polis* in religious-cultural affairs, with its rights guaranteed first by the Ptolemaic and later by the Roman authorities. The Jewish community had two sorts of special rights. The first probably referred to the right to establish its own governing body, a court of law, and some control of internal fiscal affairs; tied to expenses of the Temple. The second may have referred to the inviolability of Jewish 'ancestral religion'. This irked the Greeks in Alexandria who tried to get the status of Jews as *katoikoi*—denizens—abolished and the Jews designated *xenoi*—aliens or foreigners (Lüderitz 1994). Also, nowadays, *politeuma* cannot only refer to rights of immigrants in the country of destination and political organizations taking advantage of the liberty to assemble and to lobby for their interests. As the case of diaspora shows, *politeuma* is centrally geared towards the country of origin.

While immigrants and refugees have thus avidly followed news and remained actively interested and involved in the politics of the country of origin for ages dating back to at least the Hellenistic period, and while emigration country governments have always been interested in their populations abroad, if only to ensure the continued flow of remittances, there is a new quality to it today. It is partly due to technological changes that have enabled immigrants to maintain more frequent and closer contact with their areas of origin. Moreover, this has to do with a rush in the contemporary world to tackle the consequences of nation-state building outside Western Europe and the Americas and the claim of more and more groups toward political autonomy or even independence. Taken together, these two developments have contributed to an unprecedented flourishing of *politeuma*. This becomes obvious when looking at prominent examples of *politeuma* such as Kurds in Western Europe, Sikhs in the British Commonwealth and the USA, Armenians and Iranian refugees all over the globe.

Transnational social spaces could be a more permanent and lasting phenomenon. This leads to the development of transnationalizing civil societies, a sort of border-crossing *politeuma*. Do transnational social spaces—in their fully-fledged version of transnational communities, in particular—develop into transnationalizing civil societies? Does a transnationalizing civil society represent a counterweight to the activities of nation-states on the international level? This is most likely in the supranational framework of the EU; with a sprouting associational culture of immigrant and minority lobbying in Brussels and Strasbourg. However, it seems evident that a transnational civil society in singular or plural incarnations does not exist. None the less, activities of immigrants and refugees in transnational spaces do have implications for civil societies bounded by nation-states. Extreme cases are refugees who have ardently supported change in the political system in their emigration countries, such as Palestinian 'refugee warriors' from the 1950s to the early 1990s. Less clear-cut cases are groups advancing the Islamic *umma* or immigrants from the Caribbean in the United States who keep ties through the Catholic church.

Successful melting into the core can be quite compatible with transnational projects, especially if the foreign policy of the country of settlement is conducive. Descendants of immigrants in the USA whose great-grandparents cherished Polish or Irish nationalism and Zionism vividly illustrate that successful acculturation and the maintenance of transnational symbolic ties do not contradict each other. They not only present a short episode in the American ethnic chronology but also one column in transnational networks, circuits, and communities. Examples range from the very recent vigorous support of Polish-Americans for Solidarnosc in the 1980s, widespread sympathies and financial aid of Irish-Americans for the IRA, and the well-known donations of American Jews for the state of Israel (M. F. Jacobson 1995). Indeed, acculturation and assimilation notwithstanding, US citizens of Polish,

Irish, and Jewish descent, many in the third and fourth generation, have acted as late twentieth-century outposts of partially unfulfiled nationalist aspirations in Northern Ireland, demanding freedom from Russian dominance in Poland and shelter from Arab predators in Israel. The wary reader will question the representativeness of these examples: yet we could extend this claim to all known cases over the past hundred years, where immigrants abroad have been linked to unfinished struggles of nationalist movements to grasp state power or to efforts to secure embattled tenuous nation-states. It is exactly in the course of nationalist projects that nowadays contemporary Kurds, Sikhs, and Tamils also mobilize the prodigious energy of their future compatriots who heed the clarion calls for political action. Better transportation and communication links increase the chances of these groups to form enduring transnational linkages.

Therefore, to reduce symbolic ties in the form of ethnic and national belonging—often aided by religious fervour—to leisure time pursuit is to belittle the extent of the transnational imagination of the descendants of immigrants. Many children of immigrants still act as members of transnational circuits and communities. Underlying these examples of transnational solidarity is a vibrant original emigration country nationalism that is very much in agreement with the citizenship of the country of settlement. We have to discard one-sided notions of assimilation theory that single-mindedly focus on the acculturation of the uprooted masses. It is also time to reconsider the notions of ethnic pluralism that make too much of transplanted identities, the persistence of unaltered ethnic ties carried abroad by immigrants. Instead, we can speak of transpositionality: while immigrants and their children may be honourable and loyal American, German, or British citizens when it comes to immigration country issues, they may represent perspectives very different from their government when it comes to questions of ethnic or national or religious belonging regarding their former homeland or that of their ancestors. They position themselves according to how the political issues affect their social and symbolic transnational ties.

We can conclude that the notion of a singular political trajectory and strictly contained political spaces has to be questioned. A concept of transnational membership, for example, materialized in dual state membership and is not located on a magic carpet. It only makes sense when firmly tied to specific spaces in different nation-states. It is not a notion above nation-states but a combination of both the inside and the between. In other words, the national and transnational dimensions of dual state citizenship and membership are not like Russian dolls with no interlinks other than level of analysis differences. They are rather akin to Georg Simmel's metaphor of bridges and doors:

> Because the human being is the connecting creature who must always separate and cannot connect without separating—that is why we must first conceive intellectually of the merely indifferent existence of two river banks as something separated in order to connect them by means of a bridge. And the human being is likewise the bordering creature who has no border. The enclosure of his or her domestic being by the door means, to be sure, that they have separated out a piece from the uninterrupted unity of natural being. But just as the formless limitation takes on the shape, its limitedness finds its significance and dignity only in that which the mobility of the door illustrates: in the possibility at any moment of stepping out of this limitation into freedom.
>
> (Simmel 1997: 174)

Translated into the language used here, this would mean: the bridging function of dual citizenship or dual nationality makes no sense without doors through which persons may both enter and leave. In contrast, the dominant conception of citizenship in political theory has been rather archaic. For example, one widespread image draws on 'walls' protecting the essence of political communities, a core of cherished practices, beliefs, and rights. Yet, the true civilizational achievements are not walls—or windows for that matter—but doors. The doors delineate territorially bounded states and, in an emerging way, supra-national institutional structures such as the EU. But the match between bridges and territories is ever shifting, as are the positions of the doors.

Cultural Practices and Recognition: Acculturation, Cultural Retention, and the Strengthening of Transnationally-Induced Syncretism

Symbolic ties in cultures transmit meaningful ways of life across the full range of human activities and, as such, include both public and private realms (Kymlicka 1995: 76). As to the development of immigrant culture(s), we can discern three ideal-typical views—the acculturation thesis of the assimilation perspective, the proposition of cultural retention of ethnic pluralism, and the emergence of syncretist cultural practices and meanings, as suggested by the concept of border-crossing expansion of social space. The main problem of the strong versions of the acculturation and ethnic retention perspectives is that they espouse a container concept of culture. They do not pay sufficient attention to phenomena such as cultural diffusion and syncretism. For assimilation theory, immigrant culture is a sort of baggage brought from the 'old world'. It mainly considers adaptation of immigrants to core culture(s). Everything beyond folkloristic expressions is considered a transitory phenomenon. At first sight, cultural pluralism contradicts this view because it emphasizes cultural retention among immigrant groups. Nevertheless, this is also a rather bounded view of culture because it does not pay attention to hybrid cultural practices and cultural syncretism. Akin to an acculturation perspective that gives analytical priority to cultural core(s), cultural pluralism focuses on cultural retention at the fringes, the margins. In other words, assimilation theory surveys the main river, whereas ethnic pluralism investigates the side streams and channels.

Without any doubt both perspectives have merit, have captured important trends in the past, and do correspond to crucial aspects of present-day cultural adjustment of immigrants. We should also try to include the whole river valley with the main rivers and side streams to get a more complete picture (Conzen 1991). Nevertheless, we have to go one step further since the cultural diversity around us evolving out of international migration and transnational social spaces has been increasing. At the root of these phenomena lies the mobility not only of persons but also of cultural practices, meanings, and symbols: 'If we look at the cultures around us, I think we can discern that much of their diversity is not merely old diversity in decline, but new diversity that the global ecumene has bred' (Hannerz 1996: 64). Hence the need to supplement the two canonical views to take into account diffusion and syncretism. The concept of border-crossing expansion of social space tries to capture how immigrant cultural syncretism connects to ongoing transnationalization.

Acculturation and Assimilation: Cultural Life in a Nation-State Container

One prominent version of assimilation theory suggests that immigrant adjustment means melting of immigrants into the core culture. In the most sophisticated version (Gordon 1964) the process of assimilation starts with acculturation. In this view, acculturation is often, albeit not always, followed by structural assimilation, the entry of immigrants into primary groups of the immigration country. The last step concerns again the cultural realm, the identificational assimilation and thus the individual and collective identities of immigrants. This indicates that cultural adaptation and meanings accompany the process of immigrant adjustment all along. The final result is, more or less, overall cultural submergence.

Assimilation theory makes certain amendments to non-linear processes of adaptation. For example, ethnicity survives or is reinvented while ethnic cultures disappear. One often overlooked claim of assimilation perspectives is that persistent collective identity in the second generation does not altogether jettison the adaptive process. In essence, ethnicity expressed as collective identity can be preserved or invented for reasons that may have little to do with inherited culture (Gans 1979). Unlike language, which changes in a linear fashion—the longer you stay, the better you tend to speak it—collective self-identities vary significantly over time. Here, we are not confronted with linear developments but with reactive developments. Some research on ethnicity among immigrants suggests that it is best dealt with as an emergent category, which arises under conditions reinforcing the maintenance of kinship and friendship networks (Yancey, Ericksen, and Juliani 1976).

Transnationalization has spurred this trend: with the help of new media and interlocutors immigrants forge new symbolic ties to putative ancestors abroad, sometimes in countries other than the emigration and immigration states. For example, since the late 1980s, Hmong immigrants from Laos in the USA have discovered their roots in interior China in a people called Miao. Even though the languages of the two people are far apart the Hmong consider the Miao a pure version of their clouded past (Schein 1998). The Hmong have fostered new social and symbolic ties with the help of mechanisms such as long-distance travel and videos on the Chinese Miao marketed in the USA. It is too early to say whether this exchange, enabled by modern technologies, has lasting impacts on Hmong cultural practices and meanings.

This last example already suggests patterns of immigrant acculturation that deviate from the main path envisioned by assimilation theory. Groups with a sense of being discriminated against, such as the Hmong mentioned above, may not turn to acculturate to the core culture but to look for examples abroad to find their place. Or, groups characterized by low human capital, weak social cohesion, and poverty, such as new arrivals from Haiti and the West Indies in the USA have much more in common with African-American cultural practices than with the so-called Anglo mainstream (Portes and Zhou 1994).

Since assimilation theory assumes that immigrants discard their old country cultural baggage or dissolve it into the mainstream, it does not pay sufficient attention to cultural diffusion and syncretism. The view of culture in the acculturation perspective is one of tight boundedness. Although diffusion is possible, it is of minor analytical importance because the nation-state as a container for a societal culture acts as an assimilator for newcomers. However, we should be more careful.

Growing transnationalization may change the rules of the game, even in the cultural sphere. There is some, albeit sparse evidence, that even groups such as second-generation Germany-Turks engage in transnational syncretism.

Cultural Pluralism: From the Transfer and Retention of Culture to Culture as a Context of Choice

The early versions of cultural pluralism claimed that immigrants, after experiencing discrimination and (partial) rejection in the country of immigration, would turn back to their cultures of origin, those of the emigration countries. Evolving out of the stage process of first assimilation and then dissimilation would be distinct national cultures existing side by side. The initial insistence that immigrants are able to reconstruct autonomous cultural worlds as separate nationalities has yielded gradually to a more nuanced understanding of the selective function and character of adaptation (Bodnar 1985). Empirically, the softer versions of ethnic pluralism have seen immigrants becoming ethnics over time. This latter finding is consistent with assimilation theory which provides, as we have seen, for the fact that a group's collective identity can exist without a strong cohesion of cultural meanings. In other words, symbolic ties may refer to collective identity without necessarily being part of a rather coherent system of practices and meanings of a 'whole way of life'.

Ethnic pluralism should not be confused with multiculturalism. Nevertheless, a normative version of multiculturalism based on liberalism seeks to justify rights undergirding minority cultures. In this view, culture is important because it constitutes, as mentioned before, a context of choice (Kymlicka 1995). Cultural traditions, symbols, and practices allegedly form a cultural repertoire that enables minorities to participate in liberal democracies on a competitive basis. In order to derive rights for distinct categories of minorities, this perspective distinguishes national minorities and immigrant categories: national minorities do have national culture that has to be supported by limited rights to self-government. But most immigrants do not because they have chosen to come rather voluntarily. And even if their migration was rather involuntary, such as that of refugees, they are often oriented towards their emigration country. Nevertheless, immigrant groups should have rights—polyethnic rights—such as the right for Jews and Muslims to evade Sunday closing laws or Sikhs to wear a turban instead of a helmet when riding a motorcycle (Kymlicka 1995: 101). In sum, this extension of cultural pluralism says that national minorities do have a national and thus a complete societal culture, while immigrant minorities do not. Although the distinction proposed is fraught with many empirical and normative problems—it cannot accommodate the many hard cases in between such as slaves and conquered minorities (for pertinent criticism, see Young 1997)—it offers a sophisticated and graduated concept of multiculturalism.

But even in this latter version of cultural pluralism two main points of criticism remain. It overemphasizes cultural retention among minorities and it underemphasizes the impact of transnationalization on immigrant cultural adjustment.

Cultural retention usually goes hand in hand with adaptation of new elements. Assimilation theory has painted perhaps too strong a picture in that immigrants supposedly get rid of their cultural baggage. It is equally unlikely, however, that immigrant cultures develop without modifications, unless rigid seclusion prevails (e.g. Hutterites). Immigrant culture thus can never be identical with country of origin culture. A lot of evidence points to the thesis that cultural practices and meanings do not simply disappear quickly, reduced to folkloristic functions. Going even further, because of eased transnational exchange of meanings across social and symbolic ties, there is nowadays a higher potential that old patterns transferred and go into a synthesis with new ones. As in the Turkish-German example, Islamic organizations such as *Milli Görüş* gradually have sought to readapt to German patterns. For example, not only do they attempt to be recognized as a religious organization with a special status, a quasi-public institution (*Körperschaft des öffentlichen Rechts*). They have also developed new ideas to reach second-generation Turks in Germany and thereby eased naturalization in addition to dual citizenship.

Newer cultural pluralist approaches make room for the fact that the character of a (minority) culture can change as a result of choices of its members. For instance, cultural diffusion can enrich the opportunities for expression of meanings. But, endemic in the conception of culture as a very bounded concept, if a culture is not a societal or national culture, it will be reduced to ever-increasing marginalization (Kymlicka 1995: 80). As we have seen, this strong assumption has to be questioned because of the ever-growing transnationalization of cultural repertoires.

Beyond the Container Concept of Culture: Transnational Syncretism

Canonical assimilation and cultural pluralist views provide only a thin veneer allowing for cultural syncretism in order to achieve the desired final results of acculturation or retention. These views give short shrift to the dynamic nature of all cultures. Both theoretical traditions have described plausible and long-term real-world outcomes in the past. But in the case of contemporary immigrants in the North, there are many phenomena—even if only transitory ones—that elude such neat categorizations. They disregard the syncretist practices, mixed languages, and hyphenated collective identities.

Overall, there is a surprising similarity between strong versions of assimilation and ethnic pluralism. They overemphasize culture as a fixed and essential phenomenon; assimilation theory does so with core cultures and ethnic pluralism with minority cultures. This container concept sees culture as essentially territorial, based on a shared language and somewhat static. In this view culture stems from a learning process that is, in the main, tightly localized. This is culture in the sense of *a* culture; the culture of a social group. Moreover, they involve common institutions and practices. Such cultures are linked with processes of modernization, such as the build-up of educational systems in nation-states (Gellner 1983). In an extreme version, it imbues a hypostasized notion of places as bounded and unchanging spaces with a fixed meaning, identified with rather strong communities (for a similar characterization, see Nederveen Pieterse 1994: 176–7). Clearly, the container concept of culture has to be widened, as tolerant assimilationists and ethnic pluralists have already suggested—although they have not brought in the effects of transnationalization sufficiently. The canonical concepts of immigrant adjustment have sensitized researchers and the public to issues of ethnic and national pluralism—while neglecting the comparable pluralism of space. This has not only been true for aspects of local culture but also for those of wider transnational diffusion. Therefore, an alternative conceptualization views culture as relating to elements of a more general human 'software'; the 'tool kit' version of culture applies here (Swidler 1986). This dynamic notion of culture has been implicit in theories of evolution and diffusion, in which culture is also viewed as a translocal or even a transnational learning process. Fluidity and not fixity, spatiality and not locality mark this notion.

Immigrant culture cannot be seen as baggage or a template, not as something to be figuratively packed and unpacked, uprooted (assimilationists) and transplanted (cultural pluralists). Instead, an analytical approach looks for structures of meaning engendered by and expressed in private and public behaviours, images, institutions, languages (see also Geertz 1973: 3–30). These structures of meaning are inherent in social and symbolic ties. Such ties and their content do not vanish or merge imperceptibly nor can it be retained easily under new circumstances, unless the transactions with surrounding groups cease.

Certainly, the ongoing and spreading transnationalization of meanings and symbols through social and symbolic ties in transnational social spaces helps to keep up multifold transactions transversing borders. Under propitious conditions—such as modern technologies (satellite or cable TV, instant mass communication, personal communication bridging long distances via telephone and fax, mass affordable short-term long-distance travel), liberal state policies (polyethnic rights and anti-discrimination policies), changing emigration state policies (reaching out to migrants living abroad for remittances, investment, and political support), and immigrant capacities to mobilize resources (organizational, social, and human capital)—transnational syncretism of culture finds a fertile breeding ground.

Eventually, these two very broad understandings of culture are compatible: for to find expression, dynamic-syncretist culture definitely needs territorial boundaries implicit in models of container culture. Immigrant cultures cannot exist in a deterritorialized space. Spatially hypermobile individuals are the exception and not the rule. Nevertheless, many immigrants who have a focus on one country and not an equally strong one on the other (or others), entertain transnational links—be they social ties or symbolic ties. Strong common strands of culture are still necessary and possible within nation-states. Among other things, common national, viz. societal, cultures are necessary because a highly educated and trained workforce constitutes a functional prerequisite of a modern economy. In addition, diffuse solidarity is essential for modern welfare states, and equality of opportunity for all residents depends on common understandings of legitimate principles of justice, rights, and redistribution. In short, without a pervasive nation-state culture, immigrants would face no prospects for successful adjustment!

It is a disputed matter whether networks with improved means of communication connect communities which have been isolated from each other, with participants exchanging symbols that eventually become the foundations of a unifying culture (see Deutsch 1966 on national cultures), or whether it is not the content but the very existence of abstract, one-to-many communication systems that engender an acceptance of new forms of interpersonal links (Gellner 1983), with the substance of collective representations playing a minor role. This study connects the two approaches because both the structure and the content of ties matter for migration and adaptation.

These considerations not only apply to nation-state formation but also to the emergence of immigrant and ethnic communities across nation-state borders. Usually, community formation is the product of transferred capital, differential treatment, and subsequent organization on the part of newcomers to overcome perceived disadvantages and discrimination or to exploit new opportunities. We should not forget that many perceptions of discrimination need a climate of toleration to be expressed in the public realm. Only in liberal democracies tolerant towards cultural difference does discrimination become an issue that leads to successful transnational syncretism and transnational political organization. No multicultural*ism*, no transnational*ism*: although multicultural rights do not necessarily encourage an enduring transnationalization of migrant ties, they advance the expansion of border-crossing spaces. For sustained transnationalization the content of symbolic ties has to go beyond multicultural orientations focused on one nation-state. Syncretist content becomes very important for forging and upholding transnationally-oriented networks and organizations. This not only means that container views of culture have to be modified. It also implies that the unrealistic image of a deterritorialized and global culture has to be cast aside. This view suggests that we are all migrants now. Even those who do not move spatially are bound to experience diffusion due to the migration of cultures (Waldron 1995). While globalized professionals, intellectuals, artists, and entrepreneurs may cherish this image, it is utterly unrealistic for the majority of migrants and those who are relatively immobile.

To think of transnationally enriched syncretism as another layer of immigrants' insertion processes—in addition to acculturation and cultural retention—is to use an understanding of culture as a 'whole way of (immigrant) lives', one that emphasizes their translocal aspects without occluding the fact that cultures are still overwhelmingly nationally bounded and have mainstreams. Even eighty years ago in the USA, during the heyday of Americanization drives, a one-sided melting into the core of immigrants was unrealistic, as Randolph Bourne remarked sagaciously in 1916: 'No Americanization will fulfil this vision which does not recognize the uniqueness of this trans-nationalism of ours. . . . America is coming to be, not a nationality but a trans-nationality, a weaving back and forth, with the other lands, of many threads of all sizes and colors' (Bourne 1996: 107). Leaving aside the unrealistic image of immigrants as nations and America as a nationally pluralist state, the quote's main thrust—cultural pluralization in the wake of immigration—is relevant for today's world. Migrant and migration networks have brought forth the dual characteristic of migrant resources as both local assets and border-crossing transmission belts.

Conclusion: Capturing the Plural Experiences of Adaptation

The concept of border-crossing social expansion can be used to analyse some aspects of the sequel to international migration. It complements our rich heritage of assimilation and ethnic retention theories. If we want to avoid border-crossing expansion of social spaces to become the new codeword for ethnic retentionism, we need to self-consciously locate this concept in the midst of these two canonical, contending, and yet often complementary approaches. All in all, we should remember that far from being a cosmopolitan lot, most immigrants and even transmigrants, are rather parochial transnationals. Despite sometimes ambivalent allegiances and reproaches of dubious commitments, immigrants and their descendants retain and develop new local attachments and ties while being engaged in border-traversing activities.

Since studies on transnationalization are in their infancy, there a danger of treating ideal-typical constructs as if they were exclusive concepts. As this analysis suggests, the real potential of concepts of transnational membership is to enrich notions underlying assimilation and ethnic pluralism, and to identify dimensions of emerging transnationalizing civil societies. At this point, we have adduced plausible arguments that assimilation, ethnic pluralism, and border-crossing expansion of social space each explains important aspects of contemporary immigrant adaptation in an age of more perpetual international migration. This makes the export of ethnic conflicts from the countries of origin and the spread of transnational religious communities more attractive. With as much likelihood, however, we have found that transnationalization helps certain groups to eventually adapt in a very favourable manner, to retain advantageous aspects of their heritage and to develop new and syncretist forms. Evidence comes from diverse backgrounds, such as transnational business persons or musicians who end up commuting back and forth. Even if massive transnationalization should eventually turn out to be an evanescent phenomenon only, its contemporary manifestations force us to incorporate them in more sophisticated theories of assimilation and ethnic pluralism, at the very least. But it is equally likely that transnationalization in all walks of life, including capital investment and migration, will turn out to be a more enduring structural characteristic of today's world.

9

Elements for Multi-level Research on International Migration and Post-Migration Processes

For purposes of convenience, this book has divided three levels of analysis on migration and post-migration processes—micro, macro, and meso. This study has focused on the meso level or meso link that provides a connection between the two other levels of analysis. Such a meso link offers mechanisms for disaggregating macro- into micro and aggregating micro- into macro-level analysis. Deliberately abjuring a more ambitious synthesis for the sake of simplicity, the meso-level considerations presented in the preceding chapters are a step in linking the micro and macro levels and thus enlarge the possibilities of analysis. As the discussion of migration systems theories already indicated, more comprehensive approaches cover more than one level of analysis. It is now time to bring the other two levels back in and wrestle with connecting all three layers.

Without an awareness of how necessary multi-level theoretical constructs are, building a more systematic and comprehensive migration theory would be an anodyne plea and result in a plenteous brew. It would be too abstract and thus relatively meaningless in terms of empirical work and testability. The following synopsis is a first step towards reassembling the levels of analysis separated at the beginning of this study. It highlights the basic concepts and explains what questions are best answered on which level of analysis; a project fundamental for an auspicious re-evaluation of concepts concerning migration and post-migration processes.

The first part is divided into four sections, addressing each of the two substantive puzzles of international migration: (1) Why are there so few international migrants out of most places? (2) Why are there so many out of a few places? (3) How do transnational social spaces evolve in the course of international migration? (4) How can we think of intertwining the concomitant maintenance of transnational ties and adaptation of immigrants? To conclude, the second part of the discussion goes beyond the four cogent questions and asks what role migrant associations can play in contributing to an ideal construct called transnationalizing civil society. Since participation in civil society depends on enabling immigrants to participate, we finally ask how rules of membership can be adjusted to the reality of migrants living in transnational social spaces.

Determinants of Mobility and Immobility: Why Are There So Few International Migrants Out of Most Places?

The first question has been: Why are there relatively few international migrants out of most places in the South? Why do most potential migrants stay at home? Why is relative immobility so prevalent? (Figure 9.1) Immobility is relative when we consider international non-migration.

Analytical level	*MICRO*	*MESO LINK*	*MACRO*
Focus	peoples' desires	social and symbolic ties	structural opportunities and constraints
Key terms	– insider advantages – costs and benefits of staying and going – uncertainty and risk-reducing information – time-space resolution: stage in life course – location-specific human capital	– social ties of potential migrants; – location-specific social capital: reciprocity and solidarity – cultural variation in structure and role of meso-level units	– political (in)stability in emigration countries; – levels of economic development in emigration and immigration countries; – specific migration systems of nation-states within global politico-economic system – immigration state sovereignty and adherence to norms
Describes and explains primarily what?	relative immobility because of locally specific personal projects	various forms of social capital as locally specific assets constrain international mobility	– structural causes and direction of international migration; – effectiveness of control policies

FIG. 9.1. *Why are there so few international migrants out of most places?*

The Micro Level: Potential Migrants' Cost-Benefit Calculations and Cognitive Maps

Temporary or permanent territorial exit abroad is part of a variety of people's strategies to deal with stress and strain, to search for security and collective identity, to express political dissent, to enlarge options in various markets—in short, to engage in dilemmas and options posed over one's life course. In order to account for potential migrants' decisions, three main dimensions are of special relevance: the costs and benefits of migration, the uncertainty and risks involved, and the awareness of migrants, nestled in individual assets and guided by cognitive maps.

First, the net increase in utilities has to outweigh the benefits of staying relatively immobile and the perceived costs of migration. Various cost factors involved constitute a component to be considered, for example, costs of getting adequate information, expenditures for exit and transportation, search for jobs and housing in the country of destination—in addition to psychological costs of adapting to a new environment, the time and energy involved in forging new relationships and maintaining social and symbolic ties to the places and countries of origin.

In a preliminary way, potential migrants' decisions can be conceptualized as place utility that embraces the conditions in a specific location. Potential migrants weigh perceived costs and benefits, by comparing conditions at home and abroad. Ideally, a potential migrant balances a host of utility differences between countries by the probability of realizing different outcomes. Such an approach needs to consider factors that are less easily quantified—e.g. status, comfort, stimulation, autonomy, exit from oppression of all kinds, better life for one's children, and morality.

Second, not only objective differences matter for migration decisions, but also factors such as the subjectively-felt likelihood of fulfiling one's desires. Potential migrants face uncertainty, the degree to which a number of alternatives are perceived with respect to the occurrence of successfully adapting to a new environment in the case of migration (such as finding a job and housing abroad), or non-migration (e.g. economic future or safety of life at home), and the relative probabilities of these alternatives. Obtaining information can reduce the degree of uncertainty or risk. The availability of information depends upon various factors, such as level of education, or the strength and content of ties to other people. Interestingly, while potential migrants may have too little information to make the 'right' decision, they may also have too much information, i.e. an overload (Fischer, Martin and Straubhaar 1997*a*: 69). But overload is rare among first-time movers. It is more likely among those who know various places at home and abroad, and who need to decide where to stay. In sum, both too little and too much information can lead to second-best decisions that result in disappointment because the perceptions of the conditions in the immigration country are not accurate.

Third, potential migrants need to be aware of the various options for exit and voice. Only when we know about the mental maps of persons (Malmberg 1997: 42–5)—the total of knowledge, images, attitudes, and attachments to near and remote places—can we start to evaluate how the wider set of orders, organizations, and other opportunities impacts on choices. In other words, it is necessary to know how potential migrants frame the opportunities and constraints encountered.

A sophisticated understanding of costs, benefits, and corresponding cognitive maps allows us to take into account the transferability of individual resources such as human capital: viewed from an exchange perspective, potential migrants have invested in relations with significant others and reap continuous interest from their past investments. These insider advantages thus accumulated are often not transferable across borders. A decision to migrate would lead to their partial or complete loss. The crucial point here is that some assets such as experience, skills, educational and vocational diplomas, and other credentials, may only be used in a circumscribed local context, sometimes smaller than the nation-state.

The Meso Link: Relatively Immobile Local Assets

The previous considerations are predicated upon the assumption that potential migrants react to international differences such as wages and a host of non-tangible benefits. It is then necessary to move beyond assumptions of atomistic persons: it is more realistic to assume that people make migration decisions in a context constituted by the intensity and type of engagement in a localized set of projects and ties. People maintain strong and weak, symbolic and social ties with significant others and collectives. Control of others and valuable information travel across these ties. The very structure *and* the contents of ties between people and collective actors shape their actions.

Also, it is not enough to assume that small groups of kin or other relations instead of individuals optimize certain utilities. The decisive question arises: Who decides on who migrates and who stays in kinship or other groups, characterized by a specific social structure of authority and power? Gender, kin, and community relations mediate the causes, forms, and consequences of migration. To complicate matters, gender relations, kinship, and community dynamics vary widely across cultural groups and over time, and are in themselves the result of cultural rules played out in specific economic and political contexts (Bjerén 1997). Therefore, the decision regarding mobility or immobility of potential migrants not only depends on the existence of social units but also on the web of internal ties within groups and organizations.

Taking ties and not individual decisions as a point of departure, we look at membership in groups, participation in networks, and the co-ordination of people in organizations. Various forms and mechanisms of social capital exist within the boundaries of these spheres of action. These forms of social capital are transactions based on obligations as a pattern of social exchange, reciprocity as a norm, and solidarity. They are also critical mechanisms that translate larger structural opportunities into migrants' actual behaviour. Viewed within the dualism of people and groups, people get access to the resources of valued others, obtain relevant information, and occupy central positions to exercise control over other persons. In turn, groups and organizations supervise and monitor their members.

All these forms and benefits of social capital constitute typical local assets. Their transfer abroad involves maintenance and adaptation costs for migrants. Unless migrants transport social capital via transmission belts such as transnational migrant networks, place specificity of capital pares down mass migration and eventually results in cumulative immobility; especially among those categories of people notoriously short of economic and human capital desired by receivers in the North.

People are members of economic units, such as co-residing kinship groups. Such groups seek to diversify the risk to its economic well-being by sending members to work in different labour markets, one of which could be located abroad. The goals pursued are as diverse as the education of children or the purchase of a house and of consumer goods. The actual decision made (exit, voice, *in situ* adaptation, or a combination of all three), the strategies pursued after exit (relocate temporarily, return home after recurrent stays, or settle abroad), or staying depends very much on specific ties in kin groups. It also hinges upon decisions on reproduction and work over the life course. Moreover, larger local and symbolic communities mediate migration: either directly through authoritative decisions, or indirectly by people's loyalty, feeling of belonging to, and dependence on a certain collective.

Local ties arise in the course of an individual's involvement in and attachment to specific places. Local attachments are one of the main constituents of potential migrants' space-specific life projects. Life projects concern varied and quite tangible dimensions, such as family formation and careers. And many locally-specific assets are of a more intangible kind: for instance, belonging to an ethnic, religious, or national group gives people some sense of ontological security. Local ties may obstruct or spur migration of potential migrants, depending upon the values, viz. desires, of migrants about preferences and expectations at a specific time in a particular space. They hinder migration when space-specific projects demand attention to local ties.

Culture-specific norms not only organize when and where children are born, and to whom they are related kinship-wise. These norms also have immediate relevance for international mobility since they also influence where the new reproductive units should reside, and where and how children should be brought up in order to ensure cultural literacy (Bjerén 1997: 236–8). These norms can be exemplified when looking at the age of children as an indicator for migration and return. A possible time scheme could look like this: in many contemporary developing countries a child of up to 6 years of age is mostly socialized in the kin group. This poses few obstacles for a family living abroad. Yet in the 7–12 years bracket school starts and, if parents emphasize learning of the mother tongue, language training may induce either relative immobility or return. In the following age group, the 12–16 year-olds, gender roles are taught and in some cultures, parents prefer their daughters to return in order to be married. If the children are between 16 and 20 years old, it may be too late to migrate or to return for the children's' sake: they may want to stay because they have been reared and educated at home or abroad.

The Macro Context: The Structural Causes of Relative Immobility

Specific structural conditions—political conditions such as revolutions and civil wars, or economic inequalities and immigration policies—have caused, prohibited, directed, and accelerated migration and refugee flows at key historical junctures. In a global perspective, migration is part of worldwide and long-term processes of politico-economic competition between core and periphery, North and South (Hermele 1997: 133–6). Uneven development of capitalism as a driving force of global stratification, the asymmetries in the international system of states, and the strategic interactions of political collectives are equally decisive background conditions.

The control policies of the countries in the North have decisively shaped the onset, the direction, and the selection of migrants. It is one of the few undisputed findings of international migration research that virtually all labour-migration flows have been originally initiated by the immigration countries in the North. And one of the most crucial facts of state control of international flows of people is the fact that the nation-states in the North largely supervise entry. It is evident that migration within a nation-state is considered to be a human right and states, in principle, are not allowed to prevent emigration. However, there is no corresponding right to immigration under international law. Immigration is regarded as an issue of nation-state sovereignty. This state of affairs is an expression of the undisputed sovereignty of nation-states in the global political order to control borders and regulate which category of people is admitted and, partly, what the specific conditions are for legal status, access to work, housing, and social services.

In the country of destination, immigration raises issues of economic competition between newcomers, settled immigrants, and natives, of political incorporation into nation-states, regional institutions and citizenship, and questions of cultural diversity and difference. Basically, benefits from labour migration accrue to a few selected groups such as employers and can be considered private assets. By contrast, the costs arising from immigration usually are collectivized infrastructural costs to the public purse in education and housing. As in the first periods immigrants often behave as *homo migrans*—saving funds to return home soon—the collectivized costs mainly arise in the process of migrant settlement. Since asylum seekers most often are not allowed to work in the early stages, they totally depend on public funds. Therefore, in this case, conflicts about collectivized costs arise even earlier, and private benefits only accrue to those private enterprises providing food and shelter in the name of public agencies. Processes of policy-learning during the shift from privatized benefits to collectivized costs induces more restrictive policies.

An analysis of refugee movements can start with the efforts of state builders to establish and consolidate nation-state projects by instilling a sense of collective identity, loyalty, and cultural homogeneity. Among the more common measures taken are inducing people to speak a common language and implementing a common educational curriculum. However, as the fledgling nation-states in many parts of the world show, it is not a foregone conclusion that these projects succeed in the ambitious goal of homogenizing the population, or in the even more fundamental one of maintaining control over the territory. Although the international system of nation-states usually supports state sovereignty, there are manifold constellations that result in violent conflicts, inducing and producing refugee flows. In more dramatic cases civil war ensues, the nation-state project collapses, and widespread flight is usually one of the consequences. People then may flee for many reasons, for example, because they fear for their physical safety, want to practice their religion, escape from political, racial, or ethnic oppression, or from environmental disaster. Also, elites of ethnic minority groups seek to widen their political influence over domestic affairs by relocating abroad, especially if their political activities are restricted. Similar constellations arise out of social revolutions, civil upheaval and civil war, or dictatorships.

Nevertheless, there are several factors favouring relative immobility even in the case of involuntary movements. First, because of effective immigration control in the North, most potential South–North migrants either migrate internally or engage in South–South migration. This is quite obvious in the case of people with low degrees of freedom living in despondence. Second, regarding the international political system, there is a partial international regime that regulates the admission of refugees. The basic expression is the Geneva Convention. International law stipulates that political refugees are allowed to seek asylum. Yet, again, it is the prerogative of sovereign nation-states to grant asylum. It is not a right an individual can claim of the nation-state. Third, there are ties that transcend local communities and relate to symbolic communities of religion, ethnicity or nation. These ties most often refer to collectives within nation-states or to those in other states in the South. For example, experts estimated that there were about 18 million international refugees in the early 1990s, while approximately 24 million were internally displaced.

Reasons for Relative Immobility

To summarize the insights derived on all three levels of analysis, there are four main reasons for the high degree of relative immobility in South–North international migration:

(1) Despondence

The degree of absolute deprivation, such as utter poverty, severely restricts the degrees of freedom or choice. Therefore, widespread despondence purports that most of the people in the South completely lack resources for exit and voice, and are in a state of resignation to a hostile environment around them (Ahmed 1997: 176). Due to severe structural constraints, these persons cannot be considered to be potential migrants anymore. It is not surprising that a fair share of those internally displaced have no recourse to move abroad in the first place because of a lack of resources to overcome barriers of transportation.

(2) Location-Specific Assets: Human and Social Capital

Many assets available to potential migrants, be they economic, political, or social, are tied to certain places. A certain part of the abilities and assets of individuals and groups are location-specific, because they can only be used in a well-defined place and are not readily transferable to other places of residence abroad. This points to the fact that there are problems involved in transferring human capital. Accordingly, individual actors weigh the corresponding costs and benefits. For example, potential migrants decide to stay or to move in the country of origin because they cannot adequately deploy their educational and professional qualifications abroad.

As an alternative to migration, insider advantages allow potential migrants to reap the rewards of staying relatively immobile. Language skills are a prime example of an asset that constitutes an insider advantage. Of course, language is an indispensable means of communication in acquiring diverse resources. Migrating to another country sometimes incurs costs of learning another language. Unless a migrant is proficient in the immigration country language, there are usually serious obstacles to 'good' jobs, self-employment, and even housing.

Over time, we can observe processes of cumulative immobility: the more often a person decides to stay, the more likely she is to do so the next time the exit option is up for choice. Imagine people who have decided ten times to remain at home and improve their lot there. At the eleventh time the probability in favour of staying will be even higher than the time before. And the longer this process has been going on, the stronger the external incentives to alter this pattern must be. This is because repetition is one of the main mechanisms of reinforcing behavioural patterns (Fiske and Taylor 1984).

Bringing in social capital extends the realm of location-specific assets beyond purely individual characteristics and instrumental considerations. While people use their ties strategically, social and symbolic relations contain various mechanisms that pattern transactions. Without transnational networks mechanisms such as reciprocity and solidarity favour relative immobility because they are highly sensitive to exit. Devoid of border-crossing support networks, international migration usually contributes to their demise. Again, repeated instances of (relative) immobility can result in cumulative immobility if social capital inherent in ties is channelled towards voice and *in situ* adaptation.

(3) Alternatives to Exit: Loyalty and Voice

Loyalty to groups ranging from kin to nation-states favours relative immobility. Often, tradition is mentioned to denote this phenomenon. Yet, a host of allegiances better accounts for this connection. Take personal ties to kin or symbolic attachments to specific spaces or groups.

In addition, to better one's life, there are alternatives to geographical exit, as for example political voice. This option often antecedes, accompanies, or follows territorial exit. Voice means political expression and action in the space of origin. Moreover, exit and voice are not exclusive alternatives. They can be used in a sequence or at the same time. An extreme case are refugee warriors who seek to liberate their country of origin by force.

(4) Alternatives to International Migration: Internal and South–South Migration

Internal migration generally constitutes a viable alternative. In other words, there are a variety of time-space strategies available to potential migrants. Internal circulation and internal migration—rural–rural, rural–urban, urban–urban, urban–rural—are often well-established schemes. But while internal migration can function to restrict international migration, it can also be a first step towards long-distance migration across nation-state borders—but only if networks reaching abroad are available.

Migration Dynamics: Why Are There So Many International Migrants Out of So Few Places?

The second part of the first puzzle has been: Why are there so many migrants out of so few places? (Figure 9.2) Basically, migration can be seen as a self-feeding process with a strong internal momentum that reinforces itself and then declines over time. The master mechanism is cumulative causation: rising emigration sets off structural changes that make additional migration more likely and that accelerate changes in the economic, political, social, and cultural spheres. Cumulative mobility is the end result. In turn, feedback processes reach turning points after which flows decelerate. Cumulative mobility means to see migration processes as they go on, under their own steam, producing at every step that stage which will of itself determine the next one.

Analytical level	*MICRO*	*MESO LINK*	*MACRO*
Focus	peoples' desires	social and symbolic ties	structural opportunities
Key concepts	– rising expectations and relative frustration; – information flows	– chain migration; – migrant networks; – cumulative causation and S-shaped curve	– development and change; – 'inverted U-curve'
Describes and explains primarily what?	desire or preference change among stayers and movers	endogenous dynamics of the migration process	– effects upon economic development and political integration; – exogenously induced turning points

FIG 9.2. *Why are there so many international migrants out of so few places?*

The Micro Level: Processing Information and Relative Frustration

Once migration has been triggered, swift changes follow regarding the ease of moving abroad—provided that the costs for relocating assets decline. Here, pioneer migrants fulfil important roles as brokers. Brokers—such as labour recruiters—can trigger follow-up migration by enlisting pioneer migrants. Pioneer migrants themselves can later act as brokers in providing the necessary information on the advantages of certain locations for potential migrants, and link them to support networks. Failure of pioneer migrants to establish themselves abroad has the opposite effect. When pioneer migrants offer referrals, past migration accelerates the further likelihood among potential migrants to move abroad. All of this reduces the risks associated with international migration. As a consequence, chain migration in networks develops. Prerequisites are information flows via personal contacts. Information travels easily through migrant networks. Generally, as networks expand, as brokers gain a foothold and connect to gatekeepers in various locations in the country of destination, migration not only spreads as a behavioural pattern but also as a way of life; a crucial element of what Max Weber called the conduct of life—*Lebensführung* (Weber 1988). Since there are risks involved and cost-benefit calculations are inherently uncertain, migrant networks have an insurance function. The utility of networks is likely to be greatest where migration risks are very high in general and information on job and housing opportunities is rare and costly.

The cognitive maps of migrants radically change, as the migration process gets underway. Once brokers have initiated large-scale migration abroad, changes among the desires of potential migrants unravel. As opportunities for migration increase, the desire to move increases even faster. And the desires of the stayers to move increase proportionally to the degrees of freedom they have. This is an instance of relative frustration. Admission policies of immigration states that set the stage for migrant networks but above all the migrant networks themselves increase the opportunities to move and enhance the desire among potential migrants at home to participate in these venues. At bottom, it is the 'Tocqueville effect'. In our case, increased opportunities to move abroad, mediated by migrant networks, can be seen as setting the stage for growing equality of opportunity. However, large gains because of recruitment, coupled with limited migration opportunities because of immigration control, ultimately lead to frustration of those who could not migrate. Sometimes, an increase in unauthorized migration is a result.

A similar, yet distinct process applies to people involved in more involuntary migration. However, in their case, it is internal persecution or discrimination in the producing states *and* policies of the accepting countries that set off chains of events leading to flight and more flight. Then minority groups in nation-states come to favour a relocation abroad to escape and, perhaps, to topple the abusive and oppressive political regime in more deliberate ways from abroad. In contrast to potential migrants with relatively high degrees of freedom, the mechanism of expanding opportunities and even more rapidly snowballing desires does not necessarily lead to frustration effects among refugees. This is so because the more involuntary the movement, the lower the degrees of freedom. People then are less likely to scheme in any meaningful way and care so much about relatively minor differences in life chances.

During the stay abroad migrants try to minimize the break with the past they encounter. Many migrants start out with the expressed intention to return home—and many indeed do return. Note, however, that migrants change their views on whether they want to stay or return. Even narratives of temporariness and permanence fulfil functions other than settlement or return, such as a desire for consistent biographical trajectories. An example is the use of return as a metaphor (Çağlar 1994). On a personal level, expressions of return assuage the biographical breaks encountered by migrants living abroad. It serves to counter individual amnesia and create stable moorings. Return orientations connect time before migration with time after. The rhetoric of return transforms the meaning of the time spent abroad and makes it appear to the migrants that not only space but time too can be conquered.

The Meso Link: The Selective Function of Networks in Chain Migration

The changes in people's desires, initiated by macro conditions, take place within webs of criss-crossing ties. And increased information flows and feelings of relative frustration that foster migration flows unfold in migrant networks. It is impossible to discuss the reduction of risk without including the diverse functions of migrant networks. Therefore, in order to understand the mechanisms mediating desires and structures, we progress from people's choices to the bonds between them. The resources inherent in ties and within networks are not simply given. They require explanation. Migrant networks develop in a serial fashion of continued obligations, reciprocity and solidarity, within and beyond kinship groups. Only through migrant networks can people transform local assets into transnational ones. Migrant networks then turn into a transmission belt for social capital and its benefits. Equally important, perpendicular forms of social capital help migrants to either convert it into financial assets or to create the very conditions for deploying other assets, such as economic or human capital. Migrant networks funnelling the selection of migrants and chain migration need types of social capital that extend beyond specific reciprocity and intra-kinship or focused solidarity. That means social and symbolic ties have to reach beyond tightly-knit social units to enable travel, work, and housing abroad for masses of people. If the various forms of social capital and the corresponding benefits remain confined to closed groups, no snowballing effects supervene and the supply of migrants exhausts quickly. When only specific reciprocity and focused solidarity are available, the pool of potential migrants remains relatively small.

The very processes of international migration affect people's motivations, social structures, and cultural milieus in ways that can enhance migration but also limit it. Cumulative mobility means that international migration increases in volume and becomes socially more diverse, before it slows again. These changes accumulate over time and change the situation in which migration occurs. More and more people move abroad; positive feedback effects proceed in chains of cumulative causation. When the supply of potential migrants falls, the migration volume declines. Ideally, processes of cumulative mobility expand until the supply of all potential migrants in a given place has depleted. In sum, international migration flows turn into self-feeding processes and acquire an internal momentum of their own. Gradually, they become increasingly independent of the conditions that originally caused them. The quintessential image is one of an S-shaped diffusion curve.

None the less, when viewed retrospectively, temporary, recurrent, or permanent migration involve widely differing levels of commitment on the part of the mover to origin and destination. In the case of temporary migration, the relatively short time of absence can work to leave social and symbolic ties to the country of origin basically unchanged. These persons are temporary exiles. This could also apply to recurrent migration. In the case of permanent migration, we expect that the ties to the country of settlement gradually increase over time. This, however, does not mean that bonds to the country of origin necessarily decline. The strength and intensity of ties is not necessarily a zero-sum game. In the second generation, we expect these ties to the communities and countries of origin to be much less prevalent than among the first generation. It is an open question for empirical investigation whether facilitated means of transportation and exchange of information and goods have prolonged the period during which migrants maintain strong and symbolic social ties to the country of origin.

We can now inquire into the most likely stay-or-go strategies of potential migrants involved, which depend on the stage in their life course and their position within a set of relevant social and symbolic ties. The range of options for potential movers who do not fear persecution on political, religious, ethnic, or other ascriptive grounds seems to be clearest. When a kin group is growing and children are young, we expect, *ceteris paribus*, either no migration or temporary and recurrent migration to take place as favoured options. In contrast, settlement in the immigration country of kin groups migrating with young children tends to be a rather prolonged process and thus not as likely. Also, there are often legal restrictions to bringing the family along in the beginning. Again, all other conditions being equal, we forecast single men or women or recently married couples without children to choose this latter strategy.

The meso link is especially strong in specifying the mechanisms necessary for migration processes to develop into self-feeding loops, such as generalized reciprocity and diffuse solidarity. None the less, very often, processes of cumulative mobility do not reach their endogenously induced turning point. Exogenous macro factors such as favourable economic development and, more frequently, restrictive admission policies of the receivers impinge on these dynamics. In the short run, public policies seem to be ineffective because they cannot stop family reunification and marriage migration. However, in the long run, restrictive immigration policies can be quite effective; usually after the self-feeding dynamics of existing migration networks have started to decline. Many a time restrictive policies arise out of processes of cumulative mobility. Admission policies in the immigration countries become more restrictive when, for example, meta-politics connects perceived 'over-foreignization' (*Überfremdung*) and competition for jobs, housing, and social services, threats to external and internal security and to collective identities with the chain migration of undesired immigrants.

Not surprisingly, the strongest incentives for continued and strict immigration control are in those national welfare states with a high degree of internal regulation of congestible collective goods questioned by immigration. From all we know by now about the nexus between ethnic plurality and redistributive state activities one clear relationship emerges: the more ethnically diverse polities are, the less public money is spent on redistributive activities—and this has been true worldwide for the past decades (Alesina, Baqir, and Easterly 1997).

The Macro Level: The Direction of Flows within Migration Systems

If we extend the meaning of networks to include not only individual migrants but also collective actors such as nation-state governments and NGOs, we also get yet another view not only on how migration dynamics unfold but on their long-term impact. These migration networks consist of both migrant networks and (supra-)state and non-state institutions (see also Goss and Lindquist 1995). They shape and influence access to overseas employment and safe havens through the operation of institutional rules and resources. It is usually a complex institutional web in which knowledgeable individuals and the agents of organizations, ranging from immigrant associations to multinational corporations, and state authorities operate. Not only individuals participate in migration networks; collectives such as households, kinship groups, or organizations are also part of it.

The notion of migration system brings in elements of meso-level and macro-level analysis. Migration systems consist of the totality of migration and migrant networks spanning countries of emigration and immigration, and manifold organizations regulating the flow of people. The migration-systems approach has three main characteristics. First, the most basic concept is a migration system, defined as two or more locations—most often nation-states—connected to each other by flows and counterflows of people. International migrations cause counter-streams, i.e. remigration, that have to be considered. Migration systems are multi-tiered migratory spaces that are defined by subnational, national, inter-, and transnational elements. Second, linkages between countries other than people exist, such as trade and security alliances, colonial ties, and flows of goods, services, information, and ideas. Migration systems evolving in wider economic, political, cultural, and historical linkages pose the context in which the international movement of people occurs. These bonds mediate actions by potential migrants on whether to stay or to move. Third, movement is not a static or one-time event, but rather a dynamic process consisting of a sequence of events across time. Given the context of important factors such as economic inequalities within and between nation-states and the admission policies of the immigration states, people, kin groups, territorial and symbolic communities develop strategies to cope with stay-or-go alternatives. In short, positive feedback processes develop within migration systems.

The overemphasis of systems analysis on the flow and direction of migration within migrant networks has to be rectified by introducing the place-specific nature of various forms of personal and collective projects and local assets. Highly unequal rates of migration not only exist between developing countries but also inside—and within regions with similar levels of economic development. And migrant networks in themselves do not explain the dynamics of international migration. What we need to know is how networks form, what kind of resources flow through network ties that bind people and groups, and the mechanisms by which they translate into action—the mainstay of meso-link analyses.

By and large, macro-structural theories are particularly useful in explaining the underlying structural causes of international immobility and migration. The direction of the three great waves of international migration—from Europe to the colonized world, from Europe to the white-settler colonies, and from South to North—can all be explained by the stark extent of economic inequality and imbalance of political power between countries of origin and destination. Macro-structural theories thus give us an idea as to where migration is most unlikely or likely to occur and even a first hint as to group selection and admission. Although the immigration states in the North usually control first entries quite effectively, the situation changes for those immigrant groups who have achieved permanent residency. Norms of human, civil, and social rights, sanctioned by and often enshrined in constitutions of liberal democracies, act as critical mechanisms to enable family reunification and marriage migration.

During South–North migration processes structural dependence, typical instances of centre-periphery relations on the international level, turn into relations of unequal interdependence, characterized by gross and continued imbalances of political power, economic development, and cultural penetration. Relations increasingly metamorphose towards interdependence because citizens of the country of origin live abroad, strengthening the manifold linkages between the countries within the migration circuit.

Restrictive immigration policies which usually arise in the course of international migration tend to be counterbalanced because of the dichotomy of restrictionist and expansionist forces governing immigration policies. Restrictive policies concerning labour migrants often go hand in hand with exceptions given to employer interests in certain sectors, such as services and agriculture. These exceptions then favour new migrant networks emerging. Above all, this applies to liberal democratic systems characterized by competitive and non-consensual immigration politics. Moreover, totally effective external and internal immigration controls would require a degree of surveillance which would be incompatible with upholding basic human and civil rights for citizens and non-citizens alike.

Chain migration and the settlement of a part of the immigrants in the countries of destination tends to develop into (semi-)permanent politicization of politics concerning the welfare and security functions of the immigration states. Mass migration into liberal democratic regimes has not undermined the consensus in nationally-bounded states. Nevertheless, in a period of welfare state transformation since the mid-1970s and the end of the Cold War in the late 1980s, it has fostered meta-political debates and political conflicts related to three major forms of state integration concerning functional (perceived material costs and benefits over welfare and control), normative (social justice and crime), and expressive aspects (solidarity and collective identities). Concerning the welfarization of immigration politics, it is no coincidence that it has gradually picked up speed since the transformation of welfare states in the mid-1970s. And because of the restructuring of interstate security relations since the end of the Cold War and the musings over a 'clash of civilizations', the securitization of international migration has proceeded at a quick pace. The meta-politics of immigration evolves into endogenous dynamics: the more restrictive policies have become, especially towards asylum seekers and undocumented immigrants, the more this can be seen to be proof of the illegitimacy of members of these immigrant categories to be admitted. As a consequence of these ratcheting effects in welfarization and securitization of migration politics, immigration legislation and practice has become more restrictive, counteracting spiralling chain migration.

Reasons for So Many Out of So Few Places

We have to differentiate self-feeding effects along the degrees of freedom available to potential migrants.

(1) High Degrees of Freedom: Chain Migration

If the degrees of freedom are relatively high, movement occurs within strong inter-country linkages, and if social capital via mechanisms of generalized reciprocity and diffuse solidarity can be readily used in networks, then the prospects for chain and mass migration out of few places are excellent. Chain and mass flows out of a few places depend on relatively frustrated potential migrants, induced by the reciprocal and solidary mechanisms of social capital.

(2) Low Degrees of Freedom: Involuntary and Interrupted Migration

If the degrees of freedom are very low, as is generally the case in involuntary migrations, self-feeding dynamics are generally unlikely to evolve, or are of only very short duration. Many refugee flows attest to this pattern.

(3) Immigration States' Control Policies: Effective Control and the Meta-Politics of Admission and Membership

Exogenous factors, in this case restrictive immigration policies, often inhibit the S-shaped migration curve from running its full course. Because of the asymmetric nature of bi- and multilateral South–North relations, immigration states can unilaterally cease recruitment and thus effectively restrict the entry of new categories of migrants. In addition, the meta-politics of admission and membership develop their own dynamics, with each restriction furthering the perception of illegitimacy in admitting and legalizing certain immigrant categories, especially asylum seekers and undocumented migrants. However, the policies of liberal democratic nation-states honouring basic human and civil rights of migrants cannot totally curb follow-up effects such as family reunification and marriage migration.

How Do Transnational Social Spaces Evolve?

The second puzzle pertains to the fact that transnational ties, circuits, and communities represent familiar consequences of international migration in the process of immigrant adaptation in the immigration countries; yet they are insufficiently theorized as to their emergence and their role for immigrant adaptation. The third question raises the issue of how transnational ties beyond the well-known phenomena of migration and return and beyond historically singular instances of diaspora formation congeal in transnational social spaces. Even permanent settlement in the immigration country does not necessarily imply a complete rupture of social and symbolic ties and other forms of linkages within migration systems. The corresponding transnational social spaces are relatively permanent flows of people, goods, ideas, symbols, and services across international borders that tie stayers and movers and corresponding networks and non-state organizations; regulated by emigration and immigration state policies. The concept of transnational social space suggests that the transnational reciprocities and solidarities forged through migrant networks and groups form a critical mass evolving into new social entities and networks that cross nation-state boundaries for a considerable amount of time—for at least one immigrant cohort (Figure 9.3). Since these spaces involve a constant circular flow of people, it is useful in certain extreme instances to

Analytical level	*MICRO*	*MESO LINK*	*MACRO*
Focus	peoples' desires	social and symbolic ties	structural opportunities
Key concepts	transnational life projects	– transnational obligations, reciprocity, and solidarity; – transnational circuits; – transnational communities	interstitial transactions and nation-state projects
Describes and explains primarily what?	value or desire change among settled immigrants and return migrants	development of durable networks in migration systems	existence of transnational social spaces in and between nation-states and the international system of states

FIG. 9.3. *How do transnational social spaces evolve?*

speak of transnational migrants instead of emigrants and immigrants, such as in the case of multilocal families. Yet geographically hypermobile people are the exception and not the rule in transnational social spaces.

The Micro Level: People's Border-Crossing Time-Space Projects

Analytically, two aspects can be distinguished in how immigrants resolve their time-space situation—the stage in their life course and the various ties potential movers develop to varied local spaces. First, the stage of a person in her life course, earlier resolutions, and the strength of local and transnational attachments crucially affect not only the decision to stay or to go, whether to stay in the immigration country or return but also the likelihood of shuttling back and forth in transnational social spaces, materially and symbolically. In economic terms this means that people strive to optimize their individual or collective utilities, their quality of life in choosing the spatial dimension of their life course.

Second, local ties of immigrants and return migrants are fixed in places that signify a 'whole' to the migrant. Individual life projects are coupled with ties to specific places, attaining the meaning of space. It is plausible to assume that the more strongly persons are engaged in local projects, such as reproduction, community, work and business, religion, arts, sports, and politics, the less likely they are to migrate for long periods of time. The same should apply to return migration. Because of the transferability of social capital in migrant networks, immigrant communities in the immigration countries progressively evolve. Sometimes, these communities maintain or even establish new ties to the country of origin *and* to other places of destination.

Because of the use of various forms of social capital that serve as transmission belts, specific time-space resolutions through international migration encourage some important individual projects and ties to be simultaneously local and transnational. Quite a few international migrants start out as exiles. Exile refers to the individual situation of expatriation. However, durable transnational social spaces only develop if international migrants do not remain in a situation of exile. Transnational spaces require bonds to both the emigration and immigration countries; albeit not equally strong ones.

A transnational lifestyle provokes conflictual attachments. An Israeli accountant in the USA aptly summarized his predicament: 'Israel is my mother and America is my wife, so you can imagine the way I must feel' (cited in Gold 1997: 422). Some of the problems involved are information overload and, sometimes, conflicting identities. Initially, when making the first decision to migrate or to stay, migrants and pioneer movers usually face the problem of too few resources that can be used in the process of migration. In other words, they lack the main benefits—namely information, social control, and access to other people's assets. We have seen that in the course of international migration, adaptation to the new context of settlement and the maintenance of transnational ties usually goes hand in hand. However, for those who come to lead the life of true transnationals—often human capital migrants and businessmen—new difficulties arise as well. The easier communication flows between two or more places in a space, the more complex and vexing decisions become about where to stay, how long, and with whom.

The Meso Link: The Bridging Functions of Reciprocity and Solidarity

Transnational social spaces require a burgeoning transnational exchange of goods, ideas, and persons that is hardly imaginable without a multitude of strong and weak social and symbolic ties in migration systems. The transnationalization evolving out of international migration is not simply predetermined by facilitated transportation and communication but depends on choices and resources of collective actors. Transnational social spaces depend on twofold local assets that are located both in the countries of origin and destination—distant from the magic carpet assumptions in the globalization literature. If such transnational spaces exist for longer periods of time, beyond the first generation of migrants, effects spill over to issues of collective identity. We then speak of syncretist cultural practices, representations, and identities.

In an ideal-typical way, there are three types of transnational social spaces. From the first to the third, the density and intensity of social and symbolic ties is increasing:

1. Kinship-based transnational reciprocity and solidarity regularly arises through specific reciprocity, such as remittances in exchange for child-rearing and housekeeping. It also exists when members of cohesive village communities espouse generalized reciprocity and offer migrating members a first stop abroad to get referrals for essentials such as jobs and housing. In some cases, the mechanisms of reciprocity and solidarity enlarge the set of opportunities for migrants; but only if the ties lead to decent positions and provide non-redundant contacts—frequently outside the narrow kinship group or community. Just the

same, in cases of violent conflicts between kinship and other outside groups, reciprocity functions in a retributive manner and solidarity stifles innovative moves by kin outside the group.

2. Transnational circuits mainly entail networks of participants who depend on the exchange of information and mutual obligations along generalized tit-for-tat lines. Therefore, they are mostly operative in business ventures, and typically go beyond more narrow confines of kinship. In the transnational realm, the benefits derived from these networks crucially depend on insider knowledge of habits and customs in the emigration and immigration countries.

3. Transnational communities arise out of dense and strong social and symbolic ties of group members and organizations, ranging from local villages to nations. It is imperative that strong symbolic ties and a vivid display of public and collective representations with historically oriented narratives form the backbone of these 'we'-groups. Reciprocity and solidarity need to be institutionalized, albeit not to the same extent as formal citizenship in nation-states. Again, the types of reciprocity and solidarity matter: the more reciprocity extends from specific to generalized variants, and solidarity from focused to diffuse, the more likely it is that social capital functions to bridge places in transnational social spaces. Diasporas are specific types of transnational communities, characterized by a history of forced exodus, a high degree of social and cultural distance to other 'we'-groups in the country of immigration, and a yearning to return to the country of origin.

The existence of transnational political and religious groups suggests that geographical propinquity is not a necessary requirement for communities. However, another sort of propinquity—often going hand in hand with geographical closeness but not necessarily restricted to it—is of utmost importance: ethnic, class, national, or religious solidarity. Symbolic ties matter. The bridging functions of social capital cannot be seen without these collective representations.

The Macro Level: The Uneasy Existence of Transnational Spaces in and between Nation-States

There are two extremes on a continuum of transnational social spaces. At the one end, if the option of full adaptation is cut off for various reasons, such as fervid discrimination in the immigration state, we expect communities of exiles to turn into diasporas. These are transnational communities with a distinct cultural and social life over long periods of time. The members of diasporas refer to a common homeland they long to return to. Such communities extol a high degree of what is called ethnic, national, and religious retention. For continued survival, they need an institutionalized agreement to differ from others in the immigration state. If, at the other end, the migrants do not encounter high legal and informal obstacles in the immigration country and can easily adapt culturally and socially to the groups in the country of destination, they have a choice. Then, transnational communities can but must not rapidly dissolve; based on emergent assimilation.

The emergence of transnational social spaces impacts upon strategies of governments and migrants dealing with discrimination and xenophobia as well as putting forth and tolerating multicultural claims. Indeed, the stronger the restrictive efforts by the respective governments, the more vigorous the resistance of various immigrant groups.

Interstitial transactions across nation-state borders suggest that the diffusion of persons via migration encompasses both the formation of ethnic and national identities and emergence of novel supra-national identities. This has tremendous consequences not only for economic activities but also for political mobilization and cultural identity. For example, transnationally operating challenger groups increasingly direct their demands to at least two different governments and supranational institutions such as the EU, and diaspora communities keep a critical distance towards both cultures of origin and destination. These processes offer opportunities for political and cultural entrepreneurs to reintroduce or at least strengthen well-known religious and ethnic cleavage lines in politics that have characterized much of European political and cultural history, adding to the importance of non-class-identified groups and organizations. One of the ironies is that some of these carriers of transnationalization are self-proclaimed guardians of rigorous nationalist and religious projects. If this is the case, various forms of social capital and their benefits function as bridges for long-distance nationalism and long-range religion. At the same time, transnational ties enrich the adaptation of immigrants in manifold ways, brokering syncretist practices and identities. To conclude, the interstitial transactions both within and across the borders of nation-states belie the visions of bounded societies and nation-states as unitary entities (cf. Mann 1986: 16). While transnational social spaces do not constitute rival configurations to nation-states, they question the idea of an exclusive territorial and symbolic boundedness in at least two respects: transnational communities can serve as platforms to challenge the authority of governments in emigration states by launching opposition groups outside their reach and raise doubts about singular nation-state membership in the immigration countries.

Reasons for the Evolution of Transnational Social Spaces

(1) More Cumulation: A New Quality of Migration Systems

Similar to self-feeding effects of international migration among migrants with relatively high degrees of freedom, transnational spaces represent a new quality in migration systems. They are built upon pre-migration linkages, migrant and migration networks, and metamorphose into durable transnational bonds via processes of cumulative causation. This needs a critical mass of linkages and ties spanning a space in and between emigration and immigration states and relatively permanent communities in both countries of origin and destination.

(2) Macro Conditions Favourable to Transnational Spaces

Propitious factors such as eased international travel and communication and liberal policies in many immigration states that increasingly shy away from enforcing assimilation, have made the border-crossing expansion of social space more feasible in the past decades than between World War One and the 1960s. In particular, an increasing reluctance on the part of immigration country governments to enforce the bimodal model—assimilation or return—and strengthened multicultural voices have broadened the venues for immigrant transnationalization.

(3) Different Dynamics Accompanying Economic, Political, and Cultural Transnationalization

Various realms of transnationalization espouse different causes and dynamics. For economic transnationalization to unfold on a larger scale into transnational circuits, participants need to muster specific insider advantages that help them straddle laws and tax systems in separate nation-states. Durable political transnationalization requires the formation of transnational communities, tied by symbolic bonds in the struggle for political autonomy. Cultural transnationalization involves the evolution of syncretist cultural practices and identities found among the second and plus generations of immigrants.

(4) The Future of Transnational Social Spaces: War and Melting into the Core

The future prospects of transnational social spaces depends mainly on two sets of factors. First, they can only be sustained if relations between countries of emigration and immigration remain peaceful and are not endangered by war. Otherwise, the charge of dual loyalty will force immigrants into assimilation. Second, even in the absence of mercurial conditions, immigrants may melt into majority cores in the immigration states. Transnational communities then disappear. The prospects for transnational circuits, however, are more favourable.

How to Conceptualize the Concomitant Expansion of Transnational Social Spaces and Immigrant Adaptation?

Given the relevance of transnational social spaces for understanding post-migration processes, the fourth question then is how adaptation and transnational social spaces can proceed simultaneously. We need to counterweigh the popular idea that immigrants always gradually discard their cultural heritage in processes of accommodation and assimilation, and the equally erroneous assumption of ethnic retention after arrival up until the second or even third generation (Figure 9.4).

The Micro Level: Immigrants' Desires and Adaptation

Theories of assimilation have seen accommodation as the dominant form of adaptation for immigrants of the first generation, to be followed by melting into the majority core as the eminent mode among the more impressible second one. In this view adaptation is possible under favourable structural, political, and economic conditions and the absence of widespread discrimination. If we apply the concept of time-space resolutions to the life course of migrants, we can rephrase certain key assumptions of assimilation theory: based on the personal projects

Analytical level	*MICRO*	*MESO LINK*	*MACRO*
Focus	peoples' desires	social and symbolic ties	structural opportunities
Key concepts	individual accommodation or retention	border-crossing expansion of social space	transnationalizing civil society
Describes and explains primarily what?	reconciliation of personal projects in different nation-states; consistent biographical narrative	impact of transnational ties and projects upon immigrant adaptation in migration system	evolution of new political, economic, and cultural spheres at transnational interstices

FIG. 9.4. *How to conceptualize concomitant immigrant adaptation and border-crossing expansion of social space?*

of many international migrants, we expect the ties of the first generation to the emigration country not to dwindle to insignificance. Therefore, the most we expect of first-generation immigrants is indeed a sort of preliminary adaptation, i.e. accommodation. And among the second generation we surmise greater reference to the settlement country conditions, with eventual full assimilation in subsequent generations. Migrants' life courses and the personal projects attached to it usually do refer to the place of settlement to a very high degree. Whether these assumptions hold for all immigrant groups and whether they apply under conditions of increased opportunities and desires to maintain and foster transnational ties is an open question. For example, discriminated groups tend to keep on and reforge ties to their homeland to a much higher extent than groups who adapt well in the immigration country (e.g. Tatla 1999). In turn, opportunities to keep transnational ties alive can affect the speed and extent of the desire to fully adapt in the country of settlement. The question is how immigrants and their descendants merge or synthesize various threads of attachments and ties that cut across nation-state borders.

When considering theories competing with assimilation, such as ethnic pluralism, the litmus test is not socio-economic and political integration, in which the two canonical concepts of assimilation and pluralism hold different but quite compatible assumptions. Contentious here is whether immigrant children acquire and pass on the mother tongue, cultural practices, and traditions of their parents or ancestors.

Cultural differences thus play a key role in the adaptation process, irrespective of the viewpoint taken. The question is under what conditions they are of significance. Adaptation involves allocating people in accordance with their appearance and affiliations. Viewed in light of a simple cost-benefit analysis, people are thought to use cultural differences in order to create groups and slot individuals into categories. Only markers with recognized cultural significance become important for collective identity and action. The markers serve to draw boundaries around groups. They can be used to include group members and to deny others access to resources such as reciprocity and solidarity. If immigrants compete with the indigenous population and other immigrants on an individual basis, this may dissolve group boundaries. If they compete as groups, their common interests will lead them to reinforce these very boundaries (Banton 1983: 135–9). However, it would be short-sighted to consider cultural differences only as markers for analytical purposes. People not only have economic motives. Even more important, cultural traditions and practices may constitute crucial values to be upheld and defended in their own right, if push comes to shove. In order to determine the strategies for individuals it is therefore more fruitful to tie desires to macro conditions.

Concerning the limiting conditions, assimilation theories are not very explicit. Ultimately, for assimilation theories to work, group competition between immigrants and natives needs to be minimal, to become less and less important in an immigration situation over time, until individual competition between people finally dominates the field. By contrast, the predictions of ethnic pluralism concerning separation and cultural retention are fulfiled when inclusive group categories arise and exclusive processes proceed as regards economic resources, religion, language, and cultural practices. We now need to find out what factors contribute to the desires that range from melting into the core to cultural retention and further on to more complicated transitory or perhaps permanent phenomena of transnationally-induced syncretism.

The Meso Link: The Border-Crossing Expansion of Social Space

Since immigrant ties can be both transnational *and* local, perspectives that overemphasize the degree of adaptation to the immigration society, such as assimilation theory, may not render an accurate picture of how immigrants adapt. Also, concepts that consider ties but exaggerate the extent to which newcomers retain cultural practices virtually unaltered, such as ethnic pluralism, are not helpful either. At the very least, these theoretical approaches need to be supplemented by a perspective that places a premium upon the potential duality of orientations in the first lineage generation of international migrants, and continued transnational ties among their descendants—border-crossing expansion of social space. And while syncretism is by no means always of a transnational nature, communication flows in migration systems, nowadays often reconfigured interstitially across borders, ensure a continued cultural diffusion in both directions. Despite sometimes ambivalent allegiances and reproaches of dubious commitments, immigrants and their descendants retain and develop new local attachments and ties while being engaged in border-traversing activities.

Since studies on international migrants' transnationalization are in their infancy, there is a tendency to singularly focus not only on a misguided claim to newness of all associated phenomena connected with transnational ties and linkages. Also, there is the danger to treat ideal-typical constructs as if they were exclusive concepts. The real potential of concepts of transnational membership is not only to identify new modes of adaptation but also to enrich notions underlying assimilation and ethnic pluralism, and to identify dimensions of emerging transnationalizing civil societies. Transnationalization can minimize the extent to which contemporary immigrants adapt to the country of settlement—thinking of the constantly replenished or newly emerging immigrant communities in an age of more perpetual international migration in some parts of the world. This makes the export of ethnic conflicts from the country of origin abroad and the spread of transnational political and religious communities more attractive. With as much likelihood, however, transnationalization helps certain groups to eventually adapt in a very favourable manner, to retain advantageous aspects of their heritage and to develop new and syncretist forms. Above all, a systematic analysis of concomitant transnationalization and adaptation can help to shed light on empirically verifiable phenomena such as segmented assimilation—melting into majority cores in some fields of life while retaining old or developing new forms in others.

The Macro Level: States and Transnationalizing Membership

In all known cases, transnational social spaces emanate out of earlier colonial and hegemonic linkages and migration systems. This is the basis for cumulative chains of auxiliary transnational spaces and immigrant adaptation. Simultaneous transnationalization and adaptation come to the fore in diverse phenomena: transnational or multilocal families entertain economic niches in the global economy, based on economies of scope that use mechanisms such as kinship reciprocity and solidarity to cope with fluctuating market conditions. Furthermore, citizenship ties in the polity are being enlarged by dual state membership, both by dual citizenship and dual nationality. Over the past decades, there has been a substantial increase in dual state membership, as the number of those holding these codified symbolic ties with mutual obligations between states and citizens or denizens indicates.

Analysing these developments we need to keep in mind the triadic relationship between emigration countries, immigration states, and nationally-bounded civil societies to which immigrant and transmigrant organizations contribute. One element favouring the formation of transnational social spaces in the current period is the generally ambivalent attitude of both emigration and immigration states towards transnational ties among migrants. Overall, the liberal democratic polities are increasingly unwilling or unable to enforce assimilation, understood as conformity of immigrants to some sort of mainstream values, patterns, and achievements. It is exactly within a broader mosaicization of lifestyles in immigration states of the North where debates on multiple ethnicity, multiculturalism, and multiple religions with equal status occur. Public debates deal with how and to what extent to recognize diversity, be it culturally or politically.

The emigration country positions usually move from indifference and single-minded interests in a homeward flow of migrant remittances or continued expulsion of those who voice dissent to active involvement in the lives of their citizens abroad. If political organizations develop among its constituents they try to control it because many of these activities are directed towards politics in the country of origin. Also, international labour migration almost inevitably prompts emigration country governments to woo their migrants abroad. These rulers are usually interested in a continued and stable flow of remittances and capital investments of expatriates. This explains attempts to keep their constituencies abroad by diverse measures such as granting dual state membership, tax exemptions, or support in maintaining 'home-country' or 'home-town' associations. The concern of an emigration country government reaches its apex when in the process of adaptation their citizens accommodate to and adjust to the country of immigration. They are then almost irretrievably lost to the country of origin. Emigration country governments have practically no means of avoiding that their migrant citizens and the descendants thereof eventually acquire the citizenship of the immigration country. But they can attenuate this trend by easing dual citizenship and linking migrants and their offspring through specific mass media channels designed to reach 'their' migrants in foreign countries.

For the immigration countries the ambivalence is even more striking. Public policies develop as responses to both infrastructural and cultural integration, on the one hand, and xenophobia and various forms of backlash, on the other—once it becomes clear that immigrants are 'here to stay'. It is then that demands for multicultural rights begin to mushroom. Multicultural demands have a twofold thrust, relating to both emigration and immigration countries within the respective migration systems. It is noteworthy that activities of immigrant secondary associations in the country of settlement do not remain carbon copies of the emigration country. The exigencies of a minority situation lead to far-reaching modifications in organizations, rhetoric, goals, and behaviour. The export or import of conflicts from emigration to immigration countries is attenuated in the long run by the requirement to respond to de facto settlement. While the attention to the immigration country increases over time, involvement in the emigration country declines in some instances, while it remains high in the case of transnational communities and diasporas.

As we have seen, the implications of transnational social spaces for immigrant adaptation are most intricate in the political realm.

Resources inherent in social and symbolic ties are both territorially bounded and transnationally transferable. Yet a lot of politics are most tightly territorially circumscribed. As the famous Weberian definition of nation-states already explicates, states exercise legitimate control of violence over a bounded territory. They have a legal claim to monopoly over power and representation. And nation-states typically try to unify three elements: a state apparatus, a territory, and a people. Contemporary migration and transnational social spaces challenge the unity of this trinity. One of the most noteworthy interference is transpositional politics. Immigrants and their descendants, well-integrated in virtually all respects in the immigration country, have shown support for independence and nationhood movements in the emigration country until the fourth and fifth generations.

Crucially, emigration country citizenship is most often not easily convertible into another country's citizenship. Noteworthy, it is citizenship that is controversial and associated with charges of dual loyalty by the critics of dual citizenship, on the one hand, and hopes of multicultural democracy by its supporters, on the other. Specifically, contentious politics emanating from transnational social spaces to membership in political communities do not so much arise from differential rights between citizens and non-citizens. This becomes clear when we distinguish two dimensions, reciprocal rights and duties, and a sense of belonging. The issue of rights and duties is virulent mainly because full membership in nation-states is intimately tied with a sense of belonging and loyalty; often connected to collective identity.

How Transnationalization and Adaptation Can Proceed Simultaneously

(1) Reality of Transnational Ties and Multiple Identities

The border-crossing expansion of social space considers the possibilities of novel cross-overs in economics, politics, and culture in two respects. First, while immigrants indeed tend to develop ties in and to the immigration state, their ties to the emigration country do not decline to the same extent. There is not necessarily an inverse correlation between ties to the 'old' and to the 'new' country. Second, migrants do not simply keep up some cultural elements without being influenced by their new environment.

(2) Ideal-Typical Concepts with Many Shades

It is most useful to see the two canonical theories of assimilation and ethnic pluralism and the new apocryphal concept of border-crossing expansion of social space as ideal-typical constructs with manifold variations. This is obvious when considering multiple identities. Since identities refer to people's experiences of ties, roles, groups, organizations, and symbolic communities, they are necessarily pluralistic. These migrant identities can also span various countries. Think of segmentally assimilated businesspersons who adapt quite successfully to language and other practices in the country of immigration but engage in transnational economic circuits or even support nationalist projects in the country of origin as members of transnational communities. It would be quite difficult to slot such phenomena in only one concept of the adaptation triad.

Outlook: Transnationally Active Associations and Transnationalizing Civil Societies

If it is true that many contemporary migration and post-migration processes lead to transnational social spaces in various incarnations and that concomitant transnationalization and adaptation is the rule and not the exception, we need to inquire into the implications of these border-crossing expansions for integration of civil societies within migration systems. Within this realm of repercussions a meso-link analysis focuses on one of the bedrocks of democratic political systems, i.e. intermediary organizations in civil society. It is important because transnationally active immigrant associations can potentially contribute to or endanger the normative project called civil society.

The main proposition here is that transnational immigrant organizations can contribute to forge a new mix of exit and voice in nationally-bounded but ever more transnationally interlinked civil societies. So far, we have focused most attention on exit and mainly referred to voice as an antecedent to migration (as for example, in the case of refugees) or a consequence (as in diaspora communities). In transnational social spaces exit and voice reach a novel complementarity. Exit is an integral element of transnational social spaces because we often observe recurrent migration or migration circuits, and the continued exchange of goods and symbols. For immigrants in transnational spaces, voice gives increased possibilities, since members of transnationalizing civil societies can articulate dissent across nation-state borders. Immigrant associations are able to voice interests and opinions in two (or more) nationally-bounded public political arenas. The voice option helps migrant associations to serve as politically relevant border-crossing interlocutors in the civil societies of the immigration and the emigration countries. If immigrants can express their voice in transnationally-oriented associations, they usually do not endanger democratic institutions and civil society. These associations need to balance demands of the immigration country majorities upon their adaptation, on the one hand, and transnational orientations of leadership and followers, on the other. For all that, we should not forget that immigrant minorities need to adapt to the majority democratic norms in the countries of immigration.

This last part first discusses the impact of migration on immigration and emigration countries: What are the potentials for integration or fragmentation of existing organizational arrangements through migratory exit and entry? Second, in order to gauge the impact of international migration on civil societies we need to define what kind of civil society we can meaningfully talk about. We turn to three selected characteristics of civil societies which are necessary from a normative point of view—a modicum of guaranteed human, civil, political, and social rights for members, autonomy of organizations from the state, and an assurance for pluralistic political life. This leads to the conclusion that it is not useful to talk about transnational civil society. Instead, the term 'transnationalizing' civil society is more apt. Third, the question is which role transnationally active migrant associations fulfil for transnationalizing civil societies. And the fourth and last question is which kind of membership can best undergird a productive role of transnationally active associations.

Impact of Migration on the Integration of Emigration and Immigration Countries

Activities of immigrants in transnational social spaces can contribute to integrative or fragmental tendencies in the nation-states involved. Nowadays, contemporary migration raises issues in all integrative dimensions of nation-states: security, in terms of border and internal control; cultural, regarding the coexistence in multiethnic polities; and political, in terms of who is entitled to what kinds of rights and who can claim full citizenship. One specific nation-state dimension, welfare states, exemplifies the problems for integration and fragmentation. International migration has posed challenges to the institutionalized solidarity of national welfare states since World War Two (like domestic migration from the Middle Ages into the nineteenth century to the wielders of power). Over the past centuries, migration has played an important part in the emergence of public schemes for poor relief. 'Vagrancy' posed collective action problems for the rich in towns and cities (De Swaan 1988: ch. 2). The concerned successfully solved them by integrative welfare state measures. And we may speculate to what extent border-crossing problems such as international migration contribute to the collectivization of social rights on a transnational level (De Swaan 1994: 105–110).

The reverse train of thought has gained even more currency in public debates and academic analysis: presumably, international migration cannot be effectively channelled and plays a decisive role in fragmenting welfare states. It contributes to a perception of welfare goods as congestible and hence to a politics of conflict and exclusion over such goods. Political pressure emerges to exclude groups from welfare systems, the 'bad risks', and to form associations based on narrower mutualities. This in turn leads to further self-protective action by groups facing similar risks. A spiral of fragmentation is set in motion (Breuer, Faist, and Jordan 1995). The attendant dangers are well-known and present the key ingredient of populist politics.

Regarding the emigration states, the public debates usually revolve around whether international migration contributes to economic development (and vice versa). The issues—often culminating in charges over the deleterious effects of brain drain and the contribution of returnees to economic development—are perennially hard to settle. What is undisputed, however, is the diffusion of political ideas from democratic immigration countries to the frequently authoritarian emigration states.

No Transnational Civil Society But Transnationalizing Civil Societies

In order to evaluate the possible contribution of transnationally-oriented immigrant associations on civil society in the participating nation-states, we need to define more clearly what kind of society we are dealing with. Therefore, the question to be addressed is whether it is meaningful to speak of an entity called transnational civil society within South–North migration systems.

We first need to distinguish between understandings of civil society on the level of nation-states and on the transnational level. Existing definitions of civil society clearly refer to polities on the national level. Civil society can be seen as one of the central mechanisms of integrating plural societies, often thought coterminous with the territorial boundaries of nation-states. We can distinguish wider and narrower understandings of civil society: first, in a very broad sense, civil society connotes a sphere of relatively autonomous associations which are free from the tutelage of nation-states. A second and somewhat narrower understanding refers to civil society as a whole that can structure and coordinate itself—again, without being unduly restricted by the state authority. In a third, and more unequivocal sense, civil society means the whole of secondary associations influencing the course of state politics and policies, shape and modify them to a significant degree (Taylor 1991: 57). In most of the contemporary discussions this third meaning is dominant. It means that the articulation of interests and opinions—by intermediary organizations and in public debates—delivers crucial contributions to formal and institutionalized democratic processes.

We could define a transnational civil society as people, groups, and organizations in different nation-states who meaningfully interact across various policy arenas through dense spheres of transaction to articulate democratic interests—out of which migrants' transnational social spaces are but one constituent element. More specifically, the more extensive and liberal the exchange of goods, emigration and immigration, and the more open international competitions are to all members of all nation-states, the more lively is such a transnational society (Aron 1962: 113); with possible spill-overs for high politics travelling along silk economic threads. However, a notion of a transnational civil society only makes sense if we assume that transnational ties of persons, groups, and organizations are very strongly grounded in two—or more—national civil societies. In a very weak form such a transnational civil society has begun to evolve in supra-national structures such as the EU, in a common framework of economic and political inter- and transnationalization. Apart from this example of dense regional integration, the preliminary evidence suggests that transnational civil societies do not exist. By contrast, elements of transnational civil society in all other known migration systems lack quasi-state structures to guarantee rights of members, autonomy of organizations, and an assurance for pluralistic political life across borders. All of these characteristics would be necessary prerequisites for functioning civil societies.

It makes no sense to deal with the ideal-typical construct of a full-fledged transnational civil society in singular or plural incarnations. Taking any sensible understanding of civil society, the requirements for a transnational civil society would be exigent. Diasporas and communities of exiles complement the picture of elements of an incipient transnational civil society nourished by social movements engaged in environmental protection of the Amazon, higher autonomy for Indians in Mexico, or human rights of refugees. Some organizations in transnational spaces continually encroach on nation-state authority, especially those of the countries of origin. Yet this is still a marginal phenomenon when viewed in the grand arena of power politics, even on a purely regional level (Boulding 1991). No great hopes should therefore be invested in associations of transnational civil society as a balance to the international state system—starting from Tocqueville's (1988) idea of a strong civil society as a counterweight to a centralizing state.

Instead of using the term 'transnational' civil society in an inflationary sense, it seems more useful to speak of transnationalizing civil societies that are connected through multiple economic, political, social, and cultural linkages. Nationally-bounded civil societies have undergone transnationalization when considering international migration: border-crossing ties of migrants and their descendants reach a new quality when congealing in transnational social spaces. The latter present challenges to nation-states because they may undermine swift assimilation in the immigration state and sometimes question authoritarian elements in the emigration countries.

Transnationalizing civil societies here refer to sets of border-crossing ties bracketing secondary associations across nation-states within migration systems. Activities of immigrants in transnational spaces do have implications for civil societies bounded by nation-states. Strong cases are refugees who seek to change the political system in their countries of origin. Less clear-cut cases are groups advancing utopian and symbolic religious projects, such as the Islamic *umma*. And at the other end we find collectives who use other organizations, transnational by nature, to advance their goals. An example for the latter are immigrants in the Americas and Europe who keep transnational ties through the Catholic Church.

Speaking of a transnationalizing civil society, we have to take into account at least three normatively derived characteristics of this ideal construct. These elements can be used to show in more detail why it is useful to speak of transnationalizing civil societies. The following characteristics apply: (1) human, civil, political, and social rights for the members; (2) autonomy from states, markets, and kin groups; and (3) a pluralistic universe of collective identities.

(1) A Modicum of Human, Civil, Political, and Social Rights

There are some universally valid human and civil rights. There is, however, no overarching supranational structure effectively enforcing these rights all over the world, no global government and no global civil society. Specific kinds of nation-states ensure these rights: liberal democratic nation-states grant human, civil, and social rights indicating distance to market, and family. On the international level, nation-states partly adhere to a regime of human rights, as expressed in their consent to the Geneva Convention for refugees. On the nation-state level, basic civil and social rights are relatively independent of citizenship and are by now available to virtually all authorized or legal migrants in the liberal democratic polities in the North. And emergency help plus basic human rights are usually open to illegal immigrants, albeit partaking in these usually means deportation. It is true that there are gradations between aliens, denizens, and citizens in the extent of rights they are able to claim. Liberal democratic nation states, however, guarantee a modicum of rights for all residents irrespective of legal status, though only those can partake in political rights who have at least settled permanently and are members of the polity. This situation differs from most refugee-producing countries, in which civil—and political—rights are violated by civil wars and the persecution of minorities.

Formal rights need to be translated into substantive rights in order to be effective. Secondary associations have a role in shaping state–individual ties because they can help to transform formal rights into substantive realities, in essence. Transnational social spaces do not provide the institutional structure required for this translation. At this point, states and state-like structures set the room necessary for basic rights to be effective because these claims in themselves are not sufficient (Walzer 1992*a*). Contemporary transnationalization accompanying migration exemplifies the tension between differently developed political regimes, the extent to which human, civil, political, and social rights are realized in different parts of the world. Refugee organizations who engage in human rights work and non-governmental organizations such as Amnesty International exemplify the striving for meaningful human and civil rights across borders. Immigrant associations who sponsor development projects in their emigration country communities illustrate the quest for substantive social citizenship.

(2) Associational Autonomy from the State

In order to speak meaningfully of civil society we need to discern the autonomy of voluntary associations from other spheres like states, markets, and kin groups. Their autonomy can be conceptualized by the degree of freedom, i.e. the distance from the three endpoints of kin systems, states, and markets. In this view, churches and social movement organizations represent the most independent actors in national civil societies (Bauböck 1996: 76–84). This is one of the reasons why transnationalizing civil society cannot be coterminous with transnational social spaces because the latter grow out of, include, and are shaped by many kin group elements.

Truly transnational organizations have an exceptionally high degree of autonomy from states. However, more autonomy does not necessarily mean that transnational associations are interested in advancing crucial characteristics of any civil society, such as basic rights and liberal democratic pluralism. Some transmigrant associations evolve out of existing border-crossing structures such as the Catholic Church. For example, migrants yearn to fulfil their spiritual needs and maintain links to the country of origin. In this case, it is not immigrant ethnic groups themselves who sustain transnational organizational linkages. Instead, they take advantage of a wider transnational organizational structure. This has been possible in cases of religious affinities, such as Latin America–USA (Levitt 1996) or Italy–Germany (Schmitter Heisler 1984) migration. In addition, Muslim organizations—often based in Pakistan—rally immigrant associations under the heading of *umma*.

On the level of transnationalizing nation-states immigrant associations are not necessarily elements of civil society but can be if they enjoy a certain degree of autonomy from the respective state. We can distinguish transnationally-oriented organizations along a continuum from exclusive emigration country to complete immigration country orientation. The higher the emigration country orientation of transnationally active organizations, the more the emigration country government is likely to step up efforts of control. If these organizations engage in anti-regime activities, emigration country governments exert pressure on their counterparts in the immigration country to curtail political activities of immigrants and refugees. In this way, the autonomy of transnationally active organizations is always threatened and thus of a much weaker nature than organizations solely oriented towards immigration-country liberal democratic states.

Those migrant and refugee associations who primarily focus upon emigration country affairs usually do not survive in the long run. They have to at least supplement the emigration country emphasis with including the problems of their members in the immigration country. Over time, the balance of focus shifts from emigration countries political, religious, ethnic, and national struggles to the countries of settlement. This does not mean that political projects in the country of origin lose importance. Rather, the organizations' foci tend to shift to the country of settlement. There is one important exception: unfinished nation-state projects in the country of origin.

(3) Pluralist Liberal Democracy

A functioning civil society flourishes in a pluralistic and liberal democracy that allows its members to publicly express and pursue collective and individual interests. Political competition, partisanship, and conflicts between the various groups are basic ingredients. Civil society denotes a pluralistic society in which the sometimes varying obligations of its members, groups, and communities towards the society as a whole and central institutions and laws are recognized (Shils 1991: 4). Again, it would be presumptuous to speak of contemporary transnational structures in which these requirements are fulfilled.

The main point is that the conditions for pluralist-liberal democracy are less often met in the emigration than in the immigration countries. Indeed, one of the main causes for refugee movement are civil strife in the countries of origin and the persecution of minorities who choose the exit option. Since conflicts in the refugee-producing states are intimately tied to processes such as nation-state formation, revolutions, civil wars, and authoritarian political rule, the struggle around collective identities assumes central importance. These considerations best apply to first-generation refugees and their potential for the formation of transnational communities of the diaspora type. In a long-term transnational perspective, the sometimes syncretist collective identities of migrants' descendants matter. They have a strong transnational component and are composed of elements from both producing and accepting countries.

Transnationally active migrant associations can make a contribution to the integration of nation-states composed of members with 'multiple identities' (Walzer 1992*b*). Such a conception is far from complete melting into the core which would remove virtually all emigration country elements of identity. It is equally devoid of connotations that see—as the early cultural pluralists did—immigrant minorities as nations within a nation-state. Instead, it recognizes that syncretist identities have emerged which relate to both emigration and immigration contexts.

The Role of Migrants' Associations in Transnationalizing Civil Societies

Since a functioning civil society constitutes one of the bedrocks of democracy, we have to elaborate on the mechanisms through which the country of destination end can evolve towards a multi-ethnic democracy, and on the contribution to democratization in the country of origin.

Social capital and the various mechanisms of exchange, reciprocity, and solidarity, and its benefits of control, information, and access to other actors' social and other resources can crystallize in networks of cooperation and associations that can be part of civil society. In short, civil society requires that specific forms of social capital in associations are compatible with and represented in democratic processes. Two less sanguine notes are in order: first, it is important to remember that the essential mechanisms enabling the activities of transnationally-oriented secondary associations—such as reciprocity and solidarity—can work both ways, they can expand or stifle autonomy, rights, and pluralism of opinions. Second, civil societies made up of an array of people and groups committed to freedom of expression and personal liberties make a necessary but by no means sufficient connection between civil society and democratic voice.

The question then becomes: Under what conditions do elements of transnational social spaces strengthen democratic voice—and can thus be called elements of transnationalizing civil societies? How do secondary associations that span two or more nation-states—incipient *politeuma*—contribute to democratic political processes? The argument sometimes put forward is that transnational links inhibit the process of adaptation and thus do not contribute to peaceful and democratic resolution of conflicts; especially if secondary groups are sometimes seen to differ fundamentally from central values upheld in the immigration state (Heitmeyer, Müller, and Schröder 1997). The most obvious contemporary example are the Muslims. There are two counter arguments.

First, immigrant minorities—unless the country of destination rigidly discriminates against and segregates the minority, or the minority themself separates itself—have to adapt to certain rules of the political game in the country of settlement. Muslim migrants form minorities in the immigration states. We expect even transnational migrants and communities to adapt to a large extent to dominant patterns of political interaction in the respective countries of settlement. Therefore, if immigrants want to constitute more than a bunch of exiles, they will have to adapt to some fundamental tenets, such as respect for individual rights. Asymmetry in relationship between natives and immigrants also means that immigrant adaptation depends very much on tolerance of natives' organizations.

Second, if the associations themselves are highly undemocratic, these groups do not contribute to multi-ethnic democracy. But there need not be a complete congruity between democratic principles in nation-states and secondary associations. Most non-immigrant secondary associations ranging from religious congregations to sports clubs are not necessarily organized along democratic principles. Of course, the higher the degree of congruence or resemblance of associations with the form of democratic governance regarding control and authority, exchange of information and patterns of communication, the more likely it is that we see a positive contribution of multiple membership or even citizenship in transnationalizing societies.

In sum, the wealth of empirical evidence over the past two hundred years indicates that immigrants have never posed a challenge to established democracies. Individual immigrant groups formed small minorities who adapted to the political rules of the immigration countries. It has mostly been religion which allegedly is not compatible with democratic processes. Whether it was the Catholicism of the Irish in nineteenth century America or the Islam of contemporary immigrants from North Africa and Asia in Europe, the charge has been that they are non-democratically organized and sustain non-democratic attitudes among their members. Empirical evidence flatly contradicts this accusation. In contexts of immigration, Catholicism became (Fuchs 1990: 33–53) and there is evidence suggesting that Islam in Europe can become a religion compatible with democratic political systems (Spuler-Stegemann 1998). Catholicism has become an American religion and we can look upon Islam as an Occidental religion in Malta and the Balkans for centuries, and increasingly in the rest of Europe since the 1960s, with the large influx of labour migrants. In his treatment of the integration of Catholicism in American democracy, Alexis de Tocqueville identified two factors determining the success or failure of transplanted religions: members of this religion must not reject democracy as a principle and the social position and small number of immigrants relative to natives require them to adapt (Tocqueville 1988: 287–90).

Especially, we find that most immigrant associations in Western democracies function as lobbies for immigrants, inserting newcomers into society and polity, and are also important in fostering cultural and communal cohesion. Immigrant associations generally neither minimize nor increase conflicts between immigrants and the indigenous population. They rather point to problems of interaction, and work as transmission belts for interests of immigrants (see e.g. Rex, Joly, and Wilpert 1987).

Dual State Membership in Transnationalizing Civil Societies

As we have seen, elementary human, civil but also political and social rights undergird activities of members in civil societies. One of the questions is what kind of citizenship can support participation in transnationalizing civil societies. Normatively, citizenship has pre-eminence over membership in associations. It has become clear that transnational ties have implications for the conceptual apparatus analysing immigrant adaptation, especially for political adaptation regarding citizenship, the formalized bundling of symbolic ties in nation-states. In the assimilationist view, citizenship is a crucial part of political and civic adaptation through loyalty to a single immigration state. In the ethnic pluralist view citizenship is a means to maintain a cultural frame of reference thought to be necessary for political participation. According to the concept of border-crossing expansion of social space it is also a way to uphold vital transnational ties that foster migrants' options for voice. While full citizenship status hardly makes any difference for the socio-economic adaptation of permanently settled immigrant residents, its significance for issues of belonging and recognition is paramount (Dörr and Faist 1997).

Therefore, the idea and the spreading reality of dual state membership constitutes a grave challenge to the advocates of single nation-state citizenship, namely the claim that undivided loyalty to the principles of *one* nation-state is a high value to be retained. It reminds us that the identity of citizen is not an ineluctable consequence of a principle called citizenship. Rather, immigrants' identity reflects contested ties between emigration and immigration states, those striving to become citizens, and the respective power-holders. The more powerful the country of origin and the more closely tied the collective identity to geopolitical fault lines, the stronger the charges of disloyalty waged against its citizens abroad. From the point of view of *raison d'état*, the critics of dual state membership refer to situations in which immigrants and their descendants have to decide which side they are on. Consequently, opponents of dual citizenship and dual nationality doubt the fact that immigrants or newcomers can be loyal towards the immigration country. Prime examples are situations of war.

However, in most cases cross-cutting commitments and loyalties are a source of moderation and cohesion in democracies. In a minimalist sense, the stability of democracy requires only that people's identifications as well as the associations themselves, be pluralistic and not confined to groups representing a single class or occupational interest (Truman 1951: 168). Of course, we then wonder—to take up Randolph Bourne's metaphor once more—how a cloth can be of many threads, but still of one cloth. In other words, how can a transnationalizing civil society with many transnational social spaces at its interstices still be bounded by a nation-state that functions according to unwavering principles of democratic inclusion for all?

Dual state citizenship is mainly the institutional expression of transnational symbolic and social ties movers and non-movers entertain. The support of development projects in the countries of origin through (former) migrants and the intensification of transnational economic exchange on the level of small players are effects considered desirable by most individual and collective actors involved. Such a consensus would probably be impossible in those cases involving the import of those values and conflicts thought to be incompatible with democratic norms of the immigration country. Examples are easy to find, such as religious fundamentalism and civil war. However, it would be far-fetched to consider dual state membership as the cause of such developments. Quite to the contrary, it is mostly collective identities denied that prove to be resistant among immigrant minorities.

Statuses such as dual state membership form a solid basis upon which those actors involved in the import and export of conflicts can be critically questioned. How much do they adhere to democratic principles in liberal democratic nation-states? After all, with dual state membership they are then quasi-full members in each of the nation-states involved. Dual state membership enables persons and associations to effectively contribute to controlling politics and policies in the emigration countries. A frequent case is the military support by the North lent to the contenders for state power in the South. In such situations, immigrant groups who constitute part of the electorate can exert formal pressure on their immigration country government to modify or abandon direct or indirect intervention in the countries of origin.

The main point is that dual state membership enriches and can be used in the multi-layered cultural, economic, and social reality of immigrants. Dual state membership does not mean a radical decoupling of territory, cultures, and political representation. Rather, it signifies the fact that the nation-state of current residence is the most privileged but not the only determinator of formal citizenship. It recognizes and legitimizes the circumstance that citizens can entertain multiple ties, some of them extending into other nation-states. In some situations dual nationality may be a better solution than dual citizenship. The reason is simple: bearers of dual citizenship should be equally tied to both states which is truly a very rare case. For those migrants who tend to have stronger affiliations to one side compared to the other, dual nationality corresponds much closer to their lived experiences.

The concept of exclusive citizenship that is predicated on a single nation-state citizenship and disregards transnational ties has long been an anachronism. It is hard to realize because geopolitical factors such as the fallout of two World Wars and the development of nationally-based welfare states have counterbalanced another significant long-term trend. In the late nineteenth century, passports were not yet dominant means of regulating access of strangers and foreigners. For example, foreign travel was not controlled in Europe, with the exception of Tsarist Russia. Migrants could also take up work and residence without permits. However, it should not be forgotten that state authorities could deport foreign residents at will; for example, when they were poor. International migrants, even those with legal alien status, had no recourse to civil and social rights to the extent they are able to today. In the inter-war period, during World War Two and the two decades thereafter, we observe the climax of the exclusive nation-state form of citizenship, going along with the increasing protection of the domestic population in labour markets and social rights in a global economy. Interestingly, the protection of natives and settled immigrants against aliens in the inter-war period has been followed by an expansion of entitlements for the newcomers after World War Two; provided immigrants resided permanently in the immigration states. In other words, growing protection of the indigenous population entailed strengthening the rights of newcomers. It was a clear instance of internal transnationalization that served integrative functions. For example, it served to avoid wage competition. Even more important, this case shows that certain packages of rights and duties are decoupled from citizenship. Again, we are back to the two separate dimensions of citizenship—rights and duties, on the one hand, and belonging and collective representations, on the other.

What is remarkably similar, then and now, is the fact that not from a legal perspective but from an empirical political one citizenship has often been associated, in a more encompassing way, with collective representations, a grounding in a common civilization, and shared ways of life and beliefs, and, in its exclusive version, a common belonging—be it defined by birth, ancestry, language, culture, or religion. The more universal definition sees a wide common foundation. It may transcend nation-state borders. For to maintain transnational ties and linkages and to institutionalize symbolic ties into meaningful dual state membership, we require some sort of common understanding of membership principles, rights, and duties.

Let me suggest three propositions for further discussion: first, we can think of dual state membership to reflect the transnational ties of first-generation immigrants. There is a great wealth of empirical evidence that they entertain border-crossing social and symbolic ties over their life span (for an introduction, see Gmelch 1980). As we defined above, citizenship is a morally very demanding and institutionalized form of solidarity. Ultimately, it is a highly regulated form of a key mechanism of social capital. Therefore, the fundamental characteristics of social capital apply: it is primarily a local asset and can have a border-crossing function only when transmission belts are available such as migrant networks or transnational organizations, such as human rights groups. As such, dual state membership is neither likely to contribute to the export of conflicts from the emigration to the immigration countries, nor does it in itself further processes of democratization in the emigration states. All these processes have occurred without multiple formal membership. Crucial are the transmission belts of interstitial networks and organizations.

Therefore, second, from the point of view of the states involved, dual loyalties to different states will usually not present a problem for the states involved, unless in situations of war. These, however, are exceedingly rare between countries of emigration and immigration along the South–North axis. Generally, we have to differentiate between emigration and immigration states: the former have an interest in keeping ties to emigrants for the sake of remittances or investments. The latter, as mentioned before, have started to openly or tacitly tolerate multiple memberships in ever-increasing numbers.

Third, dual state membership directly impinges upon the public recognition of ties and not only upon state-citizen ties (go back to Figure 9.3). The majority of first-generation immigrants interested in acquiring citizenship of the immigration country favour dual state membership, viewing it as a welcome recognition of their multiple attachments (see e.g. Kılıç 1994: 75 on Germany). This is so because issues central to transnationals such as inheritance laws can be changed accordingly without bestowing full citizenship. Instead, dual state citizenship pertains to the aspects of belonging and recognition. Its main purpose is to acknowledge the symbolic ties reaching back to the countries of origin.

Bibliography

ABADAN-UNAT, NEREMIN (1964). *Bai Almanya'daki Türk İşçileri ve Sorunları (Turkish Workers in Germany and their Problems)*. Ankara: DPT.

—— (1974). 'Turkish External Migration and Social Mobility', in Peter Benedict and Erol Tümertekin (eds.), *Turkey: Geographic and Social Perspectives*. Leiden: Brill, 362–403.

—— (1985*a*). 'Der soziale Wandel und die türkische Frau', in Neremin Abadan-Unat (ed.), *Die Frau in der türkischen Gesellschaft*. Frankfurt: Dağyeli, 13–55.

—— (1985*b*). 'Die Auswirkungen der internationalen Arbeitsmigration auf die Rolle der Frau am Beispiel der Türkei', in Nermin Abadan-Unat (ed.), *Die Frau in der türkischen Gesellschaft*. Frankfurt: Dağyeli, 201–39.

—— (1988). 'The Socio-Economic Aspects of Return Migration to Turkey', *Migration*, 3/1: 29–59.

—— and KEMIKSIZ NEŞE (eds.) (1992). *Türkische Migration 1960–1984: Annotierte Bibliographie*. Translated and updated by Kirkor Osyan and Claudia Schöningh-Kalender. Frankfurt: Dağyeli-Verlag.

ADEPOJU, ADERANTI (1997). 'Emigration Dynamics in Sub-Saharan Africa: The Economic, Demographic, Political and Ecological Conditions and Policy Implications', IOM/UNFPA Project on Emigration Dynamics in Developing Countries. Geneva: International Organization for Migration.

AHFELDT, HORST (1993). 'Sozialstaat und Zuwanderung', *Aus Politik und Zeitgeschichte*, B7/93: 42–52.

AHMED, ISHTIAQ (1997). 'Exit, Voice and Citizenship', in Tomas Hammar, Grete Brochmann, Kristof Tamas, and Thomas Faist (eds.), *International Migration, Immobility and Development: Multidisciplinary Perspectives*. Oxford: Berg, 159–86.

AKER, ALI (1972). *İşçi Göçü (Labour Migration)*. Istanbul: Sander.

AKGÜNDÜZ, AHMET (1993). 'Labour Migration from Turkey to Western Europe (1960–1974)', *Capital & Class*, 51: 153–94.

AKKAYAN, TIMUR (1979). *Göç ve Değişme (Emigration and Change)*. Istanbul University. Faculty of Letters. Yayinlari.

AKPINAR, ÜNAL, and MERTENS, GABRIELE (1977). *Türkische Migrantenfamilien: Familienstrukturen in der Türkei und in der Bundesrepublik. Angleichungsprobleme türkischer Arbeiterfamilien: Beispiel West-Berlin*. Bonn: Arbeitsgemeinschadft Katholischer Studenten- und Hochschulgemeinden. Projektbereich ausländische Arbeiter. Materialien. Sonderheft No. 2.

ALBERT, MATHIAS (1998). 'Entgrenzung und Formierung neuer politischer Räume', in Beate Kohler-Koch (ed.), *Regieren in entgrenzten Räumen*, Politische Vierteljahresschrift, Sonderband. Opladen: Westdeutscher Verlag, 49–76.

Albrecht, Günter (1972). *Soziologie der geographischen Mobilität: Zugleich ein Beitrag zur Soziologie sozialen Wandels.* Stuttgart: Enke.

Alesina, Alberto, Baqir, Reza, and Easterly, William (1997). *Public Goods and Ethnic Divisions*, Working Paper Series No. 6009. Cambridge, Mass.: National Bureau of Economic Research.

Americas Watch Committee (1984). *Guatemalan Refugees in Mexico 1980–1984.* New York and Washington, DC: Americas Watch Committee.

Amin, Samir (1974). 'Introduction', in idem (ed.), *Modern Migrations in Western Africa.* Oxford: Oxford University Press for International African Institute, 65–124.

Anderson, Benedict (1983). *Imagined Communities: Reflections on the Origin and Spread of Nationalism.* London: Verso.

Andrews, Peter Alford (with the assistance of Rüdiger Benninghaus) (1989). *Ethnic Groups in the Republic of Turkey.* Wiesbaden: Dr. Ludwig Reichert.

Appadurai, Arjun (1996). *Modernity at Large: Cultural Dimensions of Globalization.* Minneapolis: University of Minnesota Press.

Appleyard, Reginald (1991). *International Migration: Challenge for the Nineties.* Geneva: International Organization for Migration.

—— (1992). 'Migration and Development: A Critical Relationship', *Asian and Pacific Migration Journal*, 1/1: 1–19.

Arendt, Hannah (1949). 'Es gibt nur ein einziges Menschenrecht', in Dolf Sternberger (ed.), *Die Wandlung.* Vol. iv. Heidelberg, 754–70 (Reprinted in Otfried Höffe, Gerd Kadelbach, and Gerhard Plumpe (eds.) (1981). *Praktische Philosophie/Ethik.* Vol. ii. Frankfurt: Fischer, 152–66).

—— (1973 [1959]). *The Origins of Totalitarianism.* New York: Harcourt Brace Jovanovich.

Arensberg, Conrad M., and Kimball, Solon T. (1940). *Family and Community in Ireland.* Cambridge, Mass.: Harvard University Press.

Aron, Raymond (1962). *Paix et guerre entre les nations.* Paris: Calman-Lévy.

ATIAD (Verband türkischer Unternehmer und Industrieller in Europa e.V.) (1996). *Türkisches Unternehmertum in Deutschland. Die unsichtbare Kraft. Bestandsaufnahme 1996 und Perspektiven für das Jahr 2010.* Düsseldorf: ATIAD.

Axelrod, Robert (1984). *The Evolution of Cooperation.* New York: Basic Books.

Ayata, Sencer (1989). 'Toplumsal Çevre Olarak Gecekondu ve Apartman' ('Gecekondu and Apartment Housing as Social Environment'), *Toplum ve Bilim*, 46/7: 101–27.

Aydin, Hayrettin (1997). 'Das ethnische Mosaik der Türkei', *Zeitschrift für Türkeistudien*, 1: 65–101.

Balán, Jorge (1988). 'Selectivity of Migration in International and Internal Flows', in Charles Stahl (ed.), *International Migration Today.* Paris: OECD, 44–59.

Banfield, Edward (1958). *The Moral Basis of a Backward Society.* Glencoe, Ill.: The Free Press.

BANTON, MICHAEL (1983). *Racial and Ethnic Competition*. Cambridge: Cambridge University Press.

BARABAS, GYÖRGY (1992). 'Gesamtwirtschaftliche Effekte der Zuwanderung 1988 bis 1991', *RWI-Mitteilungen*, 43/2: 133–54.

BARCLAY, JOHN M. G. (1996). *Jews in the Mediterranean Diaspora: From Alexander to Trojan (323 BCE–117 CE)*. Edinburgh: T & T Clark.

BARIŞIK, AYFUR, ERAYDIN, AYDA, and GEDIK, AYŞE (1990). 'Turkey', in William F. Serow, Charles B. Nam, David F. Sly, and Robert H. Weller (eds.), *Handbook on International Migration*. New York: Greenwood Press, 301–24.

BARKAN, ELLIOT ROBERT (1996). *And Still They Come: Immigrants and American Society, 1920 to the 1990s*. Wheeling, Ill.: Harlan Davison.

BASCH, LINDA, SCHILLER, NINA GLICK, and SZANTON BLANC, CRISTINA (1994). *Nations Unbound: Transnational Projects, Postcolonial Predicaments, and Deterritorialized Nation-States*. Langhorne, Penn.: Gordon and Breach.

BAUBÖCK, RAINER (1996). 'Social and Cultural Integration in a Civil Society', in Rainer Bauböck, Agnes Heller, and Aristide R. Zolberg (eds.), *The Challenge of Diversity: Integration and Pluralism in Societies of Immigration*. Aldershot: Avebury, 67–132.

BECK, ULRICH (1996). *Was ist Globalisierung?* Frankfurt a.M.: Suhrkamp.

BECKER, GARY (1975). *Human Capital: A Theoretical and Empirical Analysis with Special Reference to Education*. New York: National Bureau of Economic Research.

—— (1976). *The Economic Approach to Human Behavior*. Chicago: University of Chicago Press.

BEHRENDT, GÜNTER (1993). *Nationalismus in Kurdistan: Vorgeschichte, Entstehungsbedingungen und erste Manifestationen bis 1925*. Hamburg: Deutsches Orient-Institut.

BEISHEIM, MARIANNE, DREHER, SABINE, WALTER, GREGOR, ZANGL BERNHARD, and ZÜRN, MICHAEL (1998). *Im Zeitalter der Globalisierung? Thesen und Daten zur gesellschaftlichen und politischen Denationalisierung*. Baden-Baden: Nomos.

BENDIX, JOHN (1990). *Importing Foreign Workers: A Comparison of German and American Policy*. American University Studies. New York: Peter Lang.

BEN-PORAH, Yoram (1980). 'The F-Connection: Family, Friends and Firms and the Organization of Exchange', *Population and Development Review*, 6/1: 1–30.

Bericht der Beauftragten der Bundesregierung für die Belange der Ausländer über die Lage der Ausländer in der Bundesrepublik Deutschland (1994). Bonn.

BILSBORROW, RICHARD, and ZLOTNIK, HANIA (1994). 'The Systems Approach and the Measurement of the Determinants of International Migration', in Rob an der Erf and Liesbeth Hering (eds.), *Causes of International Migration*. Luxemburg: Eurostat, 61–76.

BILSBORROW, R. E., HUGO, GRAEME, OBERAI, A. S., and ZLOTNIK, HANIA (1997). *International Migration Statistics: Guidelines for Improving Data Collection Systems*. Geneva: International Labour Office.

BJERÉN, GUNILLA (1997). 'Gender and Reproduction', in Tomas Hammar, Grete Brochmann, Kristof Tamas, and Thomas Faist (eds.), *International Migration, Immobility and Development:. Multidisciplinary Perspectives.* Oxford: Berg, 219–46.

BLAU, PETER M. (1974). *On the Nature of Organizations.* New York: Wiley.

BÖCKER, ANITA (1994). 'Chain Migration over Legally Closed Borders: Settled Immigrants as Bridgeheads and Gatekeepers', *The Netherlands' Journal of Social Sciences,* 30/2: 87–106.

BODNAR, JOHN (1985). *The Transplanted: A History of Immigrants in Urban America.* Bloomington: Indiana University Press.

BOGARDUS, EMORY S. (1959). *Social Distance.* Los Angeles: Antioch Press.

BÖHNING, WOLF-RÜDIGER (1984). *Studies in International Labour Migration.* New York: St Martins Press.

—— and WERQUIN, JACQUES (1989). *Some Economic, Social and Human Rights Considerations Concerning the Future Status of Third-Country Nationals in the Single European Market.* Geneva: International Labour Office.

—— and ZEGERS DE BEIJL, R. (1995). *The Integration of Migrant Workers in the Labour Market: Policies and their Impact,* International Migration Papers No. 8. Geneva: International Labour Office. Employment Department.

BOISSEVAIN, JEREMY (1974). *Friends of Friends: Networks, Manipulators and Coalitions.* Oxford: Blackwell.

BOLI, JOHN, and THOMAS, GEORGE M. (1997). 'World Culture in the World Polity: A Century of International Non-Governmental Organization', *American Sociological Review,* 62 (Apr.): 171–90.

BOMMES, MICHAEL, and HALFMANN, JOST (eds.) (1998). *Migration in nationalen Wohlfahrtsstaaten: Theoretische und vergleichende Untersuchungen.* Osnabrück: Universitätsverlag Rasch.

BONACICH, EDNA (1979). 'The Past, Present, and Future of Split Labor Market Theory', *Research in Race and Ethnic Relations,* i. Greenwich, Conn.: JAI Press, 17–64.

—— (1993). 'The Other Side of Ethnic Entrepreneurship: A Dialogue with Waldinger, Aldrich, Ward and Associates', *International Migration Review,* 27/4: 685–92.

BORJAS, GEORGE J., and BRATSBERG, BRENT (1996). 'Who Leaves? The Outmigration of the Foreign Born', *Review of Economics and Statistics,* 78: 165–76.

—— FREEMAN, RICHARD B., and LANG, KEVIN (1991). 'Undocumented Mexican-Born Workers in the United States: How Many, How Permanent?', in John M. Abowd and Richard B. Freeman (eds.), *Immigration, Trade and the Labour Market.* Chicago: University of Chicago Press, 77–100.

BOTT, ELIZABETH (1957). *Family and Social Network: Roles, Norms, and External Relationships in Ordinary Urban Families.* London: Travistock.

BOULDING, ELISE (1991). 'The Old and New Transnationalism: An Evolutionary Perspective', *Human Relations,* 44/8: 789–805.

—— (1997). 'Foreword', in Jackie Smith, Charles Chatfield, and Ron Pagnucco (eds.), *Transnational Social Movements and Global Politics: Solidarity Beyond the State*. Syracuse: Syracuse University Press, ix–xi.

BOURDIEU, PIERRE (1983). 'Ökonomisches Kapital, kulturelles Kapital, soziales Kapital', in Reinhard Kreckel (ed.), *Soziale Ungleichheiten*, Soziale Welt, Sonderheft 2. Göttingen: Otto Schwartz & Co., 183–98.

—— (1990). *In Other Words: Essays Towards a Reflexive Sociology*. Cambridge: Polity Press.

—— (1992). *Die verborgenen Mechanismen der Macht*. Hamburg: VSA-Verlag.

—— and WACQUANT, LOÏC (1992). *An Invitation to Reflexive Sociology*. Chicago: University of Chicago Press.

BOURNE, RANDOLPH, (1996 [1916]). 'Trans-National America', in Werner Sollors (ed.), *Theories of Ethnicity: A Classical Reader*. London: Macmillan, 93–108.

BOVENKERK, FRANK (1974). *The Sociology of Return Migration: A Review Essay*. The Hague; Martinus Nijhoff.

BOYD, MONICA (1989). 'Family and Personal Networks in International Migration: Recent Developments and New Agendas', *International Migration Review*, 23/3: 638–70.

BREDEMEIER, HARRY C., and STEPHENSON, RICHARD M. (1970). *The Analysis of Social Systems*. London: Holt, Rinehard & Winston.

BREUER, MICHAEL, FAIST, THOMAS, and JORDAN, BILL (1995). 'Collective Action, Migration and Welfare States', *International Sociology*, 10/4: 369–86.

BRIEDEN, THOMAS (1996). 'Die Bedeutung von Konflikten im Herkunftsland für Ethnisierungsprozesse von Immigranten aus der Türkei und Ex-Jugoslawien', in FES (ed.), *Ethnisierung gesellschaftlicher Konflikte*. Gesprächskreis Arbeit und Soziales, No. 62. Bonn: Friedrich-Ebert-Stiftung.

BRINKS, HERBERT J. (1995). *Dutch American Voices: Letters from the United States, 1850–1930*. Ithaca, NY: Cornell University Press.

BROCHMANN, GRETE (1996). *European Integration and Immigration from Third Countries*. Oslo: Scandinavian University Press.

BRÖSKAMP, BERND (1993). 'Ethnische Grenzen des Geschmacks: Perspektiven einer praxeologischen Migrationsforschung', in Gunter Gebauer and Christoph Wulf (eds.), *Praxis und Ästhetik: Neue Perspektiven im Denken Pierre Bourdieus*. Frankfurt: Suhrkamp, 174–207.

BROWN, ALAN, A., and MOORE, ELIZABETH G. (1971). 'The Intra-Urban Migration Process: A Perspective', in Larry S. Bourne (ed.), *Internal Structure of the City: Readings on Urban Form, Growth, and Policy*. New York: Oxford University Press, 45–61.

BROWN, DENNIS (1997). 'Workforce Lessons and Return Migration to the Caribbean: A Case Study of Jamaican Nurses', in Patricia R. Pessar (ed.), *Caribbean Circuits: New Directions in the Study of Caribbean Migration*. New York: Center for Migration Studies, 197–223.

BRUBAKER, WILLIAM ROGERS (1992). *Citizenship and Nationhood in France and Germany*. Cambridge, Mass.: Harvard University Press.

Bruinessen, Martin van (1978). *Agha, Shaikh and State; On the Social and Political Organization of Kurdistan*. Ph.D. Dissertation. Utrecht.

Bueno, Lourdes (1997). 'Dominican Women's Experiences of Return Migration: The Life Stories of Five Women', in Patricia R. Pessar (ed.), *Caribbean Circuits: New Directions in the Study of Caribbean Migration*. New York: Center for Migration Studies, 61–90.

Bulutay, Tuncer (1995). *Employment, Unemployment and Wages in Turkey*. Ankara: International Labour Office.

Burt, Ronald S. (1986). 'Comment', in Siegwart Lindenberg, James Coleman, and Stefan Nowak (eds.), *Approaches to Social Theory*. New York: Russell Sage Foundation, 105–7.

—— (1992). *Structural Holes: The Social Structure of Competition*. Cambridge, Mass.: Harvard University Press.

Çağlar, Ayşe (1994). 'German Turks in Berlin: Migration and their Quest for Social Mobility'. Ph.D. dissertation. McGill University, Montréal, Canada.

—— (1995). 'German Turks in Berlin: Social Exclusion and Strategies for Social Mobility', *New Community* 21/3: 309–23.

Caces, Fe, Arnold, F., Fawcett, John T., and Gardner, Robert W. (1985). 'Shadow Households and Competing Auspices', *Journal of Development Economics*, 17/1: 5–25.

Cardenas, Gilbert (1976). '"Los Derragidados": Chicanos in the Midwestern Region of the United States', *Aztlán*, 24: 150–68.

Carens, Joseph H. (1997). 'Liberalism and Culture', *Constellations*, 4/1: 35–47.

Castles, Stephen (1985). 'The Guests Who Stayed—The Debate on Foreigners Policy in the German Federal Republic', *International Migration Review*, 19/4: 517–34.

—— and Miller, Mark J. (1993). *The Age of Migration: International Population Movements in the Modern World*. London: Macmillan.

Cavalli-Sforza, L. L. and Feldman, L. L. (1981). *Cultural Transmission and Evolution: A Quantitative Approach*. Princeton: Princeton University Press.

Cebecioğlu, Tarik (1995). 'Änderungen im Staatsangehörigkeitsrecht der Türkei', *Das Standesamt*, 48: 234–5.

Chaliand, Gérard, with Ghasemlou, A. R., Kendal, P., Nazdar, M., Roosevelt Jr., A., and Vanly, I. C. (1978). *Les Kurdes & Le Kurdistan: La Question Nationale Kurde au Proche-Orient*. Paris: François Maspero.

Chant, Silvia (ed.) (1992). *Gender and Migration in Developing Countries*. London: Belhaven Press.

Chavez, Leo R. (1988). 'Settlers and Sojourners: The Case of Mexicans in the United States', *Human Organization*, 47/6: 761–78.

—— (1992). *Shadowed Lives: Undocumented Immigrants in American Society*. Fort Worth, Tex.: Harcourt Brace Jovanovich.

Chepulis, Rita L. (1984). 'Return Migration: An Analytical Framework', in Daniel Kubat (ed.), *The Politics of Return: International Return Migration in Europe*. Roma: Centro Studi Emigrazione and New York: Center for Migration Studies, 239–46.

CHOLDIN, HARVEY M. (1973). 'Kinship Networks in the Migration Process', *International Migration Review*, 7/2: 163–76.

CLARK, PETER B., and WILSON, JAMES Q. (1961). 'Incentive Systems: A Theory of Organizations', *Administrative Science Quarterly*, 6/2: 126–66.

CLAYTON, RICHARD, and PONTUSSON, JONAS (1998). 'Welfare-State Retrenchment Revisited: Entitlement Cuts, Public Sector Restructuring, and Inegalitarian Trends in Advanced Capitalist Societies', *World Politics*, 51 (Oct.): 67–98.

CLIFFORD, JAMES (1994). 'Diasporas', *Cultural Anthropology*, 9/3: 302–38.

COASE, RONALD H. (1960). 'The Problem of Social Cost', *Journal of Law and Economics*, 3: 1–44.

COHEN, ROBIN (1987). *The New Helots: Migrants in the International Division of Labour*. Aldershot: Avebury.

—— (1997). *Global Diasporas: An Introduction*. London: University College of London (UCL) Press.

COLEMAN, JAMES S. (1988). 'Social Capital in the Creation of Human Capital', *American Journal of Sociology*, 94: S95–S121.

—— (1990). *Foundations of Social Theory*. Cambridge, Mass.: The Belknap Press of Harvard University Press.

—— KATZ, ELIHU, and MENZEL, HERBERT (1966). *Medical Innovations: A Diffusion Study*. New York: Bobbs-Merrill.

COLLINSON, SARAH (1994). 'Towards Further Harmonization?', *Studi Emigrazione*, 31/114: 210–37.

CONZEN, KATHLEEN NEILS (1991). 'Mainstreams and Side Channels: The Localization of Immigrant Cultures', *Journal of American Ethnic History*, 11: 5–20.

CORNELIUS, WAYNE (1991). 'Labour Migration to the United States: Development Outcomes and Alternatives in Mexican Sending Communities', in Sergio Diaz-Briquets and Sidney Weintraub (eds.), *Regional and Sectoral Development in Mexico as Alternatives to Migration*. Boulder, Colo.: Westview Press, 39–56.

—— MARTIN, PHILIP L., and HOLLIELD, JAMES F. (eds.) (1994). *Controlling Immigration: A Global Perspective*. Stanford, Calif.: Stanford University Press.

ÇÜRÜKKAYA, SELIM (1997). *PKK: Die Diktatur des Abdullah Öcalan*. Frankfurt a.M.: Fischer.

DANIELS, Roger (1990). *Coming to America: A History of Immigration and Ethnicity in American Life*. New York: HarperCollins Publishers.

DAHRENDORF, RALF (1960). *Homo sociologicus: Ein Versuch zur Geschichte, Bedeutung und Kritik der Kategorie der sozialen Rolle*. Köln and Opladen: Westdeutscher Verlag.

DAVANZO, JULIE (1980). *Microeconomic Approaches to Studying Migration Decisions*. Santa Monica, Calif.: Rand Corporation.

DAVANZO, JULIE (1981). 'Microeconomic Approaches to Studying Migration Decisions', in Gordon F. DeJong and Robert W. Gardner (eds.) *Migration*

Decision Making: Multidisciplinary Approaches to Microlevel Studies in Developed and Developing Countries. New York: Pergamon Press, 90–130.

DAVIS, F. JAMS, and HEYL, BARBARA SHERMAN (1986). 'Turkish Women and Guestworker Migration to West Germany', in Rita J. Simon and Carline B. Brettl (eds.), *International Migration: The Female Experience.* Totowa: Roman and Allanheld, 178–96.

DAVIS, KINGSLEY (1989). 'Social Science Approaches to International Migration', in Michael S. Teitelbaum and Jay M. Winter (eds.), *Population and Resources in Western Intellectual Tradition.* Population and Development Review. Supplement, 245–61.

DEJONG, GORDON F., and FAWCETT, JAMES T. (1981). 'Motivations for Migration: An Assessment and a Value-Expectancy Research Model', in Gordon F. DeJong and Robert W, Gardener (eds.), *Migration Decision Making: Multidisciplinary Approaches to Microlevel Studies in Developed and Developing Countries.* New York: Pergamon Press, 13–57.

—— and GARDNER, ROBERT W. (eds.) (1981). *Migration Decision Making: Multidisciplinary Approaches to Microlevel Studies in Developed and Developing Countries.* New York: Pergamon Press.

DE SWAAN, ABRAM (1988). *In Care of the State: Health Care, Education and Welfare in Europe and the USA in the Modern Era.* Cambridge: Polity.

—— (1994). 'Perspectives for Transnational Social Policy in Europe: Social Transfers from West to East', in Abram de Swaan (ed.), *Social Policy Beyond Borders: Essays on the European Social Question.* Amsterdam, 96–118.

DELEUZE, GILLES, and FÉLIX GUATTARI (1987). *A Thousand Plateaus: Capitalism and Schizophrenia.* Minneapolis: University of Minnesota Press.

DEMIRCAN, ÖMER (1988). *Türkiye'de Yanbaci Dil* (Foreign Language in Turkey). Istanbul: Remzi Kitabevi.

DEN BOER, MONICA (1995). 'Moving between Bogus and Bona Fide: The Policing of Inclusion and Exclusion in Europe', in Robert Miles and Dietrich Thränhardt (eds.), *Migration and European Integration: The Dynamics of Inclusion and Exclusion.* London: Pinter, 92–111.

DEUTSCH, KARL W. (1966). *Nationalism and Social Communication.* New York: MIT Press.

Deutsches Ausländerrecht: Textausgabe (1998); with an introduction by Helmut Rittstieg. München: Deutscher Taschenbuch-Verlag.

DIETZEL-PAPAKYRIAKOU, MARIA (1993). 'Ältere ausländische Menschen in der Bundesrepublik Deutschland', in Deutsches Zentrum für Altersfragen (ed.), *Expertisen zum ersten Altenbericht der Bunderegierung.* Vol. iii. *Aspekte der Lebensbedingungen ausgewählter Bevölkerungsgruppen.* Berlin: Deutsches Zentrum für Altersfragen, 1–154.

DÖRR, SILVIA, and FAIST, THOMAS (1997). 'Institutional Conditions for the Integration of Immigrants in Welfare States: A Comparison of the Literature on Germany, France, Great Britain, and the Netherlands', *European Journal of Political Research*, 31: 401–26.

DOWTY, ALAN (1987). *Closed Borders: The Contemporary Assault on Freedom of Movement*. New Haven: Yale University Press.

DUBETSKY, ALLEN (1973). 'A New Community in Istanbul: A Study of Primordial Ties, Work Organization, and Turkish Culture'. Ph.D. thesis, University of Chicago.

DUBOIS, W. E. B. (1989 [1903]). *The Souls of Black Folk*. New York: Bantam.

DUMMETT, ANN (1994). 'The Acquisition of British Citizenship: From Imperial Traditions to National Definitions', in Rainer Bauböck (ed.), *From Aliens to Citizens: Redefining the Status of Immigrants in Europe*. Avebury: Aldershot, 75–84.

DURKHEIM, ÉMILE, (1964 [1893]). *The Division of Labour in Society*. Trans. George Simpson. New York: Macmillan.

—— (1958 [1895]). *The Rules of the Sociological Method*. Ed. George E. C. Catlin, trans. Sarah A. Solovay and John H. Muller. Glencoe, Ill.: The Free Press.

—— (1965 [1912]). *The Elementary Forms of Religious Life*. Trans. J. W. Swain. New York: The Free Press.

DUSTMAN, CHRISTIAN (1996). 'Return Migration: The European Experience', *Economic Policy: A European Forum*, No. 22 (Apr.): 213–50.

DUYMAZ, ISMAIL (1988). 'Selbständige Erwerbstätigkeit von Ausländern als Integrationsindikator', *Zeitschrift für Ausländerrecht und Ausländerpolitik*, 2: 27–8.

EASTERLIN, RICHARD A. (1961). 'Influences in European Overseas Migration before World War I', *Economic Development and Cultural Change*, 9: 331–51.

ECKSTEIN, HARRY (1966). *Division and Cohesion in Democracy: A Study of Norway*. Princeton: Princeton University Press.

EISENSTADT, SHMUEL N. (1954). *The Absorption of Immigrants: A Comparative Study Based Mainly on the Jewish Community in Palestine and the State of Israel*. London: Routledge.

—— and RONIGER, LUIS (1984). *Patrons, Clients and Friends: Interpersonal Relations and the Structure of Trust in Society*. Cambridge: Cambridge University Press.

EKEH, PETER P. (1974). *Social Exchange Theory: The Two Traditions*. Cambridge, Mass.: Harvard University Press.

ELSTER, JON (1989). *Nuts and Bolts in the Social Sciences*. New York: Cambridge University Press.

ENGELBREKTSSON, ULLA-BRITT (1978). *The Force of Tradition: Turkish Migrants at Home and Abroad*. Göteborg: Acta Universitatis Gothoburgensis.

ENTZINGER, HAN (1978). *Return Migration from West European to Mediterranean Countries*. World Employment Programme, Migration for Employment Project. Working Paper. Geneva: International Labour Organization.

ERGIL, DOĞU, with YAŞAR, YAVUZ, KILIÇALP, NOĞMAN, ÇAVDAR, GAMZE, TOZKOPARAN, ADIGÜZEL, and İÇEN, ALP (1995). *'Doğu Sorunu': Teshisler ve Tesbitler ('The Eastern Question': Diagnoses and Analyses)*. Ankara: Türkiye Odalar ve Borsalar, TOBB.

ESMAN, MILTON J. (1986). 'The Chinese Diaspora in Southeast Asia', in Gabriel Sheffer (ed.), *Modern Diasporas in International Politics.* London: Croom Helm, 130–63.

ESPENSHADE, THOMAS (1994). 'Does the Threat of Border Apprehension Deter Undocumented U.S. Immigration? ' *Population and Development Review*, 20 4: 871–92.

ESPINOSA, KRISTIN, and MASSEY, DOUGLAS (1997). 'Undocumented Migration and the Quantity and Quality of Social Capital', in Ludger Pries (ed.), *Transnationale Migration: Soziale Welt*, Sonderband 21. Baden-Baden: Nomos, 141–62.

ESSER, HARTMUT (1980). *Aspekte der* Wanderungssoziologie*: Assimilation und Integration von Wanderern, ethnischen Gruppen und Minderheiten.* Darmstadt and Neuwied: Luchterhand.

—— HILL, PAUL B., and VAN OEPEN, GERT (1983). *Ausländerintegration im Ruhrgebiet—Sozialökologische Bestimmungsfaktoren.* Essen: Universität-GH Essen.

EC Communication (1994). *Communication from the Commission of the E.C. to the Council and the European Parliament on Immigration and Asylum Policies*, COM 94/33 final, Brussels, 23 Feb.

European Parliament (1994). *Deuxième Rapport sur un projet de Charte de droits et des devoirs des ressortissants des pays tiers résident dans l'Union Européenne.* Commission des libertés publiques et des affaires intérieures. Doc. PE 208.166/déf. Strasbourg, 16 Mar.

EVEN, HERBERT, YEŞILYAPRAK, KADIR, ELWERT, GEORG, and STAUTH, GEORG (1984). *Sozio-ökonomische Differenzierung und Arbeitsmigration in der ländlichen Türkei*, Bielefelder Studien zur Entwicklungssoziologie 22. Saarbrücken and Fort Lauderdale: Breitenbach.

FAINI, RICCARDO, and VENTURINI, ALESSANDRA (1994). *Migration and Growth: The Experience of Southern Europe*, Discussion Paper Series No. 964. London: Centre for Economic Policy Research.

FAIRCHILD, HENRY P. (1925). *Migration: A World Movement and its American Significance.* New York: Putnam.

FAIST, THOMAS (1991). *After the Goldrush: Organized Labour and Chinese Exclusion in California and Eastern Australia*, CSSC Papers No. 107, Center for Studies of Social Change. New York: New School for Research.

—— (1994). 'How to Define a Foreigner? The Symbolic Politics of Immigration in German Partisan Discourse, 1978–1992', *West European Politics*, 17 2: 50–71.

—— (1995). 'Ethnicization and Racialization of Welfare State Politics in Germany and the USA', *Ethnic and Racial Studies*, 18 2: 219–50.

—— SIEVEKING, KLAUS, REIM, UWE, and SANDBRINK, STEFAN (1999). *Ausland im Inland: Die Beschäftigung von Werkvertragsarbeitnehmern aus Osteuropa in der Bundesrepublik Deutschland.* Baden-Baden: Nomos.

FALK, SVENJA (1998). *Dimensionen kurdischer Ethnizität und Politisierung: Eine Fallstudie ethnischer Gruppenbildung in der Bundesrepublik Deutschland.* Baden-Baden: Nomos.

FARRAG, MAYAR (1997). 'Managing International Migration in Developing Countries', *International Migration*, 35/3: 315–36.

FAWCETT, JAMES T. (1989). 'Networks, Linkages, and Migration Systems', *International Migration Review*, 23/3: 671–80.

FEATHERMAN, DAVID L., and HAUSER, ROBERT L. (1978). *Opportunity and Change.* New York: Academic Press.

FEINDT-RIGGERS, NILS, and STEINBACH, UDO (1997). *Islamische Organisationen in Deutschland: Eine aktuelle Bestandsaufnahme und Analyse.* Hamburg: Deutsches Orient-Institut.

FERNÁNDEZ-KELLY, M. PATRICIA (1994). 'Broadening the Scope: Gender and International Development', in A. Douglas Kincaid and Alejandro Portes (eds.), *Comparative National Development.* Chapel Hill: University of North Carolina Press, 143–68.

FERTIG, GEORG (1994). 'Transatlantic Migration from the German-speaking Parts of Central Europe, 1600–1800: Proportions, Structures, and Explanations', in Nicholas P. Canny (ed.), *Europeans on the Move: Studies on European Migration, 1500–1800.* Oxford: Oxford University Press, 192–235.

FESTINGER, LEON (1957). *A Theory of Cognitive Dissonance.* Stanford, Calif.: Stanford University Press.

FISCHER, PETER A., MARTIN, REINER, and STRAUBHAAR, THOMAS (1997*a*). 'Should I Stay or Should I Go?', in Tomas Hammar, Grete Brochmann, Kristof Tamas, and Thomas Faist (eds.), *International Migration, Immobility and Development: Multidisciplinary Perspectives.* Oxford: Berg, 49–90.

—— —— —— (1997*b*). 'Interdependencies between Development and Migration', in Tomas Hammar, Grete Brochmann, Kristof Tamas, and Thomas Faist (eds.), *International Migration, Immobility and Development: Multidisciplinary Perspectives.* Oxford: Berg, 91–132.

FISHMAN, JOSHUA (1966). *Language Loyalty in the United States.* The Hague: Mouton Publishers.

FISKE, SUSAN T., and TAYLOR, SHELLEY E. (1984). *Social Cognition.* New York: Random House.

FLAP, HENDRIK D. (1991). 'Social Capital and the Reproduction of Inequality: A Review', *Comparative Sociology of Family, Health and Education*, 20: 179–202.

FORSYTHE, DAVID (1993). *Human Rights and Peace: International and National Dimensions.* Lincoln: University of Nebraska Press.

FRAZER, NANCY (1995). 'From Redistribution to Recognition? Dilemmas of Justice in a "Post-Socialist" Age', *New Left Review*, 212: 68–93.

FREEMAN, GARY P. 1986: 'Migration and the Political Economy of the Welfare State', *Annals of the American Academy of Political and Social Sciences (AAPSS)*, No. 486: 51–63.

FREEMAN, GARY P. (1995). 'Modes of Immigration Politics in Liberal Democratic States', *International Migration Review*, 29/4: 881–903.

FRÖBEL, FOLKER, HEINRICHS, JÜRGEN, and KREYE, OTTO (1977). *Die neue internationale Arbeitsteilung: Strukturelle Arbeitslosigkeit in den Industrieländern und die Industrialisierung der Entwicklungsländer*. Reinbek: Rowohlt.

FUCHS, DIETER, GERHARDS, JÜRGEN, and ROLLER, EDELTRAUD (1993). 'Wir und die Anderen: "Imagined Communities" im westeuropäischen Vergleich', Discussion Paper FS III 93–301. Berlin: Wissenschaftszentrum Berlin für Sozialforschung.

FUCHS, LAWRENCE H. (1990). *The American Kaleidscope: Race, Ethnicity, and the Civic Culture*. Hanover: University Press of New England.

FURNIVALL, JOHN S. (1948). *Colonial Policy and Practice: A Comparative Study of Burma and Netherlands India*. London: Cambridge University Press.

GANS, HERBERT J. (1962). *The Urban Villagers*. New York: The Free Press.

—— (1979). 'Symbolic Ethnicity: The Future of Ethnic Groups and Cultures in America', *Ethnic and Racial Studies*, 2/1: 1–20.

—— (1992). 'Comment: Ethnic Invention and Acculturation: A Bumpy-Line Approach', *Journal of American Ethnic History*, 12/1: 45–52.

GEERTZ, CLIFFORD (1973). *The Interpretation of Cultures*. New York: Basic Books.

GEHLEN, ARNOLD (1957). *Die Seele im technischen Zeitalter: Sozialpsychologische Probleme in der industriellen Gesellschaft*. Reinbek: Rowohlt.

GELLNER, ERNEST (1983). *Nations and Nationalism*. Ithaca, NY: Cornell University Press.

—— (1991). 'Civil Society in Historical Context', *International Social Science Journal*, 43: 495–510.

GIDDENS, ANTHONY (1991). *The Consequences of Modernity*. Cambridge: Polity Press.

GILLESSEN, GÜNTHER (1997). 'Mythos "humanitäre Intervention"', *Internationale Politik*, 9: 13–20.

GITMEZ, ALI S. (1984). 'Geographical and Occupational Re-Integration of Returning Turkish Workers', in Daniel Kubat (ed.), *The Politics of Return Migration*. New York and Rome: Center for Migration Studies, 218–57.

—— (1989). 'Turkish Experience of Work Emigration: Economic Development or Individual Well-Being', *Yapı Kredi: Economic Review*, 3/4: 3–27.

—— and WILPERT, CZARINA (1987). 'A Micro-Society or an Ethnic Community? Social Organization and Ethnicity among Turkish Migrants in Berlin', John Rex, Danièle Joly, and Czarina Wilpert (eds.), *Immigrant Associations in Europe*. Aldershot: Gower: 86–125.

GLAZER, NATHAN, and MOYNIHAN, DANIEL P. (1963). *Beyond the Melting Pot*. Cambridge, Mass.: MIT Press.

GLEBE, GÜNTHER (1997). 'Statushohe ausländische Migranten in Deutschland', *Geographische Rundschau*, 49: 406–12.

GLICK SCHILLER, NINA, BASCH, LINDA, and BLANC-SZANTON, CRISTINA (1992).

'Transnationalism: A New Analytic Framework for Understanding Migration', *Annals of the New York Academy of Science*, 645: 1–24.

GMELCH, GEORGE (1980). 'Return Migration', *Annual Review of Anthropology*, 9: 135–59.

GÖKDERE, AHMET, Y. (1978). *Yabancı Ülkelere İşgücü Akımı ve Türk Ekonomisi Üzerindeki Etkileri* (The Flow of Labour Abroad and the Impact on the Turkish Economy). Ankara: İş Bankası Yayını.

GOLD, STEVEN J. (1997). 'Transnationalism and Vocabularies of Motive in International Migration: The Case of Israelis in the United States', *Sociological Perspectives*, 40/3: 409–27.

GOLDBERG, ANDREAS (1992). 'Selbständigkeit als Integrationsfortschritt?' *Zeitschrift für Türkeistudien*, 7: 75–92.

GOLDBERG, MICHAEL A. (1985). *The Chinese Connection: Getting Plugged in to Pacific Rim Real Estate, Trade, and Capital Markets.* Vancouver: University of British Columbia Press.

GOLDRING, LUIN (1996*a*). 'Gendered Memory: Reconstructions of the Village by Mexican Transnational Migrants', Melanie DuPuis and Peter Vandergeest (eds.), *Creating the Countryside.* Philadelphia: Temple University Press, 303–29.

—— (1996*b*). 'Blurring Borders: Constructing Transnational Community in the Process of Mexico–U.S. Migration', in *Research in Community Sociology*, Vol. vi. Greenwich, Conn.: JAI Press, 69–104.

GOLDSCHEIDER, CALVIN (1971). *Population, Modernization, and Social Structure.* Boston: Little, Brown, and Company.

GÖLE, NILÜFER (1995). *Republik und Schleier: Die muslimische Frau in der modernen Türkei.* Berlin: Babel Verlag.

—— (1996). 'Authoritarian Secularism and Islamist Politics: The Case of Turkey', in Augustus Richard Norton (ed.), *Civil Society in the Middle East*. Vol. ii. Leiden: E. J. Brill, 17–44.

GORDON, MILTON (1964). *Assimilation in American Life.* New York: Oxford University Press.

GOSS, JON D., and LINDQUIST, BRUCE (1995). 'Conceptualizing International Labour Migration: A Structuration Perspective', *International Migration Review*, 24/2: 317–51.

GOULBOURNE, HARRY (1991). *Ethnicity and Nationalism in Post-Imperial Britain*. Cambridge: Cambridge University Press.

GOULDNER, ALVIN W. (1960). 'The Norm of Reciprocity: A Preliminary Statement', *American Sociological Review*, 25/2: 161–78.

GRANOVETTER, MARK S. (1973). 'The Strength of Weak Ties', *American Journal of Sociology*, 78/6: 1360–80.

—— (1978). 'Threshold Models of Collective Behaviour', *American Journal of Sociology*, 83/6: 1420–43.

—— (1979). 'The Theory Gap in Social Network Analysis', in Paul W. Holland and Stephen Leinhardt (eds.), *Perspectives in Social Network Research*. New York: Academic Press, 45–67.

GRANOVETTER, MARK S. (1985). 'Economic Action and Social Structure: The Problem of Embeddedness', *American Journal of Sociology*, 91/3: 481–510.

GROTHUSEN, KLAUS-DETLEV (1984). 'Modernisierung und Nationsbildung: Modelltheoretische Überlegungen und ihre Anwendung auf Serbien und die Türkei', *Südosteuropa-Forschungen*, Matthias Bernrath (ed.), 43: 135–80.

GRÜNER, HANS, and KÖHLER, CHRISTOPH (1992). *Mobilität und Diskriminierung: Deutsche und ausländische Arbeiter auf einem betrieblichen Arbeitsmarkt.* Frankfurt a.M.: Campus.

GUARNIZO, LOUIS E. (1994). 'Los Dominicanyorks: The Making of a Binational Society', *Annals of the American Academy of Political and Social Science*, 533: 70–86.

GUNATILLEKE, GODFREY (1997). *The Role of Networks and Community Structures in International Migration from Sri Lanka*, IOM/UNFPA Policy Workshop on Emigration Dynamics in South Asia, Geneva, 2–3 Sept. 1996.

GUNTER, MICHAEL M. (1990). *The Kurds in Turkey: A Political Dilemma.* Boulder, Colo.: Westview Press.

GÜR, METIN (1993). *Türkisch-islamische Vereinigungen in der Bundesrepublik Deutschland.* Frankfurt a.M.: Brandes & Apsel.

GURAK, DOUGLAS T., and CACES, Fe (1992). 'Migration Networks and the Shaping of Migration Systems', in Mary M. Kritz, Lin Lean Lim, and Hania Zlotnik (eds.), *International Migration Systems: A Global Approach.* Oxford: Clarendon Press, 150–76.

GURR, TED R. (1993). *Minorities at Risk.* Washington, DC: United States Institute for Peace.

—— (1994). 'Peoples Against States: Ethnopolitical Conflict and the Changing World System', *International Studies Quarterly*, 38: 347–78.

GUYER, JANE (1981). 'Household and Community in African Studies', *African Studies Review*, 24/2–3: 87–137.

HABERMAS, JÜRGEN (1981). *Theorie des kommunikativen Handelns.* 2 vols. Frankfurt a.M.: Suhrkamp.

HÄGERSTRAND, TORSTEN (1975). 'On the Definition of Migration', in Emrys Jones (ed.), *Readings in Social Geography.* Oxford: Oxford University Press, 200–10.

HAMMAR, TOMAS (1985). 'Sweden', in Tomas Hammar (ed.), *European Immigration Policy: A Comparative Study.* Cambridge: Cambridge University Press, 17–49.

—— (1990). *Democracy and the Nation-State: Aliens, Denizens and Citizens in a World of International Migration.* Aldershot: Gower.

—— (1995). 'Development and Immobility: Why have not Many More Emigrants Left the South?', in Rob van der Erf and Liesbeth Heering (eds.) *Causes of International Migration.* Luxembourg: Office for Official Publications of the European Communities, 173–86.

—— BROCHMANN, GRETE, TAMAS, KRISTOF, and FAIST, THOMAS (eds.) (1997). *Migration, Immobility and Development: A Multidisciplinary View.* Oxford: Berg Publishers.

HANDLIN, OSCAR (1973 [1951]) *The Uprooted: The Epic Story of the Great Migrations that Made the American People* (2nd edn, enlarged). Boston: Little, Brown and Company.

HANNERZ, ULF (1996). *Transnational Connections: Culture, People, Places.* New York: Routledge.

HARRIS, JOHN R., and TODARO, MICHAEL P. (1970). 'Migration, Unemployment and Development: A Two-Sector Analysis', *American Economic Review*, 60: 126–42.

HARVEY, DAVID (1989). *The Condition of Postmodernity.* Oxford: Blackwell.

HATTON, TIMOTHY J., and WILLIAMSON, JEFFREY G. (1994). 'What Drove the Mass Migrations from Europe in the Late Nineteenth Century?' *Population and Development Review*, 20/3: 533–59.

HECHTER, MICHAEL (1987). *Principles of Group Solidarity.* Berkeley: University of California Press.

HECKMANN, FRIEDRICH (1981). *Die Bundesrepublik: Ein Einwanderungsland?* Stuttgart: Klett-Cotta.

HEITMEYER, WILHELM, MÜLLER, JOACHIM, and SCHRÖDER, HELMUT (1997). *Verlockender Fundamentalismus: Türkische Jugendliche in Deutschland.* Frankfurt a.M.: Suhrkamp.

HELD, DAVID (1995). *Political Theory and the Modern State: Essays on State, Power, and Democracy.* Cambridge: Polity Press.

HERMELE, KENNETH (1997). 'The Discourse on Migration and Development', in Tomas Hammar, Grete Brochmann, Kristof Tamas, and Thomas Faist (eds.), *International Migration, Immobility and Development: Multidisciplinary Perspectives.* Oxford: Berg, 133–58.

HIRSCHMAN, ALBERT O. (1970). *Exit, Voice, and Loyalty: Responses to Decline in Firms, Organizations, and States.* Cambridge, Mass.: Harvard University Press.

—— (1984). 'Against Parsimony: Three Easy Ways of Complicating Some Categories of Economic Discourse', *American Economic Review*, Papers & Proceedings, 96th Annual Meeting 196–219.

—— (1993). 'Exit, Voice, and the Fate of the German Democratic Republic: An Essay in Conceptual History', *World Politics*, 45: 173–202.

HOBSBAWM, ERIC (1996). *Das imperiale Zeitalter: 1875–1914.* Frankfurt: Fischer.

HOCKER, REINHARD, and LIEBE-HARKORT, KLAUS (eds.) (1996). *Zur Kurdenfrage in der Türkei: Dokumente aus der Türkei und aus der Bundesrepublik Deutschland (1980–1995).* Frankfurt a.M.: Gewerkschaft Erziehung und Wissenschaft (GEW).

HOF, BERND (1993). *Europa im Zeichen der Migration: Szenarien zur Bevölkerungs- und Arbeitsmarktentwicklung in der Europäischen Gemeinschaft bis 2020.* Köln: Deutscher Instituts-Verlag.

HOFFMANN-NOWOTNY, HANS-JOACHIM (1973). *Soziologie des Fremdarbeiterproblems.* Stuttgart: Ferdinand Enke Verlag.

—— (1988). 'Paradigmen und Paradigmenwechsel in der sozialwissenschaftlichen Wanderungsforschung', in Gerhard Jaritz and Albert Müller (eds.), *Migration in der Feudalgesellschaft*. Frankfurt: Campus, 21–42.

HOLLIFIELD, JAMES (1992). *Immigrants, Markets and States: The Political Economy of Postwar Europe*. Cambridge, Mass.: Cambridge University Press.

HOMANS, GEORGE C. (1986). 'Fifty Years of Sociology', *American Sociological Review*, 12: xiii–xxx.

HPDP (Hispanic Policy Development Project) (1990). *The Hispanic Almanac: Edition Two*. Washington, DC: HPDP.

HUGO, GRAEME J. (1981). 'Village–Community Ties, Village Norms and Ethnic and Social Networks: A Review of Evidence from the Third World', in Gordon F. De Jong and Richard W. Gardner (eds.), *Migration Decision Making: Multidisciplinary Approaches to Microlevel Studies in Developed and Developing Countries*. New York: Pergamon Press, 186–224.

—— (1995). 'International Labour Migration and the Family: Some Observations from Indonesia', *Asian and Pacific Migration Journal*, 4/2–3: 273–302.

HUSA, KARL (1990/1). 'Wer ist ein Migrant? Probleme der Dokumentation und Abgrenzung räumlicher Mobilität in der Dritten Welt', in *Demographische Informationen*, ed. Institut für Demographie, Österreichische Akademie der Wissenschaften. Wien, 35–47.

HUYCK, EARL E., and BOUVIER, LEON F. (1983). 'The Demography of Refugees', *Annals of the American Academy of Political and Social Sciences*, 467 (May): 39–61.

HUYSMANS, JEF (1995). 'Migrants as a Security Problem: Dangers of "Securitizing" Societal Issues', in Robert Miles and Dietrich Thränhardt (eds.), *Migration and European Integration: The Dynamics of Inclusion and Exclusion*. London: Pinter Publishers, 53–72.

İÇDUYGU, AHMET (1991). 'Migrant as a Transitional Category: Turkish Migrants in Melbourne, Australia'. Ph.D. dissertation. Australian National University, Canberra, Australia.

—— (1998). 'Migration from Turkey to Western Europe: Recent Trends and Prospects', *Proceedings of the Mediterranean Conference on Population*. Strasbourg: Council of Europe, 23–38.

—— SIREKCI, İBRAHIM, and MURADOĞLU, GÜLNUR (1999). 'Socio-Economic Development and Mobility: Facilitating or Restricting the Emigratory Flows from a Country—a Turkish Study', *International Migration Review* (forthcoming).

Informationsdienst zur Ausländerarbeit (1994). Freiburg: Pädagogische Hochschule.

International Labour Office (1945). *The Exploitation of Foreign Labour by Germany*. Montréal: ILO.

ISAAC, JULIUS (1947). *Economics of Migration*. New York: Oxford University Press.

JACOBSON, DAVID (1995). *Rights Across Borders: Immigration and the Decline of Citizenship*. Baltimore: Johns Hopkins University Press.

JACOBSON, MATTHEW FRYE (1995). *Special Sorrows: The Diasporic Imagination of Irish, Polish, and Jewish Immigrants in the United States*. Cambridge, Mass.: Harvard University Press.

JASSO, GUILLERMA, and ROSENZWEIG, MARK R. (1982). 'Estimating the Emigration Rates of Legal Immigrants Using Administrative and Survey Data: The 1971 Cohort of Immigrants to the United States', *Demography*, 19/3: 279–90.

JEAN, FRANÇOIS (ed.) (1994). *Helfer im Kreuzfeuer: Humanitäre Hilfe und militärische Intervention. Ein Report über Völker in Not*. Bonn: Verlag J. H. W. Dietz.

JOLY, DANIÈLE, KELLY, LYNNETTE, and NETTLETON, CLIVE (1997). *Refugees in Europe: The Hostile New Agenda*. London: Minority Rights Group.

JONAS, SUSANNE (1995). 'Transnational Realities and Anti-Immigrant State Policies: Issues Raised by the Experiences of Central American Immigrants and Refugees in a Trinational Region', in Roberto Patricio Korzeniewicz and William C. Smith (eds.), *Latin America in the World Economy*. Westport, Conn.: Praeger, 117–32.

JONES, PHILIP N. (1990). 'West Germany's Declining Guestworker Population: Spatial Change and Economic Trends in the 1980s', *Regional Studies*, 24/3: 223–33.

KAĞITÇIBAŞI, ÇIĞDEM (1983). *Immigrant Populations in Europe: Problems Viewed from the Sending Country*, EPC (82) 7-E. Strasbourg: Council of Europe.

KAISER, KARL (1969). 'Transnationale Politik: Zu einer Theorie der multinationalen Politik', *Politische Vierteljahresschrift*, Sonderheft 1: 80–109.

KALLEN, HORACE (1996 [1915]). 'Democracy versus the Melting-Pot: A Study of American Nationality', in Werner Sollors (ed.), *Theories of Ethnicity: A Classical Reader*. Houndmills, Basingstoke: Macmillan, 67–92.

KARACABEY, MAKFI (1996). *Türkische Tageszeitungen in der BRD: Rolle–Einfluß–Funktionen*. Inauguraldissertation. Johann-Wolfgang-Goethe-Universität. Frankfurt a.M.

KARAKAŞOĞLU-AYDIN, YASEMIN (1997). '"Ich bin stolz, ein Türke zu sein". Bedeutung ethnischer Orientierungen für das positive Selbstwertgefühl türkischer Jugendlicher in Deutschland—Ein Essay', in Forschungsinstitut der Friedrich-Ebert-Stiftung (ed.), *Identitätsstabilisierend oder konfliktfördernd? Ethnische Orientierungen in Jugendgruppen*. Bonn: FES, 27–38.

KARPAT, KEMAL H. (1976). *The Gecekondu: Rural Migration and Urbanization*. Cambridge: Cambridge University Press.

KASTORYANO, RIVA (1994). 'Construction de communautés et négociation des identités: Les Migrants musulmans en France et en Allemagne', in Dennis-Constant Martin (ed.), *Cartes d'Identité: Comment dit-on 'nous' en politique?* Paris: Presses de la Fondation Nationale des Sciences Politiques, 229–44.

KAZANCIGIL, ALI (1991). 'Democracy in Muslim Lands: Turkey in Comparative Perspective', *International Social Science Journal*, 43: 343–60.

KEHL-BODROĞI, KRISZTINA (1988). *Die Kızılbaş/Aleviten: Untersuchungen über eine esoterische Glaubensgemeinschaft*, Islamkundliche Untersuchungen. Vol. 126. Berlin: Klaus Schwarz.

KEOHANE, ROBERT O. (1986). 'Reciprocity in International Relations', *International Organization*, 40/1: 1–27.

—— and NYE, JOSEPH S. (1977). *Power and Interdependence: World Politics in Transition*. Boston: Little, Brown.

KERNS, VIRGINIA (1983). *Women and the Ancestors: Black Caribbean Kinship and Ritual*. Urbana: University of Illinois Press.

KEYDER, ÇAĞLAR, and AKSU-KOÇ, AYHAN (1988). *External Labour Migration from Turkey and its Impact: An Evaluation of the Literature*, Manuscript Report 185e. Ottawa: International Development Research Centre.

KIBRIA, NAZLI (1993). *Family Tightrope: The Changing Lives of Vietnamese Americans*. Princeton: Princeton University Press.

KILIÇ, MEMET (1994). 'Deutsch-türkische Doppelstaatsagenhörigkeit?' *Das Standesamt*, 47: 73–8.

KLANDERMANS, BERT (1997). *The Social Psychology of Protest*. Oxford: Blackwell.

KLAVER, JEANINE (1997). *From the Land of the Sun to the City of Angels: The Migration Process of Zapotec Indians from Oaxaca, Mexico to Los Angeles, California*, Netherlands Geographical Studies 228. Utrecht: KNAG.

KLEFF, HANS-GÜNTER (1984). *Vom Bauern zum Industriearbeiter: Zur kollektiven Lebensgeschichte der Arbeitsmigranten aus der Türkei*. Ingelheim: Manthano.

KNIGHT, FRANK H. (1982 [1921]) *Freedom and Reform: Essays in Economics and Social Philosophy*. Indianapolis: Liberty Press.

KNOKE, DAVID, and KUKLINSKI, JAMES H. (1982). *Network Analysis*. Beverly Hills, Calif.: Sage.

KRANE, RONALD E. (ed.) (1975). *Manpower Mobility across Cultural Boundaries: Social, Economic and Legal Aspects. The Case of Turkey and West Germany*. Leiden: Brill.

KRASNER, STEPHEN (1983). 'Structural Causes and Regime Consequences: Regimes as Intervening Variables', in Stephen Krasner (ed.), *International Regimes*. Ithaca, NY: Cornell University Press, 1–21.

KRITZ, MARY M., and ZLOTNIK, HANIA (1992). 'Global Interactions: Migration Systems, Process and Policies', in Mary M. Kritz, Lin Lean Lim, and Hania Zlotnik (eds.), *International Migration Systems: A Global Approach*. Oxford: Clarendon Press, 1–18.

KUBAT, DANIEL (ed.) (1984). *The Politics of Return Migration*. New York and Rome (Center for Migration Studies).

KUDAT, AYŞE (1975). *Emigration Effects on the Turkish Countryside: A Representative Study of Settlement Units*, Series of Reports of the International Migration Project. Berlin: Internationales Institut für Vergleichende Gesellschaftsforschung.

KUDAT-SERTEL, AYŞE (1972). *Patron-Client Relations: The State of the Art and Research in Eastern Turkey*. Princeton: Princeton University Press.

KULU-GLASGOW, IŞIK (1992). 'Motives and Social Networks of International Migration within the Context of the Systems Approach: A Literature

Review', The Hague: Netherlands Interdisciplinary Demographic Institute (NIDI), Working Paper 3.

KUNZ, EGON F. (1973). 'The Refugee in Flight: Kinetic Models and Forms of Displacement', *International Migration Review*, 7/2: 125–46.

—— (1982). 'Exile and Resettlement: Refugee Theory', *International Migration Review*, 15/1: 42–51.

KUPER, ADAM, and KUPER, JESSICA (eds.) (1985). *The Social Science Encyclopedia*. London: Routledge & Kegan Paul, 524–8.

KÜRŞAT-AHLERS, ELÇIN (1992). 'Zur Psychogenese der Migration: Phasen und Probleme', *Informationsdienst zur Ausländerarbeit*, 3/4: 107–13.

KYMLICKA, WILL (1989). *Liberalism, Community and Culture*. Oxford: Clarendon Press.

—— (1995). *Multicultural Citizenship: A Liberal Theory of Minority Rights*. Oxford: Clarendon Press.

LALONDE, ROBERT J., and TOPEL, ROBERT H. (1997). 'Economic Impact of International Migration and the Economic Performance of Migrants', in Mark R. Rosenzweig and Oded Stark (eds.), *Handbook of Population and Family Economics*. Amsterdam: Elsevier, 241–56.

LASH, SCOTT, and URRY, JOHN (1994). *Economies of Signs & Space*. London: Sage.

LASSWELL, HAROLD D. (1948). *Power and Personality*. New York: Harper & Row.

LEE, EVERETT S. (1964). 'A Theory of Migration', *Demography*, 3: 47–57.

LEGGEWIE, CLAUS (1996). 'How Turks Became Kurds, Not Germans', *Dissent*, 43/2: 79–83.

LEMAY, MICHAEL C. (ed.) (1985). *The Gatekeepers: Comparative Immigration Policy*. New York: Praeger.

LEOPOLD, ULRICH (1978). *Sozio-ökonomische Ursachen der Migration türkischer Arbeitskräfte*, Veröffentlichung aus dem Übersee-Museum Bremen. Reihe D, Band 4. Bremen: Selbstverlag des Museums.

LERNER, DANIEL (1958). *The Passing of Traditional Society: Modernizing the Middle East*. New York: The Free Press.

LEVINE, DAVID (1977). *Family Formation in an Age of Nascent Capitalism*. New York: Academic Press.

LEVITT, PEGGY (1996). 'Transnationalizing Civil and Political Change: The Case of Transnational Organizational Ties between Boston and the Dominican Republic'. Ph.D. dissertation. Massachusetts Institute of Technology.

LEWIS, ARTHUR W. (1954). *Theory of Economic Growth*. London: Unwin.

LIGHT, IVAN H. (1972). *Ethnic Enterprise in America: Business and Welfare among Chinese, Japanese, and Blacks*. Berkeley: University of California Press.

LOHRMANN, REINHARD, and MANFRASS, KLAUS (1974). *Ausländerbeschäftigung und internationale Politik: Zur Analyse transnationaler Sozialprozesse*. München: Oldenbourg.

LÜDERITZ, GERT R. (1994). 'What is the Politeuma?', in J. W. van Henten and

P. W. van der Horst (eds.), *Studies in Early Jewish Epigraphy.* Leiden: Brill, 183–225.

LUHMANN, NIKLAS (1975). 'Weltgesellschaft', *Soziologische Aufklärung 2*. Opladen: Westdeutscher Verlag.

MCADAM, DOUGLAS, MCCARTHY, JOHN, and ZALD, MAYER (eds.) (1996). *Comparative Perspectives on Social Movements: Political Opportunities, Mobilizing Structures, and Cultural Framings.* Cambridge: Cambridge University Press.

MACDONALD, JOHN S., and MACDONALD, LEATRICE D. (1964). 'Chain Migration: Ethnic Neighborhood Formation and Social Networks', *Milbank Memorial Fund Quarterly*, 42 (Jan.): 82–97.

MCDOWALL, DAVID (1996). *A Modern History of the Kurds.* London: I. B. Tauris.

MCGINNIS, ROBERT (1968). 'A Stochastic Model of Social Mobility', *American Sociological Review*, 33/5: 712–22.

MCPHAIL, CLARK, and MILLER, DAVID (1973). 'The Assembling Process: A Theoretical and Empirical Examination', *American Sociological Review*, 38/6: 721–35.

MABOGUNJE, AKIN L. (1970). 'Systems Approach to a Theory of Rural–Urban Migration', *Geographical Analysis*, 2: 1–17.

MACKIE, GERRY (1995). 'Frustration and Preference Change in Immigration Migration', *Archives Européennes de Sociologie*, 36/2: 185–208.

MACY, MICHAEL W. (1991). 'Chains of Cooperation: Threshold Effects in Collective Action', *American Sociological Review*, 56 (Dec.): 730–47.

MAGNARELLA, PAUL J. (1972). 'Aspects of Kinship Change in a Modernizing Turkish Town', *Human Organization*, 31/4: 361–71.

—— (1974). *Tradition and Change in a Turkish Town.* Cambridge, Mass.: Schenkman Publishers.

MAGOBUNJE, AKIN L. (1970). 'Systems Approach to a Theory of Rural–Urban Migration', *Geographical Analysis*, 2/1: 1–17.

MÄLICH, WOLFGANG (1989). 'Wanderungen', in Görres-Gesellschaft (ed.), *Staatslexikon* (7th and revised edn). Vol. v. Freiburg: Herder, 876–82.

MALMBERG, GUNNAR (1997). 'Time and Space in International Migration', in Tomas Hammar, Grete Brochmann, Kristof Tamas, and Thomas Faist (eds.), *Migration, Immobility and Development: A Multidisciplinary View.* Oxford: Berg Publishers, 21–48.

MANDEL, RUTH (1989). 'Turkish Headscarves and the "Foreigner Problem": Constructing Difference through Emblems of Identity', *New German Critique*, 46: 27–46.

—— (1990). 'Shifting Centres and Emergent Identities: Turkey and Germany in the Lives of Turkish Gastarbeiter', in Dale F. Eickelman and James Piscatori (eds.), *Muslim Travelers: Pilgrimage, Migration, and the Religious Imagination*. London: Routledge, 153–71.

MANN, MICHAEL (1986). *The Sources of Social Power.* Vol. i. *A History of Power from the Beginning to A.D. 1760*. Cambridge: Cambridge University Press.

MARSHALL, T. H. (1964). *Class, Citizenship and Social Development: Essays by T. H. Marshall.* New York: Anchor Books.

MARTIN, PHILIP L. (1991). *The Unfinished Story: Turkish Labour Migration to Western Europe.* Geneva: International Labour Office.

—— and WIDGREN, JONAS (1996). *International Migration: A Global Challenge.* Washington, DC: Population Reference Bureau.

MARUYAMA, MAGOROH (1963). 'The Second Cybernetics: Deviation-Amplifying Mutual Causal Processes', *American Scientist*, 51/2: 164–79.

—— (1982). 'Four Different Causal Metatypes in Biological and Social Sciences', in William Schieve and Peter Allen (eds.) *Self-Organization and Dissipative Structures.* Austin: University of Texas Press, 354–61.

MARWELL, GERALD, and OLIVER, PAMELA (1993). *The Critical Mass in Collective Action: A Micro-Social Theory.* Cambridge: Cambridge University Press.

MARX, KARL (1973 [1859]). *Grundrisse: Foundations of the Critique of Political Economy.* New York: Vintage Books.

MASSEY, DOUGLAS S. (1990). 'Social Structure, Household Strategies, and the Cumulative Causation of Migration', *Population Index*, 56/1: 3–26.

—— (1995). 'The New Immigration and Ethnicity in the United States', *Population and Development Review*, 21/3 (Sept.): 631–52.

—— and ESPINOSA, KRISTIN (1997). 'What's Driving Mexico–US Migration? A Theoretical, Empirical, and Policy Analysis', *American Journal of Sociology*, 102/4: 939–99.

—— GOLDRING, LUIN, and DURAND, JORGE (1994). 'Continuities in Transnational Migration: An Analysis of Nineteen Mexican Communities', *American Journal of Sociology*, 99/6: 1492–1533.

—— ALARCÓN, RAFAEL, DURAND, JORGE, and GONZÁLEZ, HUMBERTO (1987). *Return to Aztlan: The Social Process of International Migration from Western Mexico.* Berkeley: University of California Press.

—— ARANGO, JOAQUÍN, HUGO, GRAEME, KOUAOUCI, ALI, PELLEGRINO, ADELA, and TAYLOR, J. EDWARD (1993). 'Theories of International Migration: A Review and Appraisal', *Population and Development Review*, 19/3: 431–66.

—— —— —— —— —— —— (1994). 'An Evaluation of International Migration Theory: The North American Case', *Population and Development Review*, 20/4: 699–751.

MAUSS, MARCEL (1954 [1925]). *The Gift.* Translated by Ian Cunnison. New York: The Free Press.

MERTON, ROBERT K. (1936). 'The Unanticipated Consequences of Purposive Social Action', *American Sociological Review*, 1: 894–904.

—— (1957). *Social Theory and Social Structure.* New York: The Free Press.

MEYER, JOHN W., BOLI, JOHN, THOMAS, GEORGE M., and RAMIREZ, FRANCISCO O. (1997). 'World Society and the Nation-State', *American Journal of Sociology*, 103/1: 144–81.

MEYERS, EYTAN (1994). 'European Migration Regimes in a Comparative Perspective', Paper presented at the Conference of Europeanists, Chicago.

MEYERS, REINHARD (1979). *Weltpolitik in Grundbegriffen. Ein lehr- und ideengeschichtlicher Grundriß*. Düsseldorf: Droste.

MILLER, MARK J. (1992). 'Evaluation of Policy Modes for Regulating International Labour Migration', in Mary M. Kritz, Lin Lean Lim, and Hania Zlotnik (eds.) *International Migration Systems: A Global Approach*. Oxford: Clarendon Press, 300–14.

MIN, PYONG GAP (1998). *Traditions and Changes: Korean Immigrant Families in New York*. Needham Heights, Mass.: Allyn and Bacon.

MITCHELL, CHRISTOPHER (ed.) (1992). *Western Hemisphere Immigration and United States Foreign Policy*. University Park, Penn.: The Pennsylvania State University Press.

MITCHELL, J. CLYDE (1969). *Social Networks in Urban Situations: Analyses of Personal Relationships in Central African Towns*. Manchester: Manchester University Press.

MOCH, LESLIE (1992). *Moving Europeans: Migration in Western Europe since 1650*. Bloomington: Indiana University Press.

MODOOD, TARIQ, and BERTHOUD, RICHARD, with LAKEY, JANE, NAZROO, JAMES, SMITH, PATTEN, VIRDEE, SATNAM, and BEISHON, SHARON (1997). *Ethnic Minorities in Britain: Diversity and Disadvantage*, The Fourth National Survey of Ethnic Minorities. London: Policy Studies Institute.

MORAWSKA, EWA (1990). 'Labour Migration of Poles in the Atlantic World Economy, 1880–1914', *Comparative Studies in Society and History*, 31/3: 237–72.

—— and SPOHN, WILLFRIED (1997). 'Moving Europeans in the Globalizing World: Contemporary Migrations in a Historical-Comparative Perspective (1955–1994 v. 1870–1914)', in Wang Gungwu (ed.), *Global History and Migrations*. Boulder, Colo.: Westview Press, 23–62.

MOROKVASIC, MIRJANA (1991). 'Die Kehrseite der Mode: Migranten als Flexibilisierungsquelle in der Pariser Bekleidungsproduktion. Ein Vergleich mit Berlin', *Prokla*, 21: 264–84.

—— WALDINGER, ROGER, and PHIZACKLEA, ANNIE (1990). 'Business on the Ragged Edge: Immigrant and Minority Business in the Garment Industries of Paris, London, and New York', in Roger Waldinger, Howard Aldrich, Robin Ward, and Associates (eds.), *Ethnic Entrepreneurs: Immigrant Business in Industrial Societies*. Newbury Park: Sage, 157–76.

MÜNCH, URSULA (1992). *Asylpolitik in der Bundesrepublik Deutschland: Entwicklung und Alternativen*. Opladen: Leske + Budrich.

MÜNZ, RAINER, SEIFERT, WOLFGANG, and ULRICH, RALF (1997). *Zuwanderung nach Deutschland: Strukturen, Wirkungen, Perspektiven*. Frankfurt a.M.: Campus.

MURRAY, COLIN (1981). *Families Divided: The Impact of Migrant Labour in Lesotho*. Cambridge: Cambridge University Press.

MYRDAL, GUNNAR (1957). *Rich Lands and Poor: The Road to World Prosperity*. New York: Harper & Brothers Publishers.

—— (1972 [1944]). *An American Dilemma: The Negro Problem and Modern Democracy.* 2 vols. New York: Pantheon.

NAUCK, BERNHARD (1985*a*). '"Heimliches Matriarchat" in Familien türkischer Arbeitsmigranten? Empirische Ergebnisse zu Veränderungen der Entscheidungsmacht und Aufgabenallokation', *Zeitschrift für Soziologie*, 14/6: 450–65.

—— (1985*b*). *Arbeitsmigration und Familienstruktur.* Frankfurt/New York: Campus.

NEDERVEEN PIETERSE, JAN (1994). 'Globalisation as Hybridisation', *International Sociology*, 9/2: 161–84.

NIELSEN, JØRGEN (1992). *Muslims in Western Europe.* Edinburgh: Edinburgh University Press.

NISBET, ROBERT (1966). *The Sociological Tradition.* New York: Basic Books.

NOGLE, JUNE M. (1994). 'The Systems Approach to Migration: An Application of Network Analysis Methods', *International Migration*, 32/2: 329–42.

NONINI, DONALD M., and ONG, AIHWA (1997). 'Introduction', in Aihwa Ong and Donald M. Nonini (eds.), *Underground Empires: The Cultural Politics of Modern Chinese Transnationalism.* London: Routledge, 3–36.

NORTH, DOUGLAS C. (1981). *Structure and Change in Economic History.* New York: W. W. Norton.

—— (1991). *Institutions, Institutional Change and Economic Performance.* Cambridge: Cambridge University Press.

OBERSCHALL, ANTHONY (1973). *Social Conflict and Social Movements.* Englewood Cliffs, NJ: Prentice-Hall.

OECD (various years). *SOPEMI: Trends in International Migration.* Paris: OECD.

OGATA, SADAKO (1992). *Lisbon 1992: The Annual Meeting of the Trilateral Commission.* New York: The Trilateral Commission, 17–19.

OLSON, MANCUR (1965). *The Logic of Collective Action: Public Goods and the Theory of Groups.* Cambridge, Mass.: Harvard University Press.

ONG, AIHWA (1992). 'Limits to Cultural Accumulation: Chinese Capitalists on the American Pacific Rim', *Annals of the New York Academy of Sciences*, 645 (July): 125–43.

—— (ed.) (1997). *Ungrounded Empires: The Cultural Politics of Modern Chinese Transnationalism.* New York: Routledge.

OSTROM, ELINOR (1995). 'Self-Organization and Social Capital', *Industrial and Corporate Change*, 4/1: 131–59.

ÖZEL, SULE, and NAUCK, BERNHARD (1987). 'Kettenmigration in türkischen Familien: Ihre Herkunftsbedingungen und ihre Effekte auf die Reorganisation der familiären Interaktionsstruktur in der Aufnahmegesellschaft', *Migration*, 2: 61–94.

PAGENSTECHER, CORD (1996). 'Die "Illusion" der Rückkehr: Zur Mentalitätsgeschichte von "Gastarbeit" und Einwanderung', *Soziale Welt*, 47/2: 149–79.

PAINE, SUZANNE (1974). *Exporting Workers: The Turkish Case.* New York: Cambridge University Press.

PARK, ROBERT E. (1950). *Race and Culture: Essays in the Sociology of Contemporary Man*. Chicago: University of Chicago Press.

—— and BURGESS, ERNEST W. (1969 [1921]). *Introduction to the Science of Sociology*. Reprint. Chicago: University of Chicago Press.

PARSONS, TALCOTT (1951). *The Social System*. Glencoe, Ill.: The Free Press.

—— (1968). *The Structure of Social Action*. 2 vols. New York: The Free Press.

PEACOCK, JAMES L. (1988). *The Anthropological Lens: Harsh Light, Soft Focus*. New York: Cambridge University Press.

PENNINX, RINUS (1982). 'A Critical Review of Theory and Practice: The Case of Turkey', *International Migration Review*, 16/4: 781–818.

—— VAN RENSELAAR, HERMAN, and VAN VELSEN, LEO (1976). 'Social and Economic Effects of External Migration in Turkey', *Studi Emigrazione/Etudes Migrations*, 13/143: 335–45.

PESSAR, PATRICIA R. (ed.) (1997). *Caribbean Circuits: New Directions in the Study of Caribbean Migration*. New York: Center for Migration Studies.

PETERS, BERNHARD (1993). *Die Integration moderner Gesellschaften*. Frankfurt a.M.: Suhrkamp.

PETERSEN, WILLIAM (1958). 'A General Typology of Migration', *American Sociological Review*, 23: 256–66.

—— (1968). 'Migration: Social Aspects', in David L. Sills (ed.), *International Encyclopedia of the Social Sciences*. New York: The Macmillan Company & The Free Press, 1968, Vol. x. 286–92.

PHILIPPOVICH, EUGEN VON (1890). 'Auswanderung', in Johannes Conrad (ed.), *Handwörterbuch der Staatswissenschaften*. Vol. i. Jena: Fischer, 1000–40.

PHIZACKLEA, ANNIE (1980). *Unpacking the Fashion Industry*. London: Routledge.

PIEHLER, THOMAS (1991). *Der unterschiedliche Umfang der registrierten Kriminalität der Arbeitsmigranten: Eine kriminologische Interpretation der statistischen Diskrepanzen im Nationalitätenvergleich*. Pfaffenweiler: Centaurus-Verlagsgesellschaft.

PIORE, MICHAEL J. (1979). *Migrant Labour in Industrial Societies*. New York: Cambridge University Press.

POLANYI, KARL (1957). 'The Economy as Instituted Process', in Karl Polanyi, Conrad M. Arensberg, and Harry Peason (eds.), *Trade and Markets in Early Empires*. Glencoe, Ill.: The Free Press, 243–70.

POPKIN, SAMUEL J. (1979). *The Rational Peasant: The Political Economy of Rural Society in Vietnam*. Berkeley: University of California Press.

PORTES, ALEJANDRO (ed.) (1995). *The Economic Sociology of Immigration: Essays on Networks, Ethnicity, and Entrepreneurship*. New York: Russell Sage Foundation.

—— (1996). 'Transnational Communities: Their Emergence and Significance in the Contemporary World System', in Roberto Patricio Korzeniewicz and William C. Smith (eds.), *Latin America in the World Economy*. Westport, Conn.: Praeger, 151–68.

—— GUARNIZO, LUIS E., and LANDOLT, PATRICIA (1999). 'Introduction',

Special Issue: Transnational Communities, *Ethnic and Racial Studies*, 22/2: 217–37.

—— and RUMBAUT, RUBÉN (1990). *Immigrant America*. Berkeley: University of California Press.

—— and SENSENBRENNER, JULIA (1993). 'Embeddedness and Immigration: Notes on the Social Determinants of Economic Action', *American Journal of Sociology*, 98/6: 1320-50.

—— and WALTON, JOHN (1981). *Labour, Class, and the International System*. New York: Academic Books.

—— and ZHOU, MIN (1994). 'Should Immigrants Assimilate?' *The Public Interest* 116 (Summer): 18–33.

PRIES, LUDGER (1996). 'Internationale Arbeitsmigration und das Entstehen Transnationaler Sozialer Räume: Konzeptionelle Überlegungen für ein empirisches Forschungsprojekt', in Thomas Faist, Felicitas Hillmann, and Klaus Zühlke-Robinet (eds.), *Neue Migrationsprozesse: politisch-institutionelle Regulierung und Wechselbeziehungen zum Arbeitsmarkt*, ZeS-Arbeitspapier No. 6/1996. Bremen: Zentrum für Sozialpolitik, 21–31.

PUTNAM, ROBERT D. (1993). *Making Democracy Work: Civic Traditions in Modern Italy*. Princeton: Princeton University Press.

RAHM, GÉRARD DE (1990). 'Naturalisation: The Politics of Citizenship Acquisition', in Zig Layton-Henry (ed.), *The Political Rights of Migrant Workers in Western Europe*. London: SAGE, 158–85.

RATH, JAN (ed.) (1998). *Immigrant Businesses on the Urban Economic Fringe: A Case for Interdisciplinary Analysis*. Houndmills, Basingstoke: Macmillan.

RAVENSTEIN, ERNEST GEORGE (1885 and 1889). 'The Laws of Migration', *Journal of the Statistical Society*, 68: 167–227 and 72: 241–305.

REHFELD, ULI (1991). 'Ausländische Arbeitnehmer und Rentner in der gesetzlichen Rentenver-sicherung', *Deutsche Rentenversicherung*, 7: 468–92.

Repräsentativuntersuchung 1995: *Situation der ausländischen Arbeitnehmer und ihrer Familienangehörigen in der Bundesrepublik Deutschland*. Berlin: Bundesministerium für Arbeit und Sozialordnung.

REX, JOHN (1991). 'The Political Sociology of a Multi-Cultural Society', *European Journal of Intercultural Studies*, 2/1: 7–19.

—— JOLY, DANIÈLE, and CZARINA WILPERT (eds.) (1987). *Immigrant Associations in Europe*. Aldershot: Gower.

RICHMOND, ANTHONY H. (1984). 'Explaining Return Migration', in Daniel Kubat (ed.), *The Politics of Return: International Return Migration in Europe*. Roma: Centro Studi Emigrazione and New York: Center for Migration Studies, 269–76.

—— (1988). 'Sociological Theories of International Migration: The Case of Refugees', *Current Sociology*, 36/2: 7–25.

—— (1993). 'Reactive Migration: Sociological Perspectives on Refugee Movements', *Journal of Refugee Studies*, 6/1: 7–24.

ROGERS, EVERETT M. (1983). *Diffusion of Innovations* (3rd edn). New York: The Free Press.

—— and Kincaid, Donald L. (1981). *Communication Networks: Towards a New Paradigm of Research.* New York: The Free Press.

Rouse, Roger (1991). 'Mexican Migration and the Social Space of Postmodernism', *Diaspora*, 1/1: 8–23.

Roy, Olivier (1996). 'Le Néo-fondamentalisme islamique ou l'imaginaire de l'*oummah*,' *Esprit*, 220: 80–107.

Rumbaut, Rubén G. (1994). 'Origins and Destinies: Immigration to the United States since World War II', *Sociological Forum*, 9/4: 583–621.

—— (1997*a*). 'Ties That Bind: Immigration and Immigrant Families in the United States', in Alan Booth, Ann C. Crouter, and Nancy Landale (eds.), *Immigration and the Family: Research and Policy on U.S. Immigrants.* Mahwah, NJ: Lawrence Erlbaum Publishers, 3–45.

—— (1997*b*). 'Paradoxes (and Orthodoxies) of Assimilation', *Sociological Perspectives*, 40/3: 483–511.

Runciman, Walter G. (1966). *Relative Deprivation and Social Justice: A Study of Attitudes to Social Inequality in Twentieth-Century England.* London: Routledge.

Rushdie, Salman (1989). *Die satanischen Verse.* München: Th. Knaur.

Safran, William (1991). 'Diasporas in Modern Societies: Myths of Homeland and Return', *Diaspora*, 1/1: 83–95.

Sahlins, Michael D. (1965). 'On the Sociology of Primitive Exchange', in Michael Banton (ed.), *The Relevance of Models for Social Anthropology.* A.S.A. Monographs 1. London: Tavistock.

Saint-Blancat, Chantal (1995). 'Une Diaspora Musulmane en Europe?' *Archives de sciences sociales des religions*, 92 (Oct.–Dec.): 9–24.

Salt, John (1997). *International Movements of the Highly Skilled*, OECD Working Papers, Vol. v, No. 91. International Migration Unit: Occasional Papers No. 3. Paris: OECD.

Sarna, Jonathan D. (1981). 'The Myth of No Return: Jewish Return Migration to Eastern Europe, 1881–1914', *American Jewish History*, 71: 256–68.

Sassen, Saskia (1988). *The Mobility of Labour and Capital: A Study in International Investment and Labour Flow.* New York: Cambridge University Press.

—— (1990). *The Mobility of Labor and Capital: A Study in International Investment and Labor Flow.* New York: Cambridge University Press.

Saunders, Harold W., (1956 [1943]). 'Human Population and Social Equilibrium', in Joseph J. Spengler and Oded Duncan (eds.), *Population Theory and Policy.* Glencoe, Ill.: The Free Press, 219–29.

Saxton, Alexander (1971). *The Indispensible Enemy: Labour and the Anti-Chinese Movement in California.* Berkeley: University of California Press.

Schein, Louisa (1998). 'Forged Transnationality and Oppositional Cosmopolitanism', in Michael Peter Smith and Luis Eduardo Guarnizo (eds.), *Transnationalism from Below.* New Brunswick: Transaction Publishers, 291–313.

SCHIFFAUER, WERNER (1987). *Die Bauern von Subay: Das Leben in einem türkischen Dorf.* Stuttgart: Klett-Cotta.

—— (1991). *Die Migranten aus Subay: Türken in Deutschland. Eine Ethnographie.* Stuttgart: Klett-Cotta.

SCHMIDT-KODDENBERG, ANITA (1989). *Akkulturation von Migrantinnen: Eine Studie zur Bedeutsamkeit sozialer Vergleichsprozesse von Türkinnen und deutschen Frauen.* Opladen: Leske + Budrich.

SCHMITTER HEISLER, BARBARA (1984). 'Sending Countries and the Politics of Emigration and Destination', *International Migration Review*, 19/3: 469–84.

SCHOULTZ, LARS (1992). 'Central America and the Politicization of U.S. Immigration Policy', in Christopher Mitchell (ed.), *Western Hemisphere Immigration and United States Foreign Policy.* University Park, Penn.: The Pennsylvania State University Press, 157–220.

SCOTT, JAMES A. (1976). *The Moral Economy of the Peasant: Rebellion and Subsistence in Southeast Asia.* New Haven: Yale University Press.

SEGAL, AARON (1993). *An Atlas of International Migration.* London: Zell.

SEN, AMARTYA (1967). 'Isolation, Assurance and the Social Rate of Discount', *Quarterly Journal of Economics*, 81: 112–24.

ŞEN, FARUK (1990). *Problems and Integration Constraints of Turkish Migrants in the Federal Republic of Germany*, World Employment Programme Research Working Paper. Geneva: International Labour Organization.

Senatsverwaltung für Gesundheit und Soziales, Die Ausländerbeauftragte des Senats von Berlin (1997). *Türkische Jugendliche in Berlin.* Berlin.

SHAH, NASRA M. (1994). 'Economic, Demographic, Sociocultural and Political Dynamics of Emigration from and within South Asia', unpublished manuscript. New York: Rockefeller Foundation.

—— (1996). *The Role of Social Networks in Migration to Kuwait among South Asian Males*, IOM/UNFPA Policy Workshop on Emigration Dynamics in South Asia, Geneva, Switzerland, 2–3 Sept.

SHEFFER, GABRIEL (1986). 'A New Field of Study: Modern Diasporas in International Politics', in Gabriel Sheffer (ed.), *Modern Diasporas in International Politics.* London: Croom Helm, 1–15.

SHIBUTANI, TAMOTSU, and KWAN, KIAN MOON (1965). *Ethnic Stratification.* New York: Macmillan.

SHILS, EDWARD (1957). 'Primordial, Personal, Sacred and Civil Ties', *British Journal of Sociology*, 8/2: 130–45.

—— (1991). 'The Virtue of Civil Society?', *Government and Opposition*, 26/1: 3–20.

SIMMEL, GEORG (1995 [1908]). *Soziologie: Untersuchungen über die Formen der Vergesellschaftung.* Band 11. Frankfurt a.M.: Suhrkamp.

—— (1955 [1922]). *Conflict & the Web of Group-Affiliations.* Translated by Kurt H. Wolff and Reinhard Bendix. New York: The Free Press.

SIMMEL, GEORG (1997). *Simmel on Culture.* Ed. David Frisby and Mike Featherstone London: Sage.

SIMMONS, ALAN B. (1985–6). 'Recent Studies on Place-Utility and Intention to

Migrate: An International Comparison', *Population and Environment*, 8/1–2: 120–40.

SIMON, HERBERT A. (1957). *Models of Man*. New York: Wiley.

SIMON, JULIAN L. (1988). *The Economic Consequences of Immigration*. Oxford: Basil Blackwell.

SIMON, RITA JAMES and BRETTELL, CAROLINE B. (eds.) (1986). *International Migration: The Female Experience*. Totowa, NJ: Rowman & Allanheld.

SJAASTAD, LARRY A. (1962). 'The Costs and Returns of Human Migration', *Journal of Political Economy*, 70/1: 80–93.

SKERRY, PETER (1993). *Mexican Americans: The Ambivalent Minority*. Cambridge, Mass.: Harvard University Press.

SMITH, ADAM (1961 [1789]). *An Inquiry into the Nature and Causes of the Wealth of Nations*. Chicago: University of Chicago Press.

SMITH, MICHAEL PETER, and GUARNIZO, LUIS EDUARDO (eds.) (1998). *Transnationalism from Below*. New Brunswick: Transaction Publishers.

SMITH, ROBERT (1999). 'Reflections on Migration, the State and the Construction, Durability and Newness of Transnational Life', in Ludger Pries (ed.), *Migration and Transnational Social Spaces*. Ashgate: Aldershot: 187–219.

SOMBART, WERNER (1969 [1916]). *Der moderne Kapitalismus*. Vol. i, Book 2. *Die vorkapitalistische Wirtschaft*. Berlin: Duncker & Humblot.

SOMERS, MARGARET R. (1994). 'The Narrative Constitution of Identity: A Relational and Network Approach', *Theory and Society*, 23: 605–49.

SOPEMI (1993–6). *Continuous Reporting System on Migration* (various issues). Paris: OECD.

SOWELL, THOMAS (1996). *Migrations and Cultures: A World View*. New York: Basic Books.

SOYSAL, YASEMIN N. (1994). *The Limits of Citizenship*. Chicago: University of Chicago Press.

SPAAN, ERNST (1994). 'Taikong's and Calo's: The Role of Middlemen and Brokers in Javanese International Migration', *Internation Migration Review*, 28/1: 93–113.

SPEARE, ALDEN (1974). 'Residential Satisfaction as an Intervening Variable in Residential Mobility', *Demography*, 11/2: 173–88.

SPULER-STEGMANN, URSULA (1996). 'Der Islam in ausgewählten Staaten: Türkei', in Werner Ende and Udo Steinbach (eds.), *Der Islam in der Gegenwart* (4th revised and expanded edn). München: C. H. Beck, 232–46.

—— (1998). *Muslime in Deutschland: Nebeneinander oder Miteinander*. Freiburg: Herder.

STALKER, PETER (1994). *The Work of Strangers: A Survey of International Labour Migration*. Geneva: ILO.

STARK, ODED (1991). *The Migration of Labour*. New York: Cambridge University Press.

Statistisches Bundesamt (ed.) (1993). *Statistisches Jahrbuch 1993 für die Bundesrepublik Deutschland*. Stuttgart: Kohlhammer.

STEIN, BARRY N. (1981). 'The Refugee Experience: Defining the Parameters of a Field of Study', *International Migration Review*, 15/1: 320–30.

STEINBACH, UDO (1993). 'Türkei', in Dieter Nohlen and Franz Nuscheler (eds.), *Handbuch der Dritten Welt*. Band 6. *Nordafrika unnd Naher Osten*. Bonn: Verlag J. H. W. Dietz Nachf., 510–37.

STERLING, CLAIRE (1994). *Thieves' World: The Threat of the New Global Network of Organized Crime*. New York: Simon & Schuster.

STINCHCOMBE, ARTHUR L. (1978). *Theoretical Methods in Social History*. London: Macmillan.

—— (1986). *Stratification and Organization*. Cambridge: Cambridge University Press.

STIRLING, PAUL (1965). *Turkish Village*. London: Weidenfeld and Nicolson.

—— (1974). 'Cause, Knowledge and Change: Turkish Village Revisited', in John Davis (ed.), *Choice and Change: Essays in Honour of Lucy Mair*. London: Athlone Press, 191–229.

STOUFFER, SAMUEL A. (1940). 'Intervening Opportunities: A Theory Relating Mobility and Distance', *American Sociological Review*, 5: 845–67.

—— (1949). *The American Soldier*. Princeton: Princeton University Press.

STRIKEWERDA, CARL (1997). 'Reinterpreting the History of European Integration: Business, Labour, and Social Citizenship in Twentieth-Century Europe', in Jytte Klausen and Louise Tilly (eds.), *European Integration in Social and Historical Perspective: 1850 to the Present*. Lanham, Md.: Roman & Littlefield, 51–70.

STRUCK, ERNST (1984). *Landflucht in der Türkei: Die Auswirkungen im Herkunftsgebiet – dargestellt an einem Beispiel aus dem Übergangsraum von Inner – zu Ostanatolien (Provinz Sivas)*. Passau: Passavia Universitätsverlag.

—— (1988). 'Migration Patterns and the Effects of Migration on Household Structure and Production in an East Anatolian Village', *Tijdschrift voor Econ. en Soc. Geografie*, 79/3: 210–19.

SWIDLER, ANN (1986). 'Culture in Action: Symbols and Strategies', *American Sociological Review*, 51: 273–88.

TARROW, SIDNEY (1994). *Power in Movement: Social Movements, Collective Action and Politics*. New York: Cambridge University Press.

—— (1996). *Fishnets, Internets and Catnets: Globalization and Transnational Collective Action*, Working Paper 1996/78. Madrid: Instituto Juan March de Estudios e Investigaciones.

TATLA, DARSHAN SINGH (1999). *The Sikh Diaspora: The Search for Statehood*. London: UCL Press.

TAYLOR, CHARLES (1991). 'Die Beschwörung der *Civil Society*', in Krysztof Michalski (ed.), *Europa und die Civil Society*. Stuttgart: Klett-Cotta, 52–81.

THAMM, BERNDT GEORG and KONRAD FREIBERG (1998). *Mafia Global. Organisiertes Verbrechen auf dem Sprung in das 21. Jahrhundert* Hilden: Verlag Deutsche Polizeileratur.

THISTLETHWAITE, FRANK (1991 [1960]). 'Migration from Europe Overseas in the Nineteenth and Twentieth Centuries', reprinted in Rudolph Jeffery Vecoli and J. G. Williamson (eds.), *A Century of European Migrations, 1830–1930*. Urbana: University of Illinois Press.

Thomas, Brinley (1973). *Migration and Economic Growth*. New York: Cambridge University Press.

Thomas, William I. (1966). *On Social Organization and Social Personality*. Ed. Morris Janowitz. Chicago: University of Chicago Press.

—— and Znaniecki, Florian (1927 [1918–21]). *The Polish Peasant in Europe and America*, 5 vols. New York: Alfred A. Knopf.

Thränhardt, Dietrich (1993). 'Die Ursprünge von Rassismus und Fremdenfeindlichkeit in der Konkurrenzdemokratie: Ein Vergleich der Entwicklungen in England, Frankreich und Deutschland', *Leviathan*, 21/3: 336–57.

Tibi, Bassam (1998). *Aufbruch am Bosporus: Die Türkei zwischen Europa und Islamismus*. München and Vienna: Diana Verlag.

Tilly, Charles (1978*a*). 'Migration in Modern European History', in William H. McNeil and Ruth S. Adams (eds.), *Human Migration: Patterns and Policies*. Bloomington: Indiana University Press, 48–72.

—— (1978*b*). *From Mobilization to Revolution*. New York: McGraw-Hill.

—— (1990). 'Transplanted Networks', in Virginia Yans-McLaughlin (ed.), *Immigration Reconsidered: History, Sociology, and Politics*. New York: Oxford University Press, 79–95.

—— (1996). 'Citizenship, Identity and Social History', *International Review of Social History*, Supplement 3: 1–17.

Tocqueville, Alexis de (1988 [1835]). *Democracy in America*. Ed. J. P. Mayer and trans. by George Lawrence. New York: Harper & Row.

Todaro, Michael P. (1969). 'A Model of Labor Migration and Urban Unemployment in Less Developed Countries', *American Economic Review*, 59: 138–48.

Toprak, Binnaz (1996). 'Civil Society in Turkey', in Augustus Richard Norton (ed.), *Civil Society in the Middle East*. Leiden: E. J. Brill, 87–118.

Truman, David B. (1951). *The Governmental Process: Political Interests and Public Opinion*. New York: Alfred A. Knopf.

Turkey Human Rights Report (1994). *The Kurdish Problem*. HRFT Publications, No. 10.

Turkish Democracy Foundation (1996). *Fact Book on Turkey—Kurds and PKK Terrorism*. Ankara: TDF.

Turner, Bryan S. (1984). 'Orientalism and the Problem of Civil Society in Islam', in Asaf Hussain, Robert Olson, and Jamil Qureshi (eds.), *Orientalism, Islam, and Islamists*. Brattleboro, VT: Amana Books, 23–42.

Ueda, Reed (1994). *Postwar Immigrant America: A Social History*. Boston: Bedford Books of St Martin's Press.

Uhlenberg, Peter (1973). 'Noneconomic Determinants of Nonmigration: Sociological Considerations for Migration Theory', *Rural Sociology*, 38/3: 296–311.

United Nations (1993). *The State of World Population, 1993*. New York: United Nations.

UNHCR (United Nations High Commissioner for Refugees) (1995). *The State of the World's Refugees: In Search of Solutions.* Oxford: Oxford University Press.

—— (1997). *The State of the World's Refugees: A Humanitarian Agenda.* Oxford: Oxford University Press.

USCR (US Committee for Refugees) (1993). *1993 World Refugee Survey.* Washington, DC: Government Printing Office.

—— (1997). *World Refugee Survey 1997.* Washington, DC: USCR.

US Commission on Immigration Reform (1998). *Binational Study: Migration between Mexico and the United States.* Washington, DC: Government Printing Office.

US Department of Commerce, Bureau of the Census (1960). *Historical Statistics of the United States.* Washington, DC: Government Printing Office.

van der Erf, Rob, and Heering, Liesbeth (eds.) (1995). *Causes of International Migration*, Proceedings of a Workshop. Eurostat. Luxembourg: Office for Official Publications of the European Communities.

Vasak, Krel, and Likofsky, Sidney (eds.) (1976). *The Right to Leave and to Return.* New York: American Jewish Commission.

Veltman, Calvin (1988). *The Future of the Spanish Language in the United States.* Washington, DC: Hispanic Policy Development Project.

Vogel, Dita (1996). *Illegale Zuwanderung und soziales Sicherungssystem—eine Analyse ökonomischer und sozialpolitischer Aspekte*, ZeS-Arbeitspaper No. 2/96. Bremen: Centre for Social Policy Research.

Voll, John Obert (1997). 'Relations among Islamist Groups', in John L. Esposito (ed.), *Political Islam: Revolution, Radicalism, or Reform?* London: Lynne Rienner Publishers, 231–48.

Wacquant, Loïcq J. D. (1997). 'Three Pernicious Premises in the Study of the American Ghetto', *International Journal of Urban and Regional Research*, 21/2: 341–53.

Waldinger, Roger (1986). *Through the Eye of the Needle: Immigrants and Enterprise in New York's Garment Trades.* New York: New York University Press.

—— (1986/7). 'Changing Ladders and Musical Chairs: Ethnicity and Opportunity in Post-Industrial New York', *Politics and Society*, 15: 369–401.

—— (1996). *Still the Promised City? New Immigrants and African-Americans in Postindustrial New York.* Cambridge, Mass.: Harvard University Press.

Waldorf, Brigitte (1994). 'Assimilation and Attachment in the Context of International Migration: The Case of Guestworkers in Germany', *Papers in Regional Science*, 73/3: 241–66.

—— (1995). 'Determinants of International Return Migration Intentions', *Professional Geographer*, 47/2: 125–36.

Waldorf, Brigitte (1996). 'The Internal Dynamic of International Migration Systems', *Environment and Planning A*, 28/4: 631–50.

—— and Esparza, Adrian (1991). 'A Parametric Failure Time Model of International Return Migration', *Papers in Regional Science*, 70/4: 419–38.

WALDRON, JEREMY (1995). 'Minority Cultures and the Cosmopolitan Alternative', *University of Michigan Journal of Law Reform*, 25: 751–93.

WALLERSTEIN, IMMANUEL (1974). *The Modern World-System*. Vol. i. New York: Academic Press.

WALTERSHAUSEN, A. SARTORIUS VON (1909). 'Auwanderung', in Eugen von Philippovich (ed.), *Handwörterbuch der Staatswissenschaften* (3rd edn). Vol. ii. Jena: Fischer, 259–302.

WALZER, MICHAEL (1992*a*). 'Was heisst zivile Gesellschaft?' *Zivile Gesellschaft und amerikanische Demokratie*. Berlin: Rotbuch, 64–97.

—— (1992*b*). 'The New Tribalism: Notes on a Difficult Problem', *Dissent* Spring 1992: 164–71.

WARNER, WILLIAM L. and SROLE, LEO H. (1945). *The Social Systems of American Ethnic Groups*. New Haven: Yale University Press.

WASSERMANN, STANLEY and FAUST, KATHERINE (1994). *Social Network Analysis: Methods and Applications*. Cambridge: Cambridge University Press.

WEBBER, MELVIN M. (1963). 'Order in Diversity: Community without Propinquity', in Lowdon Wingo (ed.), *Cities and Space: The Future Uses of Urban Land*. Baltimore: Johns Hopkins Press, 23–54.

WEBER, MAX (1980 [1924]). *Wirtschaft und Gesellschaft*. Tübingen: J. C. B. Mohr (Paul Siebeck).

—— (1988 [1924]). 'Methodologische Einleitung für die Erhebungen des Vereins für Sozialpolitik über Auslese und Anpassung (Berufswahl und Berufsschicksal) der Arbeiterschaft der geschlossenen Großindustrie (1908)', in Marianne Weber (ed.), *Gesammelte Aufsätze zur Soziologie und Sozialpolitik*. Tübingen: J. C. B. Mohr (Paul Siebeck), 1–60.

WEINER, MYRON (1986). 'Labour Migrations as Incipient Diasporas', in Gabriel Sheffer (ed.), *Modern Diasporas in International Politics*. London: Croom Helm, 47–74.

—— (1995). *The Global Migration Crisis: Challenge to States and to Human Rights*. New York: Harper Collins College Publishers.

WELLMAN, BARRY (1983). 'Network Analysis: Some Basic Principles', in Randall Collins (ed.), *Sociological Theory*. San Francisco: Jossey-Bass Publishers, 155–200.

—— and LEIGHTON, BARRY (1979). 'Networks, Neighborhoods, and Communities. Approaches to the Study of the Community Question', *Urban Affairs Quarterly*, 14/3: 363–90.

—— and BERKOWITZ, S. D. (eds.) (1988). *Social Structures: A Network Approach*. Cambridge: Cambridge University Press.

—— and WORTLEY, SCOTT (1990). 'Different Strokes from Different Folks: Which Type of Ties Provide What Kind of Social Support?', *American Journal of Sociology*, 96/3: 558–88.

WERBNER, PINA (1990). *The Migration Process: Capital, Gifts and Offerings among British Pakistanis*. Oxford: Berg.

WERNER, HEINZ (1994). 'Regional Economic Integration and Migration: The

European Case', *The Annals of the American Academy of Political and Social Science*, July: 147–64.

WHITE, HARRISON (1992). *Identity and Control: A Structural Theory of Social Action*. Princeton: Princeton University Press.

—— BOORMAN, SCOTT A., and BREIGER, RONALD L. (1976). 'Social Structure from Multiple Networks. I. Blockmodels of Roles and Positions', *American Journal of Sociology*, 81/4: 730–80.

WHITE, JENNY B. (1995). 'Civic Culture and Islam in Urban Turkey', in Chris Hann and Elizabeth Dunn (eds.), *Civil Society: Challenging Western Models*. London: Routledge, 143–54.

WIESSNER, GUNNAR (1995). 'Der Kurdenkonflikt in Ostanatolien: Eine Analyse der politischen Lage am Beispiel der Provinz Van', in Schweizer Friedensstiftung (ed.), *Friedensbericht 1995*. Zürich and Chur, 160–83.

WIHTOL DE WENDEN, CATHERINE (1997). 'Kulturvermittlung zwischen Frankreich und Algerien: Eine transnationale Brücke zwischen Immigranten, neuen Akteuren und dem Maghreb', *Soziale Welt*, Sonderband 12: 265–76.

WILLIAMSON, OLIVER E. (1981). 'The Economics of Organization: The Transaction Cost Approach', *American Journal of Sociology*, 87/4: 548–77.

WILLMOTT, WILLIAM E. (ed.) (1972). *Economic Organization in Chinese Society*. Stanford, Calif.: Stanford University Press.

WILPERT, CZARINA (1992). 'The Use of Social Networks in Turkish Migration to Germany', in Mary M. Kritz, Lin Lean Lim, and Hania Zlotnik (eds.), *International Migration Systems: A Global Approach*. Oxford: Clarendon Press, 177–89.

WOLF, DIANE L. (1992). *Factory Daughters: Gender, Household Dynamics, and Rural Industrialization in Java*. Berkeley: University of California Press.

WOLF, ERIC R. (1966). *Peasants*. Englewood Cliffs, NJ: Prentice-Hall.

WOLPERT, JULIAN (1965). 'Behavioral Aspects of the Decision to Migrate', *Papers and Proceedings of the Regional Science Association*, 15: 159–69.

—— (1975). 'Behavioural Aspects of the Decision to Migrate', in Emrys Jones (ed.), *Readings in Social Geography*. London: Oxford University Press, 191–9.

WOLTER, ACHIM (1996). 'Qualifikationsspezifische Determinanten der Migration nach Deutschland', *Mitteilungen aus der Arbeitsmarkt- und Berufsforschung* 30/4: 657–62.

WONG, LLOYD L. (1997). 'Globalization and Transnational Migration: A Study of Recent Chinese Capitalist Migration from the Asian Pacific to Canada', *International Sociology*, 12/3: 329–52.

WOOD, WILLIAM B. (1994). 'Forced Migration: Local Conflicts and International Dilemmas', *Annals of the Association of American Geographers*, 84/4: 607–34.

World Bank (1995). *World Development Report*. Oxford: Oxford University Press.

WULF, ULRIKE (1985). 'Komposition sozialer Netzwerke unter Migrationsbedingungen', Arbeitsbericht No. 7, *DFG-Forschungsprojekt Sozialisation und Interaktion in Familien türkischer Arbeitsmigranten*. Bonn: Seminar für Soziologie, Universität Bonn.

WYMAN, DAVID S. (1984). *The Abandonment of the Jews: America and the Holocaust, 1941–1945*. New York: Pantheon.

WYMAN, MARK (1993). *Round Trip to America: The Immigrants Return to Europe 1880–1930*. Ithaca, NY: Cornell University Press.

YALÇIN-HECKMANN, LALE (1994). 'Are Fireworks Islamic? Towards an Understanding of Turkish Migrants and Islam in Germany', Charles Stewart and Rosalind Shaw (eds.), *Syncretism/Anti-Syncretims: The Politics of Religious Synthesis*. London: Routledge, 178–95.

YANCEY, WILLIAM L., ERICKSEN, EUGENE P., and JULIANI, RICHARD N. (1976). 'Emergent Ethnicity: A Review and Reformulation', *American Sociological Review*, 41/3: 391–403.

YANS-MCLAUGHLIN, VIRGINIA (1977). *Family and Community: Italian American Immigrants in Buffalo, 1880–1930*. Ithaca, NY: Cornell University Press.

YOUNG, IRIS MARION (1989). 'Policy and Group Difference: A Critique of the Ideal of Universal Citizenship', *Ethics*, 99/2: 250–74.

—— (1997). 'A Multicultural Continuum: A Critique of Will Kymlicka's Ethnic-Nation Dichotomy', *Constellations*, 4/1: 48–53.

YÜCE, NILGÜN (1997). 'Die besondere Funktion der jungen türkischen Rückwanderer im Tourismus', Jürgen Reulicke (ed.), *'Spagat mit Kopftuch': Essays zur Deutsch-Türkischen Sommerakademie*. Hamburg: Edition Körber-Stiftung, 168–82.

YURTDAŞ, HATICE (1995). *Pionierinnen der Arbeitsmigration in Deutschland. Lebensgeschichtliche Analysen von Frauen aus Ost-Anatolien*. Interethnische Beziehungen und Kulturwandel. Band 23. Münster: Lit-Verlag.

ZAIMOGLU, FERIDUN (1995). *Kanak Sprak: 24 Mißtöne vom Rande der Gesellschaft*. Hamburg: Rotbuch Verlag.

ZELINSKY, WILBUR (1971). 'The Hypothesis of the Mobility Transition', *Geographical Review*, 61: 219–49.

Zentrum für Türkeistudien (1989). *Türkische Unternehmensgründungen—Von der Nische zum Markt? Ergebnisse einer Untersuchung bei türkischen Selbständigen in Dortmund, Duisburg und Essen*. Opladen: Westdeutscher Verlag.

ZOLBERG, ARISTIDE R. (1983). 'The Formation of New States as a Refugee Generating Process', *Annals of the American Academy of Political and Social Science*, 467: 73–98.

—— (1987). '"Wanted but Not Welcome": Alien Labour in Western Development', in William Alonso (ed.), *Population in an Interacting World*. Cambridge, Mass.: Harvard University Press, 36–73.

—— (1992). 'Labour Migration and International Economic Regimes: Bretton Woods and After', in Mary M. Kritz, Lin Lean Lim, and Hania Zlotnik (eds.), *International Migration Systems: A Global Approach*. Oxford: Clarendon Press, 315–34.

—— SUHRKE, ASTRI, and AGUAYO, SERGIO (1989). *Escape from Violence: Conflict and the Refugee Crisis in the Developing World*. New York: Cambridge University Press.

Index